Fourth Edition

Policy Studies for Educational Leaders

AN INTRODUCTION

Frances C. Fowler
Miami University, Oxford

PEARSON

Boston Columbus Indianapolis New York San Francisco Upper Saddle River
Amsterdam Cape Town Dubai London Madrid Milan Munich Paris Montreal Toronto
Delhi Mexico City São Paulo Sydney Hong Kong Seoul Singapore Taipei Tokyo

Vice President and Editorial Director: Jeffery W. Johnston
Senior Acquisitions Editor: Meredith D. Fossel
Associate Editor: Anne Whittaker
Editorial Assistant: Andrea Hall
Vice President, Director of Marketing: Margaret Waples
Senior Marketing Manager: Christopher Barry
Senior Managing Editor: Pamela D. Bennett
Project Manager: Kerry Rubadue
Senior Operations Supervisor: Matthew Ottenweller

Senior Art Director: Diane Lorenzo
Text Designer: S4Carlisle Publishing Services
Cover Designer: Jayne Conte
Cover Art: Fotolia
Full-Service Project Management: Christian Holdener, S4Carlisle Publishing Services
Composition: S4Carlisle Publishing Services
Printer/Binder: Courier/Westford
Cover Printer: Courier/Westford
Text Font: Minion Pro

Every effort has been made to provide accurate and current Internet information in this book. However, the Internet and information posted on it are constantly changing, so it is inevitable that some of the Internet addresses listed in this textbook will change.

Library of Congress Cataloging-in-Publication Data
Fowler, Frances C.
   Policy studies for educational leaders : an introduction / Frances C. Fowler. — 4th ed.
      p. cm.
   Includes bibliographical references and index.
   ISBN-13: 978-0-13-267811-7—ISBN-10: 0-13-267811-X   1. Education and state–United States.
2. Education—Political aspects—United States.   3. School administrators—United States.   I. Title.
   LC89.F69 2013
   379.73—dc23

                                                                                    2011050838

10 9 8 7 6 5 4 3 2 1

PEARSON

ISBN 10:   0-13-267811-X
ISBN 13: 978-0-13-267811-7

To my dear husband, Dr. Gene Collins,
with love and gratitude.

PREFACE

According to proverbial wisdom, necessity is the mother of invention. Proverbial wisdom is certainly correct in the case of *Policy Studies for Educational Leaders: An Introduction.* The idea for this book was born in the summer of 1990 when, new Ph.D. in hand, I was invited to teach a graduate course in education policy at the University of Tennessee–Knoxville. After discovering no suitable textbooks, I ordered a few paperbacks on current issues and put together a course packet consisting of articles on various aspects of education policy. However, I often longed for a good textbook that provided basic information, freeing up precious class time for substantive discussions of policy issues. Thus, the idea for this book was born. That was more than twenty years ago, and now the book is going into its fourth edition. Everything, including the world of education policy, changes with the passage of time. A number of significant changes dictated the revisions for the fourth edition of *Policy Studies for Educational Leaders.* First, the Great Recession of 2007–2009 and the subsequent faltering recovery have put unprecedented financial pressures on school districts. The 2010 Census revealed that the long-predicted demographic changes are occurring more rapidly than previously anticipated. *No Child Left Behind* is still on the books, but because Congress has failed to re-authorize the Elementary and Secondary Education Act (ESEA), it is being implemented with increasing flexibility. Hot issues of the recent past, such as site-based management, have been replaced by new hot issues such as teacher merit pay and value-added assessment. All these developments and more informed changes appear in the fourth edition.

NEW TO THIS EDITION

- All of the *News Stories for Analysis*, ever a feature of this book, have been replaced with updated news stories, making them 100% new and more practical than ever.
- Every chapter is aligned with the ISLLC Standards. A chart detailing this correlation is located on the inside front cover of this book.
- A new section in Chapter 2 examines distributed leadership.
- A detailed discussion of—and economic information about—the Great Recession can now be found in Chapter 3.
- Demographic information covered in Chapter 3 has been updated to reflect recent data contained in the 2010 Census.
- A new section on the details and long-lasting effects of the Tea Party Movement is now included in Chapter 5.
- The Democratic Party's ideological factions are presented and examined in Chapter 5.
- The *For Further Reading* sections have been revised extensively and updated with new recommended readings to promote critical thinking and further study.
- End-of-chapter *Discussion Questions* and *Internet Assignments* have been revised and updated with new assignments and suggestions for additional practice and research.

TEXT PHILOSOPHY AND FOCUS

Policy Studies for Educational Leaders: An Introduction is based on the following set of beliefs:

1. ***Educational leaders must be literate about policy and the policy process.*** The time is long past (if, indeed, there ever was such a time) when education administrators could tell themselves that, "Politics and education don't mix," and sit complacently on the sidelines while others made important policy decisions for schools. In today's rapidly changing policy environment, those who lead our schools *must* have a basic understanding of education policy and how it is made; otherwise, they will be reactive rather than proactive, and when they move into action, they are likely to make serious blunders.

2. ***Educational leaders need both theories and practical information about education policy and policymaking.*** Unfortunately, many people in education believe that theory and practice are unrelated and, indeed, opposites. I reject this view. If school administrators are truly to be reflective leaders, they need tools for thinking deeply and critically about education policy. Among these necessary tools are knowledge about major research findings, analytical frameworks, and important political theories. However, people who are politically inexperienced also need practical advice about how to apply this abstract information. Therefore, this book presents both the underlying theories and specific recommendations for practice.

3. ***Educational leaders must understand power and how to use it responsibly.*** The underlying theory behind this book is *conflict theory*—the belief that policy grows out of conflict between different individuals, groups, and institutions. Because the outcome of these struggles is shaped by the balance of power among the participants, students must understand power. Conflict theory is a large theoretical house, ranging from the pluralists who focus on the dynamics of practical politics to scholars whose thinking has been influenced by Marx and Gramsci, with many stops in between. Unfortunately, education scholars in the United States tend to set up a binary opposition between the pluralists and more critical thinkers, focusing on either practical politics or cultural politics to the exclusion of the other. In my opinion, these approaches are neither theoretically adequate nor pedagogically sound, leading either to the inevitable development of students who understand day-to-day politics (but ignore the more subtle play of power that shapes most social injustice) or to students who have a good grasp of how powerful cultural institutions shape consciousness (but do not know what happens in a legislature or court). My book transcends this unfortunate dichotomy by using Oxford University professor Steven Lukes's (1974, 2005) integration of pluralist and critical perspectives with studies of the mobilization of bias to yield a holistic theory that encompasses the many faces of power. Thus, instructors can teach their students about *both* the dynamics of everyday American power politics *and* how powerful interests use institutions and culture to perpetuate injustices based on race, gender, and class.

4. ***All public policy, but especially education policy, is value laden.*** In political science, one school of policy analysis seeks to conduct "value-free" analysis. In

my opinion, their work is misleading because it is based on a fundamental misconception about social reality. I agree therefore with those political scientists who consider policymaking to be inherently intertwined with values. This book reflects that belief. Not only is an entire chapter devoted to policy values and ideology, but also, throughout the book, I raise issues of values. Because many of the conflicts in which school leaders become embroiled turn on questions of deeply held values, this emphasis lays the foundation for a good understanding of where and when struggles over values are most likely to arise.

5. *State government has become increasingly important since the late 1970s and will probably continue to be so.* In the United States, education policy is developed at four levels: federal, state, district, and school. Although this book touches on all four levels, it emphasizes the state level, which not only is growing in importance, but also is the least understood level for several reasons: the federal focus of most civics and government courses, the split national–local focus of the media, and the patterns of practical experience that most educators develop during their careers. Therefore, filling this gap seems essential.

TEXT ORGANIZATION

This book is divided into twelve chapters that are grouped into two parts. The first of these, *The Background of Education Policy,* includes the following coverage:

- *Introductory chapters* (Chapters 1 and 2) lay a general foundation for students, most of whom have never taken a basic political science course. Chapter 1 presents an overview of education policy and the policy process. Chapter 2 deals with power, presenting Lukes's theory in detail, and applying it both to day-to-day politics and the more subtle power mechanisms that maintain inequalities based on race, class, and gender. It also provides an introduction to discursive analysis.
- *The policy environment* (Chapters 3–5): As a social phenomenon, policy grows out of a specific socioeconomic context. Chapters 3, 4, and 5 provide background for students about the most important dimensions of this context: economics, demographics, political structures, political culture, values, and ideology.

The second part, *Policy Actors and the Policy Process,* includes:

- *The policy process* (Chapters 6–11). Students can understand education policy—and how to influence it—only if they understand how it is developed, implemented, and assessed. Chapters 6 through 11 focus on this process, using the classic stage model. Chapter 6 introduces the major policy, players, and the following chapters show them in action as policy issues are defined, moved onto the policy agenda, formulated, adopted, implemented, and evaluated.
- *Retrospective and prospective*. Chapter 12 seeks to provide students, who will now have a sophisticated understanding of education policy, with a historical framework for understanding the current education reform movement and one of its major products, the *No Child Left Behind Act.*

SPECIAL FEATURES

I have tried to make this book as user friendly as possible for both students and professors. To that end, I have provided the following special features:

1. *Focus Questions.* Each chapter opens with several questions that relate to the major content of the chapter. These questions serve as advance organizers for students, helping them identify the most important points as they read.
2. *Figures and tables.* The figures and tables in this book summarize important points that would be tedious in paragraph form, give a visible form to theoretical material for visual learners, and provide an easy reference for the most important principles of political action.
3. *End-of-chapter activities.* Every chapter (except Chapter 9) ends with questions and activities for discussion and an Internet assignment. These activities can also be used as the basis for short papers.
4. *For Further Reading.* Each chapter (except Chapter 9), ends with a short, annotated bibliography of books and articles on the topic covered in that chapter. Students and professors can use it to extend and deepen their understanding of the material in each chapter.
5. *Boxed student activities.* Every chapter (except Chapter 9) includes one or two activities in boxes for student thought, writing, and/or discussion; these are news stories for analysis, case studies, or pro-con debates.

ACKNOWLEDGMENTS

A book is a monumental and often frustrating project, one that requires much assistance and support if it is ever to reach completion. Therefore, I acknowledge the contributions of the following people:

- Several anonymous reviewers, who offered valuable suggestions for the fourth edition.
- My husband, Dr. Gene Collins, who has been endlessly patient when I had to spend time on the book rather than with him, doing more enjoyable things.
- My editors at Pearson Education, Anne Whittaker and Meredith Fossel. They have been very understanding and supportive throughout the entire process.
- All the people in Anderson County and Nashville, Tennessee (their name is legion), who acted as my mentors when I was active in politics and gave me practical knowledge of how it is really done.
- The late William Boyd, Professor of Educational Leadership at the Pennsylvania State University and a fellow East Tennessean, who asked me to contribute a chapter to a *Politics of Education Association Yearbook* when I was still a sixth-grade teacher, and who supported and assisted me on many occasions after I entered higher education.
- My late parents, George and Louise Fowler, who taught me such a great love of books that even as a child I wanted to write one.

- The reviewers of the fourth edition: Hazel M. Carter, The City Colleges of New York (CUNY); Judith Faryniarz, University of Hartford; Barbara Hagler, Southern Illinois University-Carbondale; Stacey Rutledge, Florida State University
- And, finally, all those other relatives, friends, and colleagues whose support, pride, and encouragement helped me through the rough times and made sure that I finished.

BRIEF CONTENTS

CONTENTS

PART

1

THE BACKGROUND OF EDUCATION POLICY

1

POLICY: WHAT IT IS AND WHERE IT COMES FROM

Focus Questions

▌ Why do changes in the political and economic environment make understanding the policy process essential for today's school leaders?

▌ How can one determine what policy a government is actually pursuing?

▌ What roles can school leaders play in shaping and influencing education policy?

WHY STUDY POLICY?

School Leaders in Oz

"Toto, I don't think we're in Kansas anymore." A doctoral student who was taking an education policy course began one of her papers with this quotation from *The Wizard of Oz*. The student, principal of an elementary school in a large metropolitan area, had written a reflective essay about a trip that her class had taken to the state capital. This visit to the halls of power had left the students—all practicing school administrators—stunned.

The day had begun at a meeting with a state department of education official, who was supposed to brief the group on policy trends. For 50 minutes he had inundated them with facts and figures about taxes, school finance formulas, and economic growth, interspersing these statistics with complaints about how much time it took to operate a large district that the state had recently taken over. Finally, he paused and asked, "Any questions?" After a silence, another principal in the group inquired, "What about kids?" The official explained that his own background was in economics and that he had never worked in a school. This fact, he said, made it hard for him to conceptualize how education policy affects children.

After lunch, the class had an appointment with the chairman of the House Education Committee. Although the appointment had been made weeks in advance, the chairman's secretary had called just the day before to explain that the legislator's plans had changed and he would not be able to meet with them after all. Instead, they now had an appointment with a member of his staff, who nervously explained to the administrators and their professor that he did not know much about education policy. He did, however, invite them into the office of the "Great Man" himself. Standing in this room, he praised his employer's intelligence, pointing to his bookshelves and all the books on education he had read. The educators were sobered by the fact that *The Bell Curve*—widely criticized as racist in education circles—was prominently displayed. They were even more sobered when the staffer launched into an explanation of the legislator's views on special education. "Those kids shouldn't be allowed to drag down the others," he asserted. "They should be placed in special schools where they can learn at their own rate." Only with difficulty did the special education director in the group restrain an angry response.

As the students were leaving the legislative office building, they encountered another member of the legislature in the lobby. Because he was acquainted with a member of the class, he stopped to talk with them for a few minutes. At first, concentrating on his words was difficult, because everyone was distracted by the bright pink pigs patterned on his tie. He later explained that he had just worn it to a meeting with a group of hog farmers who had come to the capital to lobby him. This politician talked enthusiastically about the importance of education and jubilantly announced that the General Assembly was considering a home rule bill. If passed, this law would remove almost all state regulations from school districts, leaving them "free" to plan children's education. "Are you going to abolish the state proficiency tests?" one administrator asked hopefully, referring to the regulation that the state's educators found most burdensome. The legislator looked shocked. "Oh, no, of course not! The proficiency tests are here to stay."

On the way to the car, a member of the class commented sadly, "It's amazing— we speak two entirely different languages." A colleague answered, "And yet it's *imperative* that we learn how to communicate with them."

This true story illustrates succinctly many of the tensions and frustrations that school administrators experience as they venture into the world of education policy-making. Reacting by withdrawing into either resignation or fatalism is all too easy. The purpose of this book is to provide both potential and practicing education leaders with a basis for alternative responses if they wish to use them. It seeks to offer a knowledge base about education policy, including how it is made and how it can be influenced. It also seeks to sensitize them to some of the new dimensions of education leadership that are emerging in the twenty-first century. First, however, considering what policy is and how and why the world of education policy has changed is necessary.

DEFINING POLICY

A Brief Definition

When one begins to explore a new field, being armed with a few definitions is usually helpful. The term *policy* derives from political science, a deeply divided field (Almond, 1990). The various camps understand policy and related concepts in different ways. These disagreements grow out of philosophical conflicts over the nature of society, the meaning of power, and the proper role of government. The following series of definitions illustrates the range of interpretations of the term:

1. "[Policy] can be defined as *substantive decisions, commitments, and implementing actions by those who have governance responsibilities . . . as interpreted by various stakeholders*" (emphasis in the original) (Crosby & Bryson, 2005, p. 157).

2. Public policy is the "outputs of a political system, usually in the form of rules, regulations, laws, ordinances, court decisions, administrative decisions, and other forms. Public policy may be perceived as a pattern of activity applied . . . consistently and repetitively. . . . [It is] a dynamic process" (Kruschke & Jackson, 1987, p. 35).

3. "[A] public policy is . . . *a series of intentionally coherent decisions or activities taken or carried out by different public—and sometimes private—actors . . . with a view to resolving in a targeted manner a problem that is politically defined as collective in nature"* (emphasis in the original) (Knoepfl, Larrue, Varone, & Hill, 2007, p. 24).

4. "Policy sometimes is formed from a compromise among political participants . . . none of whom had quite in mind the problem to which the agreed problem responds" (Lindblom & Woodhouse, 1993, p. 11).

5. Public policy "includes both official enactments of government and something as informal as 'practices.' Also, policy may be viewed as the inactions of government, not simply what the government does" (Cibulka, 1995, p. 106).

6. "Policy is a very ambiguous term. . . . In its simplest sense, a policy is a decision about a course of action . . ." (Spicker, 2006, p. 15).

In this book, *policy* is understood broadly because school leaders involvement in the policy process tends to be multifaceted. *Policy,* for the purposes of this book, is defined as follows: *Public policy* is the dynamic and value-laden process through which a political system handles a public problem. It includes a government's expressed intentions and official enactments, as well as its consistent patterns of activity and inactivity.

In this definition, *government* includes elected and appointed public officials at the federal, state, and local levels as well as the bodies or agencies within which these officials work. Thus, school board members, school administrators, and classroom teachers in public schools are all part of government, as are such individuals and groups as governors, judges, and Congress.

At this point, some readers may be wondering how one can determine what a government's policy is on any particular issue. The following sections discuss in some detail how public policy relates to various aspects of government activity. Throughout these sections, the past racial segregation policy of the United States is used for demonstrative purposes because it illustrates beautifully the broad range of issues involved in determining what policy a government is following.

Policy and Expressed Government Intentions—Racial Segregation

To a great extent, politics is about communication, both written and spoken. Government officials communicate frequently—through campaign speeches, televised talk-show appearances, decisions reached in hearings and reports, and on the Internet. In determining the overall shape of a government's approach to a particular public problem, examining this communication for clues is helpful. For example, if a European scholar had visited the United States in 1950 and sought to determine the U.S. policy on racial segregation in public schools, he would probably have looked for evidence in the available body of political communication. No doubt such a scholar would have found public pronouncements made by southern leaders, who were already beginning to feel pressure from civil rights groups. Many of their statements would have clearly indicated that they were pursuing and intended to continue to pursue a policy of racial segregation in public schools. The European scholar probably would *not* have found similar public pronouncements made by such political figures as the governor of Colorado or the mayor of Columbus, Ohio. Concluding from this pattern of open expression and silence that racial segregation was a policy in the South, but not in the North, would have been wrong. During the 1970s, federal courts would find many northern school districts guilty of pursuing racial segregation policies, including those located in Denver and Columbus (Alexander & Alexander, 2008; Cambron-McCabe, McCarthy, & Thomas, 2004; La Morte, 2005).

Policy, Law, and Racial Segregation

POLICY AND STATUTES.   When most people use the term *law,* they actually mean *statutes*—laws enacted by legislatures. Fifty-one legislatures are active in the United States—Congress and fifty state legislatures—and their legislation is an important clue to governmental policy. If one seeks to determine what the policy really is, certainly one of the first sources to consult is statute law. However, law and policy are not identical. Many outdated laws are still "on the books" but are never enforced; some laws are purely symbolic (Edelman, 1964) and were passed to help citizens feel better about a problem but were never really intended to address it. Moreover, not every policy appears in statutes. The European scholar studying racial segregation policy would certainly have consulted the laws passed by federal and state governments. He would have found that in seventeen states and the District of Columbia, segregation was mandatory, and that it was optional in four other states (Alexander & Alexander, 2008; Cambron-McCabe, McCarthy, & Thomas, 2004; La Morte, 2005). The other twenty-nine states had no statutes in place regarding racial segregation in schools. This would not have meant, however, that they did not practice racial segregation. Ultimately, the U.S. Supreme Court would distinguish *de jure* segregation policies, based on statutes, from *de facto* segregation policies, based on official practice. It would rule that both were equally serious violations of the law (Alexander & Alexander, 2008; Cambron-McCabe, McCarthy, & Thomas, 2004; La Morte, 2005).

POLICY, RULES AND REGULATIONS, AND RACIAL SEGREGATION.   Most statutes are worded in general terms, and many of the details needed to put them into practice are not included in the statute itself. These details are usually provided by rules and regulations that government agencies develop. At the state level, the state department of education and state board of education usually exercise this responsibility; local school boards also have the authority to develop some rules and regulations. As with statutes, these rules and regulations provide important clues as to what the policy really is. It is especially important to note whether the rules are written narrowly or broadly. Broadly worded rules give considerable flexibility to educators who are lower in the hierarchy, whereas narrowly written ones give very little flexibility. Some rules may address issues not covered in state or federal statutes. For example, in 1973, the U.S. Supreme Court found that the Denver School Board had an official neighborhood school policy that it had used to develop a racially segregated school system

(Cambron-McCabe, McCarthy, & Thomas, 2004). This rule, passed by a local education agency, was an important clue to the policy that the system was really following. Chapter 8 explains the relationship between statutes and rules and regulations.

POLICY, COURT DECISIONS, AND RACIAL SEGREGATION.   Under the U.S. judicial system, courts have the right to review statutes in order to interpret them and evaluate their constitutionality; they can also overturn earlier court decisions. This means that court decisions are part of the law; in fact, they are called *case law*. Our European scholar, researching segregation policy in 1950, would have discovered that U.S. school segregation policies had first been upheld in the 1850s in a Massachusetts case, *Roberts v. the City of Boston* (Alexander & Alexander, 2008). This early decision had been reinforced by a related 1896 Supreme Court case, *Plessy v. Ferguson* (163 U.S. 537). In this suit, an African-American resident of Louisiana challenged racial segregation on trains, alleging that this practice violated the equal protection clause of the Fourteenth Amendment. The court's majority disagreed, ruling that racial segregation was constitutional as long as the facilities provided the races were "equal" (Alexander & Alexander, 2008; Cambron-McCabe, McCarthy, & Thomas, 2004). Later decisions applied the "separate but equal" doctrine to education. In this situation, case law was a more reliable indicator of policy than statute. It suggested that racial segregation could be legally practiced anywhere in the country. Our European scholar would have been mistaken, however, if he had concluded that the education facilities provided for children of different races were always—or even usually—equal.

POLICY, BUDGETS, AND RACIAL SEGREGATION.   Virtually all government bodies and agencies adopt budgets either annually or biennially. In legislatures, the committees that determine the level of funding to support an education statute are different from the committees that determine its wording. In essence, two battles occur during the passage of any statute—a battle over words and a battle over dollars. Both are important clues to the seriousness with which a government is pursuing a policy. Moreover, funding levels for most education policies are reconsidered regularly and are subject to upward or downward revision. This means that, in order to determine what policy a government is pursuing, considering both the initial funding level and funding trends over time is essential. Our European scholar would have been well advised to consider budgets, financial reports, and other documents relating to education funding in his efforts to figure out the real policy on racial segregation. Financial studies carried out at the time clearly demonstrated that separate but equal education for the races was not the policy that U.S. states and school boards were pursuing. African-American children were consistently disadvantaged in resource allocation, being assigned to the oldest school buildings and provided with outdated textbooks and equipment. Careful analyses of spending trends suggested that the real policy was "separate and unequal" education.

IMPLEMENTATION, POLICY, AND RACIAL SEGREGATION.   Policies are usually developed close to the top of the political system. Presidents and governors make speeches; legislators develop statutes and pass budgets; judges issue court decisions; but policies are put into practice close to the grass roots. In education, the implementers of most policies are superintendents and their staffs, principals, and classroom teachers. Educators are not robots who mechanically carry out orders issued from above. They are human beings with minds of their own making decisions in a specific social and cultural context that they understand better than presidents, governors, legislators, and judges. All policies are therefore mediated through the context in which they are implemented; in the process, changes happen. These changes may take the form of minor adjustments or major transformations, but policies are *always* altered during implementation (Hamann & Lane, 2004). In determining what the real policy is, then, considering how the policy is implemented is essential. Our European researcher would have been wise to visit schools for both races to see what was happening and talk with people working there. Direct observation would probably have confirmed the inequalities suggested by the financial records. Conversations with grassroots implementers might also have provided insights into why separate but equal education tended to become separate and unequal when put into practice. No doubt the values of the implementers and their communities, as well as political and economic pressures, would have emerged as part of the explanation.

SEGREGATION POLICY AS GOVERNMENTAL ACTION AND INACTION.   Sometimes the nature of the policy being followed becomes apparent only after an analysis of consistent patterns of government action and inaction. Our European scholar would have found it relatively easy to determine that racial segregation in public schools was the government's policy in the seventeen states with statutes mandating segregation. Little doubt existed in such states, since statements of government intent, statutes, the U.S. Supreme Court's decisions, and the allocation of education funds were all consistent, making the policy clear. The European scholar would have found determining the policy followed in northern states more difficult, for there signals were mixed. However, a study of repeated patterns of action would have made it clearer. Eventually, the U.S. Supreme Court relied on such patterns in ruling that many northern school districts were practicing segregation. For example, in *Keyes v. School District No. 1, Denver* (413 U.S. 189), the court identified several tactics that Denver used to create a segregated school system. In addition to the neighborhood school policy mentioned earlier, the Denver School Board habitually manipulated attendance zones, selected sites for new buildings that maintained racial segregation, and used mobile classroom units to avoid integration. The result of all these actions, repeated consistently and over time, was a racially segregated system. Thus, Denver was following a policy of racial segregation in its schools and was declared in violation of federal law in 1973 (Alexander and Alexander, 2008; Cambron-McCabe, McCarthy, & Thomas, 2004).

Patterns of government inaction became evident after *Brown v. Board of Education of Topeka* (347 U.S. 483) declared racial segregation illegal. Although the U.S. Supreme Court's decision became the law of the land, superseding all laws inconsistent with it, neither southern nor northern school districts rushed to dismantle segregation. Instead, they adopted patterns of inaction that, in some cases, endured for many years. Fifteen years after *Brown,* a federal district court ordered the Charlotte–Mecklenburg School District in North Carolina to create a desegregation plan (Alexander & Alexander, 2008). Ten years later, other federal courts gave the Columbus, Ohio, district similar instructions (Cambron-McCabe, McCarthy & Thomas, 2004). What was happening in those districts during the years after the *Brown* decision was handed down? School administrators in Charlotte–Mecklenburg and Columbus were certainly not unaware of the U.S. Supreme Court decision or of the possibility that their practices were violating it. Nor is it likely that legislators, governors, and judges in North Carolina and Ohio were unaware of the court's ruling, or of the fact that some districts in their states continued to practice segregation. Rather, we must conclude that school officials had adopted a pattern of inaction that was tacitly supported by the inaction of their state governments. In those states—and many others—racial segregation continued to be the policy long after it had ceased to be lawful.

THE TRANSFORMATION OF THE EDUCATION POLICY ENVIRONMENT

The Way It Used to Be

If the world of education policy changed from a relatively quiet and predictable "Kansas" to a rapidly changing and unpredictable "Oz," we must understand the way it used to be. Until the 1980s, public schools were among the most respected institutions of U.S. society. At times, public leaders severely criticized them and offered suggestions for improvement. For example, in the late 1950s, the former Soviet Union launched *Sputnik,* an artificial satellite, provoking frantic calls for better science and mathematics instruction in U.S. high schools. However, this critique and virtually all others were offered within a framework that took public education itself for granted. Few people raised questions about its fundamental legitimacy. Until the early 1980s, funding for schools was more or less adequate, although this varied by district and region. At times, as in the 1960s, public funding was even generous. Moreover, until the beginning of the Reagan Administration, state governments delegated most of their authority over public education to local school districts without requiring them to do much to demonstrate accountability. In state legislatures, education policy was commonly developed within what was called an *iron triangle*, consisting of the education committees of the legislature, the state department of education, and the major education lobbying groups. Policy changes were usually slow and incremental. When political bodies considered new policies, all three corners of the triangle became involved in the discussion. Educators were considered experts with valuable opinions about education policy.

The New Policy Environment

Since the late 1980s, every aspect of this situation has changed. Presently, business, media, and political leaders generally consider public education to be in crisis. Many of its critics propose changes that would either alter it in profound ways or, over time, cause it to disappear in some areas and among some populations. Many school districts—and not just poor or urban ones—find themselves in ongoing financial emergencies. In states where school choice programs have been implemented, school leaders find themselves grappling with market pressures to which they are unaccustomed. State governments have asserted their authority over public schools by issuing a bewildering array of new policies and policy proposals. More often than not, they did not ask public school educators for input. Instead, they defined educators as a major part of the problem, rather than as professionals qualified to offer solutions, and sought input from business leaders and think-tank researchers instead. Many public school teachers and administrators feel confused and even resentful as they cope with the resulting policy climate. Many also have become fatalistic about the new environment, perceiving it as a storm to be weathered passively because no one can do anything about it.

Reasons for These Changes

ECONOMIC CHANGES.   The reasons for the changed education policy environment are complex and multifaceted. However, most observers agree that major economic changes, not only in the United States but around the world, played an important role. World War II was followed by an unprecedented boom, during which many countries experienced economic growth for nearly thirty years. That period ended about 1975 and was succeeded by a period of slow to stagnant growth. During times of slow growth, citizens become increasingly reluctant to pay taxes; since the late 1970s, the United States has seen several low-tax movements and tax rebellions. In such a climate, politicians are unwilling to increase taxes or even keep public spending steady. Instead, they try to reduce spending on public services, including public education. Although an economic boom occurred during the 1990s, the "no new tax" mentality persisted. The September 2001 terrorist attacks on Washington, D.C., and New York City ushered in a period during which already lean government resources have been more frequently directed toward military action and domestic security than public education. By 2007 the country had entered a serious recession, and the recovery has been slow and uneven. The economic problem has been compounded in the United States by a well-documented increase in the disparity between the wealthiest and the poorest sectors of the population, as well as a higher percentage of children falling below the poverty line. Educating poor children well is costlier than educating those whose families have abundant or adequate resources. Thus, schools find themselves shouldering additional burdens at a time when their own resources are declining. These new facts contribute to the overall sense of crisis in education (Bartlett, 2009; Krugman, 2009; Reich, 2010).

DEMOGRAPHIC TRENDS.   Demographics have also contributed to a change in the policy environment. Since the early 1980s, the composition of the U.S. population has changed greatly. One demographic phenomenon of special importance is the aging *baby boom generation*, people born between 1946 and 1964. As babies, teens, and young adults, this segment of the population had enormous cultural impact on the nation. Now the oldest baby boomers are in their sixties and beginning to retire. Political leaders are concerned about financing their retirements as well as their health-care costs. Significant funds, both private and public, will be spent on the baby boom generation over the next forty years, thereby reducing the amount of money available for schools. Moreover, older people tend to be poorly attuned to the current needs of education because they have no young children. This means that political support for public schools, which has declined as the population aged, will probably continue to decline.

Another important demographic change is the increasing diversity of the population, a trend apparent in the 2010 Census. Because of high levels of immigration and differential birth rates, the nation is becoming more multicultural. Racial, ethnic, religious, and linguistic diversity are an important part of the context in which public schools operate and in which political decisions about them are made. This diversity means that new demands are being made on public schools. Bilingual programs, the accommodation of a wider range of religious practices, and pressures for multicultural curricula are just a few manifestations of the complexity resulting from diversity. Although diversity enriches society, some find it threatening. In fact, it has led some to question whether a single system of public schools can or should meet the needs of so many diverse groups. Faced with conflicting demands from different segments of the population, some people suggest that public education be fragmented into multiple, freestanding schools of choice, each specialized to meet the needs of a specific group (Chubb & Moe, 1990).

IDEOLOGICAL SHIFT.   Since the late 1970s, a major shift in political ideas has occurred in the United States and, indeed, throughout the English-speaking world. In general, the focus of education politics shifted from issues of equality to issues relating to excellence, accountability, and choice (Boyd & Kerchner, 1988). This shift has influenced both Republicans and Democrats, and affected education policy not only under Reagan and both Bushes, but under Clinton and Obama as well. In policy debates, politicians have embraced the ideas pushed by business leaders, sometimes sounding as if they discern no differences between public schools and private firms. They criticize schools for their alleged inefficiency and insensitivity to the market—concerns that have not traditionally been high priorities for public educators. Moreover, for the first time in decades, traditional conservatives—such as the Religious Right—emerged as a major force in U.S. politics. In many communities across the nation, in many state capitals, and in Washington, D.C., these conservatives began to play an active role in policy development. For many reasons, this group is also often critical of public education. The ideologies of both the business community and the Religious Right lead them to be skeptical of government involvement and government initiatives. Public schools are, of course, a part of the government and are therefore automatically defined as part of the problem. As a result of these shifts in values, school leaders find themselves at the center of the attention of two groups that formerly had less to say about education.

Finally, the tone of U.S. politics has changed, becoming increasingly harsh. Lowi (1995), a political scientist at Cornell University, argues that since the 1980 presidential election, U.S. politics has been "Europeanized," by which he means that it has become both more polarized and more focused on ideas. Not only are American politicians pushing narrower ideologies, but they are pursuing them more aggressively than before. For school leaders who grew up when political discourse was more civil, this harsh tone can be disconcerting.

PRO-CON DEBATE: SHOULD POLITICS BE KEPT OUT OF EDUCATION?

YES: The education of our children is much too important to permit it to become entangled with politics. Of course, because public money funds public schools, some form of government oversight must exist. Ideally, this oversight should be provided by a governing body chosen through nonpartisan elections with the authority to provide general policy guidelines for the schools. However, those policies should be carried out by professional educators who have considerable freedom to act without interference. After all, professionals are knowledgeable about children, curriculum, and teaching methods. They may make mistakes, but they are more likely to make decisions in the best interests of children than are politicians. Politics and education don't mix.

NO: Public schools are funded by tax money and are under the authority of state legislatures, school boards, and the courts. This means that politics *cannot* be kept out of public education. Even when education is governed by "nonpartisan" boards, political activity continues. However, it is relatively quiet and hidden, making it difficult for ordinary citizens to understand and influence it. Openness about the political nature of education is more democratic, and can encourage leaders to develop governance structures and laws that facilitate healthy political activity. The idea that politics and education do not mix is an illusion.

• *What do YOU think?*

Changed Roles of School Leaders

REALLOCATION OF AUTHORITY.   To complicate matters even further during this time of rapid change, education authority was reallocated in several ways. Because the Reagan Administration devolved, or handed down, much authority to the states—a trend reinforced by every administration since then—in some ways the federal government has less authority over education than it did in 1980. For example, the shift from categorical to block grants gave state governments more discretionary power over federal education funds than they previously exercised. The states, however, did not usually pass their new power on to districts and their school boards. Not only did they keep power in the state capitals, often they also took it away from local districts and made it their own. The *No Child Left Behind Act* (NCLB) intensified this trend. Of course, states have long had the ultimate legal authority over U.S. school systems. Legally, local school districts are "state agencies." Even so, until recently, most states delegated much of their authority to school boards. As long as they worked effectively with their boards, district office administrators had considerable latitude to develop education policy within school districts.

In the early 1980s, state legislatures began to take back some of their authority. Curriculum policy, for example, was traditionally the domain of local educators. This changed. During the 1980s, states such as Florida and Texas—in which state governments had traditionally said little or nothing about curriculum—passed basic skills curricula and statewide testing programs. In the 1990s, state standards became commonplace in many places. States such as New York and California, where legislatures historically exercised some jurisdiction over curriculum, intensified their control over it. Several states also passed "state takeover" legislation. Under such laws, school districts that are deemed "deficient" according to state criteria can be taken over and operated by state officials. New Jersey and Illinois are just two of the states in which takeovers occurred. Additionally, in the mid-1980s, many education reformers started advocating site-based management. At least one state, Kentucky, mandated it, and numerous districts in other states practice it. Site-based management moves considerable authority from the district to the building level. In the new configuration of education authority, then, the federal and district levels lost power, and state and building levels gained it (Fowler, 2000).

DISTRICT LEADERSHIP. Not so long ago, most superintendents and other district leaders could do their jobs effectively while largely ignoring the rest of the world. They needed to understand how to work with their school board, manage district finances, select competent personnel, and build community support. Two or three times a year they visited the state capital for a legislative briefing, and once a year they attended a national conference to hear about the latest innovations. The rest of the time, they tended the shop at home.

The extent to which these changes had occurred by the mid-1990s is suggested by Kowalski's (1995) study of seventeen big-city superintendents. To his surprise, he found that most of the major problems that these school leaders identified were not local issues, but state and national ones, such as the funding of education and the impact of child poverty on public schools. Not surprisingly, a decade later Björk and Gurley (2005) argued that contemporary superintendents must be prepared to act as both educational statesmen and political strategists. They stated that today's super-intendents have to understand "the dynamics of human political behavior at macro and micro levels of government and organizations" (p. 181). Moreover, in a study of female superintendents and women who aspired to become superintendents, Brunner and Grogan (2007) found that almost 30% of the women in their sample believed that the perception that women are "weak politically" was a major barrier to being hired for the position.

BUILDING LEADERSHIP. Even more than district leaders, building administrators have traditionally been insulated—and isolated—from the pressures of the outside world. For the most part, they stayed within their four walls, making occasional forays to district meetings. No one expected them to follow state politics, or even the policy developments in neighboring districts. In the 1990s, however, several education re-form movements began to break down this isolation. Under site-based management policies, for example, principals and assistant principals are likely to find themselves dealing directly with state **policymakers.** Goode (1994) studied two high schools in Kentucky, one of the first states to mandate site-based decision making. She found that the principals frequently had direct dealings with officials in the state capital. The principals and their councils attended training sessions offered by the state depart-ment of education, and they had to submit their professional development plans to the state for approval, not to their school board. One of the principals had even applied for waivers from certain board policies. In order to do so, she first had to obtain rulings from the state attorney general's office. Current reforms that imply a need for greater sensitivity to the state policy environment on the part of building leaders include early childhood education, charter schools, and state-mandated standards. For principals, too, the days when they could close their doors and forget everything else have ended.

PUBLIC LEADERSHIP. Public school administrators are being transformed from bureaucratic leaders into what Crosby and Bryson (2005) call *public leaders.* They argue that bureaucratic leaders rely heavily on authority and rational decision mak-ing because they work within organizations that accord them high hierarchical status. Of course, superintendents, principals, and other administrators still function bureaucratically within their school districts. Increasingly, however, they are called on to act outside their districts and to function as leaders in networks of organizations. For school leaders, these networks often include the leaders of organizations such as the state legislature, the juvenile justice system, other school districts, local chapters of national advocacy groups, and city or state human services departments. In these networks they have no hierarchical status; rather, they must rely on such leadership tools as persuasion, coalition building, and political strategies. Effective action in such arenas requires an understanding of the broader socioeconomic context within which schools are located and an awareness of the policy environment. In short, it requires an understanding of policy issues and processes.

THE POLICY PROCESS

The *policy process* is the sequence of events that occurs when a political system considers different approaches to public problems, adopts one of them, tries it out, and evaluates it. Political scientists often use game metaphors to describe it. Like a game, the policy process has rules and players. Like a game, it is complex and often disorderly. Like a game, it is played in many arenas and involves the use of power. And like a game, it can have winners and losers (Lindblom & Woodhouse, 1993). The process is driven by policy issues (Crosby & Bryson, 2005). Therefore, we begin our discussion with policy issues, then present briefly the classic stage model of the policy process. Each stage is developed later in this book—although a weakness of this model is that it suggests that the policy process is more orderly, as well as more rational than it really is (Knoepfl et al., 2007). However, it does provide a helpful framework for organizing information and investigating how policies change.

Policy Issues

CONTROVERSIAL ELEMENTS. A policy issue is, by definition, controversial. An issue exists only if social groups disagree about how government should approach a given problem (Coplin & O'Leary, 1981). Most education policies are not *policy issues* at all. For example, the policy goal of teaching all children to read is not an issue today. Virtually everyone in the United States—liberal and conservative, rich and poor, male and female, white, African American, or Hispanic—agrees that children need to learn to read. Two centuries ago, however, the proposal that all children should attain literacy *was* a policy issue. At that time, most people considered reading an appropriate skill only for children from relatively affluent backgrounds. In many states, teaching slaves to read was illegal, and Native Americans were widely believed incapable of learning. Moreover, children from the large rural segment of the population—especially girls—often did not learn to read. The goal of universal literacy ceased to be a policy issue over the next 200 years, but only after hard-fought battles in courts and state legislatures.

PUBLIC ELEMENT. Many disagreements about how children should be socialized are not policy issues, either. Policy issues are problems that the government can address legitimately. For example, psychologists disagree about the appropriateness of toy guns and war weapons for children. Some argue that such toys encourage violence, whereas others deny that allegation. However, this disagreement is not currently a policy issue because no government in the United States is likely to deal with it. In the U.S. political culture, a sharp line of demarcation runs between private problems that concern the family and public issues that fall within the scope of government authority. Few Americans—even those who disapprove of toy weapons—believe that government policies about them would be appropriate.

EXAMPLES OF EDUCATION POLICY ISSUES.   Today a large number of education policy issues are under debate. One especially controversial issue is merit pay for teachers. Traditionally, teachers have been remunerated on a "single-salary scale," which bases their pay on the number of years of experience and the level of professional education attained. However, many people believe that this approach neither motivates good teachers to excel nor penalizes weak teachers. They argue therefore that teachers' pay should be "linked" to the quality of their work. Opponents of such plans argue that teacher quality is hard to determine and that merit pay might encourage unhealthy competition among teachers and be based on favoritism rather than on true merit (Johnson & Papay, 2010; Ritter & Jensen, 2010). Another education policy issue relates to establishing national curriculum standards, advocates of which assert that such standards provide clear criteria for excellence throughout the country and reduce the negative impact of mobility on children's schooling. They also argue that most other advanced industrial countries have national curricula, and that because of global economic competition, the United States should follow suit. Opponents of such a policy believe that it would weaken local control of education and lead to an undesirable standardization of education throughout the country. They also argue that the federal government lacks the constitutional authority to establish national curriculum standards or develop national tests to evaluate it. Both merit pay for teachers and a national curriculum are policy issues because they are controversial and because they are policies that governments might adopt.

Applying the Stage Model to Standards-Based Reform

Figure 1.1 represents the classic stage model of the policy process, with minor modifications. It begins with issue definition, the first stage in the process chronologically. The heavy arrows move from left to right, following the order of the classic model. However, dotted arrows move from right to left because sometimes a policy issue advances for a time and then moves back to an earlier stage. The diagram is shaped like a funnel because the process functions selectively; at each successive stage, fewer issues or policies are involved. In the following sections, each stage of the process is discussed briefly. Throughout these sections, a single policy issue—standards-based reform—is used as an example, for it is relatively easy to trace the history of this issue from the early 1980s to the present.

ISSUE DEFINITION.   At any given time, every society has numerous social problems, but only a few are ever identified as public policy problems. For many reasons, government never addresses most problems. Sufficient political support may not exist, for example, or the potential costs of addressing certain problems may be too high.

Standards-based reform provides a good example of a policy area that for many decades was not an issue. Although states set up public school systems and mandated school attendance during the nineteenth century, they delegated almost all of their

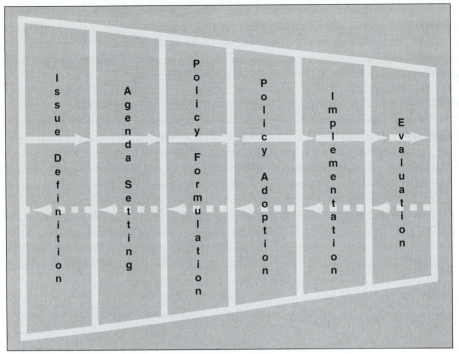

FIGURE 1.1   A diagram of the policy process

authority to local school districts (Fowler, 2000). Throughout most of the twentieth century, they continued to let local school districts have broad latitude in the areas of curriculum and pedagogy, concentrating most of their regulatory efforts on educational inputs such as pupil-teacher ratios, teachers' qualifications, and per-pupil expenditure. However, in the mid-1970s, national organizations and leaders began to express concern about performance. For example, many politicians worried about the fact that SAT scores had been declining since 1963. In 1981, the Southern Regional Education Board—which represented fifteen southern states—published a report called *The Need for Quality,* attacking the minimum competency reforms of the previous decade (Ravitch, 1995). However, it was the *Nation at Risk* report that most dramatically defined the quality issue in 1983. President Reagan used it as a springboard for redefining the key education issues not as access and equity, but as the need for increased excellence (Cook, 2001; Fuhrman, 2001; Ravitch, 1995).

Spearheaded by presidential rhetoric, the states launched numerous incremental reforms such as increasing graduation requirements. By the end of the 1980s, however, these reforms were generally perceived as inadequate. Concerns about the poor performance of American students on international tests in science and mathematics led leaders to examine the education policies of other nations. Learning that most developed countries had national content standards and tests, they began to redefine the problem of the supposedly poor quality of education in the United States as the lack of clear curriculum standards and tests to assess curriculum mastery (Ravitch, 1995). Issue definition is discussed in greater depth in Chapter 7.

AGENDA SETTING.   Not every problem defined as an education policy issue is acted on by a government. In order to have a chance of eventually becoming policy, an issue must be placed on the policy agenda, or "list of subjects or problems to which governmental officials, and people outside government closely associated with those officials, are paying some serious attention at any given time" (Kingdon, 2003, p. 3). The policy agenda is usually set by powerful politicians, such as presidents, governors, and legislators.

Unlike many policy issues, standards-based reform reached the national policy agenda not long after it was defined as an issue. In the mid-1980s, Secretary of Education William Bennett was a vocal spokesman for higher intellectual standards in the nation's schools. In 1987, two books that were read and discussed widely, Allan Bloom's *The Closing of the American Mind* and E. D. Hirsch, Jr.'s *Cultural Literacy*, pushed the issue into the national limelight. In the fall of 1989, President Bush and the nation's governors, who were under considerable pressure from business leaders, developed a set of national education "goals" that the president announced in his 1990 State of the Union Address. He also set up a National Education Goals Panel to monitor progress toward achieving them. Although the term used at this point was *goals* rather than *standards,* the issue was now squarely on both the state and national policy agendas (Jennings, 1998; Ravitch, 1995). Sometimes the activities of grassroots organizations influence political leaders', agendas. For example, in both Milwaukee and Cleveland, the voucher issue was placed on the state policy agenda at least in part because of the efforts of local African-American organizers. However, no evidence of any grassroots activity in support of standards-based reform is available. Agenda setting is also discussed in Chapter 7.

POLICY FORMULATION.   Before a policy can be adopted formally, it must be expressed in written form. The first written text developed is usually a *bill,* a draft of a proposed statute. Most legislators in Congress and state legislatures do not write the bills they sponsor. Bills may be developed by members of their legislative staff, by lawyers retained for that purpose, or by advocacy groups who support the legislation. Often rival bills on the same subject are introduced into a legislature for consideration. Rules and regulations are written after statutes have been adopted. They, too, may pass through several drafts before becoming official. Those groups and individuals who advocate standards-based reform cooperated nationwide to influence policy formulation. This is why, for example, there is a strong resemblance among the curriculum standards and testing programs of many states (Ravitch, 1995). Policy formulation is described in Chapter 8.

POLICY ADOPTION.   In order for a policy to take effect, its written formulation must be adopted officially by the appropriate government body. Statutes are adopted by a majority vote in Congress and in state legislatures. In public education, rules and regulations are adopted by authorized officials within such agencies as the U.S. Department of Education, state departments of education, and local school districts. Some district policies require a majority vote by a school board.

Under the first Bush Administration, two bills that endorsed standards and tests were introduced in Congress; both failed. Clinton defeated Bush in the 1992 election, but he advocated national standards and tests during his campaign. His administration tried to get Congress to pass a standards-based reform bill in 1993, but failed. However, a rewritten version of that bill was passed in 1994 as the *Goals 2000: Educate America Act.*

It set up an agency called the National Education Standards and Improvement Council to develop voluntary national standards; national tests were not included because of strong political opposition. Moreover, in 1994, the reauthorization of the *Elementary and Secondary Education Act (ESEA)* linked Title I funds to standards-based reform (Jennings, 1998; Ravitch, 1995). The second Bush Administration's reauthorization of ESEA, called the *No Child Left Behind Act* of 2001, further strengthened the policy language in support of standards and testing. Policy adoption is presented in detail in Chapter 8.

IMPLEMENTATION.   The passage of a statute and accompanying rules and regulations does not mean the new policy automatically goes into operation. Education policies must be implemented at the grassroots level by district administrators, principals, and classroom teachers. These educators are not necessarily enthusiastic about new laws and rules from Washington or their state capital. Therefore, the success of implementation depends on motivating educators to implement the new policy and providing them with the resources to do so. Research suggests that often new policies either are not implemented at all or are substantially modified during implementation. By 2000, forty-nine states had adopted legislation establishing curriculum standards. However, research by the Urban Institute and the Consortium for Policy Research in Education (CPRE) about that time suggested that implementation at the district and school levels had been uneven, with some aspects of the reforms used more widely than others (DeBray, Parson, & Woodworth, 2001; Fuhrman, 2001; Hannaway & Kimball, 2001; McGuinn, 2006). When the democratic Obama Administration took office in 2009, it soon revealed that it also favored standards-based reforms, as evidenced by its Race to the Top competition and proposals for amending NCLB (Obama Administration's education reform plan emphasizes flexibility, resources and accountability for results, 2010; Noguera, 2010). Policy implementation is discussed in Chapter 10.

EVALUATION.   Ideally, policies are evaluated in order to determine if they work as they are intended. *Evaluation* is a form of applied research designed to achieve this purpose. Sometimes policies are evaluated by a research office within the government that passed the policy. Evaluations may also be conducted by outside groups that do this kind of work. Although standards-based reform is supposed to raise student achievement, its effectiveness is still unclear. A number of programs have been evaluated, generally by curriculum writers who have a vested interest in the success of their own curricula. In 2002, the National Science Foundation (NSF) commissioned a review of existing evaluations that was released in 2003. However, these findings may also be biased because the NSF has been a major advocate of standards (Hoff, 2002, June 12). For the time being, at least, standards-based reform has not been evaluated adequately. Policy evaluation is the subject of Chapter 11.

THE SCHOOL LEADER AND POLICY STUDIES

School administrators act as hierarchical leaders within their organizations and as public leaders in the broader community. In both roles, they play, or can play, a significant part in defining, developing, and implementing education policy. Although their multidimensional role is developed in detail in later chapters, understanding the general nature of that role from the outset is helpful.

Administrators as Policymakers

Legally, school districts are agencies of the government of the state within which they are located, just as the bureau of motor vehicles and the state highway department are state agencies (Alexander & Alexander, 2008). As a result, school administrators play a major role in the development of rules and regulations. In most policy areas, the state legislature and its state education agency provide a broad framework of legislation. School boards, administrators, and classroom teachers are responsible for filling in many of the details of that framework. Their policy making takes such forms as recommending a policy revision to the school board, developing a manual of rules for classified staff, or writing a student discipline code for a school. No matter what the situation, knowledge of policy and the policy process is helpful to administrators in their policy-making role. For example, if a principal perceives that insufficient parking is becoming an issue for her faculty, knowledge of the policy process suggests several courses of action. If it is still in the early stages, she may choose to participate in defining the issue, and knowledge of policy studies suggests some ways to do that. If the issue is already defined clearly and she agrees with the definition, she may appoint a committee to work with her to carry out an informal **policy analysis** and generate alternatives for discussion. An understanding of the range of policy instruments available enables her to enter the discussion with several creative ideas and assess alternatives suggested by others. Ultimately, her expertise should permit her and the teachers to develop a sound rule that deals effectively with the problem.

Administrators as Implementers of Policy

Within their organizations, school administrators also play a major role in implementing new policies. Regardless of whether the new policy originated at the federal, state, or local level, they are expected to develop a plan to carry it out, motivate teachers and others to cooperate, marshal the necessary resources, and provide feedback about the process. Change is always difficult, so administrators who are responsible for implementing a new and possibly unpopular policy find themselves in a challenging situation. Under stress, they are likely to make mistakes. However, much research has been done on implementation, and specifically on the implementation of education policy. The major mistakes that implementers make were identified long ago; so were sound approaches to organizational change. School administrators familiar with this literature are well equipped to avoid the most obvious pitfalls of implementation. They also know some ways to reduce the stress and confusion that are inevitable components of putting any new policy in place.

Administrators as Followers of Policy Issues

School leaders of the twenty-first century cannot restrict themselves to building and district level concerns. State governments are more active in education policy than ever before, and education is considered a "hot" issue at both the state and federal levels. This means that administrators who try to ignore the outside world find themselves on the receiving end of many policy surprises and may also feel as if they have no input into many of the reforms occurring. Today, therefore, following policy issues is essential for school leaders. They must be aware of the major changes occurring in their social and economic environment and of how those changes may eventually give rise to education policy issues. They must know what issues are being defined in think tanks, universities, and foundations, and must also follow the legislative process at the federal and state levels. More than ever, then, it is essential for school leaders to be active and informed. Such activity is the indispensable foundation for being a knowledgeable participant in the policy process beyond the limits of the district.

Administrators as Influencers of Policy

In their capacity as public leaders (Crosby & Bryson, 2005), school administrators are in a position to exercise influence on the policy process at the state and federal levels. This influence can take many forms. A superintendent may call the state department of education to discuss the problems he is having implementing a program, which may lead to a change in the department's rules and regulations. A special education supervisor may believe that a new bill in the legislature is unfair to the state's handicapped children, which may lead her to identify several other supervisors and leaders of parent organizations who share her views. Together, they may make an appointment with the chair of the House Education Committee to discuss the issue, and may alert several professional organizations to the problem and obtain their support. These efforts may lead to the defeat of the bill or to amendments that reduce its negative impact. At the building level, a principal may become involved in a school-university partnership that includes a number of agencies that work with children. This collaboration may make him and everyone else aware of overlaps and contradictions in the services delivered to at-risk children. After defining the issue carefully, the principal and other participants may coordinate a simultaneous approach to all their respective state agencies to inform them of the problem.

FINAL POINTS

Today's school leaders have a different role than they did in the past. In part, this new role involves exercising public leadership. School leaders who do not learn how to exercise this new role are likely to be the passive recipients of policy surprises. Today, effective public leadership requires a solid foundation of knowledge about education policy and how it is developed and changed. This book provides that foundation.

QUESTIONS AND ACTIVITIES FOR DISCUSSION

1. Develop a list of current policy issues in your state, district, or building. Situate each in a stage of the policy process.
2. What major education policy initiatives has your state government made during the past decade? How have the initiatives affected your school and district?
3. Select one of the following policy issues and describe the current status of your state's policy regarding this issue: early childhood education, high school graduation rates, merit pay for teachers, improving teacher quality, or value-added evaluation. Be sure to consider not only formal laws but also funding levels and patterns of government inaction.
4. Identify and describe an instance in which school administrators you know have acted as public leaders to influence the policy process.

INTERNET ASSIGNMENT

Locate three reviews of Davis Guggenheim's 2010 documentary film, *Waiting for Superman,* and read them critically. In what ways do they reflect the new education policy environment discussed in this chapter?

FOR FURTHER READING

Björk, L. G., & Gurley, D. K. (2005). Superintendent as educational statesman and political strategist. In L. G. Björk & T. J. Kowalski (Eds.), *The contemporary superintendent* (pp. 163–185). Thousand Oaks, CA: Corwin Press.

 The authors discuss the political dimensions of the job of school superintendents in the new millennium. Arguing that the job has become increasingly political and involves a sophisticated understanding of education policy, they provide a valuable overview of the superintendent's job in both the micro- and macropolitical arenas.

Marshall, C. (2000). Policy discourse analysis: Negotiating gender equity. *Journal of Education Policy, 15*(2), 125–156.

 Marshall applies standard policy analysis procedures as well as discourse analysis to the passage and implementation of gender equity policies in Australian schools. Her article provides a good example of how a policy can be analyzed systematically.

Sykes, G., Schneider, B., & Plank, D. N. (Eds.). (2009). *Handbook of education policy research.* New York: Routledge.

 This edited volume contains 76 articles on a wide range of policy topics, from the impact of politics on policy to research on current issues. It provides a good resource for exploring various dimensions of policy studies and identifying up-to-date findings in the field.

Weimer, D. L. (2009). Making education research more policy-analytic. In G. Sykes, B. Schneider, & D. N. Plank (Eds.), *Handbook of education policy research*, pp. 93–100. New York: Routledge.

 While acknowledging the value of general policy research, Weimer argues that more *policy-analytic* research is needed. Such research would provide several concrete policy alternatives as solutions to a given problem, giving policymakers several informed choices to consider.

Yanow, D. (2000). *Conducting interpretive policy analysis.* Thousand Oaks, CA: Sage Publications.

 Yanow, a professor of public administration, shows how interpretive policy analysis can provide insights into the values and ideological stances of the different stakeholders in a policy environment. Of particular interest is her use of interpretive policy analysis to reveal the "architecture of policy arguments" (p. iii).

2 | POWER AND EDUCATION POLICY

Focus Questions

▌ What is power?

▌ What are the major types and sources of power?

▌ How is power used in school organizations and to shape education policy?

▌ What ethical issues does power raise?

INTRODUCTORY COMMENTS

Power and education policy cannot be separated because the exercise of power shapes the outcome of the policy process. Moreover, because power relations are institutionalized in school systems, school administrators have power through their organizational positions. They have that power in order to carry out the government's education policy as it relates to schools and school systems. In doing so, they also regularly interact with powerful individuals and groups, many of whom wish to influence or circumvent that policy. All school leaders, then, must understand power and the complex issues it raises.

DEFINING POWER

A "Contested" Concept

Power is an "essentially contested" concept (Lukes, 2005, p. 30), which means that one's understanding of it is shaped by one's theory of human nature and society, leading social scientists from different theoretical traditions to argue about its meaning. At one extreme, some utilitarians deny the very existence of power. At the other, some post-structuralists, such as Foucault, believe that power so permeates every human activity that truth itself is determined by it. Between these extremes one finds many positions.

Political scientist Robert Dahl proposed a classic definition: "*A* has power over *B* to the extent that he [*sic*] can get *B* to do something that *B* would not otherwise do" (Lukes, 2005, p. 16). Although many people have found Dahl's definition helpful, it leaves certain points obscure: Does *A* have to be consciously aware of exercising power over *B*? Does *B* have to be consciously aware of *A*'s power? Can *A*'s exercise of power cause *B* *not* to act? Has *A* exercised power if *B* believes that what *A* wants is good, and eagerly performs the desired action? Is it ethical to exercise power over another? The controversy over power swirls around issues such as these. In the next section, a working definition of *power,* situated somewhere between the extremes represented by the utilitarians and some poststructuralists, is developed for use in this book.

A Working Definition of Power

Despite the scholarly controversy, a working definition of *power* is essential in a book about education policy. The starting point for this definition is Muth's (1984) statement that *power* is "the ability of an actor to affect the behavior of another actor" (p. 27), a somewhat broader definition than Dahl's. The term *actor* includes both individuals— such as superintendents, governors, and teacher union presidents—and groups—such as school boards, state legislatures, and Parent–Teacher Associations (PTAs). The ability to exercise power depends on possessing appropriate resources, such as money, social status, and information. Power resources are discussed in detail later in the chapter. Because power resources are limited and a "cost" is attached to using them, actors are not always willing to expend them. Thus, the ability to exercise power includes the willingness to deploy resources. Finally, behavior can be affected in many ways, using one or more types of power. Possible effects include causing an actor to act, preventing an actor from acting, and shaping the nature of the actor's action. An actor may be conscious, unconscious, or partially conscious of the use of power (Bachrach & Baratz, 1962; Delpit, 1988).

Because power is a relationship, it always exists in a concrete social context. An actor who is relatively powerful in one context may not be in others. For example, a superintendent may be powerful in her community but have little power with the state legislature. Power relationships may be symmetrical or asymmetrical. Actors who have similar degrees of power are symmetrically related, having a "shared power" relationship (Crosby & Bryson, 2005). In symmetrical relationships, people commonly use persuasion and bargaining with economic resources. Actors with significantly different amounts of resources have an asymmetrical power relationship. Although they may use persuasion or bargaining, more powerful actors may also use force, appeals to authority, or reward-and-punishment strategies to affect less powerful actors. Even in very asymmetrical relationships, however, weaker actors are rarely powerless. Various forms of resistance are available to them. For example, teachers who resent a state legislature's new testing program may find ways to sabotage it.

Power may be exercised either distributively or facilitatively (Mann, 1992). In using power distributively, one actor exercises power over the other. For instance, a superintendent may decide unilaterally that all teachers in his district must punch time clocks, proceed to have the clocks installed, and distribute a memo describing the new procedure. However, power may be exercised facilitatively to "create or sustain favorable conditions, allow[ing] subordinates to enhance their individual and collective performance" (Dunlap & Goldman, 1991, p. xx). For example, a supervisor may work facilitatively with a group of teachers to establish a computer lab, providing support in the form of information and release time.

Power, like automobiles, can be abused easily, but it is ethically neutral. Although some types of power and some power resources can never be used ethically, leaders can exercise power in an ethical manner. Ethical issues surrounding power are discussed in the final section of this chapter.

DISCOURSE AND POWER

School Administration as Talk

Language is important in school leadership. To a great extent school administration is achieved through talk: talk in meetings, talk in random hallway encounters, talk on the telephone, talk to the media, and talk on the grapevine. Research indicates that principals and superintendents spend 67% to 75% of their time talking (Gronn, 1983). This means that when school leaders exercise power or experience its pressure on their own behavior, that power is usually communicated through language. As Corson (1995) puts it: "All kinds of power are directed, mediated, or resisted through language" (p. 3).

Since about 1970, scholars in every branch of the social sciences have devoted much attention to the study of language, or discourse, in society. Because they have made more obvious the linguistic mechanisms through which people exercise power, their research provides valuable tools for exploring power in school leadership and the education policy process. Throughout this book, then, discursive exercises of power are identified and discussed.

Texts

What is *discourse*? According to Fairclough (2003), every instance of discourse has three aspects. The first is the *text*, which can consist of written, spoken, or a combination of written and spoken language. For example, when a superintendent holds his weekly meeting with the district office staff, a text is produced that includes everything he and the other participants said at the meeting, as well as documents associated with the meeting, such as the agenda and written versions of committee reports. Looking at this text alone may provide important clues to power relationships in the central office and the community. For example, the text may reveal that the superintendent and the business manager dominated the meeting, talking far more than anyone else. It may reveal that cost was the determining consideration in 90% of the decisions reached. The language used by participants may be full of terms borrowed from business, such as *payoff, bottom line,* and *biggest bang for the buck.* Such findings suggest a school system dominated by a superintendent and business manager who have been influenced by the business community. One would expect district policy to reflect this influence and the values implicit in it.

Social Events

The second aspect of any instance of discourse is the social event that shapes the production of the text (Fairclough, 2003). Because meetings are frequent social events in U.S. society, rules and traditions shape them. For example, a chairperson usually runs a meeting, determining who gains the floor, how long each issue is discussed, and how issues are resolved. Someone usually takes notes, which are later converted into minutes. Motions are usually made and seconded. Moreover, each organization has its own traditions about meetings. These traditions may include how items are placed on the agenda and how long the meeting can last. All of these formal and informal rules and traditions constitute a *social event* (Fairclough, 2003). They influence what can be said and done as the text is produced. In order to interpret a text accurately, one must not only have the text, but understand the social event that produced it as well. For example, in interpreting the meeting previously described, knowing how items were placed on the agenda and who appointed the committee chairpersons provides important clues to power relationships.

Social Practice

The third aspect of discourse is the *social practice* in which both the text and the discourse practice are embedded (Fairclough, 2003). The superintendent and district office staff attending the meeting are part of a larger organization, a school system. If it is like most U.S. school systems, it has both a formal structure, consisting of differentiated roles arranged hierarchically, and an informal network of relationships and influence. Beyond the school system, other relevant social practices can be found. The formal organization of most school systems reflects the Scientific Management Movement, popular in U.S. business circles in the early 1900s. This movement included definitions of the appropriate roles for people at various hierarchical levels, and U.S. culture also includes ideas about how men and women and people of different races should relate to each other. All these elements—and many others—constitute the social practice in which the superintendent's meeting is situated. They, too, must be taken into account in developing a sensitive interpretation of what happened at the meeting. Of course, savvy school leaders have always understood that conversations, meetings, and official documents provide important clues to organizational power relationships and behind-the-scenes happenings. They have long conducted informal analyses of discourse in order to figure out what is really going on. However, recent research on discourse provides some useful and systematic ways to approach this task.

THE THREE-DIMENSIONAL MODEL OF POWER

Because power is a popular subject for research, many theories concerning it have been advanced. Lukes (2005) and Gaventa (1980) developed a three-dimensional model of power that includes all the major theories, including the Weberian theories Bendix (1960) and Wrong (1995) summarized. Table 2.1 summarizes the three dimensions of power discussed in this section. Although the three dimensions of power, types of power, and power resources are presented separately, real life is more complex than textbook models. In most social settings, all three dimensions operate simultaneously, and several types of power are used.

The First Dimension of Power: Explicit Uses of Power

In Table 2.1, the first dimension of power consists of explicit exercises of power, which are often observable directly. For example, a state legislature uses first-dimension power visibly when it passes a law making graduation requirements more stringent. Some exercises of first-dimension power are not directly observable, however; nonetheless, they can be readily deduced from observable evidence. For example, in many schools, untenured teachers perform much extra work, such as chaperoning dances and sponsoring clubs. Their principals ask them to do these tasks because these teachers are in a precarious situation and are more likely to say "yes" than are tenured

TABLE 2.1 The Three Dimensions of Power

First Dimension: Explicit Exercises of Power	Second Dimension: Mobilization of Bias	Third Dimension: Shaping of Consciousness
Mechanisms	*Mechanisms*	*Mechanisms*
Force	Customs	Communication processes
Economic dominance	Norms	Myths
Authority	Organizational structures	Symbols
Persuasion	Procedures	
	Rules of the game	
	Social usages	
	Traditions	

Source: Based on Bendix (1960), Gaventa (1980), Lukes (2005), Weber (1986), and Wrong (1995).

teachers. For their part, nontenured teachers know they need the principal's support to be rehired and, eventually, tenured. The principal may never explicitly point this fact out to them, because it is not necessary—the procedures for rehiring and obtaining tenure are spelled out in board policy and state law. Therefore, the power relationship is explicit, although not immediately observable (Gaventa, 1980; Lukes, 2005).

TYPES OF POWER. As Table 2.1 shows, four general types of power operate in the first dimension: force, economic dominance, authority, and persuasion. They should be understood as ideal types or abstract descriptions based on many concrete examples. Real-life instances of each type include most, but not necessarily all, of the characteristics of the ideal type. Moreover, in real life, two or more types of power can be used simultaneously.

Force.   There are two kinds of force: *physical force* and *psychic* force. Exercising power through physical force involves using, or threatening to use, physical actions to impose one's will on others. Such actions include killing, injuring, or causing pain to another; restricting another's freedom; preventing another from satisfying basic biological needs; and using one's body to block another's movement. Examples of physical force in education include corporal punishment, detention halls, and in-school suspension. Psychic force is used to damage another person's self-concept. Common forms include verbal or symbolic insults, nagging, malicious gossip, and negatively stereotyping an entire group. Although the use of psychic force is never ethical, it is common at all levels of education (Wrong, 1995).

Economic Dominance.   According to Weber (1986), two types of power are especially important in modern societies: economic dominance and authority. *Economic dominance* involves using one's influence over the jobs, careers, or economic prosperity of others to affect their behavior. Anyone who is in a position to hire, fire, evaluate, or promote employees has access to this type of power, as do those who are likely to be asked to write job recommendations. Another form of economic dominance is using one's influence over such working conditions as schedules, job assignments, and vacation dates to encourage people to comply with one's wishes. On a broader scale, some corporations use their economic dominance to gain tax abatements and other concessions from local governments by threatening to relocate, taking jobs with them.

Authority.   *Authority* is operational when one observes "unquestioning recognition by those who are asked to obey; neither coercion nor persuasion is needed" (Arendt, 1986, p. 65). Authority depends on *legitimacy*, the belief that the person in authority has a right to special power. Students of power identify several sorts of authority. *Patriarchal authority* is one; a more contemporary term is *parental authority*. Because most people grow up in families, they first experience power in their relationships with parents and other relatives. In most families, people assume that parents and other older family members have a right to exercise power over children because this right is grounded in tradition. Therefore, children usually accept it as natural. People often transfer elements of parental authority to other settings, especially in elementary schools, where children may project it onto teachers and principals (Bendix, 1960).

A second form is *legal authority*, which is conferred on those who hold positions of responsibility within an organization. *Legal authority* is usually described and limited by official documents such as policy manuals and job descriptions. As long as an officeholder acts within the scope of legal authority, other members of the organization will probably comply readily. To a great extent, the relationships among teachers, principals, and district office administrators are based on legal authority (Bendix, 1960).

Competent authority is a third form. Based on expertise, it is often the only type of power professionals use with their clients. Few people challenge the medical recommendations of their doctors or the legal advice of attorneys. Although educators have less competent authority than doctors or lawyers, many individual teachers and administrators succeed in establishing a high level of competent authority in their communities (Wrong, 1995).

Finally, some people are able to affect the behavior of others through *charismatic authority*, based on purely personal qualities. Some people, through a combination of personality, appearance, and manner, evoke spontaneous confidence and enthusiasm from others. The most striking examples of charismatic authority surface in emergency situations, and charismatic authority may evaporate as soon as the emergency ends. Educators often draw on charismatic authority for some of their effectiveness; but because this is the most unstable form of authority, relying on it heavily is unwise (Bendix, 1960).

Many writers argue that the legitimacy of all forms of authority has declined steeply since World War II. Evidence for this "legitimation crisis" includes widespread cynicism about government and other institutions, juvenile delinquency, and increased crime rates. Educators experience the decline of their authority every day, both in education settings and beyond them. Forced by the weakening of their authority to use other forms of power, they nonetheless may feel uncomfortable exercising them.

Persuasion.   The final type of first-dimension power is *persuasion,* the overt attempt to affect the behavior of others by convincing them that the desired behavior is good. A common form of persuasion is *socialization,* which can be offered

TABLE 2.2 Major Power Resources

Material Resources	Social Resources	Knowledge Resources
Control over careers and working conditions	Access (to money, the media, the legal system)	Control over information
		Information
Energy	Control over votes	Intelligence
Money (cash or credit)	Numbers (allies or followers)	Skills
Patronage	Official position	Understanding how the system works
Time	Organization	
	Personal impact	Verbal ability
	Popularity	
	Social status	
	Visibility	

Source: Based on Dahl (1986), Mann (1992), Robinson (1995), and Wrong (1995).

in several formats. Many organizations require new employees to participate in an induction program, the purpose of which is to socialize newcomers to group norms (Wrong, 1995). In education, orientation sessions for new students and teachers serve this purpose. Many organizations that influence education policy also use socialization. For example, school board associations usually offer training programs for newly elected board members, and teachers unions provide training conferences for local leaders.

A second form of persuasion is *rational persuasion,* in which one individual marshals arguments and pertinent facts in order to convince another individual to take a course of action. Finally, *manipulative persuasion* may be used. On the surface, manipulative persuasion looks like rational persuasion; in fact, it is so intended. However, manipulative persuaders withhold important facts from the actors they are trying to affect. Most often, the hidden information relates to the persuader's true goal or to the potentially harmful impact of the suggested course of action (Wrong, 1995). For example, one reason many teachers are skeptical about implementing new programs is that they have been manipulatively persuaded to do so in the past. Like psychic force, manipulative persuasion is always unethical.

POWER RESOURCES.   Power depends on resources (Mann, 1992). Therefore, people who wish to build a power base do so by amassing appropriate resources for the arenas in which they wish to exercise power. Table 2.2 summarizes the major power resources. Because power is cumulative, powerful people and groups usually control a wide range of resources and may deploy several simultaneously. Although these resources can be important in the first dimension of power, some operate in other dimensions as well. In the following discussion, only a few resources are described in detail.

Material Resources.   Material resources, shown in the first column of Table 2.2, are essential to most exercises of power. Most important is money, because its possessors can easily convert it into other resources (Dahl, 1986; Wrong, 1995). For example, a school district with a large "war chest" for a funding campaign can convert money into knowledge resources by hiring a professional campaign consultant. It can also convert money into access to the media by purchasing newspaper advertisements and television and radio spots. Using control over hiring to build and exercise power, or *patronage,* is unfortunately still an important source of power in many places (Dahl, 1986). In her study of superintendents in the Northeast, Johnson (1996) found that patronage was used frequently in about one third of the districts. *Time* is a material resource because of the relationship between time and money (Wrong, 1995). Because the majority of people spend most of each day earning a living and performing unpaid labor necessary for their household, they do not have time to build and maintain a power base. Those few people who do not have to work have a considerable advantage. Among these individuals are the independently wealthy; retired people on pensions; college students supported by their families, scholarships, or loans; and married people whose spouses earn enough to support them. Therefore, people in these social categories often exercise disproportionate influence on public policy, including education policy.

Social Resources. Even if one has abundant material resources, having social resources is important as well. People who lack significant material resources can compensate for this deficiency by building and deploying social resources. The middle column of Table 2.2 lists the major social resources. One of the most important social resources is *numbers,* or numerous allies and followers. Johnson (1996) describes one superintendent's skillful use of numbers. Soon after Dick Fitzgerald began his superintendency, the town council cut the school budget by $500,000. Fitzgerald enlisted his central office staff to go out into the school buildings to tell teachers about the problem and win their support. At their superintendent's request, the teachers packed the next meeting of the town council; the money was restored to the budget. The impact of numbers can be magnified by *effective organization.* An organization is effective when it has skillful, committed leaders; respected decision-making procedures; and a planned, systematic communications system (Mann, 1992). The Religious Right has been able to influence curriculum policy in many places because it is highly organized (Apple, 2006).

Knowledge Resources. French philosopher Michel Foucault's term *power/ knowledge,* which equates power and knowledge, vividly demonstrates the importance of knowledge as a source of power (Fendler, 2010). The last column of Table 2.2 lists the most important knowledge resources. In almost any arena, people can build power by gathering pertinent *information*. Information can be of many types, including facts about relevant laws, the demographic composition of a population, the state of public opinion, and voting patterns in recent elections. Accurate information facilitates the development of realistic plans and programs. Unethical uses of information to build power include gathering "dirt" on opponents in order to smear their reputations or to blackmail them. Once an information database has been created, the issue of *control of the information* arises. Those who exercise control over information gain power because they can choose with whom they share their knowledge, as well as when and how they use it strategically (Wrong, 1995).

DISCURSIVE POWER IN THE FIRST DIMENSION. The possession of many knowledge resources can give a person considerable discursive power. In the first dimension, as in the other two, people exercise power through language, or discourse. In the first dimension, language is obviously used as an instrument of power, and the actors are usually aware of it. One frequently used discursive power technique is to produce a text designed to limit the scope of a discussion at a meeting. The person who has the authority to produce such a text—usually called an *agenda*—has a powerful tool. At most meetings, the other participants can amend the agenda, and important debate sometimes occurs around suggested amendments. Even so, people usually hesitate to propose sweeping changes in an agenda, much less suggest that it be abandoned altogether.

Nonetheless, skillful users of discourse can sabotage well-planned agendas. Waite (1995) observed a conference in which Faye, the supervisor, came armed with an agenda in the form of a checklist because she considered Bea, the teacher under supervision, "argumentative." Although Faye sought to control the discussion of Bea's teaching with her checklist, Bea successfully used other discursive techniques, finally causing the supervisor to give up all attempts to influence her. Among the teacher's discursive uses of power were raising her voice, interrupting her supervisor, talking simultaneously with her, changing the subject, and getting up from the table to look out the window. Bea's most successful discursive technique was a series of innuendos suggesting that Faye was out of touch with the realities of the classroom. This anecdote is particularly interesting because it demonstrates that the person with legal authority does not always prevail when power is exercised.

The Second Dimension of Power: The Mobilization of Bias

UNDERSTANDING THE SECOND DIMENSION: RACE. In contrast to the first dimension, in which exercises of power are explicit, power exercised in the second dimension is implicit. Table 2.1 shows some ways of exercising power in the second dimension. In this dimension, few or none of the actors may realize that power is being exercised. Exercises of power in this dimension usually limit the meaningful participation of certain groups or restrict the issues that can be raised for debate through devices less obvious than agendas (Bachrach & Baratz, 1962; Bachrach & Botwinick, 1992). This way of exercising power is called the **mobilization of bias** (Gaventa, 1980).

A historical example clarifies the difference between the two dimensions. In the 1890s, the participation of both women and African-American men in elections was limited. Although a few states had laws permitting women to vote, most did not; and the women's suffrage amendment to the U.S. Constitution had not yet been passed. Using their legal authority, Congress and most legislatures explicitly rejected bills that would have given women the right to vote. Women's low participation in voting therefore resulted from exercises of first-dimension power.

The case of African-American men was different. After the Civil War, amendments to the U.S. Constitution gave them the right to vote, and they exercised this right during Reconstruction. Their tendency not to vote in the 1890s resulted from intervening exercises of second-dimension power. Instead of passing laws outlawing African-American suffrage—which would have been unconstitutional—many states and local communities erected ingenious barriers to voting that disproportionately affected African Americans. For example, citizens who wanted to register to vote often had to pay a poll tax or pass a literacy test. Because higher percentages of African Americans were poor and illiterate, these rules affected them more than they affected whites. Sometimes voting places were located in the white residential districts of cities. Because African Americans found getting there difficult and felt intimidated if they did, they often decided not to vote. Thus, although the laws officially permitted African Americans to vote, other rules and practices made doing so difficult. In other words, a strong bias against their participation had been mobilized. When such rules were first established, most people understood their real purpose. However, after decades passed, many citizens did not. Some people sincerely believed that literacy tests would ensure an informed electorate; they did not recognize them as an exercise of second-dimension power.

NEWS STORY FOR ANALYSIS

Teachers' Union Fears Tenure Bill

CHEYENNE, WY—A legislative proposal to end teacher tenure in Wyoming would devastate school reform efforts in the state, teachers union officials say. "I think teachers are going to be less apt to take risks; they're going to be less apt to try new and different approaches," Wyoming Education Association President Kathryn Valido said at a news conference at the Capitol on Thursday. "Teachers are going to be less apt to advocate for students who may not be getting the services they need because they're not sure how their supervisor is going to react."

Lawmakers are set to debate a proposal to end tenure when the general session of the Legislature begins next week. But that would give school districts the power to fire good teachers without good reason, said Valido. Lawmakers need to kill the proposal, she added.

Currently, teachers earn "continuing contract" status after three straight years of effective teaching and good evaluations, Valido said. But, she added, that doesn't guarantee teachers a job for life. It's also nonsense to say that continuing contract teachers can't be fired, added the WEA's attorney, Pat Hacker. Districts already have the power to fire them for things like incompetence, insubordination, and unsatisfactory performance. And teachers under threat of a termination hearing often leave quietly before the process is completed, he added. Valido said the legislative proposal would allow districts to get rid of teachers even when it's unjustified or unfair.

But the termination process is so long and expensive that it overwhelms school board members, said the bill's co-sponsor Rep. Matt Teeters, R-Lingle. He is chairman of the House Education Committee. Because of that, most districts don't even start the process, he said. He added that he believes a majority of teachers are doing the job. But there also are bad teachers. "To say this legislation will be used to eliminate good teachers is ridiculous," Teeters said. "School board members are elected to run their schools."

(Adapted from M. Dynes, "Teachers' union fears tenure bill," from the *Wyoming Tribune-Eagle*. Reprinted from the January 7, 2011, edition of the *Wyoming Tribune Eagle* with permission of Cheyenne Newspapers, Inc. All rights reserved. Copyright 2011.)

QUESTIONS

1. What kind of power does tenure represent for teachers?
2. Identify the power resources available to school boards.
3. Identify the power resources available to the Wyoming Education Association.
4. To what extent is Rep. Teeters right when he says, "School board members are elected to run their schools?"

SECOND-DIMENSION POWER IN EDUCATION: PARENTAL INVOLVEMENT.   Public education in the United States is an old institution, having been established in the first half of the nineteenth century. Organizations usually bear the marks of the beliefs and social positions of their founders, and public education is no exception. As Schattschneider (1960) pointed out, "Organization is itself a mobilization of bias" (p. 30). The organizational structures of public schools and the traditions, proce-dures, customs, and "rules of the game" associated with them, therefore, encourage the participation of some while discouraging others.

Public education was established when only white men who owned a certain amount of property had full citizens' rights; therefore, the major figures in the Common School Movement were white, middle- to upper-class men. As a result, much of the organizational bias mobilized in public education is advantageous to those who belong to one or more of these social categories and disadvantageous to those who do not. This does not mean that Horace Mann and others deliberately conspired to create an institu-tion that would discourage participation by females, working- and lower-class people, and members of racial minority groups. Rather, they established public schools for the people who worked in schools and attended them at that time. They also established schools that reflected their beliefs and the characteristics of other large nineteenth-century organiza-tions, such as the U.S. Army and businesses. All these factors taken together cause the pub-lic school to mobilize bias for and against certain social groups. Other biases are inherent in public school organization as well. Because most adults were barely literate in the early 1800s, school teachers were often the most educated people in the community. Therefore, the founders of public schools did not think that building in mechanisms for broad parent or community participation was necessary. As a result, the organization of public schools also mobilizes bias in favor of professional educators and against other stakeholders.

Although Horace Mann and other early reformers did not deliberately design schools to enhance participation by educators and limit participation by others, structures and customs from the past are often perpetuated today in order to do so. For example, many educators complain about parents lack of participation in school activities; but many parents complain just as loudly that the school sends them mixed messages about participation. Teachers and principals say that they want parents to come to school more often, but their actions often relay a different message. In the typical U.S. public school, bias is mobilized against parent participation in many ways. Educators often expect parents to participate in school activities on the school's sched-ule. Parents who do come to school may have to park blocks away. On a first visit, they may find locating the entrance or the principal's office difficult. When they finally find the office, it may lack a suitable waiting area. In the unlikely event that a teacher per-mits them to observe a class, adult-size chairs may not be available. Finding out when the PTA or school council meetings are held, much less what is on the agenda, may also be difficult for parents. Procedures for electing officers for these groups may be unclear. Communication from school officials may be couched in incomprehensible "educationese." Most teachers and principals are unaware that their school mobilizes bias against parent participation; indeed, many would be shocked at the suggestion that by maintaining the status quo they are exercising power to keep parents out. Yet, as Delpit (1988) writes, "Those with [second-dimension] power are frequently least aware of—or at least willing to acknowledge—its existence" (p. 282). Many parents experience these barriers as an exercise of power and believe that educators should remove them if they sincerely desire parent participation.

THE MOBILIZATION OF BIAS: RACE, GENDER, AND CLASS.   This section presents three concrete examples of the mobilization of bias in education: bias experienced by minority children in schools, bias encountered by women who enter school administration, and bias in school choice policies.

Mobilization of Bias and Minority Children.

Delpit is an African-American educator who has written eloquently about the mobilization of bias against children of color in U.S. schools. Although she calls the phenomenon the *culture of power,* political scientists call it the *mobilization of bias.* She argues in a seminal 1988 article that schools reflect the "cultural code" of the white middle class. As a result, children from that social group start school knowing the rules of the education game well. They feel comfortable in the classroom, can interpret the teacher's indirect way of expressing himself or herself, and understand the rules. However, children from other backgrounds are disadvantaged from the beginning. At school they are expected to speak and write an unfamiliar form of English. The teacher's indirect way of expressing himself or herself—typical of the middle class—confuses them. Their modes of presenting themselves differ from modes of self-presentation favored by the school's culture. For example, their dress may stand out as unusual, and their patterns of social interaction may differ from those of white, middle-class students.

This means that minority children face a double task at school: learning the cognitive material that is explicitly presented to them and deciphering the implicit but unfamiliar "codes" in which it is embedded. This mobilization of bias against their effective participation in the classroom often leads to frustration, alienation, and failure. Delpit (1988) suggests that teachers should explicitly teach the cultural codes of the white middle class to minority children while simultaneously teaching them to understand and treasure their own cultural heritage. In that way, children can overcome some of the bias that has been mobilized against them if they wish to do so.

Bias Against Women in School Administration.

Public education in the United States was feminized early; the deaths of more than 500,000 men in the Civil War meant that women were needed to staff schools. As a result, classroom teaching was institutionalized consistently with social roles deemed appropriate for women. Because teachers often functioned as "public mothers" (Wodak, 1995), women felt comfortable in classrooms. Today, most women do not sense much mobilization of organizational bias against them as long as they remain there. In fact, male classroom teachers probably encounter it more than females.

School administration, however, has traditionally been a male-dominated field. Its rules, customs, norms, and discourse were shaped by several generations of men. Therefore, women who become administrators soon begin to feel the mobilization of bias against them. In this respect, they share the experience of women in all fields who move into management. For example, in an early book for women moving into business management, *Games Mother Never Taught You,* Harragan (1977) describes the unwritten rules of the business "game" for women. (Note that Harragan does for women exactly what Delpit recommends doing for minority schoolchildren: She makes the rules explicit.) In the first chapter, she writes:

> Most women are completely unaware that once they pass through the gates [of management], they have entered an alien land with customs, traditions, security forces, and mores of its own. What's more, the natives speak a strange, oblique tongue, and the signposts are in cryptic ciphers. Although the terrain is crisscrossed with well-trodden paths, there are few visible directions to guide the unfamiliar strangers. (p. 33)

New female school administrators usually experience a similar sense of strangeness in their jobs. They feel they no longer know the rules or understand what people say to them. Colleagues often misunderstand their attempts at communication. In her study of three female superintendents who had left the superintendency, Skrla (2000) found that these women encountered great difficulty because of the mismatch between traditional expectations for women and the demands of the superintendency. For example, one of them said:

> The passivity that we see in the general perspective for the woman is antithetical to what we would expect the role of the superintendent to be, which would be more aggressive, more assertive, more intervening. I have been told that I needed to be more assertive, speak up more—which, then when I did it, it seemed like I got slapped back down. (p. 308)

In the terms of this discussion of power, this woman was experiencing a mobilization of bias against women achieving success in the superintendency.

Bias in School Choice.   Since the early 1980s, one of the most popular education reform proposals has been school choice. In theory, permitting parents to select the schools that their children attend is supposed to make high quality schools accessible to all children, including the children of the poor and uneducated. Therefore, legislators across the country have passed laws establishing such policies as inter- and intra-district open enrollment, charter schools, and vouchers. However, those thinkers who developed the theories underlying school choice did not take the mobilization of bias against poor and uneducated parents into account. A growing body of research indicates that middle-class parents are better able to identify high-quality schools for their offspring than are poor parent, because they have access to more resources. For example, Bell (2009) found in her study of how parents choose schools for their children that poor parents lacked access to the social networks that middle-class parents used to narrow their choices to schools with good reputations; instead, they tended to select schools that did not perform well. She concluded that if school choice is to enhance equity, then "our policies must take better account of the almost invisible social and historical inequities that constrain the schools parents are willing to consider" (p. 207). In other words, policymakers and school leaders must develop ways to reduce the mobilization of bias against poor parents and help all parents choose schools wisely. Similarly, in his research on the New Orleans school system after Hurricane Katrina, Garda (2011) found that providing parents with dozens of schools to choose from did not necessarily empower them. Bias was mobilized against poor and minority parents by such barriers as "lack of information" (p. 89), "complex enrollment procedures"

(p. 89), "parent contracts" (p. 90), and "first come, first served admission practices that favor[ed] the informed parent with resources and time" (p. 90).

The Third Dimension of Power: The Shaping of Consciousness

UNDERSTANDING THE SHAPING OF CONSCIOUSNESS.   The third column of Table 2.1 lists the mechanisms of third-dimension power. In a discussion of the third dimension of power, Lukes (2005) asks, "Is not the supreme exercise of power to get another or others to have the desires you want them to have—that is, to secure their compliance by controlling their thoughts and desires?" (p. 23). We have all been on the receiving end in this dimension of power, for all of us have undergone the acculturation that is the main business of childhood. Several social institutions are especially important in shaping consciousness. The family is the most crucial, in part because people first learn language within it. Language has long been recognized as a major shaper of consciousness, determining the basic categories of meaning that one imposes upon the world (Cherryholmes, 1988). The family also inculcates beliefs and values, and its patterns of interaction shape the child's personality structure. However, other institutions also shape consciousness. The mass media are increasingly important today, bombarding everyone with a barrage of messages, both explicit and implicit (Giroux, 1999). Schools and religious organizations also play a major role in shaping the way people see the world (Bernstein, 1996; Corson, 1995; Lemke, 1995). Questions about how consciousness is shaped and how it can be transformed preoccupy contemporary social science. A thorough discussion of this subject would go well beyond the scope of this book; however, school leaders must understand that many of the people they deal with have been either unusually empowered or unusually disempowered through the shaping of their consciousness.

Unusual Empowerment.   Among the most important messages communicated by institutions that shape consciousness are messages about who should hold leading positions in society and who should be dominated by others. Some people receive a steady stream of messages suggesting that they are privileged, with natural rights to positions of power and prestige. For instance, in his ethnographic study of an elite, private prep school that he called "Edgewood Academy," Peshkin (2001) found that students in this school were surrounded by symbols of their importance. Although the school only had 900 students, its "pristine" and "elegant" facilities were located on a 312-acre campus. In addition, the school owned 270 acres of mountainous terrain where students engaged in "experiential education." Edgewood recruited its teachers—many of whom held PhDs—in national searches, and each faculty member had a well-equipped office with a personal computer. The school's library had a staff of nine, an online catalog, and microfiche readers. Among the field trips offered was a two-week trip to Paris to practice French in an immersion situation. All these symbols communicated the high worth of the students. They also implicitly informed these adolescents that they were the future leaders of American society. In some instances, the students were fully conscious of the message the school was sending them. When Peshkin asked one student what Edgewood's parents thought the school could give their children, he answered very directly: "They want [us] to be on the top of the food chain. They want us to be the bosses, not the employees. . . . We are going to be the leaders" (Peshkin, 2001, p. 9).

School leaders do not find many people of this type within their school systems as students, employees, or parents. In their roles as public leaders in the broader community, however, they encounter some. In working with them, keeping their socialization in mind is helpful.

Unusual Disempowerment.   At the other end of the social spectrum are people who have been unusually disempowered through the **shaping of consciousness**. They have grown up surrounded by messages that communicate their low status and unsuitability for leadership.

A good example is provided by Gaventa's (1980) award-winning study of rural Appalachia, *Power and Powerlessness.* In the area of Kentucky and Tennessee he investigated, the people had experienced generations of exploitation. During the Civil War, both armies terrorized them. Later, the lumber companies tricked them out of their land; still later the coal companies gave them menial jobs in the mines, keeping them under strict control in company towns. Local governments sold out to the companies, and newspapers, churches, and schools praised the status quo with a united voice. The Appalachians had adapted to their powerlessness by sinking into passivity, dependence, and apathy, expressing fatalism about the future and openly stating that they were stupid. Moreover, they had internalized the views of the powerful people around them, ironically blaming themselves for their own poverty.

Gaventa worked with a group of these people to produce a film about their situation. While working on the film and seeking to get it broadcast on television, project participants emerged from their apathy. As their consciousness about their situation was raised, they developed greater self-confidence. Community leaders felt very threatened by these activities, however. Eventually, the homes of several of the people working on the film were burned—an exercise of first-dimension power. In response, the people sank back into their original apathy.

Many public school leaders work in settings where they deal with people who have been disempowered to an unusual degree. When one encounters massive apathy, a natural response is to become angry and complain about the deficiencies of the population, which often amounts to blaming the victims. School leaders should consider apathy, fatalism, self-deprecation, and other signs noted by Gaventa as symptoms of a deeper problem. Reflection and a little investigation may reveal a tragic history that explains their disempowerment. Research suggests that the best way to handle such problems is to initiate projects in which the people can participate and in which they are empowered to make bona fide decisions. Through working in such projects, they gain self-confidence, skills, and knowledge, as well as a more realistic understanding of their situation. In short, they gain power. Progress will probably be slow, but it can be made (Bachrach & Botwinick, 1992; Gaventa, 1980).

POWER IN EDUCATIONAL SETTINGS

The Power of Education Policy Actors

Power permeates the education system, and although some actors are more powerful than others, all have power. Table 2.3 depicts the major types of power accessible to education actors and their most important power resources. In interpreting this table,

TABLE 2.3 The Power of Major Actors in Educational Settings

Actor	Types of Power	Power Resources
Governance bodies (e.g., legislatures, school boards, departments of education)	Economic dominance Budget proposal Budget adoption Tax policy Withholding funds Legal authority Adoption of laws, rules, policies Court decisions	Access to money Control over information Information Official positions Organization
School administrators	Economic dominance Legal authority	Control over careers and working conditions Control over information Information Official positions Patronage Visibility
Teachers	Economic dominance Work stoppages Work slowdowns Tenure (job protection) Legal authority Control over classroom	Control over information about classroom activities Numbers Official positions Organization
Support staff	Economic dominance Work stoppages Work slowdowns	Numbers Organization
Students	Force Physical (i.e., threat of disruption, actual disruption, fights) Psychic (i.e., heckling, verbal insults)	Numbers
Parents	Persuasion	Numbers Organization
Public	Economic dominance (e.g., voting on funding issues) Legal authority (e.g., voting in school elections)	Numbers Organization

readers should understand that it summarizes those forms and sources of power that are most readily available to each actor. If a type of power is not listed for a given actor, that definitely does not mean that he cannot have it; rather, it means that the actor must exert special effort to obtain it.

For example, according to the chart, school administrators have two types of power: economic dominance and legal authority. These types of power are built into the system for administrators. However, wise school leaders build their power by working to add to what the system provides them. Many administrators work to establish their competent authority, which can be done in several ways. Some people obtain a doctorate for this purpose; another approach is to stay up-to-date in professional reading and work actively in one or more professional organizations. Administrators can also establish their competent authority by pointing out clearly the educational reasons for the decisions they make. Persuasive power is important, too. Learning how to make a convincing presentation at a meeting or polishing writing skills in order to be able to draft effective news releases can enhance a school leader's power, as can making a serious effort to gain more knowledge about the community and its population. Administrators can use other types of power and obtain other resources, but they are not given; they must be achieved.

Building Power

Achieving a policy goal often requires building power. People build power by obtaining more, or different, power resources. They also build power by obtaining access to new types of power. Ways to build power in education are illustrated by the following fictional story; a running analysis of power-building techniques appears in brackets.

"Building Power for Kids."

Dr. Dolores Hernandez, superintendent of a suburban district in a southwestern state, got angry when she read the February issue of the newsletter published by the superintendents association. A bill requiring second graders to take a basic skills proficiency test had been introduced in the General Assembly. [Hernandez builds power by gathering knowledge.] *"We test these kids to death," she muttered. She supported accountability and high performance, but under No Child Left Behind the state already required multiple tests. "Enough already," she thought.*

Dolores called the man who represented the district in the legislature. Four busy signals, two holds, and three secretaries later, she reached a legislative staffer said to specialize in education issues. She registered her concern with this individual, who replied: "I'll leave a note in the representative's box." [Her call signals possible lost votes to the representative and his staff.]

Over the next two weeks, Dolores also contacted lobbyists at the superintendents and school board association's headquarters. She gained the support of four other superintendents. The elementary teachers in her district seemed apathetic, but the teachers union president agreed with her. [Dolores builds power by gaining numbers; some of her new allies have better access to resources than she does.] *This handful of people generated several letters and phone calls to members of the legislature. In early April, a phone message from one of the lobbyists came through: "The bill has been defeated in committee. They'll probably get their ducks in a row and try again next year."*

"I don't have time to fight this fight any longer," Dolores thought as she drove home late that evening. But the next day she asked the central office supervisor who handled government relations, a retired social studies teacher, and an active parent to spearhead a committee to get their own ducks in a row. She selected the retired teacher and the parent— a woman whose husband's income permitted her to be a full-time mother—because she knew they would have lots of time to devote to the project. [She increases her numbers and adds to her time and knowledge resources.]

The committee considered establishing a special organization called something like Spare Our Kids, but decided instead to work through existing organizations. Before school ended, they gained a sympathetic hearing from the associations representing superintendents, principals, and school boards, as well as the two teachers unions. The state chapters of the PTA and the International Reading Association were also supportive. Several of these organizations considered amending their legislative agendas to include opposition to additional testing. [The power of numbers is magnified through effective organization. These organizations also have wealth, knowledge, and access to resources to contribute to the cause.]

During the summer the state PTA developed a flyer against excessive testing, which cited research about the stress caused by tests. [Knowledge has been gained and is deployed.] *By attaching a price tag to testing all the state's second graders, the flyer suggested that more testing "would be a waste of taxpayers' dollars."* [The child-centered discourse is preserved, but a new, cost-conscious discourse is added. This broadening of the discourse increases the persuasiveness of the argument.]

Meanwhile, Dolores told her committee about how difficult it was to contact their representative. Soon the committee members had tales of their own to add to hers. Everyone agreed that people who tried to contact anyone in the legislature or find out what was going on in the statehouse wasted a lot of time and energy jumping through hoops. Several committee members wrote letters to legislators complaining about this problem. They also sent three letters to the editor of the nearest city newspaper. The last letter ran under the heading, "Do They Really Want to Hear from Voters?" [The mobilization of bias against effective participation in state politics is explicitly identified and made public.] *In September, the local representative revamped his system for handling phone calls and letters.*

Dolores was also concerned about the apathy of the elementary teachers in her district. She realized that most were women who might have grown up believing the myth that "Women do not belong in politics." Moreover, the district had previously had several authoritarian elementary principals who ruled "their teachers" like benign dictators. She felt these old ideas and behavior patterns needed to change, so she pushed the committee to actively recruit some elementary teachers. She was delighted when several agreed to participate and began to develop more confidence in their leadership potential. [A disempowered group is identified and becomes active. Numbers and knowledge resources are increased.] *As the opening of the next session of the legislature approached, Dolores did not know what the future held. She did know, however, that the opponents of pointless testing "had their ducks in a row." She thought they had done their best to protect the state's children from an unnecessary test.*

CASE STUDY

Satanism and Witchcraft in the Schools

Bob Mathews is the superintendent of a school district that includes a small city and the surrounding rural area. The district is about thirty miles from a large metropolis; but recently, many former city dwellers purchased houses in two new subdivisions. About ten days ago, Bob received a phone call from a man who identified himself as Clyde Ruggles. Saying that he had some concerns about the language arts books used in the district, Ruggles requested an opportunity to address the school board at its next meeting. Because Ruggles spoke with a "country" accent and made several grammatical errors, Bob thought, "Just a harmless crackpot." He agreed to place him on the agenda and forgot about him.

At last night's school board meeting, Bob was astonished to see that every seat in the meeting room was occupied. Many in the crowd were wearing red, white, and blue buttons that read, "Save our children from the devil." Some were holding up professional-looking signs containing the same words. As he made his way through the crowd, someone shoved a leaflet into his hand and a camera snapped. Looking around, Bob recognized several reporters in the audience.

Because Bob had placed Ruggles first on the agenda, Ruggles strode to the microphone right after the Pledge of Allegiance and read a brilliantly written speech to the school board. In it he claimed that the language arts series used by the system taught Satanism, magic, and witchcraft. After citing several examples, Ruggles concluded: "This school district systematically teaches our children a heathen religion: Satanism. Under the Establishment Clause of the First Amendment of the U.S. Constitution, this practice is illegal. I therefore request that the school board immediately stop using this textbook series." The room rang with thunderous applause.

Then Ed Zabriski, one of the board members, said, "I move that we stop using this series." After considerable hesitation, Jay Bullock seconded the motion, and the audience applauded again. The motion failed, 3–2, on a roll call vote. Then, in a voice not much above a whisper, Dr. Dale Attali said, "I move we adjourn to the superintendent's office to discuss personnel matters in an executive session." This motion passed, 3–2. Bob did not know if this motion was legal or not, but he did not care. He, the board members,

and the treasurer hurriedly left the room to calls of "Cowards! Cowards!" In his office, Bob learned that Zabriski strongly supported Ruggles and his group. Bullock, however, supported the motion because many voters from his district were present. Attali and the other two board members, both from the new subdivisions, were appalled by Ruggles's ideas.

The next morning, Bob attended a Kiwanis pancake breakfast before meeting with the city manager. When he reached his office at 10:00 A.M., he found a stack of telephone messages on the desk. They included: (1) "Jane Cohen, president of the REA called. Several English teachers have contacted her, concerned about censorship after last night." (Eighty-five percent of the teachers belong to the union, which has been bargaining for twenty years.) (2) "Harold Brook of Realtors Association—concerned about declining home sales in new subdivision if 'kooks' take over." (3) "Jasper Powers, pastor of the Four Square Solid Bible Gospel Temple called. Concerned about Satanism in our schools." (This church has 800 members, mostly from working-class families.) (4) "George P. Trotwood, president of First Home Fidelity Bank called—wants to know what in h— is going on around here? Have you lost control?" (5) Every elementary principal had left a message to the effect that several students were refusing to participate in reading class. (6) "Robert Bachfeld, pastor of the Holy Light Tabernacle, wants an appointment to discuss the curriculum with you." (This church has about 600 members.) (7) "Tammy Brouillette, Channel 7 News Reporter, wants to interview you about Satanism."

QUESTIONS

1. Analyze the power relationships in this district.
2. Apparently, Bob Mathews based his behavior on a faulty analysis of power relationships. Describe his apparent analysis. In your opinion, why did he make these mistakes?
3. In what ways do the second and third dimensions of power probably operate in this district?
4. Develop a plan that Bob Mathews and the majority on the board could use to alter power relationships so that this conflict can be resolved in a positive, ethical manner. ■

Power and Distributed Leadership

In recent years, distributed leadership has been a popular subject for thought and research among educators. Some readers may wonder, then, how distributed leadership relates to the concepts of power presented in this chapter. Although distributed leadership is often confused with "shared" or "democratic" leadership, it is actually a leadership theory that focuses on the *practice* of leadership rather than on a single leader who is in charge of everything in a school. It explicitly rejects the idea of "heroic" school leaders (usually principals) who are able to work wonders in failing schools in a short period of time; such dramas are a staple of the entertainment industry but rarely occur in real life (Spillane, 2005, 2006). According to this theory, leadership practice is "a product of the joint interactions of school *leaders, followers*, and aspects of their *situation*" (Spillane, 2006, p. 3; emphasis in the original). In his research, Spillane (2005, 2006) has discovered that most schools have multiple leaders; these include both formal leaders (such as administrators and lead teachers) and informal leaders (such as teachers who have a great deal of influence with their colleagues).

In terms of power theory, it does not matter whether a school has a single leader or several, or how many of them are informal rather than formal leaders. Their sources of power and their power resources are the same as those discussed above. True, administrators can exercise economic dominance and have legal authority as well as any other types of power they have managed to develop. However, usually there are at least a few teachers or staff members in every school who are very charismatic, or have developed considerable expert authority, or have strong supporters among the faculty, students, or parents. In terms of distributed leadership, such persons will inevitably be involved in some sort of leadership within the school. Wise administrators are able to identify these people and welcome their cooperation in building a good school; foolish ones seek to dominate them, showing them "who's the boss." This analysis of power in schools presented here is therefore consistent with Spillane's emphasis on leadership as the product of the *interaction* of leaders and followers, constrained by their situation.

ETHICAL ISSUES SURROUNDING POWER

The Dangers of Power

"Power tends to corrupt, and absolute power corrupts absolutely," wrote Lord Acton about a century ago (Tripp, 1970, p. 713). Acton belongs to a long tradition of thinkers who have expressed moral reservations about power. Under the Roman Empire, Jesus said: "You know that among the gentiles the rulers lord it over them, and great men make their authority felt. Among you this is not to happen" (Matt. 20:25–26, *New Jerusalem Bible*). Sixteen centuries later, English philosopher Thomas Hobbes argued that human beings have "a perpetual and restless desire of power after power, that ceaseth only in death" (Hobbes, 1958, p. 86). In the twentieth century, German sociologist Max Weber wrote about politicians who "enjoy the naked possession of the power [they] exert" (Gerth & Mills, 1946, p. 84).

Such doubts have led many to conclude that all exercises of power are unethical by nature. Writing specifically about power in education, Burbules (1986) asserts:

> Power is a seductive, even addictive tonic, and anyone who takes it, ostensibly for a limited time and for a limited purpose, invariably finds it easier and easier to justify retaining and exercising it beyond these limits. . . . Educators have been notably susceptible to this temptation. (p. 105)

Burbules's solution to the ethical problem posed by power is to refuse to exercise it. On the surface, this conclusion appears high-minded; deeper reflection suggests that it does not resolve the ethical dilemma surrounding power after all. If every person with moral reservations about power refused to exercise it, power would not cease to exist. Rather, it would be exercised only by those people who lack moral reservations about it. The result would be more abuses of power than exist today, and those who refused to exercise power on moral grounds would be partially responsible. Thus, the refusal to exercise power because of its corrupting potential is itself an unethical exercise of power.

Another answer to the dilemma posed by power is to exercise it consciously— that is, with awareness of its corrupting potential and of one's own susceptibility. Peck (1978), a psychotherapist, advocates this course of action, writing: "Awareness . . . comes slowly, piece by piece, and each piece must be worked for by the patient effort of study and observation of everything, including [one's self]" (p. 285). This means that school leaders should consider power a useful but potentially dangerous tool, similar to an automobile. Just as one should never drive thoughtlessly, so leaders should never fall into the habit of exercising power without thinking about what they are doing. The next two sections offer guidance for using power.

Power as Means and End

Wrong (1995) identifies four purposes for which power can be used and discusses the ethical implications of each. His major points are summarized here.

POWER AS INDIVIDUAL MEANS.   An individual may exercise power to pursue an individual goal. For example, for financial reasons, a superintendent near retirement may want to finish his career in the district that currently employs him. In order to enhance his job security, he may build personal power within the district. Exercising power to achieve a personal goal is not necessarily unethical. Even so, over time, the temptation will be strong to sacrifice the good of the district to the personal goal. In order to behave ethically, the superintendent must monitor his behavior closely to make sure that pursuing his personal goal is always consistent with district goals.

POWER AS INDIVIDUAL END.   An individual may exercise power solely because of the sense of importance she experiences as she does so. For example, a principal may enjoy demonstrating her power over parents, teachers, students, and staff by making unilateral decisions and suddenly reversing them without explanation. Such a use of power as an end in itself is always unethical.

POWER AS MEANS FOR A GROUP.   An individual may exercise power to advance the goals of a group. For example, a secondary science supervisor may use her power to obtain funds to purchase lab equipment for her district's chemistry teachers. Assuming that the group's goals are ethical, this use of power is the least susceptible to abuse.

POWER AS END FOR A GROUP.   A group leader may exercise power to enhance his group's power solely because the group enjoys being influential. For example, the president of a teachers' union may engage in numerous activities to build the union's power. He does so because he and other leaders enjoy packing board meetings, walking out of bargaining sessions, and threatening strikes. This behavior feeds their sense of self-importance. Exercising power for such a purpose is unethical.

Using Discursive Power Ethically

Discourse, especially speech, has always been an important instrument of power for school leaders. With the introduction of site-based management in many districts, it is more important than ever. Like other power resources, discourse can be used both ethically and unethically.

Robinson (1995) provides valuable guidelines for exercising discursive power ethically, suggesting that people must adhere to three values in responsible discourse:

- *Respect.* The more powerful actors must understand that the less powerful ones have the same basic rights that they do. The less powerful actors must be given the opportunity to suggest issues for the agenda, speak in discussions, and question positions taken by the more powerful actors.
- *Commitment to valid information.* All participants in the discourse should be willing to change their opinions in response to new and valid information.
- *Freedom of choice.* Less powerful actors should be genuinely free to take positions or choose courses of action without fear of negative repercussions.

Robinson (1995) believes that people find acting consistently with these values difficult because they lack the necessary skills. People must know how to be open about their intentions and how to place their opinions under public scrutiny. Moreover, leaders must be able to facilitate open discussions and group decision making. Several facilitative skills are important, including

- the ability to listen well;
- the ability to invite contributions from others;
- open and receptive body language;
- the ability to test and revise ideas; and
- the ability to guide a group toward closure.

To illustrate her points, Robinson (1995) describes a school council meeting that she observed. The topic of discussion was adopting a school uniform, a subject that had been discussed at length previously. The principal, Tony, who chaired the meeting, was receptive to everyone's opinion, and many people participated. However, Tony was unwilling (or unable) to facilitate the meaningful discussion of different suggestions or to guide the group toward closure. As a result, after a second entire meeting had been devoted to the uniform issue, faculty felt frustrated. One of them later told Robinson that although Tony tended to listen to everyone's opinion in meetings, he later made decisions unilaterally. Robinson concludes that both excluding voices and failing to lead a group to a sound decision are abuses of discursive power.

Using power ethically requires considerable maturity, self-awareness, and effort, yet school leaders must make the effort if they wish to avoid becoming victims of power's insidious lure. Only by exercising power thoughtfully and with deep respect for others can education leaders build healthy and humane organizations.

FINAL POINTS

Power permeates education systems and the policies that shape them. Much of that power is wielded by individual employees of the system, acting in their capacity as government officials. Their power ultimately rests on their institution and the policies and traditions behind it, not on their personal characteristics. Traditionally, much of the power wielded by educational institutions has been authority—a type of power that society considers right and legitimate. However, authority rests on legitimacy, and legitimacy is easily lost. In the twenty-first century, the legitimacy of all authority—including educational authority—is in crisis. When their authority is weakened, educators must learn to use other types of power, and understanding the power relations in their policy environment becomes more important than ever. Developing an understanding of power is therefore crucial for education leaders.

QUESTIONS AND ACTIVITIES FOR DISCUSSION

1. List the types of power to which your educational position entitles you and the major power resources at your disposal. How could you make more effective use of your power? What ethical challenges have you encountered because of your power?
2. Call your representative in the state legislature and request some information from the office. Keep a list of everything that happens, starting with locating the representative's phone number. Analyze the bias mobilized against public participation in legislative policy making.
3. What evidence suggests that some people in your district have been disempowered through the shaping of their consciousness? How does their disempowerment affect district education policy?
4. Identify a current issue in your district or state as well as the major players in the controversy around the issue. Which side seems more powerful? Why?

INTERNET ASSIGNMENT

Find the web sites of three education groups that try to influence policy in your state. Using the information in Tables 2.2 and 2.3, rank them from most to least powerful. Be prepared to explain your rankings.

FOR FURTHER READING

Addi-Raccah, A., & Arviv-Elyashiv, R. (2008). Parent empowerment and teacher professionalism: Teachers' perspective. *Urban Education 43*, 394–415.

Recent education reforms have redistributed power in various ways; parents are one group that has gained power in the process. This article explores the impact of more powerful parents on teachers in Israel and describes the strategies teachers have developed to deal with their new situation.

Bell, C. A. (2009). All choices created equal? The role of choice sets in the selection of schools. *Peabody Journal of Education 84*, 191–208.

In this study, Bell interviewed parents from different social class backgrounds, asking them which schools they had considered when choosing one for their child. She found that social background determined the quality of the schools parents considered.

Delpit, L. D. (1988). The silenced dialogue: Power and pedagogy in educating other people's children. *Harvard Educational Review, 58*, 280–298.

In this classic and widely cited article about the mobilization of bias, Delpit describes "the culture of power" that children of color encounter in public schools and suggests ways to reduce its negative effect.

Duffy, F. M. (2006). *Power, politics, and ethics in school districts*. Lanham, MD: Rowman & Littlefield Education.

Duffy addresses a subject that has rarely merited book-length treatment: the ethical use of power in public school systems. After providing a theoretical overview of the issue in the first half of the book, Duffy provides seven essays by other people about using power to bring about change in schools.

Gaventa, J. (1980). *Power and powerlessness*. Urbana, IL: University of Illinois Press.

Gaventa's award-winning classic poignantly describes disempowered people in a valley in Appalachia. His sensitive portrayal of their past and present promotes understanding of why some people seem unable to help themselves.

3 | THE ECONOMY AND DEMOGRAPHICS

Focus Questions

▌ What is the business cycle?

▌ How does the business cycle affect spending on education?

▌ According to the 2010 Census, how is the U.S. population changing?

▌ What are the implications of these demographic changes for education policy?

WHY ANALYZE THE POLICY ENVIRONMENT?

Defining Policy Environment

Every public policy, including every education policy, is a response to a specific social setting that includes a wide range of phenomena studied by the social sciences: economic forces, demographic trends, ideological belief systems, deeply held values, the structure and traditions of the political system, and the culture of the broader society. Although these phenomena change over time, most of them also reveal historical continuity. The complex social dimensions of a specific place at a particular time constitute its policy environment.

Policy and Its Social Context

In Greek mythology, Zeus, the king of the gods, suffered from a severe headache one day. As he agonized in pain, his head split open and a new goddess emerged. Athena, as she was called, was already fully grown and appeared to have no mother; she was dressed in a complete set of armor and ready for battle. Since that time, Athena has provided a useful symbol for ideas or social forces that suddenly appear, full-blown, as if from nowhere. Public policies, including education policies, are not like the goddess Athena. They do not suddenly emerge from nowhere, taking everyone by surprise. Public policies are responses to the complex dynamics of a specific social setting. Although shifts in policy are not fully predictable, people who are knowledgeable about a policy environment are usually not taken completely by surprise. Their understanding of broad social trends prepares them for certain types of change.

As public leaders, school administrators must be keenly attuned to their social context and how it is changing (Crosby & Bryson, 2005). Such knowledge permits them to ready themselves to respond intelligently to relatively predictable changes in policy. For example, a superintendent who knows that the economy is sliding into a recession realizes that tax revenues will drop, and as a result, school boards, state legislatures, and Congress will probably lose interest in expensive education programs. These bodies may also be strongly motivated to increase accountability for education expenditures. If the superintendent understands this, she may be able to modify district plans to suit the changing economic climate.

Another reason for understanding the policy environment is that such knowledge can help school leaders avoid wasting time, energy, and resources as educational Don Quixotes tilting at policy windmills. Some school leaders, unaware of a changed environment, continue to push for policy changes that have become unrealistic. For example, a curriculum supervisor who has been working with the state department of education to get funds for a professional development program may think he does not have time to follow the news. Unaware of economic indicators that a recession is looming, he may plow ahead with his project, not realizing that developing alternative strategies for this changing policy environment would be wise. If the legislature cuts the department's budget, eliminating the money he had hoped to obtain, he may be caught by surprise and even perceive this legislative action as sudden. Caught off-guard without a contingency plan, he may feel he wasted many months of hard work. Sensitivity to the changing policy environment makes avoiding such disappointments easier.

Finally, understanding the relationship between the social environment and education policy helps school leaders conceptualize the broad direction of education policy. Humans have a need to make sense out of their experience, especially in periods of rapid change. School leaders who develop an intellectual framework for thinking about policy issues are equipped to interpret the flow of policy change; the policy world no longer seems like Oz to them. Such understanding builds their confidence in their own abilities to act constructively as public leaders in a changing world.

THE ECONOMIC ENVIRONMENT

The Importance of the Economy

Two of the most important aspects of the policy environment are the structure of the economic system and the current economic climate. In fact, some believe that, ultimately, the economy is the only aspect of the social environment that matters and that all other social phenomena are determined by it. Although this book does not take this extreme position, it does assume that the economic environment is important. In trying to understand why a policy has been proposed or what its real purpose is, one should always consider the economic dimension of the social environment first. Although the economy does not determine public policy, it does establish important parameters within which policy must be adopted and implemented. The next section provides a brief overview of the economic history of the United States and permits readers to situate the discussion of economic issues that follows within a meaningful intellectual framework.

An Overview of U.S. Economic History

THE EARLY DAYS.   The British colonies that became the United States and the early republic that succeeded them did not have a capitalistic economic system. Based on an agrarian economy of small farms, the early U.S. economy still bore traces of Europe's feudal past, particularly in institutions such as slavery and indentured servitude. Market forces were severely constrained by government regulation of prices and other aspects of the economy (Galbraith, 1994).

THE EMERGENCE OF CAPITALISM.   During the last decades of the eighteenth century, the Industrial Revolution began in the British Isles before gradually spreading to North America and the European continent. Capitalism was born with the Industrial Revolution, causing not only major economic changes but also the development of new ideas about economics. One of the most important economic thinkers of this period was Adam Smith (1723–1790), who published his masterpiece, *The Wealth of Nations,* in 1776. In it, Smith argued that humans have a natural desire to pursue their own economic self-interest. Government should not interfere with natural human tendencies, but permit them full play. In the resulting free-market economy, both self-interest and broader social purposes are served, for although each person "intends only his [*sic*] own gain, . . . he is . . . led by an invisible hand to promote an end which was no part of his intention" (Smith, 1976 [1776], p. 456). Smith's invisible-hand theory and other ideas were used to justify the relatively unregulated development of industrial society in the nineteenth century (Buchholz, 1989).

PROBLEMS DEVELOP.   Industrial development in an atmosphere of relative economic freedom led to the development of great wealth and unprecedented standards of living. It also led to serious problems; urban slums, huge inequalities between the rich and poor, and consumer fraud were major issues by the 1890s. Another issue was the wild swings of industrial economies between periods of rapid economic growth and periods of sudden economic "crashes" leading to joblessness, hunger, and social unrest. In this country, a few reforms were put in place in the early 1900s, but they were insufficient to prevent the onset of the Great Depression in 1929 (Bartlett, 2009; Frieden, 2006).

THE NEW DEAL AND ITS AFTERMATH.   Many U.S. economists interpreted the Great Depression as proof that capitalism did not work well without considerable government intervention. Franklin Roosevelt's New Deal Administration accepted this interpretation, and as a result adopted much activist economic legislation. By 1940 or so, the necessity for government intervention in the economy had become economic orthodoxy in the United States. The result was a long period during which the federal government pursued policies that regulated the economy in order to minimize the risk of another major depression. These policies were generally effective because, although many economic slowdowns or recessions have occurred since 1933, no major depression has happened. The New Deal culminated in twenty-eight years of unprecedented economic growth, stretching from 1945 to 1973. This does not necessarily mean that government economic policy caused the growth, although some economists support that interpretation. Other economists argue that the long period of prosperity was caused by factors such as World War II, the rebuilding of Europe and Japan, and the Baby Boom (Bartlett, 2009; Frieden, 2006).

ECONOMIC TROUBLES REAPPEAR.   By 1973, the postwar boom was clearly ending. In all developed countries, economic growth slowed and an array of puzzling problems appeared. Both inflation and unemployment rates were high, although, according to prevailing economic theory, this should not have happened. The rate of productivity growth declined, and wages stagnated. Table 3.1 shows unemployment rates by decade for the six decades immediately after World War II; Table 3.2 shows changes in the consumer price index (CPI), an indicator of inflation, during the same period. In both tables, the strength of the economy between 1950 and 1969 and its problems during the 1970s and 1980s are apparent. Why political leaders of the 1980s and early 1990s were concerned about the U.S. economy is easy to understand.

In part, these problems were caused by the actions of the Oil Producing and Exporting Countries (OPEC), which raised oil prices in the early 1970s. However, as the 1970s wore on, it became clear that other, deeper problems were also causing economic growth to slow. Many economists began to question the theories that led to New Deal policies and to advance new theories or revive old ones (Bartlett, 2009; Frieden, 2006).

TABLE 3.1 U.S. Unemployment Rates, Averaged by Decade, 1950s–2000s

Decade	Average Rate (%)
1950s	4.5
1960s	4.8
1970s	6.2
1980s	8.4
1990s	5.2
2000s	5.5

Source: Based on information from Plotkin and Schuermann (1994), p. 44, *Historical Labor Force/ Unemployment Data for United States* (2006), and *United States Unemployment Rate by Year* (2011).

TABLE 3.2 Increases in U.S. Consumer Price Index by Decade, 1950s–2000s

Decade	Change (%)
1950s	20.7
1960s	23.9
1970s	87.1
1980s	33.3
1990s	32.5
2000s	25.6

Source: Based on information from Plotkin and Schuermann (1994), p. 52, and U.S. Department of Labor (2011).

REAGANOMICS.   One of the new theories was called *supply-side economics;* in many ways this "new" theory was a revival of traditional, pre–New Deal economics. In fact, workers in the Reagan Administration who advocated supply-side economics wore ties adorned with pictures of Adam Smith (Buchholz, 1989). Supply-side economics recommends pursuing a four-part economic policy: (1) indexing taxes to inflation, (2) reducing taxes, (3) reducing government expenditures, and (4) deregulation (Bartlett, 1981). After the Reagan Administration adopted supply-side economics in the early 1980s, this economic policy was nicknamed *Reaganomics*. In many respects, Reaganomics succeeded. As Table 3.2 demonstrates, during the 1980s inflation was reduced, many jobs were created, and taxes were cut. As early as the fall of 1983, however, some economists started warning about the rising federal deficit (see, e.g., Summers, 1984). By 1990, concern about the deficit was widespread, and it was not limited to economists. In their 1992 presidential campaigns, both Democrat Bill Clinton and Independent Ross Perot made the deficit an issue, promising to reduce it if elected. The Republican Congress elected in 1994 also ran on a deficit reduction platform. By the late 1990s, the deficit had been greatly reduced; but political leaders, fearful of driving it up again, were still unwilling to support lavish government programs (Bartlett, 2009).

THE BUSHES AND CLINTON.   To a great extent, George H. W. Bush lost his 1992 bid for the presidency because the recession of 1990–1991 caused voters to perceive him as an ineffective leader. Bill Clinton's campaign team seized on the economy as its major issue, going so far as to display a sign in their campaign headquarters that read, "It's the economy, stupid." In actual fact, the economy had bottomed out in March 1991; and the longest economic expansion in U.S. history had begun before Clinton took office. It was to last until the spring of 2001, shortly after George W. Bush took office. During this period, the gross domestic product grew about 4% per year, unemployment fell to 4.1% by 1999, and inflation dropped to its lowest level since the early 1960s. The value of the stock market tripled. To a certain degree, this flourishing economy resulted from the policies of the Clinton Administration; for example, economists believe that its deficit reduction plan had a positive impact on economic expansion. Many experts also attributed this strong economy to decisions made by Federal Reserve Board Chairman Alan Greenspan, who raised and lowered interest rates to keep the system from either overheating or slipping into recession. However, Clinton and Greenspan also reaped the benefits of some of their predecessors' policies. Moreover, they were lucky; although the steep declines in the prices of oil and computer equipment that occurred during the 1990s did not result from public policy, they contributed significantly to the prosperity of the period. All was not rosy during the 1990s, however. The trade deficit reached unprecedented levels in 1998, and wealth became increasingly concentrated in the top 1% of the population (Blank, 2000; Brouwer, 1998; Hatch & Clinton, 2000; Penner, Sawhill, & Taylor, 2000).

In economic terms, the George W. Bush Administration got off to a shaky start, as the country slid into a recession in March 2001, just two months after the new president took office. This downturn lasted until the following November, but the economy recovered strongly after that. Under the second President Bush, inflation was low and labor productivity grew significantly; in addition, the stock market reached record highs. This strong economic performance may have been partially the result of a $1.35 trillion tax cut put in place by laws enacted in 2001, 2002, and 2003. However, the economic picture under George W. Bush was not entirely beautiful. Many economists called attention to troubling economic symptoms during the Bush years: enormous trade and budget deficits; a growing poverty rate; the skyrocketing costs of health care; and a crumbling infrastructure, dramatically demonstrated in 2005 when the levees supposed to protect New Orleans failed during Hurricane Katrina. Toward the end of his administration, a serious recession began (Bartlett, 2009; Domestic policy of the George W. Bush Administration, 2007; Economic policy of the George W. Bush Administration, 2007; Krugman, 2009; House Committee, 2006).

THE GREAT RECESSION.   In December 2007, the U.S. economy slipped into a recession, where it stayed until the summer of 2009. Economists and others have dubbed this period "the Great Recession" because it was the longest recession since the 1930s, it was unusually severe, and it was international in scope. It was preceded by a rapid increase in housing prices in the United States, accompanied by the unprecedented use of unconventional mortgages, such as mortgages that required a minimal—or even no—down payment. As a result, this recession was marked by a severe financial crisis in both the United States and Europe. For example, in the United States, the Bear Stearns investment bank and mortgage lenders Fannie Mae and Freddie Mac faced bankruptcy in part because of their heavy involvement in subprime mortgages, and were bailed out by the federal government. Other investment banks, such as the venerable Lehman Brothers, were allowed to fail. Numerous banks in Europe failed as well, and poorer countries there went heavily into debt. In the United States, the unemployment rate rose to 10%, and many families faced foreclosure on their homes (Gross, 2009; Isidore, 2008; Pew Center on the States, 2010).

The Obama Administration took office in early 2009 and soon developed an economic stimulus program, passed by Congress as the American Recovery and Reinvestment Act. The bulk of the stimulus money went to states, which used much of it for school systems, preventing massive layoffs of teachers and other school employees in 2009. Although the recession officially ended in the summer of 2009, recovery has been slow, and unemployment rates remain high. As a result, state tax revenues shrank and as the stimulus money began to run out, public education began to sustain large budget cuts. For example, Florida's public schools lost 10% of their state funding for the 2011-2012 school year, and Ohio school systems were projected to lose 14% of their state funds between 2011 and 2013 (Cavanagh, 2011). In a 2010 report, researchers at the Pew Center on the States predicted that the Great Recession would affect school funding for years to come, saying, "It will take years for states to return to normal, whatever the new normal will be" (Pew Center on the States, 2010, p. 2).

CONCLUSIONS.   This brief overview suggests several general conclusions of importance to those interested in education policy. The first is that economic systems are not stable; they change over the short, intermediate, and long terms. The short-term changes of the business cycle are discussed in the next section. Major changes in the direction of general economic policy such as the New Deal or Reaganomics occur less frequently. Economic upheavals such as the Industrial Revolution happen only occasionally in history. A second conclusion is that although economic changes are somewhat predictable, economics is not an exact science, like chemistry. Economists adhere to different schools of thought and hold conflicting theories about why economic phenomena occur. Moreover, no simple formula exists for eliminating unemployment, reducing inflation, or achieving prosperity. Finally, economics is closely intertwined with politics. Ultimately, most economic decisions have political implications, which is why economics cannot be ignored in the study of any area of public policy, including education policy.

Short-Term Economic Changes

BUSINESS CYCLES. Business cycles are a structural feature of capitalistic economies, resulting from the fact that most economic decisions are made by private businesses rather than by governments. A business cycle consists of two parts: an expansion and a recession. During an expansion, production rises, more jobs are available, and business profits increase; prices are also likely to rise more quickly than usual. The earliest phase of an expansion, which occurs right after the end of a recession, is called a *recovery,* and the high point of an expansion is termed its *peak.* After the expansion peaks, production, profits, and employment begin to fall. This part of the business cycle is called a *recession,* and its lowest point is the *trough.* If an economic contraction becomes extremely severe, it is labeled a *depression.* In the United States, the last depression occurred in the 1930s.

Table 3.3 provides a graphic example of how the business cycle consists of alternating periods of growth and contraction. It illustrates the business cycles in the United States for the 61-year period from 1948 to 2009. As of this writing, the economy has been expanding since the summer of 2009 although the recovery has been slow and uncertain, leading some to fear a double-dip recession.

TABLE 3.3 U.S. Recessions, 1948–2011

Years	Length of Recession in Months
1948–1949	11
1953–1954	10
1957–1958	8
1960–1961	10
1969–1970	11
1973–1975	16
1980	6
1981–1982	16
1990–1991	8
2001	8
2007–2009	18

Source: Based on data drawn from ECRI: Economic Cycle Research Institute, 2011.

In the economic history of the United States, thirty-three complete business cycles occurred through 2009. Expansions usually last about four times longer than recessions. The longest expansion lasted ten years, running from 1991 to 2001; the second longest lasted eight years, from 1961 to 1969. The longest recession lasted six years, from 1873 to 1879. The 18-month, 2007-2009 recession was the longest economic downturn since the 1930s. As Table 3.3 suggests, since 1948 expansions have become considerably longer and recessions considerably shorter than before the war. Neither the length of the phases of a business cycle nor its peak and trough are predictable; however, the recurrent pattern of the cycles is. "Business cycles are as intrinsic to capitalism as earthquakes are to the earth's geology," writes Massachusetts Institute of Technology economist Lester Thurow (1996, p. 211).

ECONOMIC INDICATORS.   Economists use various statistics, known as *indicators,* to track the general trends of the economy. The most important is probably the gross national product (GNP), a measure of a country's total economic output. When adjusted for inflation, this indicator is called the *real GNP*; real GNP figures for two or more consecutive years can be compared. The *unemployment rate,* which is the percentage of residents older than age 16 who want to work but lack jobs, is another important indicator, as is the Consumer Price Index (CPI), a general measure of the prices of goods and services prepared regularly by the U.S. Bureau of Labor Statistics. It suggests the inflation rate. Other indicators of the economy's direction include (1) sales of durable goods such as furniture, cars, and major appliances; (2) consumer installment credit; (3) business investment in plant and equipment; and (4) new housing starts (Foldvary, 2007).

In general, an economic expansion is indicated by such signs as strong growth in the real GNP, a decline in the unemployment rate, and important increases in the sales of durable goods, consumer installment credit, new housing starts, and business investments. A recession is indicated by declines in these signals. The CPI increases during both expansions and recessions; however, it increases more slowly during recessions (Foldvary, 2007).

MONITORING BUSINESS CYCLES.   Education leaders must be aware of where the economy is in the business cycle, and they can use many methods to maintain such awareness. Most daily newspapers include a business section that covers both national and regional economic news. Major metropolitan newspapers periodically publish a summary of indicators for their area. Cable and commercial television channels as well as some radio stations broadcast shows about business. Many online services and Web sites also offer up-to-date business and economic news. Today, following economic trends is easier than ever.

Tracking the local economy in informal ways is also wise because national and regional trends do not always predict local economic situations. Alert school leaders know where new subdivisions are being built in their districts and how much the houses cost. They notice how many shoppers are at the mall on weekends, and are aware of business closures and neighborhoods full of "For Sale" signs. In thinking about the economic environment, they consider information that they have gathered from both the media and their own observations. Figure 3.1 provides a set of questions for analyzing the economic environment.

Which of these is rising? Falling?

- Real GNP (over the last two years)
- Unemployment
- Misery Index
- New housing starts
- Sales of durable goods
- Business investment

What is the current inflation rate?

From local observation, what is happening?

- Are businesses moving in or leaving?
- Are any businesses expanding?
- Are shopping areas busy or relatively deserted?
- Are new houses being built?
- Are sales of existing houses moving well or slowly?
- Are restaurants and recreational facilities doing a lot of business?

FIGURE 3.1 Analyzing the economic environment

Long-Term Economic Trends

SLOW GROWTH. Unfortunately, relatively slow growth has been a characteristic of the world economy since the early 1970s, and experts have no reason to believe that this trend will reverse itself in the foreseeable future. In the United States, the absolute growth of the economy from year to year, as measured by increases in the per capita GNP, has declined since the 1950s and 1960s, as has the growth of productivity, as measured by increases in the GNP per employed worker. During the long expansion of the 1990s, the growth rate in the United States improved significantly; nonetheless, it was just average when compared to the entire post–World War II period (Penner, Sawhill, & Taylor, 2000). Most mainstream economists expect, therefore, that growth will eventually slow to the pre-1990s level, an expectation that seems to be supported by the arrival of the Great Recession.

FROM MANUFACTURING TO SERVICE AND INFORMATION. For more than a century, heavy industry provided the driving force of the U.S. economy, with U.S. factories producing cars, machinery, steel, and chemicals for domestic use and export. However, by 1980, the industrial sector was clearly in decline. Factories were beginning to lay off large numbers of workers; eventually, many closed altogether. A poll conducted by the *New York Times* in the mid-1990s found that since 1980, 72% of the respondents had either been laid off themselves or had seen a member of their household or close circle of friends and relatives laid off (1996). Factory workers have not been the only ones to lose their jobs; by the early 1990s, people in white-collar and middle-management jobs were being caught in massive "downsizings" as well. Although several causes for these layoffs have been identified, a major reason is the transformation of the U.S. economy into one based primarily on service and information rather than on manufacturing. The statistics are rather staggering.

According to figures from the United Nations, between 1980 and 1993 alone, 6.2% of U.S. manufacturing jobs were lost, whereas the number of jobs in financial and insurance services grew by 55% and the positions in the hospitality industry (largely hotels and restaurants) went up 22.7% (Reif et al., 1997). Although many of these new jobs—such as hotel maids and kitchen workers—were low paying, others—such as financial planners—commanded respectable salaries.

The development of new technologies, such as robotics, computers, and electronic telecommunications, is also transforming both the manufacturing and the service industries. No doubt, these new technologies offer unparalleled opportunities to human individuals and societies, but the transition from an industrial economic base to a service and information base can be difficult. For example, in an information economy, a few highly-skilled, knowledge workers tend to prosper, but many other types of workers tend to flounder, especially if they lack technological skills. As Reif et al. (1997) put it: "Job creation in the United States is skewing along educational and high-skill lines. The 'middle ground' may be losing way, especially in traditional manufacturing. The fastest growing employment sectors in services are now educationally based—in high . . . technology sectors" (pp. 2–3). Although some people predict that virtually all jobs will be eliminated by the new technologies of the Information Age, avoiding specific predictions is more prudent. We can, however, safely suggest that as the Information Age unfolds, virtually every aspect of the U.S. economy will change.

GLOBALIZATION.   Another major long-term trend of the U.S. economy is *globalization,* meaning that our economy is increasingly not independent, but rather part of a larger, worldwide economic system. Many causes for this trend have been identified; however, the most important ones are probably technological. Because of advances in computer science and telecommunications, information, money, and processed data can move thousands of miles in seconds. As a result, "for the first time in human history, anything can be made anywhere and sold everywhere" (Thurow, 1996, p. 115). This means that businesses—which are increasingly likely to be parts of large multinational corporations—can move their factories and offices to places where labor is cheap, taxes are low, and regulation is minimal. This also means that national governments have lost much of their power to influence their own economies through national economic policies. By providing them with stiff international competition, globalization forces many businesses to restructure, merge, or even go bankrupt. The collapse of the former Soviet Union and its Eastern European satellites in the early 1990s further accelerated the globalization process (Galbraith, 1994; Thurow, 1996).

HEAVY DEBT.   In the United States, increasing indebtedness, both public and private, has been a trend since the 1970s. A major indicator of public indebtedness, the soaring federal budget deficit, was much in the news during the late 1980s and early 1990s and is back in the news today. It grew from about half a trillion dollars in 1975 to more than four trillion dollars in 1992, an eightfold increase in fewer than twenty years (Perot, 1993). It increased under every president during that period, but growth was most rapid after 1982. Under Clinton, the federal budget deficit declined substantially and was eventually replaced by surpluses. However, the terrorist attacks of September 11, 2001, led to greatly increased spending on domestic security as well as to military action in the Middle East. As a result, the federal government moved once more into deficit spending; and by 2010 the national debt had reached $13.9 trillion, or 94% of the gross domestic product for that year (Tucker & Wilson, 2011).

Although business leaders and private citizens enjoy criticizing the federal government's spendthrift habits, when they do so they are really the proverbial pots calling the kettle black. Both corporate and personal indebtedness have also soared since the 1970s. For example, levels of consumer loans and personal mortgage debt nearly tripled between 1976 and 1985. To a great extent, this growth was fueled by the rapid expansion of the use of bank credit cards. During the 1980s, millions of U.S. families became overextended financially, and the rate of personal bankruptcy increased dramatically. Private indebtedness continued to accelerate during the 1990s, with credit card debt an increasingly important dimension of the phenomenon. By 2010, household debt in the United States had reached $13.4 trillion, or 107% of household income (Tucker & Wilson, 2011). High levels of individual debt lead to such personal calamities as bankruptcy and mortgage foreclosures; they also raise resistance to taxes.

INFLATION.   Since the end of World War II, the United States has experienced what some economists call *endemic inflation*—persistent and ongoing price increases that cannot be controlled completely (Heilbroner, 1985). In fact, since 1945, the CPI has increased in every year but three. It was relatively low until the 1970s, when it exceeded 10% in some years; under Reagan's supply-side economics, it dropped again. During the 1990s, the inflation rate averaged about 3%, although by the very end of the decade it was running between 1% and 2% (Blank, 2000; Makin, 1996, 1997). Inflation continued during the 2000s, as shown in Table 3.2. Although high inflation weakens an economy and disturbs citizens, a certain amount of inflation is helpful to debtors. They can pay off their loans in dollars that are cheaper than the dollars they borrowed. However, even a relatively low inflation rate makes financial planning difficult.

GROWING GAP BETWEEN RICH AND POOR.   One of the most troubling trends of the U.S. economy is the increasing difference in income between the top 20% of the population and the bottom 80%. This trend is well documented and has provoked concerned commentary from conservatives such as Kevin Phillips (1994), liberals such as Lester Thurow (1996), and independents such as Ross Perot (1993). It began in 1968 and accelerated with time, caused by a complex set of factors. First, the top 20% of the population is doing better than ever: They are well-educated, highly skilled workers who can command good salaries in the emerging information economy. However, the lower 80% is less skilled and is therefore doing less well; in fact, the less skilled a worker is, the more difficulty he or she has earning a decent wage. According to U.S. Census figures, the distribution of wealth among the five quintiles (or fifths) of the U.S. population and the wealthiest 5% of the population changed significantly between 1950 and 1997. The richest 5% and the richest 20% of the population have become richer, whereas everyone else has experienced a decline in their share of the national wealth. By 2000, the top 1% of households owned as much wealth as the bottom 95% (Draut, 2005). In 2007, the top 1% of the population earned 24% of the total income in the United States (Reich, 2010). An especially distressing aspect of this problem is its impact on children. Between 1974 and 1994, the child poverty rate in the United States increased by 49%. Although it dropped slightly during the long expansion of the 1990s, it still hovers around 20%—the highest rate among industrialized nations (Brouwer, 1998; National Center for Children in Poverty, 2009; Penner, Sawhill, & Taylor, 2000; UNICEF, 2007).

DEMOGRAPHICS AND THE POLICY ENVIRONMENT

The Importance of Demographics

Those who wish to understand education policy must pay as much attention to demographics as they pay to the economy. *Demography* is the scientific study of the characteristics of human populations and how they change over time, and *demographics* refers to the characteristics of a specific population, such as U.S. residents or U.S. schoolchildren (*The American Heritage Dictionary of the English Language,* 2000). Demographers record and analyze information about the size of a specific population, its growth patterns, age distribution, and vital statistics.

Like the economy, the demographic context can create severe constraints for education policy. After World War II, for example, the U.S. birthrate soared. Suddenly, school systems accustomed to demographic stability because of the Great Depression and World War II faced the challenge of educating unusually large numbers of children. They had little choice: most of the available resources had to be channeled into constructing school buildings, hiring additional staff, and equipping new classrooms. A declining school enrollment presents a different set of challenges, and an aging population creates special pressures for schools. School leaders must be aware of broad demographic trends not only in the nation, but also in their own geographic area, because, as demographer Harold Hodgkinson (2000/2001) puts it: *"Nothing is distributed evenly across the United States.* Not race, not religion, not age, not fertility, not wealth, and certainly not access to higher education" (p. 6, emphasis in the original). Figure 3.2 provides a set of questions for analyzing the demographic environment.

Which of these is rising? Falling? Remaining stable?

- The percentage of people older than 50?
- The percentage of people between ages 5 and 18?
- The percentage of high-income families?
- The percentage of low-income families?
- The percentage of white population?
- The percentage of people whose native language is English?
- The total population?

What is happening to rural, urban, and suburban populations?

What is happening to family composition and life style?

FIGURE 3.2 Analyzing the demographic environment

Long-Term Demographic Trends

AN AGING POPULATION WITH A "MINI BABY BOOM."   In the United States, as in most developed countries, the population is aging: the average age is increasing and increasingly higher percentages of the population are found in older age groups. This phenomenon is partly the result of better health care and nutrition; in wealthy countries, people often enjoy eighty years or more of active, productive living. Another reason is the presence of the "Baby Boom" generation—people born between 1946 and 1964. The oldest members of this unusually large age cohort of 75 million people are now in their sixties, pushing the median age of the general population higher. Based on the 2010 Census, demographers expect a major shift in age distribution, with a massive increase in the percentage of the population over the age of fifty. Meanwhile, the percentage of children under eighteen is declining; in 2010 it was 24.3%, down from 25.7% in 2000 (It's all relative, 2000; Mather et al., 2011; Morrison, 2001). One result of the changing age distribution is that a lower percentage of households include school-age children; according to the 2010 Census, that figure dropped from 36% in 2000 to 33.5% in 2010. In fact, in the United States today, more households have dogs than have children (El Nasser & Overberg, 2011).

However, the absolute *number* of school-age children will *not* decline. Rather, the U.S. Department of Education predicts that it will expand rapidly through 2020. This growth will result from what is called the *Baby Boom Echo* caused by the youngest boomers, many of whom had their children late, and the growing families of new immigrants, most of whom are young and have a higher birthrate than the native-born population. The growth will not, however, be evenly distributed across the country. Metropolitan areas are growing more rapidly than rural and small-town ones, and some states will see huge growth whereas others will see their school-age population decline. As Figure 3.3 shows, most of this growth will occur in the West and South (It's all relative, 2000; Mather et al., 2011; Morrison, 2001; U.S. Department of Education, 1999).

IMMIGRATION AND MIGRATION.   We live in a period of enormous population movement. The United States and several other nations receive hundreds of thousands of immigrants each year, many of them from Third World countries. Many immigrants to the United States are illegal, making it difficult even to determine

Alaska	Maryland
Arizona	New Jersey
California	New Mexico
Colorado	Oregon
Florida	Texas
Georgia	Utah
Hawaii	Virginia
Idaho	Washington
Kansas	Wyoming

FIGURE 3.3   States whose school-age populations will grow, 2000–2015

how much immigration is occurring. As a result of this massive and partially uncon-trolled immigration, the percentage of the American population that is foreign-born today is similar to the percentage in the early 1900s, when millions of Europeans im-migrated to this country. However, the immigrants of the late twentieth and early twenty-first centuries do not usually come from Europe, but from Latin America and Asia; the three countries that have contributed the most to this growth are Mexico, the Philippines, and Vietnam. A great deal of internal migration has occurred as well. States in the South, West, and Southwest have been drawing large numbers of people away from states in the Northeast, Midwest, and North-Central regions since the mid 1960s. This internal migration, combined with the arrival of many new immigrants in the West and South, contributed to the uneven growth patterns shown in Figure 3.3 (Mather et al., 2011; Mixed needs of immigrants pose challenges for schools, 2000; The immigration wave, 2000).

SUBURBANIZATION.   Another internal population shift that has been occurring for decades is suburbanization. The rural population has been in decline for a long time, but, in the twenty-first century, the urban population is also dwindling. City dwell-ers are not, however, fleeing to the country, but rather settling in the suburban belts that girdle large cities. As a result, suburbs are no longer the sheltered havens from the pressures of modern life they once were. Most large cities are surrounded by at least three rings of suburbs: (1) older suburbs that sprang up between 1920 and 1945; (2) the suburbs of the post–World War II era; and (3) newer suburbs, often many miles from the inner city. Many of the older suburbs have taken on the character-istics of the inner city. Not surprisingly, then, since the mid-1970s, the poverty rate has increased most rapidly in suburban areas. According to the 2010 U.S. Census, the suburban poverty rate grew by 37% between 2000 and 2010, considerably higher than the overall growth in the national poverty rate of 26.5%. However, cities—which have a poverty rate of 19.5%—are still poorer than suburbs, where 10.4% of the population lives below the poverty line (Dreier, Mollenkopf, & Swanstrom, 2001; Hodginkson, 2000/2001; Orfield, 2002; Yen, 2010).

INCREASING DIVERSITY.   Because of both immigration and differential birth rates, the U.S. population is becoming more diverse ethnically, linguistically, and religious-ly. The fastest-growing ethnic groups are Hispanics and Asians/Pacific Islanders, but immigration from Eastern Europe and the Middle East has also increased. The 2010 Census found that 46% of American children under 18 belong to a minority group; half of those children are Hispanic. In addition, the number of Americans who con-sider themselves bi- or multiracial is growing. People like golfer Tiger Woods—who is Asian, Black, Caucasian, and Native American—are becoming increasingly com-mon. Table 3.4 compares the ethnic composition of the school-age population in 2000 to the composition of this population in 2010. Because immigration levels vary considerably among states, some areas have experienced the challenges of greater cultural diversity for years. For example, in 1990, 40% of the children enrolled in the New York City public schools belonged to racial minority groups. In the same year, 31.4% of public school pupils in California were Hispanic, 11% were Asian, and 8.9% were African American. Until recently, in fact, five states (California, Florida, Illinois,

TABLE 3.4 The Ethnic Composition of the School-Age Population in 2000 and 2010

Ethnic Group	2000 (%)	2010 (%)
White, non-Hispanic	65	54
Hispanic	15	23
Black, non-Hispanic	15	14
Asian/Pacific Islander	4	4
Other	2	2

Source: Based on data from the U.S. Census Bureau, *Series A: Population Projections by Age, Sex, Race, and Hispanic Origin for 1999 to 2100, and* Mather et al., 2011. Figures do not add up to 100 because of rounding.

New York, and Texas) received most new immigrants, so the impact of this new diversity was geographically restricted. Today, however, this wave of immigration is fanning out into other areas that are less experienced in dealing with it. For example, due in large part to the growth of the Hispanic population, the 2010 Census showed that the populations of Arizona, Florida, Georgia, Maryland, Mississippi, and Nevada were already more than 40% minority. Moreover, the Hispanic population had more than doubled in nine states, including North Carolina, South Dakota, and Tennessee (Mather et al., 2011).

With ethnic diversity comes other kinds of diversity. In many schools, linguistic diversity is a daily reality, with most pupils speaking Spanish or an Asian language more fluently than English. Religious diversity is also growing. The old formula "Protestant–Catholic–Jew" is remote from the reality of classrooms in which many children come from Orthodox Christian, Muslim, Buddhist, or Hindu traditions. And the challenges of ethnic, cultural, linguistic, and religious diversity are spreading as the new immigrants and their children migrate out of the states that originally welcomed them.

PRO–CON DEBATE: SHOULD THE SCHOOLS TEACH ALL CHILDREN A CORE CURRICULUM?

YES: Today, more than ever, children in all U.S. public schools must be exposed to the same core curriculum. This curriculum should include the basic skills of reading, writing, and mathematics as well as exposure to the cultural heritage of the United States and its European antecedents. Two reasons exist for adopting such a curriculum. First, U.S. schools have historically been common schools because all children could attend them and also because they provided all children with a common experience. In a nation as diverse as ours, continuing this tradition is essential. How else can we develop in children the understanding that we are all part of the same culture and should be loyal to other Americans? Second, our society has become extremely mobile. A core curriculum would make life easier for children who move from school to school and from district to district without falling behind.

NO: The genius of the United States has always been its diversity. We have citizens whose ancestors came from many continents, and we also have many fine local traditions of education. Honoring this rich tradition by adapting the curriculum to the needs of the specific children who will use it is important. In some places, this will mean including much material about the African American experience; in others, it will mean an emphasis on our European roots; in still others, it may mean delving into the history of the labor movement. Each school, each ethnic group, and each community should have the freedom to develop a curriculum tailor-made for the needs of its children. Let a thousand flowers bloom!

- *What do YOU think?*

CONCLUSIONS.   The U.S. population and its lifestyle are changing rapidly. As a result, today's children are growing up in a world that differs substantially from the world in which school administrators—even relatively young ones—grew up. Moreover, this world is one that changes very quickly. The experience of the children of 2000 was somewhat different from the experience of their younger siblings in 2010. The experience of 2020 will differ from that of 2010. In thinking about the demographic policy environment, school leaders are truly dealing with a moving target. Those who do not stay abreast of these changes risk creating the impression that they are hopelessly out of date. Wise school leaders read newspaper and magazine articles about changing demographics with keen interest and ask themselves: What does this mean for children? For schools and teachers? For districts and administrators? What policy changes are needed in order to better deal with this trend?

IMPLICATIONS FOR EDUCATION POLICY

Implications of the Business Cycle

Because tax revenues expand and contract with the business cycle, that cycle has important implications for the level of funding that is likely to be available for public education. Guthrie and Koppich (1987) analyzed the political economy underlying each of four national education reforms: (1) the passage of the *National Defense Education Act* in 1958; (2) the passage of the *Elementary and Secondary Education Act* in 1965; (3) the passage of Public Law 94–142, the *Education for All Handicapped Children Act,* in 1975; and (4) the education excellence movement of the 1980s. They compared these four reform periods in relation to nine variables of the political and economic environment, finding that only two of the variables were consistent across all four cases. The first was that all four reform periods were sparked by a catalyst, such as the launching of *Sputnik* or the release of a commission report. The second was that "an upbeat economy undergird[ed] enactment or initiation of all four reform efforts" (p. 37). They concluded: "It may well be that economic buoyancy is a precondition of widespread change" (p. 38).

This finding has both reactive and proactive implications for school leaders. The reactive implication is that, although "economic buoyancy" does not always stimulate reforms in education, reform periods almost always occur against the backdrop of a strong economy. Thus, whenever the national, state, or local economy enters a strong expansion, school leaders should anticipate that proposals for major changes in education policy may be made. During such periods, keeping abreast of what is happening in Washington, D.C., in the major think tanks, and in professional publications is especially important. However, school leaders should not sit by passively, watching new policy proposals unfold. Leaders who wish to work for changes in education policy should lay the groundwork for such changes during slow economic times and try to catch the groundswell of the next expansion as they start to push publicly for reform. With more public resources available and an upbeat mood in the air, they will find persuading others to support their proposed policy change easier. Even more important, if their timing is right, they not only have a better chance of getting the policy change adopted, but may also have sufficient funding for the early years of implementation. Working with the business cycle is always easier than working against it.

Implications of Long-Range Trends

THE ECONOMIC/DEMOGRAPHIC SCENARIO.   Policymakers and policy scholars are fully aware of the broad outlines of the economic and demographic data discussed previously and have been for a long time. For example, in their introduction to the first *Politics of Education Association Yearbook,* Boyd and Kerchner (1988) wrote of "the serious implications of current social and demographic trends in the United States" (p. 2). To a considerable degree, concern about these trends has driven U.S. education policy since the early 1980s.

The demographic trends suggest that the task of public schools is going to become increasingly difficult. First, about one out of every five schoolchildren is growing up in poverty with all its associated problems: poor nutrition, inadequate health care, transience, and stress. Moreover, many children—and not just poor ones—have special social and educational needs, which might include bilingual or English-as-a-second-language programs; activities to introduce their parents to the expectations of U.S. schools; academic curricula that include more coverage of Eastern Europe, Asia, Africa, and Latin America; before- and after-school programs; tutors to help with homework; remediation; and mentoring. In short, the probable needs of today's and tomorrow's schoolchildren are such that educators could easily justify spending more money in the near future than they do today.

However, the economic and demographic trends together suggest that raising more money will not be easy, and that even raising as much as was raised in the recent past may be impossible. For complex reasons, including slower economic growth, stagnating wages, the aging of the population, the threat of unemployment, and heavy consumer debt, Americans have become averse to tax increases—and even to maintaining the current level of taxation. So-called tax revolts were common in the late 1970s, and as a result, many states passed tax and expenditure limitation laws that are still on the books. Experts see no signs that these will be lifted soon; in fact, such limitations are likely to be made more restrictive. Moreover, increased concerns about terrorism and military actions to counter it have diverted public funds that might have gone to education under different circumstances. Another problem is that a growing percentage of the population has no school-age children. Of course, most senior citizens fall in this category; the tendencies to marry late, start a family late, or decide not to have children at all further increase the number of childless households. These economic and demographic trends interact, intensifying opposition to paying taxes to support schools. Finally, although few people admit it openly, the changing social, racial, ethnic, religious, socioeconomic, and linguistic compositions of the school-age population probably makes identifying with today's children and feeling any responsibility for their education or general welfare hard for some Americans.

"Do More with Less"

Three broad reactions can be found to the implications of long-term economic and demographic trends. One can be described as the "Do more with less" philosophy. Those who hold this position believe that public schools already receive more money than they need; the real problem is that educators waste it. This position was espoused by Reagan's second secretary of education, William Bennett, who stated in a February 1988 speech: "Money doesn't cure school problems" (Baker, 1991, p. 628). His opinions were based largely on studies conducted by economist Eric Hanushek (1989, 1994), who analyzed dozens of studies of the relationship between educational expenditure and student achievement, concluding that: "There is no consistent relationship between the resources applied to schools and student performance" (Hanushek, 1994, p. 464). He argued that the incentive structure in education must be changed, not the amount of money available.

Many of the reforms of the 1980s, 1990s, and 2000s can be understood as attempts to alter the incentive structure in order to encourage more effective educational practices. For example, in the early days of the excellence in education movement, graduation requirements were increased and statewide testing programs were initiated or revised. Other popular policy proposals during this period included merit pay for teachers and career ladders. Many states also began to gather detailed education performance statistics and use them to publish "report cards" for school districts and individual schools, making them available to parents and the general public.

More recently, the desire to change the incentive structure in education has led to numerous school-choice proposals, including charter schools, intradistrict open enrollment, interdistrict open enrollment, and vouchers. Another widely suggested change is merit, or performance, pay for teachers and perhaps for administrators as well. The common thread linking these policies is competition; many proponents of school choice believe that if schools and educators have to compete for students and money, they will be motivated to improve their performance. Inadequate schools will either get better or go out of business; and weak teachers and administrators will leave the field. Moreover, competition will force educators to use their resources more efficiently than they do now. Ultimately, schools will both be better and cost less.

"Do a Lot More with a Little More"

Others have been willing to provide a little more money for schools, but only if it is used in certain ways. Representative of this school of thought is policy scholar William H. Clune (1994a, 1994b). Two decades ago, he argued both for a funding level that would promote "high minimum outcomes" for all children and for curricular and structural changes to support such outcomes. In his view, additional funding would be "targeted": low-performing districts—whether poor or not—would be eligible for extra financial support, but only if they used it to implement specific improvement plans (Clune, 1994a, 1994b). Proposed and actual education policies that reflect ideas similar to Clune's include (1) standards-based reform; (2) authentic assessment;

(3) school-linked services; (4) curricula that emphasize higher order thinking skills; and (5) professional development to support new curricula and pedagogies. Indeed, the *No Child Left Behind Act* of 2001 provides an excellent example of this approach.

"Do a Lot More with a Lot Less"

In an era of layoffs and budget cuts, educators may feel that they are actually being asked to do a lot more with a lot less in the way of resources. Budgets are being slashed . . . but state accountability programs are not. Class sizes are being increased . . . but teachers must prepare more students for the same tests. States are pressuring districts to achieve better high school graduation rates . . . but states are also cutting the support services that would help districts meet this goal. In short, often policymakers seem not even to notice the contradiction between simultaneously increasing demands and reducing resources. Truly, today's educators are living in interesting times.

Reading Between the Lines

Most readers have no doubt been struck that many of the economic and demographic issues discussed in this chapter are politically charged. As a result, policymakers do not always make fully explicit their rationales for adopting policies that touch on these areas. For example, openly advocating a reduction in teachers salaries would be tantamount to political suicide in most states. However, legislatures sometimes quietly reduce teachers hourly pay by increasing their work load without providing additional clerical support. In effect, some of the testing programs of the 1980s, 1990s, and 2000s did exactly this. Similarly, parents would rise up in anger at the suggestion that they assume a greater share of the costs of transporting their children to school, yet this is one hidden effect of some school-choice proposals. Figure 3.4 contains questions to use in assessing some of the hidden implications of actual or proposed education policies.

- What are the financial implications of this policy?
- Will it cost the same as, more than, or less than alternative policies?
- Will anyone gain financially from the policy? If so, who?
- Will anyone lose financially because of this policy? If so, who?
- Will this policy shift costs—as measured in money, materials, or time—from government to parents, teachers, administrators, or others?
- Will this policy shift costs from one level of government to another?
- Could this policy be used to cut costs in ways not intended by its advocates?
- How will this policy affect the affluent, the middle class, and the poor?
- Will this policy encourage more diversity, less diversity, or leave the current degree of diversity unchanged? (Consider racial, ethnic, religious, linguistic, and social class diversity as well as handicapping conditions.)
- Will this policy support family life? If so, how? If not, why not?

FIGURE 3.4   Ten questions to help in reading between the lines of education policies

FINAL POINTS

As this chapter has made clear, public schools are facing some unprecedented challenges. The American economy is not bouncing back from the 2007-2009 recession. At best, the country seems to face a slow and prolonged economic recovery; at worst, it may sink into a second, or "double dip," recession. At the same time, state education funding is being cut. However, as the population ages and fewer voters have school-age children at home, passing local school finance issues will probably become more difficult. And, the children who will increasingly fill our classrooms will be poorer and less likely to speak English at home than the children of the not-so-distant past. In short, we live in a time when outstanding leaders will be needed in public schools—leaders who know how to use resources skillfully and how to motivate and inspire children from backgrounds very different from their own. The challenges are great; but so are the opportunities for creative leadership.

QUESTIONS AND ACTIVITIES FOR DISCUSSION

1. Using a daily newspaper, find several indicators of the health of the economy. What are the implications of your findings for education policy?
2. In class, brainstorm ideas for gaining senior citizens support for public schools.
3. Identify a major problem of at-risk children in your geographic area, and suggest a policy for dealing with it.
4. What evidence do you see in your own district of the impact of the Great Recession? How have local leaders responded to this challenge?

INTERNET ASSIGNMENT

Search the Internet for information about how the Great Recession has affected school funding in your state. What conclusions can you draw from your findings?

FOR FURTHER READING

Bartlett, B. (2009). *The new American economy.* New York: Palgrave Macmillan.

The author, a treasury official under the first President Bush and one of Reagan's public policy advisors, offers a surprising analysis of what has gone wrong with the U.S. economy. He concludes with political and economic advice for the future.

Buchholz, T. G. (1989). *New ideas from dead economists.* New York: New American Library.

Written from a conservative perspective, this book explains the ideas of important economists of the past and tells how they are important today. It provides a readable introduction to some of the conservative economic concepts that have shaped public policy in the United States since 1980.

Draut, T. (2005). *Strapped.* New York: Doubleday.

In a very readable book, Draut explains why people under 35 have so much trouble making it financially in contemporary America. After describing the economic pressures of school loans, credit card debt, unaffordable housing, and the cost of raising a child, she movingly argues that the issue is fundamentally one of values and urges her readers to bring about change through political action.

Ginsberg, R., & Multon, K. D. (2011). Leading through a fiscal nightmare. *Phi Delta Kappan, 92*(8), 42–47.

The authors surveyed 93 principals and 100 superintendents, trying to determine the impact of state budget cuts on them and their schools. They reported considerable job satisfaction, but also great stress; they offer school leaders some survival tips.

Krugman, P. (2009). *The return of depression economics and the crisis of 2008.* New York: W. W. Norton.

Krugman, the 2008 winner of the Nobel Prize in Economics, situates the Great Recession in a global framework. His very readable book explains how the recession occurred and recommends policy changes to prevent a future recession of the same type.

4 THE POLITICAL SYSTEM AND POLITICAL CULTURE

Focus Questions

▌ What are the distinctive characteristics of the U.S. political system?
▌ How can school leaders work most effectively within this system?
▌ What is political culture?
▌ Why should school leaders take into account the political culture of the geographic area in which they work?

THE IMPORTANCE OF THE LESS OBVIOUS

The importance of economic conditions and the demographic situation is relatively apparent. However, other aspects of the education policy environment are considerably less obvious to casual observers, and may even seem insignificant at first glance. This chapter deals with two of these less obvious factors: the political system and political culture.

The United States has a distinctive *political system* that was devised in the late eighteenth century by men with a good knowledge of political theory but few contemporary models available for study. Although many Americans idealize the system of separated powers that the Founding Fathers developed, some political scientists believe that, as the first modern attempt at representative government, it is clumsier than the parliamentary system that evolved in Great Britain during the nineteenth century. Indeed, today most democratic countries use the parliamentary system because it is widely considered more efficient and responsive than our system (Coulter, 1997). Be that as it may, the United States is unlikely to change its political system, which means that school leaders must understand this system's strengths and limitations in order to work intelligently within it. The first portion of this chapter, therefore, deals with the U.S. political system, describing how it constrains and shapes education policy and suggesting ways education leaders can function effectively within it.

Even less obvious than the political system is **political culture.** Daniel Elazar (2003), well known for his research on U.S. political culture, defines *political culture* as "the particular pattern of orientation to political action in which [a] political system is embedded" (p. 256). He identified three basic political cultures in the United States: individualistic, moralistic, and traditionalistic. Although on paper the formal political systems of the fifty states resemble each other greatly, in practice, those structures operate somewhat differently in each of the three political cultures. This means that a school leader who moves from Pennsylvania (which has an individualistic culture) to Tennessee (which is traditionalistic) must relearn many principles of practical politics in order to work well in the new setting. These issues are discussed in the second part of this chapter.

THE U.S. POLITICAL SYSTEM

Federalism

FEDERALISM DEFINED.   The fundamental characteristic of the U.S. political system is that it has a federal structure. The best way to define **federalism** is to contrast it with unitary government, the other major modern political structure. Under a unitary system, such as that in France, Japan, and the United Kingdom, only one government in the country exercises sovereign power by taking such actions as passing laws and levying taxes; this is the national government, headquartered in the country's capital. Local governing bodies exist, but they are subordinate to the national government that created them and can also overrule, or even abolish, them. Unitary governments also exist in the United States; the relationship between the fifty state governments and their respective local governments is unitary (Coulter, 1997; Isaak, 1987).

In contrast, under a federal system, several governments share sovereign powers among themselves and the national government cannot abolish the subsidiary governments. In the United States, for example, the states actually founded the national government, and the Constitution clearly delineates which sovereign powers belong to the states and which belong to the federal government. The federal government does not have the authority to overrule state governments when they are acting within their area of sovereignty, nor can it abolish them (Coulter, 1997; Hanson, 2004; Isaak, 1987). Federalism is often used by countries with strong regional traditions. The young United States, for instance, consisted of thirteen former British Colonies with distinctive histories and cultures. Two centuries later, regional traditions are still strong, a fact school leaders should always bear in mind, especially if they are "transplants" to the region in which they work.

HISTORY OF U.S. FEDERALISM.   The relationship between the federal and state governments is not fixed and unchanging, but dynamic. During the more than two centuries since the signing of the Declaration of Independence, U.S. federalism has gone through several distinctive phases. Because the Founding Fathers were suspicious of centralized political power, they established an extremely weak federal system under the Articles of Confederation. This structure was so glaringly inadequate that after just a few years the current Constitution was written and ratified, establishing a stronger federal government. However, the new Constitution was controversial from the start; several major leaders, including Thomas Jefferson, had serious reservations about it. For decades the amount of power appropriate for the federal government was a central issue in national politics. Indeed, one major party called itself the "Federalists" because strengthening the national government was one of its major objectives. The early arguments over federalism culminated in the Civil War, when the Southern states exercised what they considered their sovereign right to secede from the Union. The Northern victory in that war meant that the weakest interpretation of federalism was seriously discredited. However, other weak interpretations still flourish today alongside stronger ones.

During the sixty-four years between the end of the Civil War and the beginning of the Great Depression, the federal government enjoyed a new legitimacy that it used to promote the construction of railroads, the settlement of the West, and the conquest of numerous Native American tribes. Even so, it was relatively weak by contemporary standards; it did not even begin to levy a significant income tax until the United States entered World War I. The Great Depression, followed by World War II, led to an enormous increase in federal power. The economic collapse of 1929 caused bank failures as well as business and personal bankruptcies across the nation, leading to widespread unemployment. Because these economic problems were of such magnitude that state and local governments were unable to address them effectively, the federal government stepped in, assuming an enhanced role in economic and labor policy. This tendency to strengthen federal power at the expense of state and local governments was further accelerated by another crisis, World War II. For more than twenty years after the end of the war, Washington played an activist role, taking the lead in such areas as civil rights and urban policy. The tide began to turn in 1968, with the election of Richard Nixon to the White House. His successors, Gerald Ford and Jimmy Carter, also sought to alter the federal relationship by empowering the states. However, under Ronald Reagan, elected president in 1980, the shift in the balance of power between the states and the federal government accelerated (Bowman & Kearney, 2008; Gray, 1996; Lewis & Maruna, 1996; Van Horn, 2006). It is possible that the enactment of the *No Child Left Behind Act* (NCLB) in 2002 marked a reversal of this trend, but as of this writing, it is too soon to be certain. If NCLB is strengthened when it is reauthorized, then it will probably be reasonable to conclude that the balance of power is beginning to shift away from the states and back to the federal government.

FEDERALISM TODAY. In his 1982 State of the Union address, Reagan called for a "New Federalism," which involved giving the states more power in several policy areas and more discretion over the use of federal funds (Bowman & Kearney, 2008). Because education is a major function of state government, the New Federalism had a great impact on education policy. At the most tangible level, it meant decreased federal funding. In 1978, just before the beginning of the Reagan Administration, the federal government provided 8.1% of all money for U.S. schools; under Reagan, the government's share dropped to 6%, a decline of more than 25% (Sroufe, 1995). Moreover, under Reagan, the federal government streamlined the administration of education funds by consolidating thirty-seven programs into a single block grant entitled Elementary and Secondary Education. Under this new approach, federal guidelines for spending education funds were relaxed, empowering state governments to make decisions about the direction of education policy in several new areas (Kaplan & O'Brien, 1991). The overall effect of the New Federalism was to reduce the relative importance of the federal government in education policymaking, while increasing the relative importance of the states.

However, Reagan's New Federalism was not the only factor that led to increased state power over education policy. Starting in the early 1960s, several changes strengthened state governments and gave them more capacity for exercising political leadership. *Baker v. Carr,* a 1962 U.S. Supreme Court decision, was an important first step in this process. By affirming the one person–one vote principle, it required the reapportionment of state legislative districts, making state legislatures more representative of the general population. As these bodies became more representative, they also began to attract young, well-educated people. This new breed of state officials worked hard during the 1970s and 1980s to professionalize state government; today, therefore, most states have more efficient and modern governments than they had thirty years ago. The professionalization of state government occurred simultaneously with the growth of intergovernmental lobbies such as the National Governors Association (NGA) and the National Conference of State Legislatures (NCSL). Such organizations facilitate communication among state officials and provide a forum in which information about policy can be disseminated and discussed.

As a result of these changes in state government, state leaders were able to spearhead a national education reform movement beginning in 1983. Although the federal government played an important role—notably by sponsoring the 1983 commission report *A Nation at Risk*—governors such as Lamar Alexander and Bill Clinton worked through the NGA to push steadily for the reform of public education. In many states their efforts led to the adoption of such policies as increased graduation requirements, proficiency tests, career ladders, and school choice. Such an intense and coordinated level of activity in education policy on the part of state governments was unprecedented in U.S. history (Bowman & Kearney, 2008; Mazzoni, 1995).

Historically, states delegated much of their authority over education policy to local school districts. However, since about 1980, this traditional allocation of power has shifted, primarily because local government is often in crisis. Economic stagnation and the widespread adoption of tax and expenditure limitations during the 1970s reduced tax revenues, and many local governments find continuing to provide high-quality public services difficult. This crisis is particularly severe in large cities, where the loss of tax revenues, deterioration of infrastructure and housing stock, and growing impoverishment of the population combine to create problems so overwhelming that few municipal governments have the capacity to address them. However, the crisis has also hit other areas hard; many small-town, suburban, and rural communities that were self-sufficient a generation ago find themselves struggling today.

As one type of local government, school districts represent an important dimension of this crisis. Indeed, some big city school districts collapsed under the weight of financial and social problems, and many rural districts are in ongoing bankruptcy. In a crisis of such proportions, state governments have been obliged to take unprecedented steps. In some cases, state departments of education take over the daily administration of floundering school districts. More often, they provide emergency loans or assign state consultants to work with troubled districts. Of course, when one government gives resources to another, it also expects to have some say about how those resources are used. As a result, state governments are playing a more active role than ever in spelling out how districts should educate children and in monitoring their activities (Bowman & Kearney, 2008).

Separation of Powers

Another important characteristic of U.S. government is that it is based on the *separation of powers* rather than on a structure of fused powers. Ever fearful of powerful government, the Founding Fathers constitutionally delegated the executive, legislative, and judicial functions of government to separate branches that could check or restrain each other. Moreover, although the states were free to adopt any form of republican government they pleased, all fifty states wrote constitutions that separated government functions into three branches. This pattern is also imitated to a certain degree at the local level. For example, school boards and superintendents sometimes work at cross purposes because of a formal or informal separation of powers. The Founding Fathers thus succeeded admirably in establishing a "political system . . . designed to frustrate central power" (Cohen & Spillane, 1993, p. 38). However, they also raised an interesting question for the public leaders who must work within the system: How does one build coalitions across the system in order to bring about needed change? Cohen and Spillane (1993) observe that the greatest challenge in developing education policy in the United States is "bridging vast political chasms artfully designed to frustrate central power" (p. 43).

Fragmentation of Governance

FRAGMENTATION OF LOCAL GOVERNMENT. Public leadership in the United States is further complicated by *fragmentation,* both the fragmentation of local government and the proliferation of governance structures. Units of local government are established by law in the state in which they are located, and usually their powers and responsibilities are spelled out in either a charter or a special act of the legislature. Figure 4.1 lists the five types of local government. Most U.S. school districts are *special districts,* which are governed by an elected *school board*. Other types of special districts include park districts and water districts; and they, too, are often governed by elected or appointed boards. Although some states do not use all five types of local government, many do. As a result, school leaders must deal not only with the different branches of government at the state and federal levels, but also with numerous local governments whose geographic borders may overlap those of the school district and whose officials may perceive the school district as a competitor rather than an ally (Bowman & Kearney, 2008; Hanson, 2004).

The relationship between a school system and local government can take one of two general forms: independence or dependence. Ninety-two percent of U.S. school districts are independent. This means they are completely autonomous in relationship

Counties
Municipalities
Towns
Townships
Special Districts

FIGURE 4.1   Five types of local government

to other local governments; in particular, it means they are financially autonomous, or *fiscally independent*. They have the power to levy school taxes within a regulatory framework established by their state legislature. The school board of an independent district also develops its own budget and is not required to submit it to any other unit of local government for approval. Although fiscal independence has some advantages, it also has drawbacks. One of the most important is that an independent school district lacks a natural ally at the local level. Leaders in independent districts must work especially hard to build positive relationships with other units of local government; not infrequently, they find themselves alone when the time comes to increase school taxes (Berkman & Plutzker, 2005; Bowman and Kearney, 2009).

Only 8% of school districts are dependent; however, this pattern is more important than the percentages suggest because many of the largest districts in the nation are dependent. In five states (Alaska, Hawaii, Maryland, North Carolina, and Virginia), all school districts are dependent; in thirteen others, many districts are. *Fiscal dependence* is especially common in the South. A fiscally dependent school district is actually an education agency operated by a unit of local government, usually a city or county. Its school board does not have the power to either raise taxes or approve its own budget; instead, it depends on the controlling government unit to do so. Although this approach has obvious drawbacks, it also has one great advantage: the school system has a natural ally among local governments. For example, if the Virginia House of Delegates is considering legislation that would negatively affect the Fairfax County schools, leaders of the school system will probably work side by side with Fairfax County leaders to try to blunt this effort (Berkman & Plutzker, 2005; Bowman & Kearney, 2008).

FRAGMENTATION THROUGH SEPARATE STRUCTURES.   A second aspect of the fragmentation of U.S. school governance is the splitting of responsibility among various official or semiofficial boards and agencies. In part, this fragmentation can be attributed to the reforms put in place during the Progressive Movement of the early 1900s. In an attempt to depoliticize school governance, Progressive reformers established separate boards, especially at the state level. State boards of education, for instance, are largely a legacy of the Progressive period. However, scholars also identify a more general tendency in the United States to establish separate governance structures, both in education and in other policy domains. What happens is that leaders, working within an already fragmented system, become frustrated with its unresponsiveness, so they establish new structures. For a while, the new structures are relatively responsive; as time passes, however, they, too, become unresponsive. The result is a proliferation of boards, agencies, and commissions. In education, these structures often cluster around specific policy areas or professional interests. For example, a variety of structures have arisen around P.L. 94–142 (the *Education for All Handicapped Children Act*), around the compensatory programs established by the *Elementary and Secondary Education Act* of 1965, and around vocational education and high school athletics. In recent years such education policy developments as privatization and governors with a strong interest in education have weakened state boards of education; in fact, many governors have reduced the power of their state boards (Henig, 2009). Nonetheless, the governance structure is still very fragmented.

PRO–CON DEBATE: SHOULD SCHOOL BOARDS BE ABOLISHED?

YES: The school board was a wonderful institution for nineteenth-century America. It was appropriate at a time when only a few rudiments of the "three R's" were necessary for most children and when teachers themselves were not well educated. In an age of global competition, however, school boards are an anachronism. Most states do not even require that school board members be literate, much less knowledgeable about education. Putting more and more accountability measures in place for teachers and administrators while still giving the ultimate control of the school system to people who mean well but know very little about the learning process no longer makes sense. Nor does it make sense to raise the standards for teacher and administrator training and then put professional educators under the supervision of a lay school board. Can you imagine what our health care system would be like if doctors had to follow the policy dictates of elected "medical boards"? It is time to modernize our governance system by eliminating the old-fashioned school board!

NO: The school board is one of the last bastions of democracy in the United States. It also is an important way of building community support for public schools. Electing school board members gives people an interest in their school system and in their local community. It also provides a way for them to express their views on one of the most important functions of government—providing education for children and youth. Moreover, elected school boards help prevent education from becoming the preserve of a few professional experts. The education of our children is every citizen's concern because it shapes the future of our whole society. Therefore, everyone should have a chance to participate in the governing of the school system by electing people to school boards. Abolishing school boards would be a disastrous step for us to take; it would remove education from public control and cause many citizens to lose all interest in it. Ultimately, this could mean considerable financial loss for our public schools.

• *What do YOU think?*

Focus on Elections

Another unusual characteristic of our political system is its focus on elections rather than on governing, a phenomenon that has been nicknamed "the permanent campaign" (Fuhrman, 1993, p. 9). This preoccupation with elections results from two structural factors. First, U.S. elections occur at fixed time intervals established by law. No matter how high a president's or state legislator's public approval ratings are, he or she must run for reelection when the fixed election date comes around. In contrast, under the parliamentary system of government, most elected officials serve as long as their party has public support and is able to govern effectively. Elections are held when a "crisis of confidence" occurs. Although parliamentary systems can experience periods of instability during which several short-lived governments replace each other in rapid succession, they do focus attention on maintaining public support and governing well rather than on elections. The U.S. system, however, encourages everyone—politicians, the mass media, and the general public—to concentrate on elections and campaigns. Another structural factor that focuses attention on elections is short terms of office. Members of the U.S. House of Representatives and of the lower house in most state legislatures have two-year terms; quite literally, they are always campaigning for office. Governors, who usually serve four-year terms, and U.S. senators, who serve six-year terms, feel somewhat less electoral pressure. Judges— some of whom are appointed for long terms and some of whom are elected in low-key, infrequent elections—feel the least electoral pressure (Coulter, 1997; Fuhrman, 1993).

Judicial Review

A final characteristic of the U.S. political system is that courts have the power of *judicial review,* meaning that they can declare legislation unconstitutional. Although most democratic countries have procedures for evaluating the constitutionality of legislation, because of their power of judicial review, courts in the United States are unusually influential in the policy-making process. In fact, the U.S. Supreme Court has been called the most powerful court in the world (Isaak, 1987). Nor should the power of the fifty state court systems be overlooked. "State courts are important and highly visible participants in the making of public policy," insists political scientist Lawrence Baum (2006, p. 96), identifying education policy as a domain in which state courts are particularly active. Indeed, in many states, education interest groups consider the court system and the state legislature alternative routes for reaching policy goals. State courts have played an especially important role in school finance policy, having declared the finance systems of several states unconstitutional. Frequently, legislators are more than willing to let judges make unpopular decisions, for in their ever-recurring electoral campaigns they can blame the black-robed justices. Because judges are subject to less electoral pressure than legislators, they are sometimes willing to take some political heat for them (Baum, 2006).

IMPLICATIONS OF THE POLITICAL SYSTEM FOR SCHOOL LEADERS

Competition Among Governance Bodies

NATURE OF THE COMPETITION. Dutch sociologist Geert Hofstede (Hofstede & Bond, 2001) conducted a cross-cultural study of organizational behavior in IBM offices in sixty-seven countries, finding that Americans prefer an organizational structure that he described metaphorically as a "village market." In a village market, numerous vendors compete for customers and sales by shouting loudly, bargaining to make attractive deals, and inventing creative ways to display their goods. The structure of the U.S. political system establishes a sort of village market among the various components of government, leading to competition among the three levels (federal, state, and local), the three branches (executive, legislative, and judicial), the many local governments, and various quasi-independent governance bodies.

These political entities compete primarily for two things: resources and power. One major resource for which competition is especially keen is, of course, money, which may take the form of a generous line in a budget proposal, a grant, or approval of a tax increase. Nevertheless, readers should remember that other resources can spark competition. Agencies and branches of the government frequently jockey for desirable perquisites such as office space in a prestigious or convenient location, new equipment, and skilled personnel. Power is the second major stake in this competition. Governance bodies and government agencies often struggle with each other for jurisdiction over specific policy areas or for the right to representation on a board or committee. Sometimes policy decisions that make little sense from a purely rational perspective make a great deal of sense when interpreted as the outcome of a competition among a set of specific government actors striving for resources and power.

IDENTIFYING AND MONITORING COMPETITORS.   Clear-headed political thinking by school leaders thus depends on accurately identifying actual and potential competitors. One way to identify them is to ask, "If our district (or school) wanted a budget increase (or to submit a grant proposal, or to hold a referendum to raise school taxes), what government bodies or officials might openly or covertly oppose us?" Figure 4.2 lists possible competitors who should be considered in developing a detailed answer to this question.

Simply identifying one's competitors is not enough, however; monitoring them is also important. One way to do this is to read local newspapers, including weeklies, regularly, because they are often the only media outlets that cover local government consistently. In reading newspapers as part of a monitoring effort, school leaders should be sure to pay particular attention to reports of local government meetings and to public notices that announce upcoming bids for construction projects, because these items frequently contain important information about competitors goals. Another way to monitor competitors is to establish a good network of local contacts and maintain positive relations with them. Developing friendships in the community and participating in organizations such as the Kiwanis, Rotary, and Soroptimist clubs are good ways to ensure that one is involved in "grapevine" communication. Sometimes information is available through these channels weeks or months before

City governments
County governments
Fire departments
Health departments
Human services departments
Infrastructure (roads, bridges, sewers)
Institutions of higher education
Justice system
Museums
Other school districts
Other schools
Park systems
Police departments
Prisons
Public hospitals
Public libraries
Recreation programs
Senior citizen programs

FIGURE 4.2   Government entities that often compete with public schools it is discussed in a public meeting or becomes the subject of a newspaper article. School leaders general goal should be a sensitive awareness of all the local demands on public resources most likely to be made in the near future. Such an awareness can facilitate their intelligent planning in a number of areas and help them avoid mistakes. For example, a superintendent who knows the city police department is cooperating with police departments throughout the region to lobby the legislature for funds to purchase new computer equipment may decide this is not the best time to lobby for increased spending on school libraries. Instead, she may conclude that her district's energies would be better applied to writing a grant proposal to a foundation to obtain financial support.

Multiple Veto Points

The complex, multitiered structure of the U.S. political system creates numerous sites in which a policy proposal can be sidetracked or defeated. As a result, moving an idea from the proposal stage to the official policy stage can take years. For a proposal to be introduced several times before it finally passes a major legislative committee is not unusual; indeed, the large majority of bills introduced in a U.S. legislature not only never become laws, but they are never even voted on by the full legislature. They "die" in one of the many committees through which they must pass (Ohio State University [OSU], 1991). Outside the formal legislative process, various additional veto points exist. Strong opposition to a proposed policy change by a powerful interest group or by the agency that must implement it can slow down the process as much as any legislative committee can. Opposition by a teachers union or an accrediting association can also throw up roadblocks. As a result, school leaders who wish to influence education policy must be persistent, and must build a broad strategic base of support for their ideas as well. They should not expect that they as individuals or the professional groups in which they are active will be able to influence policy in a short time. They should anticipate a process that may take several years. Usually, policymakers must be educated, support among key policy actors must be built, and negotiations with other stakeholders must take place. In the United States, policy changes are the outcome of patient, long-term efforts and broad-based coalitions. Leaders who want quick results or who like to play "Lone Ranger," shunning all alliances, are unlikely to succeed.

Timing Policy Concerns with Elections

Given the tendency of the U.S. political system to focus on elections, school leaders must be closely attuned to the electoral cycle. First, they must know precisely when all the elections that could affect them occur at the federal, state, and local levels. Table 4.1 provides a sample chart that can be used to organize this information for easy reference. Second, school leaders must know the electoral status of every public official with whom they interact. However, they must know more than just when that official will next stand for election. With elected leaders, questions such as how long they have already served, party affiliation, margin of victory in the last election, and the probability of seeking reelection are also important. In states with term limits, knowing how many years or terms politicians have left to serve is also essential. Table 4.2 provides a sample chart for organizing such information.

TABLE 4.1 Offices and Election Dates

Offices	Date of Next Election
U.S. Representative	
U.S. Senator #1	
U.S. Senator #2	
Governor	
State Representative	
State Senator	
Chair, House Education Committee (State)	
Chair, Senate Education Committee (State)	
Mayor	
City Council Members	
County Executive	
County Commission Members	
Tax Assessor	

TABLE 4.2 Key Information on the Electoral Status of Officials

Official	Years in Office	Party Affiliation	Last Margin of Victory	Likely to Run Again?
U.S. Representative				
U.S. Senator #1				
U.S. Senator #2				
Governor				
State Representative				
State Senator				
Chair, House Education Committee (State)				
Chair, Senate Education Committee (State)				
Mayor				
City Council Members				
County Executive				
County Commission Members				
Tax Assessor				

SELECTING THE TIME AND THE PEOPLE.   Both research and years of practical experience suggest that timing is often the key to successfully influencing policy. The electoral cycle is an important aspect of this timing (Kingdon, 2003). As a rule of thumb, the closer a politician is to an election the less likely he is to support a policy change that would require increasing taxes. Conversely, the most propitious time for advocating such a change is immediately after an election. Similarly, most politicians shy away from supporting controversial policy issues right before an election; those whose position in their district is shaky are generally unwilling to support such issues at any time. Therefore, school leaders who wish to bring about a policy change that is likely to provoke opposition from a segment of the electorate should reflect carefully before asking elected officials for support. Most likely to take a strong stance on a controversial issue is a politician who has been in office for a long time, has a comfortable margin of victory in her district, and does not face reelection in the near future. Another type of politician who may be willing to take chances is one who either cannot run for reelection or does not intend to do so. However, the temporary status of such "lame ducks" limits their power and effectiveness. Although a lame duck may be the right person to approach for a vote in a key committee, he would probably make a poor sponsor of legislation.

Political party affiliation is another variable to consider in timing policy activity. Democratic politicians and legislatures controlled by the Democratic Party are more likely to support increased spending on public education than are Republicans. Thus, school leaders should consider the presence of Democrats in office an opportunity to work for policy changes with significant price tags attached. However, Republicans are usually more sympathetic to management, including school management, than are Democrats. School leaders should therefore consider the presence of Republicans in office an opportunity to work for policy changes that enhance their own power, such as changes in the tenure and collective bargaining laws.

WINDOWS OF OPPORTUNITY.   John Kingdon (2003) found that success in influencing policy often depends on recognizing the opening of a *window of opportunity,* or a period during which both politicians and the public are especially receptive to a specific policy idea. Because policy windows open suddenly and do not remain open long, moving quickly when one opens is essential. One predictable policy window is related to the electoral cycle; whenever a change in administration occurs, an opportunity to seek innovative policy changes occurs. This is because a new administration wants to make a name by initiating reforms that are popular with the public. Moreover, in future reelection campaigns, members of the administration will be able to mention these reforms in their list of accomplishments. Politically alert school leaders are aware of impending changes in administration, especially at the state level. Because most governors serve four-year terms and can be reelected once, such a change usually occurs every eight years. Well before such an election, school leaders—working through their professional organizations and other networks—should begin to discuss needed education policy changes that might appeal to a new administration. Through their legislative liaisons, professional organizations can then bring these ideas to the attention of potential candidates. Although such policy proposals should not be controversial, they can require additional expenditures; new administrations are especially likely to reallocate public funds. Examples of education policy changes brought about by new administrations include teacher testing, career ladders, preschool programs, and NCLB.

Network and Coalition Building

Because of the fragmentation of U.S. educational governance, effectiveness in the policy realm requires building both networks and coalitions. As Kaplan and Usdan (1992) observed twenty years ago:

> To function largely in isolation—which has been the norm in some sectors of education, is to volunteer for obscurity—even extinction. . . . Finding and making common cause with people and groups of similar purpose and vision and so rising above the professional roles and governmental jurisdictions is a necessity. (p. 672)

In thinking about building networks and coalitions, education leaders may find Crosby and Bryson's (2005) concepts of forums and arenas helpful. A *forum* is a venue in which ideas are presented, discussed, and debated. As a result of such exchanges, people may change their minds, find that their beliefs are stronger than they thought, or learn that those beliefs are more widely shared than they ever imagined. Issue definition, the earliest stage of the policy process, occurs in a wide range of forums, including think tanks, scholarly journals, talk shows, professional organizations, and online bulletin boards and chat rooms. People who do not participate in forums where policy issues important to them are discussed are excluded from an important phase of the policy process—some would say the most important phase.

Arenas are venues in which decisions about policies are made. Rules, laws, and various procedures are established in them. Arenas are far more restricted domains of activity than are forums. Examples of arenas include state legislatures, school boards, the board of directors of a corporation, and the executive committee of a labor union. Forums and arenas are connected with each other because the people who make decisions in arenas also participate in numerous forums.

BUILDING RELATIONSHIPS WITH EDUCATION PROFESSIONALS.   The fragmentation of education in the United States into 15,000 school districts in fifty states means that education leaders must deliberately develop ways to establish and maintain relationships with other professionals in their field. In Crosby and Bryson's (2005) terms, they must find (and sometimes create) forums in which the educational ideas and problems that concern them can be discussed. At the state level—and sometimes at the local level as well—professional organizations often provide such forums for discussion. Indeed, this is one of their major functions. After carefully considering the professional organizations that he or she is entitled to join, each school leader should select a few with which to affiliate, and at least one or two in which to become truly active.

Leaders can participate at several levels in the forums offered by these organizations. Simply reading a professional magazine regularly is an easy way to participate in a forum. A higher level of participation involves attending conferences, workshops, and dinners. An even higher level encompasses presenting at conferences or organizing workshops. The highest level of involvement is assuming a formal leadership role in the organization. At every level of activity, members have opportunities to participate in forums where policy issues are discussed and clarified. As an outgrowth of such discussions, many organizations take official policy positions, which their lobbyists then communicate to politicians. Active members help determine what these official positions are.

Often, however, forums in which educators can discuss ideas do not exist at the local or regional level. Therefore, in order to address local or regional policy issues effectively, education leaders may first need to create a forum, which can take many forms. In some places, all the high school principals in the county meet for lunch once a month. The superintendents in the southeastern corner of the state may golf together regularly. Sometimes people establish formal councils, roundtables, or task forces. Often, broader forums develop out of more limited ones. For example, in many states, the rather informal forums established by superintendents have evolved into statewide forums used to discuss school finance issues. In some states—Ohio and Tennessee are just two examples—such forums eventually led to organizations that retained legal counsel in order to challenge the constitutionality of school finance systems. In such cases, the close link between forums and arenas becomes clear.

BUILDING RELATIONSHIPS WITH OTHER GOVERNMENT AGENCIES.   Unfortunately, the relationship between local government agencies tends to be a competitive one, more often marked by the determination to "protect turf" than by a desire to cooperate in serving the public (Bundy, 2005). As a result, agency programs often overlap and duplicate each other, wasting precious resources. For more than two decades, both federal and state governments have encouraged local agencies, including school districts, to work together more collaboratively. For example, in 1988, New Jersey initiated a School-based Youth Services Program at every school site, which had to offer several social and educational services (First, Curcio, & Young, 1994). The pressure to collaborate will most likely continue in the coming years. In addition, if resources remain meager, officials in public service agencies will increasingly understand the rationale for cooperating rather than competing.

However, launching and sustaining collaborative efforts are notoriously difficult, in part because of the absence of appropriate forums and arenas at the local level. Boston provides an illuminating example of how one can go about overcoming this problem by first creating a forum. Responding to a challenge issued by Superintendent Tom Payzant, who wanted to know how full-service schools could be multiplied across the entire Boston school system, twenty people began meeting to find answers to his question. They represented the school district, five nonprofits, three agencies of city government, and two universities—institutions that "were routinely engaged in the hardscrabble competition for foundation, corporate, and public sector dollars" (Bundy, 2005, p. 75). Even so, over time they learned to trust each other and cooperated in founding the Full-Service Schools Roundtable. With a full-time executive director, its own offices, and a steering committee, the Roundtable was well positioned to overcome "the 'silo effect' of vertically organized, non-cooperating systems of care and education" (Bundy, 2005, p. 77) and to launch initiatives to establish more full-service schools in the city (Bundy, 2005). Although the creation of a single forum in Boston was adequate, in some situations it may be necessary to create multiple forums in order to overcome fragmentation and encourage people to begin to communicate with each other.

The possibilities for establishing local forums in which representatives of several government agencies can interact are endless, and include activities such as monthly luncheons with a speaker, an ongoing discussion group, an annual conference, and a newsletter. Whatever form a local forum takes, at least one forum should exist in which education leaders communicate with people from other public agencies. A long history of communication and interaction facilitates networking and the development of eventual coalitions if leaders need them in order to collaborate or seek policy change.

POLITICAL CULTURE

Defining Political Culture

In order to understand what a *political culture* is, one should first have a general understanding of what a *culture* is. Sociologists Hofstede and Bond (2001) define *culture* this way:

> [It] is the collective programming of the mind which distinguishes the members of one group or society from another. . . . We begin to acquire the mental programming we call culture from the day we are born. . . . (p. 34)

A more informal, but also useful, definition was offered by a business executive, speaking of organizational culture: "the way we do things around here" (Deal & Kennedy, 1982, p. 4). A political culture, then, is a collective way of thinking about politics that includes beliefs about the political process, its proper goals, and appropriate behavior for politicians. Over time, political culture becomes crystallized in institutions such as the campaign fund raiser, the party machine, and the town meeting; over time, such political "products" as campaign speeches, laws, and education policies increasingly reflect it. A political culture is not the same as a *political system*, which consists of a set of formal structures and constitutional laws; the first part of this chapter describes the U.S. political system. Even if two groups of people have political systems that appear identical on paper, they play the political game differently within those identical structures if their political cultures differ.

Political scientists identify three basic political cultures in the United States: the traditionalistic, the moralistic, and the individualistic. Although each of these cultures is associated with particular geographic areas, they are of roughly equal importance in national politics. Moreover, in several states, educational leaders can best understand many political conflicts as confrontations between parts of the state with different political cultures. In the following sections, the three cultures are briefly described; they are arranged in chronological order according to their appearance in the United States.

Traditionalistic Political Culture

As suggested in Table 4.3, traditionalistic political culture is dominant in the South and in regions of the country where southerners originally settled. One major characteristic of this culture is ambivalence toward the market and unrestrained commercial

TABLE 4.3 The Predominant Political Cultures of the Fifty States

Traditionalistic	Moralistic	Individualistic
Alabama	California	Alaska
Arizona	Colorado	Connecticut
Arkansas	Idaho	Delaware
Florida	Iowa	Hawaii
Georgia	Kansas	Illinois
Kentucky	Maine	Indiana
Louisiana	Michigan	Maryland
Mississippi	Minnesota	Massachusetts
New Mexico	Montana	Missouri
North Carolina	New Hampshire	Nebraska
Oklahoma	North Dakota	Nevada
South Carolina	Oregon	New Jersey
Tennessee	South Dakota	New York
Texas	Utah	Ohio
Virginia	Vermont	Pennsylvania
West Virginia	Washington	Rhode Island
	Wisconsin	Wyoming

Source: Based on Elazar (1994), p. 136.

enterprise. It is no coincidence, for example, that the first major American critique of capitalism was produced by a southern politician, John C. Calhoun, whose analysis of the social ills produced by industrialization anticipated some of Karl Marx's ideas. A second major characteristic of traditionalistic political culture is the belief that an established elite should provide political leadership. Although the exact nature of this elite can vary—it may consist of the local "good ol' boys" in one place and of a group of highly educated patricians in another—membership in it is achieved through family or other social ties. The overriding political goal is maintaining the established order or, if it must change because of changing circumstances, bringing about the transition with minimal disruption.

In traditionalistic political cultures, government is seen as a positive force in society—as long as it restricts its activity to maintaining the status quo. Active participation in politics is considered a privilege that should be restricted to the members of the elite and those whom they invite to become involved. Political parties and political ideology are unimportant; typically, traditionalist areas have a one-party system, and major issues are fought out between factions of the dominant party. However, kinship, social connections, and personal relationships are extremely important. In this culture, politicians are expected to have and steadily maintain a wide-ranging network of personal relationships. Although the traditionalistic political culture is not as likely to become corrupt as is the individualistic culture, domination by corrupt elites is sometimes a problem in traditionalistic areas.

Traditionalistic political culture brings several strengths to U.S. politics. Its skepticism about unrestrained commercial activity sometimes causes its representatives to raise important questions, and its concern for continuity provides needed balance in a rapidly changing society. Moreover, elite political systems occasionally produce courageous, even brilliant, leaders who probably would never succeed in politics in the other two cultures. Senators William Fulbright of Arkansas and Robert Byrd of West Virginia come to mind. Because their power was rooted in a base comprising kinship and other social ties, they were sometimes able to take unpopular stands, secure in the knowledge that they would be reelected anyway. Obviously, the traditionalistic political culture also has major weaknesses. Its resistance to change has been a major factor in perpetuating racism, and its elitism discourages widespread political participation, including high voter turnout (Elazar, 2003).

Moralistic Political Culture

The moralistic political culture is dominant in New England and in areas where New Englanders settled originally. It is also dominant in areas that received large numbers of Scandinavian immigrants in the nineteenth century, such as Minnesota and Wisconsin. Members of this culture believe politics is (or should be) "one of the great activities of man in his search for the good society" and "a public service" (Elazar, 2003, p. 262). People in a moralistic political culture favor an activist government that initiates new programs when necessary. They also believe participation in politics should be as widespread as possible; the New England town meeting is typical of the participative institutions this culture tends to produce. Ideas and issues are important in this culture, and its members often debate them with great intensity. Unlike representatives of the other two cultures, members of the moralistic culture view government bureaucracies and civil service systems positively because they believe that they encourage the fair and impartial implementation of government policies. Clean government is of great importance in this culture, and political corruption is seen as a shocking betrayal of public trust.

Historically, the moralistic political culture has been the source of most of the "clean government reforms" in U.S. society, such as laws requiring the publication of campaign finance records or forbidding nepotism (the hiring of relatives in government jobs). The moralistic belief in widespread political participation has also had a positive impact on U.S. government, leading to such institutions as citizens's advisory councils and public debates of important issues. Sometimes, however, members of the moralistic political culture become overly rigid in their beliefs or veer toward fanaticism. Representatives of the other two cultures often perceive them as too idealistic and out of touch with the realities of practical politics (Elazar, 2003).

Individualistic Political Culture

The individualistic political culture developed in Middle Atlantic states such as Pennsylvania and New Jersey; settlers from this area spread it westward. Moreover, in the twentieth century, its influence spread into southern New England, changing the flavor of politics in Massachusetts, Rhode Island, and Connecticut. In the individualistic culture, politics is understood as a type of marketplace in which the government should serve utilitarian—primarily economic—purposes. Members of this culture believe government should keep to a strict minimum its intervention in "private" spheres such as business, the family, and churches; however, they do want it to provide the framework needed to keep the economy working efficiently. In this culture, politics is seen as a business like any other; individuals enter it in order to advance themselves socially and financially. The political process is based on an exchange of favors that exists within a system of mutual obligation. For example, in exchange for a large campaign contribution from a corporation, a state representative may vote against a law that the corporation opposes. Or, at the local level, a city councilman may help the son of a loyal party worker get a job teaching in the city schools. The party machine—based on a complex system of mutual obligations and strong party loyalty—is an institution typical of this culture. Issues, ideas, and ideology are unimportant in it, as is tradition. Loyalty and strict respect for the system of mutual obligation are what really count. At its best, politics in this culture operates in a smooth, efficient, and businesslike manner; at its worst, it becomes corrupt. The individualistic culture is more susceptible to corruption than are the other two cultures, which is perhaps why people in the individualistic culture frequently consider political activity morally questionable or "dirty."

The individualistic political culture has made important contributions to the nation as a whole. In particular, its emphasis on smooth, efficient, businesslike government has had a national impact, as has its preference for nonideological politics. However, it is vulnerable to the criticism that its practitioners have no principles and believe that everything is for sale to the highest bidder (Elazar, 2003). Several of the political developments of recent years, including the rise of the Religious Right, Ralph Nader's visibility during presidential campaigns, and the Tea Party Movement can be understood in part as a rejection of individualistic politics by people from the traditionalistic and moralistic cultures.

Political Culture and Education Policy

In the late 1980s, Marshall, Mitchell, and Wirt (1989) conducted a cross-state comparative study of education policymaking, using a cultural framework for their analysis. One portion of their research specifically explored the impact of political culture on both policymakers and education policy. Indeed, they selected the six states for their study to include two states with a predominantly traditionalistic culture (Arizona and West Virginia), two with a predominantly moralistic culture (California and Wisconsin), and two with a predominantly individualistic culture (Illinois and Pennsylvania). Marshall et al. (1989) made two major findings with regard to political culture and education policy. First, they discovered that powerful national policy movements can overwhelm the importance of political culture in state-level policymaking. For example, the impact of national movements in such policy areas as school desegregation and special education was apparent in all six states, regardless of their political cultures. Their second major finding, however, was that in the absence of a national movement, policy differences related to political culture do emerge. For example, policymakers in the traditionalistic states reported that their legislatures were considering reforms in areas such as student testing, stronger student discipline, and weakening the power of education professionals.

More recently, Karen Seashore Louis and her colleagues studied how the political culture in ten states shapes both their education policies and their policy processes. They found that political culture exercises a considerable influence in both areas. For example, traditionalistic states like Texas, Mississippi, and North Carolina had relatively closed policy processes, dominated by elite insiders, and policymaking tended to be centralized. In contrast, moralistic Oregon and Iowa used open processes that involved numerous participants. Differences in political culture also influenced how states constructed their policies. Both North Carolina and moralistic Minnesota adopted accountability policies. However, the approach in North Carolina was centralized, in contrast to that used in Minnesota, which gave schools considerable freedom to interpret and use test score data as they wished (Febey & Louis, 2008; Louis et al., 2006, 2008). The authors concluded that in order to understand state education policy, it is necessary to "move beyond descriptive reports . . . by using the lens of political culture to interpret the types of policies . . . , stakeholders involved, and the specific mechanisms . . . employed" (Febey & Louis, 2008, p. 69). Thus, political culture seems to be an important variable in education policymaking at the state level, but it is constrained by the national education policy agenda.

NEWS STORY FOR ANALYSIS

There's No Question About What's Wrong with Education!

LOWELL, MA—One basic principle of self-government is still alive at local school committee* meetings. Committee members, parents, and others argue in public about whatever the superintendent is proposing. What a contrast with the Massachusetts Board of Elementary and Secondary Education (BESE). Although adopting national "Common Core" K-12 mathematics and English language arts (ELA) standards will have far-reaching implications for every public school and college in the state, minutes of the past year's meetings attest that most of the board members who voted in July to adopt them were utterly indifferent to the academic and financial implications of their votes.

A state education board is analogous to a local school committee. Members oversee the professionals in the agency. Professionals propose; citizen boards dispose. At the very least, the boards are expected to safeguard the public interest by asking tough questions about important issues. However, it isn't clear that any of those voting on July 21 actually read the final version of Common Core's standards. The record doesn't reveal one searching question asked by the members who approved them.

There was no shortage of questions to ask. For example, what does it mean to be "college-ready" in mathematics and ELA? Or what will the long-term cost of the transition to national standards be? It isn't the first time members failed to ask cogent questions since the board was stripped of its independence in 2008, expanded, and packed with Gov. Deval Patrick appointees. That year, a board subcommittee "report" presented to the BESE demanded a complete overhaul of our educational system to integrate "21st century skills." No Patrick appointee questioned the lack of evidence to support clearly self-serving recommendations ginned up by representatives of the special interest groups appointed by Secretary of Education Paul Reville, who then chaired the BESE, to a subcommittee the board never even authorized.

Nor were questions raised by Patrick-appointed board members about the influence of high tech companies who stand to profit from changes that would hand them a huge captive market—our public schools. The report was

(Continued)

There's No Question About What's Wrong with Education! (*Continued*)

never voted on by the board, but Elementary and Secondary Education Commissioner Mitchell Chester nonetheless signed a $146 million contract to assess mastery of 21st century skills.

Patrick appointees also haven't asked why the BESE never voted on the state's two applications for federal Race to the Top grant funds. Perhaps a pre-vote discussion might have uncovered information useful to local school and finance officials about what winning a grant would mean or the cost for new textbooks and extensive changes to teacher professional development.

How can we get a board that is willing to ask hard questions? Perhaps the Commissioner of Elementary and Secondary Education should report to both the BESE and the Legislature's Education Committee; legislators ask questions about costs and their constituents's concerns. Massachusetts needs board members willing to raise basic questions about initiatives proposed by the Governor or Commissioner of Elementary and Secondary Education if we are to restore the purpose behind a state board of education.

*In Massachusetts, school boards are called *school committees*.

(Adapted by permission of the publisher from S. Stotsky, "There's no question about what's wrong with education" from the *Lowell [Massachusetts] Sun*, 19 September 2010.)

QUESTIONS

1. What is the predominant political culture in the state of Massachusetts?
2. Briefly summarize the major characteristics of this political culture.
3. In what ways does the behavior of the people and groups mentioned in the article reflect this culture?
4. What political culture does the author of the article seem to sympathize with most? Justify your opinion.

Implications for School Administrators

SUGGESTIONS FOR IDENTIFYING POLITICAL CULTURES.   Because school leadership involves considerable interaction with local and state politicians, education leaders find reflecting on the political culture in which they work and also on their own cultural assumptions helpful. Figure 4.3 provides a framework for such reflection. In using this framework, however, leaders should be careful not to approach these issues in a simplistic manner.

Recognizing that the traditionalistic, moralistic, and individualistic political cultures are examples of what social scientists call *ideal types* is important. An *ideal type* is an abstract description of a social phenomenon that depicts that phenomenon in a simple, purified form. Although ideal types provide useful frameworks for analyzing concrete situations, they are less complex than the real world, in which phenomena overlap and mingle with each other. For example, although in every state a dominant political culture can be identified, elements of the other cultures are often present as well. In Illinois, the individualistic pattern is most important; however, many communities along the Wisconsin border are moralistic, whereas people in the southernmost tip of the state tend to be traditionalistic. Similarly, California— basically a moralistic state—has strong individualistic elements in the San Francisco Bay and Los Angeles areas and traditionalistic tendencies around San Diego. Thus, it would be a mistake to assume that because political scientists have assigned one's state a particular label, the other cultures are totally absent from it. Particularly in metropolitan centers, where many people are mobile and well traveled, a rich mix of political cultures is often found. Moreover, some evidence suggests that well-educated people, no matter where they live or originally came from, tend to accept the values of

For each of the following categories, "yes" answers suggest the presence of a given culture; the more "yes" answers there are in each category, the more dominant is the culture.

Traditionalistic Political Culture

Is political participation viewed as a privilege for an elite few?
Do most political leaders belong to an elite group based on kinship or social ties?
Are government bureaucracy and civil service systems viewed negatively?
Are most political conflicts played out within a single dominant party?
Is government's major role seen as maintaining the existing status quo?

Moralistic Political Culture

Is widespread political participation valued?
Are issues and principles important, especially in political conflicts?
Are government bureaucracy and civil service systems viewed positively, as a way to have impartial government?
Do two parties exist with different ideological platforms, supplemented by occasional third party activity?
Is government's major role seen as advancing the common good?

Individualistic Political Culture

Is politics viewed as a "dirty" marketplace best left to a few professionals?
Do two political parties exist that are businesslike organizations, characterized by a high level of cohesiveness and competition between themselves?
Is remembering one's political debts and paying them off in an appropriate manner important?
Are government bureaucracy and civil service systems viewed ambivalently—efficient but too restrictive of the system of mutual favors?
Is government's major role seen as favoring economic development?

FIGURE 4.3   A framework for reflection on the dominant political culture(s)

the moralistic political culture (Elazar, 2003). As a result, university towns and other communities with a high percentage of college-educated people are likely to contain strong moralistic elements regardless of their geographic location. This means that school leaders who are trying to determine the political culture in which they work should not jump to conclusions, but should instead observe carefully the political behavior around them before attaching labels to it. They may conclude that two or even three of the cultures are present in their area, and they may actually be able to distinguish community groups or individuals on the basis of their political culture.

LEADING IN A TRADITIONALISTIC SETTING.   Men and women selected to serve as school leaders in traditionalistic settings are usually people who are acceptable to the local elite either because they are already part of the established order or because they come from a similar environment elsewhere. Even so, leaders in traditionalistic places are not always as traditionalistic as the local elite; their education, reading, and travel have often caused them to develop new ideas about education that differ considerably from the views of the local establishment. As a result, even "down-home boys" and "girls next door" may encounter problems if they do not think through their situation carefully.

This reflection should include three major components. First, in a traditionalistic setting, identifying the members of the local elite is essential. Although they probably are not openly active in school affairs, they are interested in them and have close associates who are active. To a great extent, success in the traditionalistic setting depends on gaining and keeping the support of this group. In addition, school leaders who work in a traditionalistic area must recognize that personal contacts and social ties provide the basis for political effectiveness in this environment, and must invest their energies accordingly, paying special attention to the ruling elite and its close allies. Leaders should never spring unexpected policy surprises on the elite; rather, they should use their social network to prepare for change, laying a foundation through many conversations, offhand comments, articles in newsletters, and other channels. Finally, school leaders in a traditionalistic setting should make a point of finding out what the local education traditions are, and when arguing for needed changes, they should draw on these traditions to justify them. For example, a superintendent who wants to improve the computer education program of his school system should not make the mistake of arguing primarily that such a change will cause graduates to be more productive workers in the local economy (an individualistic argument) or that it contributes to the development of a more enlightened citizenry (a moralistic argument). Rather, the major arguments for the proposed change should relate it to successful past changes in the school district and to other local traditions.

LEADING IN A MORALISTIC SETTING.   In a moralistic environment, school leaders usually have the advantage that citizens consider education an important contribution to the common good and are inclined to support it. However, people who are part of this culture also expect to be very involved in government, including school government. A major challenge for school leaders in this environment is providing numerous opportunities for local citizens—and not just parents—to provide input on school policies and practices. Advisory councils, citizen task forces, and town meeting–style debates of issues are popular in this culture; leaders should take care to develop them if they do not already exist, and to use them frequently if they do. Leaders must also open channels of communication and keep them open, using frequent newsletters, a Web site, a series of articles in the local paper, and other communication devices. Thorough reports of official meetings and understandable copies of school and district budgets should be readily available for public perusal. In a moralistic setting few secrets should exist; most school activities and problems should be well publicized and openly discussed. The development of—or even the appearance of—a ruling clique that makes decisions behind closed doors should be avoided at all costs. Avoiding any hint of favoritism or scandal is also important, because in this culture both government impartiality and government honesty are highly valued. Finally, in a moralistic setting, school leaders should identify themselves clearly with certain education principles and ideals; they should also be prepared to defend their ideas with principled arguments as well as with facts and figures. Neither a pragmatic orientation nor appeals to tradition work as well in this culture as do good ideas that can be supported in an ethically convincing way.

LEADING IN AN INDIVIDUALISTIC SETTING. School administrators who find themselves in leadership roles in a predominantly individualistic political culture should bear in mind that people in this culture tend to have a pragmatic, economic orientation. One of the leader's highest priorities should therefore be running a smooth, efficient, and businesslike operation that offers area taxpayers a good value for their tax dollars. In this environment, school leaders would also do well to develop strong relationships with local business leaders and with local business organizations such as the Chamber of Commerce and the Jaycees. Although school–business partnerships can be an effective device for building community support in any setting, they are especially appropriate in an individualistic environment. In developing long-range plans for education, leaders should be sure to consider the needs of the local economy and the job market. Although rationales for change could—and indeed, should—include noneconomic arguments, economic arguments should always be included as well. Moreover, having a clear concept of the potential financial costs of any proposed change is essential. Finally, remembering that people in the individualistic culture consider politics a "dirty" business, education leaders in this environment should keep a low profile when they engage in political activity or meet with well-known political figures. In fact, in all their dealings with politicians, education leaders should bear in mind that the individualistic political system operates on the basis of mutual obligation and the exchange of favors. Although at times requesting a favor may be necessary, school leaders should be careful who they ask and should give serious thought to the nature of the favors they may be asked in return. In particular, they should bear in mind that, of the three political cultures, the individualistic culture is the most prone to corruption. Indeed, in some individualistic settings school leaders would be wise to hold themselves somewhat aloof from local politics, justifying their stance with the old saw, "Politics and education don't mix," if necessary.

FINAL POINTS

In order to be effective as public leaders, education administrators must understand both the political structure and the political culture within which they work. The political environment in the United States is a complex one, filled with many potential pitfalls for the unwary. Even so, it offers many opportunities for those who possess a sensitive understanding of it. School leaders should always strive, therefore, to work with the system rather than against it.

QUESTIONS AND ACTIVITIES FOR DISCUSSION

1. What evidence of the fragmentation of governance have you seen in your state? How have people involved in education politics tried to overcome this fragmentation?
2. Identify a policy change that would be beneficial to your school system and estimate its probable cost. Then develop a list of all other agencies, offices, departments, and programs at the state and local levels whose support would be helpful if you were to try to bring about this change.

3. Use the information in Table 4.3 to develop a chart that summarizes key information about elected political leaders in your area. What are the implications of your chart for education policy at this time?
4. Use Figure 4.3 to analyze your own political beliefs and attitudes. Then use it to analyze the political culture of the area in which you work professionally. What conclusions can you draw from these analyses?

INTERNET ASSIGNMENT

Find the Web sites for three state departments of education, one in a state with a traditionalistic political culture, one in a state with a moralistic political culture, and one in a state with an individualistic political culture. Do you find any differences that could be attributed to differences in political culture? Explain your findings.

FOR FURTHER READING

Berkman, M. B., & Plutzker, E. (2005). *Ten thousand democracies*. Washington, D.C.: Georgetown University Press.

   Political scientists Berkman and Plutzker draw on national statistics to explore the responsiveness of school districts to the general public's preferences in the area of educational policy. In doing so, they address several interesting issues related to local school governance.
Henig, J. R. (2009). The politics of localism in an era of centralization, privatization, and choice. *Yearbook of the National Society for the Study of Education (Wiley-Blackwell) 108*(1), 112–129.

   Although many believe that the role of local government in education is disappearing because of increased state and federal power, Henig argues that this is not the case. Rather, the "special governance structure" of public education is weakening as education is absorbed into the general political system—which, however, includes powerful local actors.
Louis, K. S., Thomas, E., Gordon, M. F., & Febey, K. S. (2008). State leadership for school improvement: An analysis of three states. *Educational Administration Quarterly, 44*, 562–592.

   Political culture is one of the theoretical frameworks that the authors use to study how three states (Indiana, Nebraska, and Oregon) develop policies to improve schools. They found that political culture shaped how the states went about adopting new policies as well as which political values they emphasized.
Manna, P. (2006). *School's in: Federalism and the national education agenda*. Washington, D.C.: Georgetown University Press.

   Manna's study of educational policymaking in a federal system demonstrates how federal and state officials interact to develop education policy. His book includes an in-depth analysis of the development and adoption of *No Child Left Behind*.
Marshall, C., Mitchell, D., & Wirt, F. (1989). *Culture and education policy in the American states*. New York: Falmer Press.

   This is the earliest full-length book to apply the concepts of political culture to education policymaking. The still relevant findings regarding political culture and the discussion of the culture of state legislatures cause this book to continue to be a valuable source of information on the deep background of education policy.

5 | VALUES AND IDEOLOGY

Focus Questions

▌ What values shape education policy?

▌ How do these values relate to the major U.S. political ideologies?

▌ How can education leaders identify the values and ideological positions behind policies and policy proposals?

▌ In an increasingly ideological policy environment, how can education leaders act both effectively and democratically?

THE IMPORTANCE OF IDEAS

An aspect of the policy environment as intangible as political culture is ideas: those values and thought systems located, not in the outer world, but in human minds. Because for generations politics in the United States was generally considered non-ideological, or unconcerned with ideas, early policy analysts advocated the "value-free" analysis of public policies. In part, this mindset was a product of the individualistic political culture that dominated mainstream U.S. politics for several decades. In part, too, it resulted from a widespread consensus around a few central ideas and values that grew out of the Great Depression and World War II experiences of the 1930s and 1940s. Seen from an international perspective, this U.S. consensus was always ideological be-cause it was based on values such as individualism, limited government intervention in society, and the free (though regulated) market. Since the early 1980s, however, this consensus has eroded, primarily because of the resurgence of conservatism. Although today's conservatives value individualism at least as much as the supporters of the ear-lier ideological consensus did, many advocate severely restricting government power to regulate the economy. Some also support increased government power over moral behavior. This growing conservative influence, conflicting with the older belief system, has thrown into sharp relief the ideological and value conflicts that were latent earlier. Today politics in the United States can no longer accurately be described as nonideo-logical, nor is it any longer realistic to ignore values when studying policy (Boyd, 1984; Lowi, 1995). As a result, today's school leaders must have a general understanding of the political ideas that swirl around them in order to think intelligently about education policy.

"Ideas operate as the proximate driving force in American politics, in particular in domestic affairs and consequently in the politics of education at every level of American government," insists Iannaccone (1988, p. 49). Ideas, beliefs, and values are important for at least two reasons. First, they shape the way people define policy problems. For example, one of the most fundamental American ideas is individualism, a high value placed on "independence and self-reliance above all else" (Bellah, Madsen, Sullivan, Swidler, & Tipton, 1996, p. viii). Americans' individualistic orientation encourages them to understand problems in terms of personal rather than social responsibility. Faced with evidence that many parents struggle to find adequate day care for their preschoolers, Americans are more likely to define the problem as "too many working mothers" rather than as "inadequate social support for young families." Second, ideas, beliefs, and values constrain people's ability to perceive possible solutions to policy problems. Having defined the child-care problem at the individual level, most Americans are likely to see possible solutions such as a public relations campaign encouraging mothers to stay home with their children or a tax break for private businesses that provide day care for their employees. They are unlikely to perceive possible solutions such as government-operated nursery schools or government subsidies to families to make staying home with young children easier for parents—policy solutions that are in effect in several Western democracies. Even if they did perceive such solutions, U.S. politicians would probably not support them. In their research on policymaking at the state level, Marshall et al. (1989) found that policymakers do not consider ideas "that diverge from the prevailing dominant values" (p. 42) because advocating such ideas makes them sound "irrelevant." As a result of the importance of ideas in the development and **implementation** of education policy, no policy or policy proposal can be fully understood without considering the values and ideological system that undergird it. In thinking about education policy, therefore, school leaders must ask questions such as: What values led people to propose this policy? Are any value conflicts inherent in it? What assumptions about society, government, and economics lie behind it? With what broader ideological position is this policy consistent?

BASIC VALUES IN U.S. POLITICS

Self-Interest and Other Values

Starting in the 1950s, utilitarian social theories derived from economics began to dominate political science in the United States. According to utilitarian philosophy, all human behavior is determined by *self-interest;* therefore, the only values operative in the policy environment are those that directly advance the interests of particular individuals or groups (Fowler, 1995b). Since the late 1980s, however, many scholars have challenged the utilitarian position, producing research evidence in support of their contention that other values also shape political behavior (e.g., Jackson & Kingdon, 1992; McDonnell, 1991; Perry, 2009). This book takes a position consistent with this newer research and also with the Weberian tradition in social theory, which insists that human behavior is shaped by *both* self-interest and other values such as commitments to ideological, philosophical, or religious principles. Weber used a railroad metaphor to compare the relationship between self-interest and other values, describing self-interest as the fuel that made the engine's operation possible and the other values as the switchmen who decided on which tracks the train would actually run (Schroeder, 1992). This means that, in analyzing the values that undergird an education policy or policy proposal, one must always consider issues of self-interest. Nevertheless, one must also always move beyond mere self-interest to consider other values, as well as the general belief systems of the advocates of the policy. Only in this manner can the underlying ideas behind a policy be determined accurately.

Self-Interest Values

ECONOMIC.   Many people are motivated almost entirely by their own *economic interests* or by the economic interests of a group with which they identify. Moreover, very few people act without considering how their behavior affects their economic situation. Therefore, one of the first steps in the analysis of any education policy or policy proposal should be to ask: Who benefits economically from this policy? Who is penalized economically by it? The beneficiary may be an individual; a broad class of individuals, such as businesspeople; or an organized group, such as a teachers' union. The economic benefit may be obvious (e.g., tax breaks for businesses, salary increases for teachers). Sometimes, however, the benefits are not immediately clear; a complex piece of special education legislation may benefit lawyers financially by establishing an ambiguous legal situation that increases their business. Similarly, who suffers economically from a policy may be immediately clear or may require considerable reflection in order to identify those who are penalized. Figure 5.1 summarizes some of the more common economic benefits related to education policy; the most common economic penalties are the reverse of these benefits.

POWER.   Individuals and groups also often act to increase their power. Therefore, additional questions that should always be asked early in the analysis of an education policy or policy proposal are: Who gains power as a result of this policy? Who loses power? Answering these questions often requires considerable thought, because power plays are frequently well hidden beneath seemingly neutral policies or cloaked in high-flown rhetoric. Figure 5.2 summarizes some major policy devices for increasing power; again, the loss of any of these privileges constitutes a loss of power.

Salary increases
Increases in fringe benefits—leaves, insurance,
    retirement, etc.
Tax reductions or waivers
Increased demand for one's services
Increased number of jobs in a department or field
Shifts of costs from one institution to another
Increases in available materials, clerical aid, etc.

FIGURE 5.1 Types of economic benefits

A new legal right
Representation in a decision-making group
Veto power over decisions
Access to information
Access to channels of communication
The right to serve long or indefinite terms
Authority to advise decision makers
An extension of one's jurisdiction
An increase in job security

FIGURE 5.2   Types of power benefits

General Social Values

General social values pervade a society and are held by virtually all people, regardless of their ideological, philosophical, or religious commitments. Often, members of the society see these values as so self-evident that they do not even try to explain or justify them.

ORDER.   Coplin and O'Leary (1981) consider *order* an overarching value of such central importance that it is a high priority in every society—developed and developing, democratic and nondemocratic, Eastern and Western. The reason is clear: Human beings want and need to live in an environment in which they are relatively safe from physical harm and in which their property is relatively secure. Few places are more frightening than those in which social order has broken down; therefore, most governments go to great lengths to prevent such an occurrence. The United States is no exception; crime, terrorism, war, and other threats to order always rank high on the public policy agenda. Because broader social problems spill over into the schools, order is also a major education policy concern. For example, bullying has become a major policy concern in American schools. The widespread nature of this concern is suggested by the fact that in May 2011, a Google search using the terms "parents + bullying" yielded 14,100,000 hits. One Web site located by this search, operated by parents in Bartow County, Georgia, reveals the seriousness of parental anxieties about bullying. The organization states that its mission is "to monitor bullying and to evaluate the effectiveness of the bullying policies" in the school system in which it operates. It even offers free legal help to parents with problems (Bartow Parents Against Bullying, 2011). Explicitly or implicitly, then, the high value that most Americans—including practicing educators—place on orderly schools is always an important influence on education policy.

INDIVIDUALISM.   "Individualism lies at the very core of American culture," wrote Bellah et al. (1996, p. 142) in their modern classic, *Habits of the Heart.* The findings of Dutch sociologist Hofstede are consistent with this assertion: In a study of IBM employees in sixty-seven countries, Hofstede found that Americans were the most individualistic (Hofstede & Bond, 2001). Valuing *individualism* means both tending to consider the single person and his or her needs before those of the group, and emphasizing self-reliance. Bellah and his coauthors describe two forms of U.S. individualism.

Utilitarian individualism refers to the belief that people can—and should—take the initiative to advance their own economic success, even at the expense of other worthwhile pursuits such as family life, friendship, and community involvement. *Expressive individualism* is in many ways a reaction against this emphasis on one's economic interests; expressive individualists stress the "deeper cultivation of the self" (p. 33) and the freedom to express that self and its feelings with minimal restraint from social conventions. The quintessential American utilitarian individualist is the "self-made man," Benjamin Franklin, whereas poet Walt Whitman, author of the poem "Song of Myself," represents expressive individualism.

U.S. education policy reflects the underlying individualism of the culture and tends to swing between the utilitarian and expressive forms of the value. The very structure of the system, with its thousands of small local school districts, is an expression of individualism; resistance by Americans to policies such as national standards, curriculum, and examinations can be understood as a desire for individualistic rather than group-oriented policies. The current emphasis on the pragmatic purposes of education and the tendency to reject subjects such as music and art as "frills" are consistent with the utilitarian orientation. Periodically, however, expressive individualism resurges. For example, in the 1960s and early 1970s, many U.S. school districts established open-space schools and expanded the number of high school electives. These policy approaches—designed to encourage children's self-actualization—were largely abandoned during the more utilitarian 1980s. Whether utilitarian or expressive, individualism is a major value underlying U.S. education policy. Although strong rational arguments can be advanced for a more group-oriented or "systemic" approach to education policy, the deeply ingrained individualism of U.S. culture makes the adoption and implementation of such policies difficult.

Democratic Values

The great rallying cry of the French Revolution of 1789 was "Liberty, Fraternity, Equality!" Political scientists agree that this slogan provides a succinct summary of the values essential in a society that wishes to have a democratic government. Each of these three values is, however, multifaceted and can be defined in several ways. Many of the value conflicts in democratic countries, and in their education policies, center around these values—around what they mean and how they can best be achieved, protected, or expanded.

LIBERTY. *Liberty*—sometimes also called *freedom, independence,* or *choice*—is a fundamental principle of democracy, and these words resonate deeply in the hearts of most people. The U.S. Bill of Rights guarantees several basic freedoms essential to the operation of our form of government, including the freedoms of speech, the press, religion (or conscience), and association (Rawls, 1971). The U.S. Constitution also implicitly grants citizens the freedom to own property and to engage in commercial activity. Although the freedom to lead one's private life without interference is not guaranteed by the literal wording of the Constitution, twentieth-century courts developed a body of case law defining various privacy rights, which constitute a general freedom to select one's lifestyle. Included among these freedoms are the rights to marry (or not marry), to have children, to make major decisions about the upbringing of one's children, and to protect one's privacy.

These freedoms do not exist in splendid isolation from each other, however; political philosopher John Rawls (1971) argues in *A Theory of Justice* that "liberty is a certain structure of institutions, a certain system of public rules defining rights and duties" (p. 202). This means that no freedom is unrestricted; each freedom has limits, and all the freedoms must constantly be balanced against each other in law and custom. As the popular saying goes, "Your freedom to swing your arm ends where my nose begins."

Liberty is a major education policy value (Guthrie, 2002). During the 1960s and 1970s, for example, a series of court decisions clearly stated that students and teachers do not lose their political freedoms when they enter a school building. As U.S. citizens, they have the constitutional right to speak out, to form organizations, and to assemble peacefully. Students' and teachers' civil liberties are not unlimited, however; they can be asserted at school only insofar as their exercise does not disrupt the learning process or infringe on the freedom of other people. Thus, students do not have the freedom to run around the room while the teacher explains a lesson, and a teacher's religious freedom does not include the right to proselytize students. Since the early 1980s, many people have advocated the adoption of school-choice policies, arguing that such policies are an inherent aspect of parents' freedom to raise their children and also of freedom of religion (conscience) (Guthrie, 2002). This freedom, too, has limitations. No parents are free to choose to raise their children in illiteracy or to send them to a school in which they are abused physically or emotionally. Figure 5.3 provides some questions to use in evaluating the aspects of an education policy that relates to freedom.

EQUALITY.   The second central democratic value is *equality;* the Declaration of Independence reads in part, "All men are created equal." Of course, this statement does not mean that all human beings have equal intelligence, physical strength, power, wealth, or other attributes people value. Rather, it means that all people are equally human and are therefore entitled to an equal standing before the law and to an equal opportunity to live their lives in a way not too remote from the norms of their society.

How does this policy affect the political freedoms (speech, press, association, assembly) of teachers?

How does this policy affect the political freedoms (speech, press, association, assembly) of students?

How does this policy affect the range of choices open to parents?

How does this policy affect the range of choices open to students?

How does this policy affect freedom of thought in areas such as access to knowledge, encouragement of open debate, and presentation of a range of ideas in school?

How does this policy affect the religious freedom of students? of faculty?

How does this policy affect the autonomy of the faculty as a decision-making group?

Is the policy justified with discourse that includes words such as *free, freedom, choice, independence, autonomy,* and *liberty?*

FIGURE 5.3   Questions to ask in evaluating the freedom issues in a policy

Democracy depends on a certain degree of social equality because extreme variations in wealth and power lead to distrust and also to social conflict. Not coincidentally, medieval Europe and nineteenth century India were not governed democratically—the enormous social inequalities that characterized both societies made democracy impossible.

Equality—sometimes called *equity* or *social justice*—has several meanings. *Political equality* is the equal right to participate in the political system, whereas *economic equality* means equal wealth. Neither is an absolute; both political equality and economic equality are relative terms. Countries and historical periods are often systematically compared in order to determine the relative degree to which they have achieved both forms of equality. In such a study of equality, Verba and Orren (1985) found that the United States is politically rather egalitarian because, compared to citizens of other developed countries, Americans have great access to participation in the political system. The United States compares less favorably on measures of economic equality, however; of all developed countries, it has the largest gap between rich and poor.

Equality can also be analyzed in terms of *equality of opportunity* and *equality of results*. Equal opportunity exists when everyone has a similar chance to get a good education or find a decent job, regardless of race, sex, sexual orientation, handicapping condition, age, or national origin. Where equal opportunity really exists, unequal results are caused largely by factors under the control of the individual, such as effort and extra study. Most Americans strongly believe in equal opportunity. Equality of results exists when the range from high to low is relatively narrow. For example, when the range between the seventy-fifth and twenty-fifth percentile scores on a standardized mathematics test is small, rough equality of educational results has occurred. Or, when the difference between the salaries of an average worker and an average CEO is relatively small, rough equality of income results has occurred. This form of equality cannot be achieved by permitting children to compete freely in school or by allowing the market to determine salaries; it requires some form of intervention. Relatively equal mathematics scores might be achieved by providing special tutoring programs for weaker students; relatively equal salaries could be achieved by legislating minimums and maximums for wages. Although many democratic countries use such policies to increase equality of results, the United States generally does not. According to Verba and Orren (1985), the major reason is that most Americans dislike the concept of equality of results because it is inconsistent with the ideal of individual achievement.

Equal opportunity has always been a major value in U.S. education policy. Guthrie (2002) argues that few Americans desire *absolute* equality between citizens but rather that they believe that people should have a fairly equal opportunity to obtain wealth and power. In the nineteenth century, the pursuit of educational equality took the form of providing every child with access to a public elementary school; in the early twentieth century, this ideal was expanded to include secondary education. As the twentieth century progressed, education policies were adopted to improve the access of minority children, girls, and the handicapped to various portions of the school program. In the last decades of the twentieth century, the struggle for equality expanded to include greater financial equality between school districts; in several states, courts struck down the finance system on the grounds that it was inherently

Does the rhetoric surrounding the policy or policy proposal include words such as *fair, just, justice, equal, equality,* or *level playing field?*

Is *equality* understood as equality of opportunity or as equality of outcome?

Will this policy advance political equality by facilitating participation in the school or in the broader society?

Will this policy advance economic equality by preparing a broader range of young people to participate effectively in the workplace?

How will this policy affect members of racial minorities?

How will this policy affect girls and women (both students and employees)?

How will this policy affect families with low incomes?

How will this policy affect children and parents from working-class backgrounds?

How will this policy affect people (students, parents, and employees) with disabilities?

How will this policy affect people whose native language is not English?

How will this policy affect members of religious minority groups?

FIGURE 5.4   Questions to ask in evaluating the equality issues raised by a policy

unequal. Although education in the United States has made progress toward greater equality, the battle is far from over, and experts can safely predict that it will continue well into the twenty-first century and perhaps beyond (Guthrie, 2002). Figure 5.4 provides some questions to use in identifying the implications of an education policy for equality.

FRATERNITY.   The third democratic value is often called *fraternity,* but a more accurate translation of the French word *fraternité* is *brotherhood.* An alternative term used in the political discourse of many countries today is *solidarity,* and in the United States the concept is increasingly subsumed under the term *social capital* (Putnam, 2000). *Fraternity* means the ability to perceive other members of one's society as brothers and sisters, to have a sense of responsibility for them, and to feel that in difficult times one can turn to them for help. Perry (2009) calls it "cohesion," saying that it "is the glue that holds individuals together as a greater whole—community, group, or nation" (p. 442). People develop feelings of fraternity through social interactions in relatively small groups such as the family; the classroom; the church, synagogue, or mosque; local chapters of political parties and labor unions; civic organizations; athletic clubs; and the like. In *Bowling Alone,* Putnam (2000) analyzed a rich database of sociological information that spanned the twentieth century, concluding that civic and social involvement peaked in the 1960s and has been in decline since. Organizations of all types, including local groups like bowling leagues and bridge clubs, have experienced dramatic decreases in both membership and participation. Similarly, voter turnout is down, and people express less trust in their neighbors and in government than they did in the 1960s. His analysis suggested that one major cause of this phenomenon is the gradual dying off of the "long civic generation" that was born between 1900 and 1940 and developed norms of solidarity during two world wars and a severe depression. Another major cause is heavy use of television and other electronic media for entertainment; two-career families and longer commuting time are additional, though less important, factors. Putnam suggested in his book that a major national crisis might reverse this trend; therefore, after the September 2001 terrorist attacks on New York City and Washington, D.C., he surveyed 500 Americans to see if their values and behavior had changed since the attacks. He found that trust in neighbors and the government had increased dramatically, and several other indicators of social involvement, such as giving blood and attending political meetings, had increased somewhat. He suggested that "a window of opportunity has opened for a sort of civic renewal that occurs only once or twice a century" (Putnam, 2002, p. 22). However, he expressed concern that the United States might not take advantage of this opportunity to build community.

Fraternity has traditionally been a central goal of U.S. education policy, however; the nineteenth-century Common School Movement advocated that everyone attend public elementary schools in order to promote a sense of common identity among Americans (Spring, 2005). More recently, the movements for racial integration and the inclusion of the handicapped in regular schools—although most often justified on the basis of equality arguments—have also been understood as ways to promote positive social interactions and feelings of brotherhood among children who might otherwise never meet. Especially at a time when fraternity is being weakened by several broad social trends, evaluating education policies to determine to what extent they foster brotherhood—and to what extent they weaken it—is important. Figure 5.5 provides some questions to use in evaluating the aspects of an education policy relative to fraternity.

Economic Values

Like most developed countries, the United States has a democratic political system and a capitalistic economic system; a different set of values undergirds each. In some ways these values reinforce each other; for example, the democratic value of freedom is especially compatible with some of the central values of capitalism. Even so, the combination

Does the discourse supporting this policy include terms such as *brotherhood, group, solidarity, belonging,* or *community?*

Does this policy make developing social relationships in an ongoing, relatively small group easier for students?

Does this policy make developing social relationships in an ongoing, relatively small group easier for teachers and other employees?

Does this policy make factual information about different social groups widely available?

Does this policy support the development of clubs and other social organizations?

Does this policy protect or provide the time and space necessary for face-to-face social interaction?

Does this policy encourage people from different social groups (racial, religious, age, class, gender, disability) to interact in relatively small groups and facilitate their doing so?

FIGURE 5.5 Questions to ask in evaluating the fraternity issues raised by a policy of democratic and capitalistic values in the United States occasionally leads to interesting value conflicts. During some historical periods, democratic values are emphasized more than capitalistic ones, and during others the situation is reversed. Some of the major conflicts between democratic values and capitalistic ones are discussed later in this chapter.

EFFICIENCY. Because making a profit is the central purpose of capitalistic enterprises, efficiency is always an important value in a capitalistic society. In its most fundamental sense, *efficiency* means obtaining the best possible return on an expenditure or investment. Closely related terms are *cost-effectiveness* and *output maximization* (Boyd, 1984; Fowler, 1995b). An education system is efficient when it achieves high levels of student learning with relatively low expenditures. Technical methods for assessing efficiency, such as cost analysis and cost-effective analysis will be discussed in Chapter 9.

Over the years, education policy experts have agreed that efficiency is one of the most important values driving U.S. education policy (Boyd, 1984; Guthrie, 2002; Kahne, 1996). At every level, policymakers are extremely concerned about the cost of education and about whether various policies are worth the financial outlays they entail. As a result, they frequently complain about the inefficiency of schools and develop policies designed to achieve higher levels of efficiency. In finance and budgeting, this search for efficiency can take forms such as strategic planning and zero-based budgeting. In other policy areas, the drive for efficiency often means accountability measures such as state proficiency tests, the allocation of funding for districts on the basis of student test performance, and merit pay for teachers. Requiring schools and districts to gather statistics on indicators such as student attendance, teacher attendance, and pupil-teacher ratios and then to report them to the state government is another measure designed to improve efficiency. A popular slogan reflecting an emphasis on efficiency is "You must do more with less." Figure 5.6 provides some questions to use in evaluating the aspects of an education policy that relate to efficiency.

ECONOMIC GROWTH. An underlying assumption of every capitalistic economy is that the economy should expand; therefore, economic growth in and of itself is a major policy value. This growth can be achieved in three interrelated ways: by increasing production,

Does the discourse supporting the policy include terms adopted from business discourse such as *effectiveness, cost–benefit analysis, accountability, output maximization,* or *performance?*

Does this policy cost less than the previous policy (policies) that it replaced?

Does this policy include close monitoring of "inputs" such as direct costs, instructional time, and materials?

Does this policy include close monitoring of "outputs" such as student achievement, student or teacher attendance, college scholarships awarded, or jobs attained by graduates?

Does this policy encourage competition among students, teachers, schools, or school districts as a way to improve performance?

FIGURE 5.6 Questions to ask in evaluating the efficiency issues raised by a policy stimulating domestic consumption, and expanding foreign trade. Education contributes to economic growth in various ways. First, and most important, is the fact that a modern economy requires a highly skilled workforce. Rudimentary literacy and numeracy are necessary even for most unskilled jobs, and many jobs necessitate advanced knowledge such as computer skills, the ability to read and write at sophisticated levels, and specialized mathematical knowledge. Seen from a historical perspective or from the perspective of contemporary developing countries, our educational requirements are enormous. A major task of the school system, then, is to guarantee the perpetuation of an educated workforce; otherwise, production eventually drops and economic growth slows.

However, education contributes to economic growth in other ways as well. Schools are expensive enterprises that purchase large numbers of products: building materials, books, computers, buses, and so on. Moreover, the millions of children and young people who attend schools are already the consumers of many products and constitute the adult consumers of the future. Recently, the privatization of many school services has also contributed to making education an area of economic growth. All these trends mean that schools aid economic growth both by purchasing products and by providing a setting in which children can be encouraged to become willing consumers of the many products marketed to them.

Economic growth is, therefore, an important value behind many education policies, whether this fact is made explicit or remains implicit. For example, many of the policies proposed during the education reform movement of the 1980s were justified in terms of how they would contribute to economic growth. The high productivity of Japan and a few European countries was praised in the U.S. press, and their school systems were given much of the credit for their economic success. Experts suggested that U.S. schools needed to improve so that the country's economy could continue to grow and compete against these foreign powerhouses. During the 1990s, other policies that were advocated and adopted were designed to exploit schools in order to stimulate consumption. For example, soft-drink machines and advertisements appeared in many schools; and computer manufacturers became deeply involved in campaigns for education policies promoting computer literacy. Economic growth remains a major policy value. For instance, in 2002, President Bush argued that a better educational system would stimulate economic growth and pull the country out of recession; more recently, figures in the Obama Administration have made similar suggestions. Figure 5.7 provides some questions to use in evaluating the aspects of an education policy that relate to economic growth.

Does the discourse supporting the policy include references to the need for economic growth and more jobs at the local, state, or national levels?
Does this policy require major purchases of new materials or equipment?
Does this policy include provisions for training students for relatively specific jobs in one or more growth industries?
Does this policy provide businesses with new access to young consumers, using the school as a site for various forms of marketing or advertising?

FIGURE 5.7   Questions to ask in evaluating the economic growth issues raised by a policy

QUALITY. *Quality* is a policy value frequently invoked in public rhetoric such as speeches and commission reports; often, the closely related terms *excellence* and *high standards* are used instead. However, quality is not necessarily an economic value (Gewirtz, 2000). In *Reframing Education Policy,* Kahne (1996) argues that U.S. education policy debates are almost always framed in the terms of either a utilitarian or a rights-based philosophy. Drawing on other major philosophies, he demonstrates how changing the philosophical framework of education policy discussions also changes one's definition of many values. For example, proponents of a humanistic philosophy that emphasizes self-actualization define a quality education as one that stimulates creativity and autonomous learning. However, the utilitarian philosophy that has been in ascendance since the early 1980s defines quality in economic terms and draws on business concepts of quality such as Total Quality Management (TQM) (Gewirtz, 2000); therefore, it is listed among the economic values in this chapter.

Discussions of quality entered the popular business literature in the 1980s as Americans discovered that workers in several other countries—most notably Japan and Germany—were manufacturing products of higher quality than Americans were. Much of the public debate focused on the automobile industry. Because Americans had figured out that Japanese cars required fewer repairs than American ones, they were—not surprisingly—purchasing more Japanese automobiles, making Toyota and Honda common makes on U.S. highways (Halberstam, 1986). Before long, popular writers and politicians made a connection between the "shoddy" products of U.S. industry and the allegedly low quality of education in the United States. The argument ran that U.S. schools emphasized a lowest common intellectual denominator through basic-skills curricula, "dumbed-down" textbooks, and multiple-choice tests. As a result, young people in the United States were not being challenged to think critically or engage in difficult problem solving. Later, when they entered the workplace, they were unable to make high-quality products or provide high-quality services. In contemporary political discourse, then, a concern about the quality of education usually takes the form of seeking higher, more intellectually demanding standards in schools. Policy proposals such as including essay questions on state proficiency tests, introducing portfolio assessment, developing curricula that stress critical thinking, and requiring more study of advanced mathematics reflect a concern for educational quality. Figure 5.8

Does the discourse supporting the policy include such terms as *standards, world-class, excellence, quality control, total quality management,* or *high performance?*

Does the policy include measures to raise the cognitive or conceptual level of the curriculum?

Does the policy include measures to raise the cognitive level of assessment procedures, requiring more essay questions, performance testing, and problem solving?

Does the policy include measures designed to raise standards in areas such as Carnegie units required for graduation, number of instructional hours required, or level of education required of teachers?

FIGURE 5.8   Questions to ask in evaluating the quality issues raised by a policy provides some questions to use in evaluating the aspects of an education policy that relate to quality.

VALUES INTERACTING WITH EACH OTHER

Cyclical Shifts in Dominant Values

A high percentage of Americans support all the values discussed thus far. Who is against more choice, social justice, cost-effective management, or order and safety? Virtually no one! Americans differ not in whether they believe in these values, but in how they prioritize them. The way people prioritize the major values is crucially important; in the real world of limited choices and resource constraints, one cannot pursue all the values at the same time. Rather, policy advocates must emphasize a few central values, ignoring or at least downplaying the others. Because all the values cannot be pursued simultaneously with equal vigor, the set of dominant values behind education policy changes cyclically over time (Guthrie, 2002). The history of education in the United States beautifully illustrates this shifting emphasis. Speaking in general terms, U.S. education policy tends to alternate between a focus on achieving more equality, and an equally strong focus on advancing the economic values. The most recent period of emphasis on equality occurred between 1945 and 1980. The United States emerged from World War II as one of two superpowers and as a major player on the international stage, yet one aspect of U.S. life was painfully embarrassing—the segregation of African Americans in every social domain, including public education. When urging other nations to adopt democratic constitutions or protect human rights, Americans lacked credibility because their own record was so poor. In the postwar years, then, powerful reasons existed for abolishing the most obvious forms of segregation, and public schools and universities were among the easiest institutions to influence. As a result, during this period, members of racial minorities as well as women and handicapped individuals made important advances.

Perhaps in part as a reaction against the gains made by members of racial minorities, women, and the handicapped, the pendulum began to swing in the other direction in the late 1970s. Under the leadership of business and conservative politicians, a new educational discourse developed. It stressed one of the democratic values—freedom, interpreted primarily as choice among alternatives—and all three economic values (Carl, 1994; Fowler, 1992). The eventual result was an education reform movement generally considered to have begun in 1983 with the publication of *A Nation at Risk*. Arguing that public schools had failed, business and political leaders called for a wide-ranging package of reforms including school choice, proficiency testing, merit pay for teachers, a national curriculum and tests, and up-to-date technology. Words and phrases such as *choice for parents, educational freedom, accountability, world-class schools, more bang for the buck,* and *greater productivity* studded their discourse (Carl, 1994; Fowler, 1992). How long this emphasis on economic values and freedom will continue is impossible to predict; however, history suggests that eventually the pendulum will swing back toward equality again.

Important Value Conflicts

THE SEARCH FOR BALANCE. "The political problem of mankind is to combine three things: Economic Efficiency, Social Justice, and Individual Liberty," wrote British economist John Maynard Keynes in 1925 (as cited in Kuttner, 1984, p. 1). Although many policy scholars would argue that more than three things should be combined in public policy, most would agree with Keynes that the art of developing good policy involves finding a good equilibrium among competing values. As suggested earlier, the democratic values sometimes conflict with the economic ones. In a broader sense, any value, when pursued to an extreme, conflicts with other values (Boyd, 1984). A central goal of sound education policymaking is therefore to establish a *balance* among the most important values so none is seriously compromised. In contrast, fanatics and ideologues often pursue one or two values with such single-minded zeal that their policies endanger or negate other important values. Although any of the values discussed here can conflict with the others, this chapter focuses on the conflicts associated with the two values currently in ascendance: freedom and efficiency.

CONFLICTS INVOLVING FREEDOM. *Freedom* never exists in a vacuum. As philosopher John Rawls (1971) argues, an unrestricted freedom always conflicts with other freedoms. Therefore, freedom is most truly enhanced when all the freedoms are intelligently balanced against each other in order to protect all. His argument can be extended to assert that, ultimately, any unrestricted freedom compromises all the other values. This is probably most obvious with the value *order*. If laws and social custom did not set limits on human behavior and enforce those limits when necessary, social order would completely break down—a fact brutally apparent in situations where governments have collapsed or are incapable of meaningful intervention, such as in war zones, during riots, and after major natural disasters. In 2005, a tragic example occurred in New Orleans after Hurricane Katrina. Although such extreme situations rarely occur in education, conflicts between freedom and order occur frequently. In the 1960s and 1970s, for example, such conflicts sometimes developed during the implementation of policies designed to introduce the open pedagogy of the British infant school in the United States. The emphasis on the freedom of children to choose their own activities sometimes led to classrooms that some observers deemed chaotic. Teachers and parents quickly reasserted the importance of order; in some schools they actually erected walls, turning large open classrooms into smaller spaces where they believed maintaining order would be easier.

Unrestricted freedom also conflicts with *efficiency*. Freedom by its very nature requires choices, options, and the means to permit people to follow several paths; yet variety is more costly than a single, one-size-fits-all program. For example, a curriculum policy that reflects Americans' love for freedom is the high school elective system. Americans build large high schools offering a wide range of courses, allowing students to select among many course offerings and programs. Such a curriculum involves many extra costs. Some large high schools print booklets describing all the choices, guidance counselors must spend much time explaining different options, some specialized courses have low enrollments, and teachers spend time developing new courses. Because of these and other costs, many high schools have had to restrict their course offerings. In some cases, when schools did not voluntarily impose limits, cost-conscious school boards and state legislatures have done so.

Freedom can also conflict with *quality*. The fact that everyone is free to do his or her own thing does not mean that all those things conform to high standards. Indeed, the very idea of a standard of excellence runs counter to the value that Bellah et al.'s (1996) expressive individualists place on the freedom to develop one's "authentic self" through spontaneous, creative endeavor. As soon as a high standard is recognized and rewarded, many people abandon their freedom of expression in order to compete for the rewards offered for "excellence." The result may be a desirable increase in quality, but it is achieved at some cost to freedom. In the debate over national standards, the latent conflict between quality and freedom often emerges in sharp relief. For example, Febey and Louis (2008) found that Iowa, a state with a long history of valuing the freedom of local districts to make most of their own decisions, resisted the standards movement for many years. In fact, in 2005 *Education Week* accorded the state a grade of "F," based on its standards and accountability program. Iowa education officials were quick to point out that although their standards and accountability program might be "failing" in the eyes of *Education Week*'s editors, Iowa consistently scores well above average on national tests!

Finally, an inherent tension exists between freedom and *equality*. Because people do, in fact, differ with regard to traits such as intelligence, motivation, energy, physical strength, and unscrupulousness, unrestricted competition among them leads to unequal outcomes. As good elementary teachers know, if they do not make some rules about sharing toys and playground equipment, the same children play with the most desirable items day after day, leading to a festering sense of resentment among the others. On a broader scale, unrestricted freedom for individuals to compete for wealth and power leads to a society in which a few people are very wealthy, whereas many live in poverty. As suggested earlier, this situation is not compatible with political democracy. Because it is also incompatible with long-term social stability, most societies—democratic or otherwise—seek to prevent the development of great social inequalities. However, when equality is imposed by law, as in the former Soviet Union, the almost complete lack of freedom that results can lead to a loss of motivation and low morale. The goal in sound public policy, then, is not to pursue either freedom or equality to an extreme, but to seek a judicious balance between the two.

CONFLICTS INVOLVING EFFICIENCY.   When zealously pursued for whatever reason, *efficiency*—the attempt to keep costs low and productivity high—is likely to come into conflict with all the other values. A central question in the social sciences concerns the relationship between efficiency and equality; it is "the contested terrain of several disciplines" (Kuttner, 1984, p. 3). The dominant school of economics argues that limiting social equality is necessary in order to promote the efficiency of the economic system. This position, supported by conservatives such as Milton Friedman (1962) as well as by moderate liberals such as Arthur Okun (1975), is based on several assumptions about the way markets operate. One is that if the market is permitted to operate with minimal government regulation, people will receive economic rewards in proportion to how hard and how well they work. As a result, they have an incentive to do their best—to exert a serious effort, to produce the best quality of which they are capable, and to work as efficiently as they know how. One side effect of this operation of the market is that some people achieve more than others, and inequality inevitably results.

However, this inequality is necessary for workers to remain motivated and for the system to function at a high level of efficiency. Okun (1975) calls this conflict between efficiency and equality "the big trade-off." Advocates of this position are critical of the welfare state and other social programs that try to reduce the unequal results of market competition. In education policy, Friedman (1962) and others support introducing more market mechanisms into public education in order to increase its efficiency. They have been leaders in the movement to adopt school-choice policies such as charter schools and vouchers (Cookson, 1994).

Although they represent a minority opinion in the United States, other thinkers such as Kuttner (1984) and Thurow (1985) have attacked the notion that an inherent trade-off exists between efficiency and equality. On the contrary, they argue that over the long run, a relatively high degree of social equality promotes efficiency and is a major prerequisite for productivity growth. In their view, great economic inequality creates resentment, undermining worker commitment and willingness to produce high-quality work. In support of this argument, they cite the productivity of Japan and Germany, two countries with a much higher degree of economic equality than the United States.

The pursuit of efficiency can also undercut quality. No matter how one defines a high-quality education—as high academic standards, encouraging the natural unfolding of the child's personality, or developing democratic citizenship—relentless pressures for efficiency will most likely undercut it because education is expensive. Upholding academic standards requires up-to-date teaching materials, well-educated teachers, relatively small classes, and much teacher preparation time. Similarly, educational programs for developing well-rounded children or well-informed citizens require the facilities, personnel, and materials to achieve these goals. Pressures to cut expenditures lead to reductions in all these areas, often causing such increased workloads for teachers and administrators that they change their goal from achieving quality to meeting minimum standards. Many of the policy battles in local school districts and state legislatures revolve around this value conflict, with professional educators upholding some vision of quality, and policymakers seeking to bring public budgets under control.

Finally, an overemphasis on efficiency can also weaken *fraternity*. Building relationships, developing a strong organization, and establishing a collegial atmosphere in a school all require time, and, as the saying goes, time is money—at least it is in the United States. In his research, anthropologist Edward T. Hall (1990) found in cross-cultural studies of attitudes toward time that, compared to Europeans, Americans schedule time very tightly, do not schedule much free time, and allow little time for the cultivation of relationships. More recent studies show that the growth in the number of single-parent households and two-career families has increased the time pressures on Americans (Jacobs & Gerson, 2000); therefore, Hall's findings are probably more relevant today than they were when he made them. Although he did not speculate about the reasons for these differences between Americans and Europeans, generations of concern about efficiency may have led many Americans to consider time spent building relationships with colleagues a waste of money. Yet, good communication and teamwork in schools and districts do not develop in a vacuum; they flourish in an environment where fraternity is valued enough to provide time for it.

IDEOLOGY

Defining Ideology

Most people do not accept a hodgepodge of unrelated ideas and beliefs; usually their major ideas about society, politics, and economics are organized into a structured but simplistic set of ideas called an **ideology.** "[A] political ideology [is] an action oriented model of people and society. . . . [It] contains prescriptions for public policy" (Grafton & Permaloff, 2005, p. 173). An ideology includes a criticism of the status quo, a vision of a better world, and a plan for achieving that vision (Heywood, 2007). Although all ideologies are based on several core assumptions about human nature and the nature of the universe, these ideas remain implicit. Adherents of the ideology take them for granted, perceiving them as common sense (Susser, 1995). Ideologies do, however, provide an analysis of the current social situation, a vision of the ideal society, and a plan for bringing society closer to this ideal. All ideologies contain at least a few shreds of truth, and some offer their adherents a relatively sophisticated worldview, but no ideology is completely consistent with reality. Nonetheless, the adherents of an ideology accept its major tenets without question and react emotionally rather than rationally when someone challenges them (Susser, 1995). In modern societies, ideologies are widely disseminated through the school system, the mass media, and advertising; therefore, most people's thinking is at least partially ideological. People who reach full intellectual maturity may continue to accept some elements of the most prevalent ideologies; however, they have also subjected their beliefs to rational analysis and are willing to change them if presented with compelling evidence. Their belief systems are more accurately described as *political philosophies* than as *ideologies* (Levine, Carmines, & Huckfeldt, 2005). Because U.S. education policy is more ideologically driven than it used to be, school leaders must have a general understanding of the ideological positions that they are likely to encounter.

MAJOR U.S. IDEOLOGIES

Conservatism

THE DIVIDED HOUSE OF CONSERVATISM.   Although several types of conservatism exist, two are dominant in the United States today: *business conservatism* and *religious conservatism.* Together, believers in these two ideologies constitute the core of the modern Republican Party. A very recent conservative movement, the Tea Party, sometimes operates within the Republican Party and sometimes acts independently of it. The open quarrels between business and religious conservatives reflect the basic contradictions between their ideologies, contradictions that led political scientist Lowi (1995) to predict the eventual fall of U.S. conservatism in *The End of the Republican Era.* As of this writing, the two main conservative groups are living under an uneasy truce, but how long the truce will last is unclear. The Tea Party often disagrees with both of the larger groups.

BUSINESS CONSERVATISM.   Once regarded as a discredited economic theory that had caused the Great Depression of 1929, *business conservatism* experienced a renaissance in the last quarter of the twentieth century. During the 1980s, President

Reagan and Prime Minister Thatcher of the United Kingdom based both their public discourse and their official policies on the core beliefs of business conservatism, contributing to the renewed legitimacy of this ideology (Apple, 2006; Bellah et al., 1996; Heywood, 2007).

Business conservatives believe human beings are motivated almost entirely by self-interest, especially their own economic interests, and that the achievement of material well-being is the central goal of society. In their view, if people can pursue their individual interests by competing freely in the marketplace, the economy flourishes because the market's "invisible hand" regulates the process naturally. No need exists for government interference in economic matters; in fact, such interference is detrimental. Business conservatives interpret current global economic problems as the natural result of the misguided policies of the welfare state. As solutions to the problems, they advocate numerous policy measures, all of which would reduce the government's influence over the economy: tax reductions, deregulation, privatization, eliminating or reforming welfare programs, abolishing many government agencies, and expanding "market discipline" into previously protected domains of society. The result of following these prescriptions would, in their view, be a prosperous society in which individuals and businesses would operate freely, pursuing their own interests with minimal government regulation. In their discourse and policy proposals, business conservatives emphasize two values: efficiency and freedom. They believe the free operation of the market produces a high level of economic efficiency. They define *freedom* as economic freedom, the liberty to compete in business and make consumer choices. They say little about the political freedoms (Heywood, 2007).

Business conservatives have a well-thought-out education policy agenda consistent with their ideology. They have been leaders in the push for higher standards, more accountability in schools, merit pay, and proficiency testing—all policies designed to improve the economy. They also advocate policies that would turn education into a competitive market, such as vouchers, charter schools, monetary awards and publicity for high-achieving schools, and deregulation. Although they also say the U.S. Department of Education (USDOE) should be abolished, their failure to abolish it during the twenty years of the Reagan and first and second Bush administrations suggests that their commitment to this policy proposal is not strong (Spring, 2010).

RELIGIOUS CONSERVATISM.   The last quarter of the twentieth century also saw a resurgence of religious fundamentalism in many parts of the world. Examples that come readily to mind include the Moslem fundamentalists who restored the ancient principles of the Koran in several Middle Eastern countries, as well as the power of Jewish fundamentalists in Israel. In the United States, one manifestation of this trend is the increasing influence of the Religious Right—a largely Protestant expression of the fundamentalist mentality (Boyd, Lugg, & Zahorchak, 1996). Like all orthodox Christians, adherents of the Religious Right believe that humans, although created in the image of a good God, are sinners who often fall short of God's will. Also, like all orthodox Christians, they believe Christians should make moral decisions based on religious teachings. However, the leaders of the Religious Right leave classic Christian doctrine behind and move into the realm of ideology when they depict the United States as a once-Christian nation that has fallen into moral chaos because it has rebelled against God and traditional Christian values. In their view, the solution to this problem is for Christians to wage a "cultural war" against the forces of moral corruption, thereby winning the country back to God. In order to prevail in this battle, Christians must work through the political system to restore traditional values—especially traditional family values—to American life, imposing them by law if need be. The value that religious conservatives most emphasize is order, understood as moral order in the traditional Protestant, American sense (Apple, 2006; Heywood, 2007).

The Religious Right has advanced its education policy agenda with some success. Like its conservative business allies, it supports school choice and wishes to abolish the USDOE. However, its rationale for these policies is different; it supports both as a way to strengthen parents' right to raise their children without interference. They support an amendment to the U.S. Constitution that would make school prayer constitutional and oppose most sex- and drug-education programs on the grounds that they are inconsistent with Christian family values. Moreover, adherents of the Religious Right are against all school policies or programs that seem to reflect the relativistic values of "secular humanism"; often they are leaders in movements to introduce creationism or intelligent design into science courses (Apple, 2006; Boyd et al., 1996; Myers & Cibulka, 2008; Spring, 2010).

FEATURES STORY FOR ANALYSIS

Tea Party Intramural Skirmish

There were always tensions within the Tea Party, but mostly they got glossed over in the run-up to the 2010 elections. Just as all political groups do when the scent of power is in the air, members of the Tea Party with widely differing views supported each other as the great march against the Usurper Obama marched on. To be fair, as far as I know, only the Birthers call him the Usurper. Other people call him a socialist, a fascist, and the anti-Christ.

I would say there are three main branches of the Tea Party. The first is libertarians, who left their own party, which was never going to win anything, and tried the Republican Party. They are mainly concerned with individual liberty and taxes—they're for one and against the other. That's why there are libertarians who support legalizing marijuana, same-sex marriage, and abortions—they believe the government should not get involved one way or the other in people's personal decisions. They also believe that the government itself is evil, and that the way toward true economic and personal happiness is through very small government, mostly involved in foreign affairs, and an unburdened populace. It's an interesting idea, but it goes along with this "we

don't need taxes" stuff that is currently destroying our large but shaky infrastructure.

Another branch is more socially and religiously conservative. They believe in the larger government they need to bolster their activist social conservative agenda, including laws against illegal immigration and working against social service unions. They also like the idea that the United States should be run according to Christian principles, which they would be happy to define for you.

The third side should be discussed, too. That's the rich guys. The rich guys want to stay rich. They don't want taxes either, and they also want a weak regulatory structure in the federal government. Sometimes they care about social issues and sometimes they don't, but if they're making common cause with their new best friends, sure, why not?

But sometimes the issues do not break themselves into easy categories. In Pennsylvania, some conservative legislators have proposed a school voucher program, which is always a cheaper substitute than actually improving schools. FreedomWorks, a large feather of the rich-guy wing, is in favor of the school voucher program

(Continued)

Tea Party Intramural Skirmish (*Continued*)

and is urging its friends to get on board. But the libertarians in the Tea Party don't like the voucher program. It's more big government; specifically, it is big government taking money from one person (a citizen taxpayer) and giving it to another (a poor parent).

According to the *New York Times*, Matt Kibbe, the president of FreedomWorks, called the conservative opponents of the bill "bed-wetters." This quite understandably enraged the opponents in attendance. Said one: "It's one thing to go against the left, but this is taking it up against your own family, the people who stood side by side with you. The whole reason the Tea Party came up is that we were tired of people coming in and telling us what to do. Now they're coming in here and trampling on the very people they take credit for creating."

So, welcome to the real world, and yes, the game is fixed. The people with power will try to convince you that they're on your side, but they will not be telling the truth. Of course, 2012 is coming up and the lure of power once more twinkles on the horizon. Will the Tea Party members paper over their differences one more time for the good of the party? What happens to ideological purity then? Is it possible to be too cynical in politics? Let's see: "I really want limited government unless there's something else I want more."

(Adapted by permission of the publisher from J. Carroll, "Tea Party intramural skirmish," from *The San Francisco Chronicle*, July 11, 2011, p. E10. Several paragraphs have been omitted from the original, and quotation marks have been added around the last sentence.)

QUESTIONS

1. According to this article, what is Libertarians' central value?
2. According to this article, what value is most important to the "rich guys" in the Tea Party?
3. What values do you think are most important to the author of the article?
4. Where would you situate the author ideologically? Why?

THE TEA PARTY MOVEMENT. A recent development in American conservatism has been the birth and rapid rise to prominence of a group officially called the Tea Party Patriots. This loosely organized national network holds a populist, Libertarian ideology. As populists, Tea Party members are deeply suspicious of all elites, whether they are in government or in business. They favor less government, lower taxes, and a greatly reduced national debt. Their relationship with the Republican Party is often contradictory. At times they have verbally attacked the party and endorsed third party candidates to run against Republicans. However, many members of the Tea Party operate within the Republican Party, and a Tea Party Caucus was recently established in Congress. The value that the Tea Party emphasizes most is freedom. Education is not high on the Tea Party's current policy agenda, but the overall ideological stance of the movement suggests that it would favor reducing public spending on education (Bannon, 2011; Barstow, 2010; Bowen, n.d.; Fabian, 2010; Fraser & Freeman, 2010).

Liberalism

ANOTHER DIVIDED HOUSE. *Liberalism* is the dominant ideology of the modern Democratic Party. Because two major variants of liberalism—that represented by the New Democrats and that represented by the Progressive Democrats—are dominant, many conflicts within that party play out between these two ideologies. However, the two major factions of the Democratic Party share a broader consensus than do the two wings of the Republican Party and disagree less intensely; therefore, their battles are reported by the popular media less often.

NEW DEMOCRATS. The New Democrats established their wing of the party in the mid-1980s, in reaction against the New Left, which had dominated the party since the early 1970s. They believe that race-and-gender identity politics alienates working-class citizens and largely ignores growing economic inequality in the United States. Nonetheless, New Democrats do not wish to restore New Deal or Great Society liberalism, even though they believe that the New Deal and Great Society programs were appropriate for their times. They consider such policies poorly adapted to the problems of today. Like earlier liberals, they accept the basic soundness of capitalism, believe government has an important role to play in a modern society, and are deeply concerned about equality issues. New Democrats differ from the opposing wing of their party about the best way to bring about greater equality in U.S. society. They are skeptical of many entitlement programs, especially those designed to give special help to disadvantaged groups, feeling that they address symptoms rather than causes. To them, the basic problems are a slow growth economy and growing disunity in the United States. In a content analysis of articles and books by four leading thinkers among the New Democrats, Fowler (1995b) found that they most emphasized the values of economic growth and fraternity. They understood progress toward realizing these values as the key to achieving greater equality, or equity, in U.S. society. With the election of Bill Clinton to the presidency in 1992, the United States had an administration strongly influenced by New Democratic thought. Clinton and his secretary of education put forth an education policy agenda consistent with their beliefs. They advocated programs of national and community service for young people as one way to strengthen their sense of brotherhood. They were also interested in improved vocational and technical education as a way to stimulate economic growth. Currently, their support for national curriculum standards and assessments reflects both their desire to improve education in order to spur the economy and their commitment to policies that build a sense of national unity (Fowler, 1995b; Lind, 1996; Peters, 1983). Since the defeat of Al Gore in the 2000 presidential election, the New Democrats have lost power within their party, although their ideas are still influential. In education policy, they support national curriculum standards and assessments as well as the expansion of charter schools (Foer, 2004; Fowler, 1995b; Halston, 2004; Reeve, 2011).

PROGRESSIVE DEMOCRATS. Founded at the 2004 Democratic convention, the *Progressive Democrats* include the heirs of the New Left, people who were active in the presidential campaigns of Howard Dean and Dennis Kucinich, and some former members of the Green Party. As of this writing, they have more members in Congress than do the New Democrats. Suspicious of big business and large corporations, they advocate numerous reforms that would enhance widespread participation in the political system by ordinary citizens and restrict the influence of Wall Street and large corporations. They also support universal health care. Their major values are equality and solidarity, especially solidarity with the poor and minority groups. Currently, the Web site of the Progressive Democrats does not even mention education policy; clearly, other issues are more important to them. However, given their general ideological stance, it is reasonable to infer that they would support public education, oppose the privatization of educational services, and seek to advance equal opportunity for education for all children, regardless of their background (Progressive Democrats of America, n.d.).

OTHER IDEOLOGIES

Extremist Ideologies in the United States

Extremist movements of both the Left and Right have a long history in the United States. However, experts on extremism agree that currently right-wing extremism is more widespread and influential than the left-wing variety. Usually, extremist ideologies are not involved directly in mainstream policymaking; however, they often exercise considerable influence in the background. For example, policymakers who live in areas where extremist groups are active may take care not to advocate policies that might provoke them, leading to public demonstrations of their power or to civil disorder. Moreover, in such areas, a few policymakers are likely to have covert connections with extremist organizations. Therefore, education leaders must be aware of extremist activity in their state and of its possible influence on education policy.

LEFT-WING EXTREMISM. *Left-wing extremists* feel deeply alienated from the social mainstream and oppose many of its major institutions. They are especially likely to blame social ills on large corporations, the military, modern technology, or the institution of private property. Their most typical solution is to withdraw from society to establish an ideal or utopian community, which they hope will serve as a shining example for everyone else. In this community—often called a *commune*—property is usually shared, few hierarchical relationships exist, and everyone works together to provide the material necessities of life. Their major political values are equality and fraternity. Although left-wing extremists are often pacifists, sometimes they are violent. In the 1960s and 1970s, such left-wing groups as the Weathermen and the Symbionese Liberation Army engaged in violent behavior, including bombing buildings, kidnapping hostages, and robbing banks. They usually targeted persons or institutions connected with large corporations or involved in the military-industrial complex. The Extreme Left tends to be suspicious of public education, seeing it as a major instrument of government and corporate propaganda. Insofar as it has an agenda for public schools, it supports "free" schools that impose minimal restraints on children and teachers. Today, left-wing extremists are not particularly active in the United States, and those that are active should not concern most K-12 educators, as their major issues are animal rights and Puerto Rican independence. However, in a time of economic uncertainty, there is always the possibility that the Extreme Left could become more active (Bailey, Rich, & Bennett, 2010; Masters, 2011; Sargent, 1995).

RIGHT-WING EXTREMISM. Like the extremists on the Left, those on the Right feel deeply alienated from the social mainstream and oppose many of its major institutions. Unlike the Left, they are likely to blame social problems on racial, religious, or ethnic minority groups, often believing that these groups are conspiring to destroy the way of life they hold dear. Many contemporary extremist groups are also very antigovernment, going so far as refusing to pay their taxes or respond to a court summons. *Right-wing extremists* advocate solving the problems they have identified by restricting the rights of the offending minority groups, eliminating or severely controlling immigration, and reducing the power of the government or overthrowing it. Their broad purpose is often to maintain or restore a mythical white Christian nation that, in their opinion, is threatened by "alien" conspirators supported by the government. Their major political values are order, interpreted as adherence to the norms of their mythical tradition, and a version of fraternity that is limited to their own group. The Extreme Right is likely to support violent action to achieve its aims; indeed, right-wing groups are often paramilitary organizations. Timothy McVeigh, who bombed the Federal Building in Oklahoma City in 1995, killing 168 people, had ties with right-wing extremist groups. One of the oldest right-wing extremist organizations is the Ku Klux Klan. Since the late 1980s, the Klan has been joined on the Extreme Right by a variety of similar groups; among them are the Aryan Nation, the Posse Comitatus, and various militias. Because public schools are agencies run by the hated government and have been a major force for racial integration, right-wing extremists are usually hostile toward them (Mulloy, 2004; Quarles, 2004; Sargent, 1995).

Ideologies in Other Countries

The study of the ideologies of other countries is fascinating, but one that far exceeds the scope of this book. However, for the sake of comparison, the major ideologies of the countries with which Americans are most likely to have contact are briefly presented. *Social democracy* and *Christian democracy* are the dominant ideologies of Western Europe and several Latin American countries.

SOCIAL DEMOCRACY.   The *Social Democrats* are the most moderate contemporary descendants of nineteenth-century socialism. As early as 1875, some German social-ist leaders began to point out that many of Marx's predictions about capitalism were not coming true, and suggested that elements of his economic analysis were probably wrong. Therefore, they eventually developed *reformist socialism*. Like all Socialists, Social Democrats believe the cause of most contemporary social problems is capital-ism. They do not, however, want to overthrow it through a revolution; rather, they hope to transform it from within by implementing a series of strategic reforms over a long period of time. One set of reforms is political. Major social democratic goals include both a fully democratic political system and full workplace democracy based on strong trade unions and representative councils in firms and factories. Another set of desired reforms is economic: the nationalization of some key industries, proportional income taxes, inheritance taxes, economic planning, full employment, and a welfare state. Social Democrats are supportive of public education, advocating policies such as extending compulsory education, abolishing tracking and ability grouping, and pro-viding students with free books and materials. Equality and fraternity—understood as national solidarity—are the key values for Social Democrats, but they also advocate economic growth. Social democracy has been a major force in Scandinavia, Germany, and Austria and has exercised considerable influence in the United Kingdom, Japan, France, and Canada. Indeed, the United States is the only major developed country that has never had a strong social democratic party (Heywood, 2007).

CHRISTIAN DEMOCRACY.   In the early 1900s, *Christian democracy* emerged in Europe as a reaction against the monarchist stance of the Roman Catholic Church between 1600 and 1900. Its founders were Catholic intellectuals who wished to develop a "third way": a political program that would be progressive but not socialistic, and modern but not procapitalist. Like the Social Democrats, Christian Democrats have serious reservations about capitalism, but their concerns grow out of the Judeo-Christian religious tradition rather than Marxist teachings. For example, they object to business conservatism on the grounds that it is based on a cynical view of human nature, attributes quasi-divine qualities to the market, and encourages immoral behavior such as consumerism and the pursuit of self-interest. They believe that democratic leaders should seek to build a humane and just society in which everyone's basic needs are met, yet people are free to develop their full potential without undue interference from either government or employers. Therefore, they advocate full political democracy, a mixed economy, a moderate welfare state, and participative governance structures in both the private and public sectors. They are usually anti-Communist, but are often willing to cooperate with social democrats to pursue desirable social goals. Their major values are fraternity and equality, understood as social justice. Since 1900, the Christian democratic movement has been progressively secularized; today, many parties have dropped the word Christian from their name and welcome as members Protestants, Jews, Moslems, and sympathetic unbelievers. Instead of drawing solely on religious traditions, they are also inspired by a broad range of humanistic and humanitarian thinking. Although Christian Democrats generally support public schools, they also advocate the right of religious organizations to operate private schools and to offer religious instruction in public ones. Countries with important Christian democratic movements include France, Germany, Italy, Chile, Venezuela, and El Salvador (Heywood, 2007).

CASE STUDY

An Unintelligent Approach to Teaching Intelligent Design

In August 2004, the Dover [Pennsylvania] Area school board divided over the adoption of textbooks for ninth-grade biology. Board member William Buckingham, who had chaired the curriculum committee that had reviewed biology textbooks, refused to vote to adopt *Prentice Hall Biology* unless a companion text that presented the theory of intelligent design was also adopted. He strongly objected to teaching young people about evolution without also teaching them about the possibility that God or an "intelligent designer" was behind the natural world. In a board meeting he stated, "Two thousand years ago, someone died on a cross. Can't someone take a stand for him?" After some arguing, the board finally voted 5–3 to approve *Prentice Hall Biology,* but agreed that at its next meeting it would vote on whether to adopt a book about intelligent design, *Of Pandas and People,* as

well. Ultimately, the board adopted the latter book as a "biology reference text." As it turned out, the board did not even have to purchase the book with public funds because an anonymous resident of the community donated fifty copies to the district.

However, by October it was apparent that the decision was dividing this once peaceful rural community about twenty miles from the state capital. At a school board meeting, open quarrelling broke out between Buckingham and another board member, and two members resigned in protest of the decision to require the teaching of intelligent design. Carol Brown, one of those who resigned, told reporters: "We have a vocal group within the community who feel very strongly in an evangelical Christian way that there is no separation of church and state." Buckingham insisted that all he wanted was "a balanced presentation." By Thanksgiving,

(Continued)

An Unintelligent Approach to Teaching
Intelligent Design (*Continued*)

national attention was fixed on the Pennsylvania district: *The New York Times*, *Philadelphia Inquirer*, MSNBC, and NPR had run stories about the controversy; the American Civil Liberties Union (ACLU) and Americans United for Separation of Church and State (AUSCS) were pondering a lawsuit against the district; and the Anti-Defamation League had sent the district's administrators a letter criticizing the board's action. "The teacher's desk may not serve as a pulpit for religious doctrine," the letter declared.

In the chaotic weeks that followed, the Fox News Channel began covering the story, another board member resigned, and eleven parents sued the district with the support of the ACLU and AUSCS. Meanwhile, the board decided to back down a little and require science teachers only to read a statement about the problems with the theory of evolution to their biology classes. When all the district's biology teachers refused to do so, the board assigned the task to administrators. Even so, the controversy continued. In May, eighteen candidates ran in a primary for the seven board seats that were open. Seven of the candidates had formed a slate called "Dover Citizens Actively Reviewing Educational Strategies"; they opposed teaching intelligent design. Never before had a Dover school board election attracted so much interest.

In September, at a trial covered by news agencies from around the world, prominent scientists, theologians, and philosophers from across the country testified to a packed courtroom about intelligent design. In November, all the proponents of teaching intelligent design who were running for the board were defeated. And just five days before Christmas, Judge John E. Jones ruled that the district could not require students to listen to a statement about intelligent design as part of their biology classes. He accused the board members of lying to cover up the fact that a church had donated the fifty copies of *Of Pandas and People* to the district and stated, "Their asserted purposes are a sham." Not surprisingly, the proponents of intelligent design saw things differently. "Why the apparent fear to allow students to hear a simple statement saying that Darwinism is a theory?" asked one of them. ∎

(Based on: Bernhard-Bubb, 2004a, 2004b, 2004c, 2004d, 2004e; Kauffman, 2005a, 2005b; Lebo, 2004; Maldonado, 2005; Mauriello, 2005; Raffaele, 2004, 2005.)

QUESTIONS

1. Identify and contrast the values of the original majority of the Dover area school board and its opponents.
2. Identify and contrast the ideological stances of these two groups.
3. Analyze the role the media played in this ideological battle.
4. Describe any similar ideological struggles with which you are familiar.

SCHOOL LEADERS CAUGHT IN IDEOLOGICAL CROSSFIRE

Schools as Contested Terrain

Since the late 1980s, public schools have become a major site of ideological conflict; increasingly, principals, superintendents, and other school leaders find themselves in the middle of heated disputes that appear to have erupted out of nowhere and to turn on points that are (to people from other ideological camps) nonissues. More often than not, such quarrels are fundamentally ideological and can be understood only within an ideological or philosophical framework.

In an article significantly entitled "Caught in the Middle," Kate Beem (2006) describes the problems of school administrators who found themselves under fire because of conflicts that erupted "over religion and personal values" (p. 16). She details fourteen controversies in eleven states in all regions of the country that flared up over such issues as sexually explicit language in a required book in a high school English course, an invitation to a creation scientist to address science students, and prayers offered over a PA system before a football game. In some instances the citizens or group that led the attacks against a school system were social conservatives; in others, they were social liberals. In some instances lawsuits were ultimately filed, and in one case a school board placed its superintendent on administrative leave for three years. Clearly, then, the stakes can be high when ideological conflict rocks a school district.

However, these controversies were not random; a high percentage of them centered on issues in two areas: sexuality and religion. Of the situations Beem describes, one related to sexual language and situations in a required book, four related to the teaching of evolution or creationism in science classes, and the rest were directly religious, involving such issues as the distribution of religious literature at school by students, and Christmas celebrations. Darden (2007) mentions other sensitive areas in which conflicts have arisen, such as programs addressing obesity and the display of advertising on school grounds; both of these issues are related to personal values, rather than to sexuality or religion. This means that school leaders who keep up with what is going on in this area can to a great extent anticipate when an ideological conflict is likely to arise; this permits them to be prepared.

Dealing Effectively with Ideological Conflicts

ASSESSING YOUR OWN IDEOLOGICAL STANCE. The indispensable precondition for effective action during an ideological conflict is recognition of your own ideological position. Otherwise, you see your own beliefs as self-evidently true and find understanding differing perspectives impossible. Therefore, this section contains three activities designed to raise your consciousness of where you stand. You should engage in these activities reflectively and, ideally, in written form. If you write them out, later you will be able to return to your responses for further reflection and, perhaps, elaboration.

First Activity.   The section of this chapter entitled, "General Social Values" discusses eight values: order, individualism, liberty, equality, fraternity, efficiency, economic growth, and quality. Rank these eight values to reflect their relative importance to you, with the value most important to you first and the least important value last. Now, consider the values that you ranked first through fourth as a group. If equality is in this group, you probably have leanings toward liberalism. If both equality and fraternity appear, those leanings are probably strong; you may even be close to one of the two foreign ideologies described. However, a group containing two or more of the economic values suggests leanings toward business conservatism, especially if liberty or individualism or both also appear. Most religious conservatives are likely to include order in their top four values; they may also include fraternity (understood as community), or liberty (understood as religious freedom), or both.

Second Activity.   Briefly answer these three questions:

1. In your opinion, what is the major cause of current social, economic, and political problems in the United States?
2. How would an ideal society differ from contemporary U.S. society?
3. Which two or three public policy changes would do most to move U.S. society toward this ideal?

Now, carefully compare your responses to the positions of the eight ideologies described in this chapter. You will probably find your answers are similar to the positions of one or two of the ideologies. You should not feel concerned if you are unable to identify clearly with a single ideology. The descriptions offered in this chapter are what social scientists call *ideal types:* abstract, simplified versions of a more complex and ambiguous reality. Thus, in real life, people often hold mixed positions; however, those positions usually belong to the same broad ideological camp. For example, a person who is basically a business conservative may share some of the views of religious conservatives, one reason why both types of conservatives have been able to work together in the Republican Party.

Third Activity.   Imagine that during a presidential campaign you hear eight candidates speak, each of whom espouses a different platform similar to one of the eight ideologies described previously. Now, reread the eight descriptions, seeing them as political platforms. For which two candidates would you be most likely to vote? For which two candidates would you be least likely to vote? Did you find yourself getting angry or disgusted as you reread some of the platforms? If so, which ones provoked this response?

The two platforms for which you would vote are probably close to your own ideological position. Now ask yourself: Which portions of these platforms most appealed to me? What facts could I mention in support of the validity of those portions? What portions of these platforms do you consider "self-evident," "a part of nature," or "what everyone with common sense believes"? Any ideas you accept on the basis of few or no facts or consider self-evident point toward areas of your thinking that are especially ideological.

Now, make a list of the two platforms for which you would be least likely to vote, plus all of the platforms that contained ideas that angered or disgusted you. For which of your negative reactions could you produce facts, including well-documented examples from history, to support your feelings? Eliminate the platforms containing them from your list. The remaining ideologies are ones that you probably have special difficulty understanding or relating to.

AN OUNCE OF PREVENTION.   Although no one can totally prevent the eruption of ideological conflicts, school leaders can do several things to minimize the likelihood of one occurring, or at least to make sure they are on solid ground in that event. Most local conflicts over ideology relate to one of two things: curriculum policy or religious issues. Ensuring that all formal policies and procedures in these two areas are clear and consistent with current legal opinion is therefore essential for schools and school districts. Moreover, curriculum adoption policies, including the adoption of supplementary materials by classroom teachers, should provide opportunities for the general public or parents to provide input. Periodically, an attorney should review all policies and recommend needed changes.

However, merely having sound policies on the books is never enough; steps must also be taken to increase the likelihood that they will be followed. School leaders should make brief copies of the guidelines available to building administrators and classroom teachers and provide in-service education about these issues regularly. Moreover, school leaders should deal quickly and effectively with policy violations. At one time, administrators could afford to ignore the high-school biology teacher who mocked the creation account in Genesis, or the fifth-grade teacher who entertained her pupils with a dramatic account of the séance in which she had recently participated. Those days are over. Today such irresponsible teacher behavior could land a whole school district in a prolonged and costly conflict; therefore, school leaders must clearly state what is acceptable and what is unacceptable. At the same time, however, they should urge teachers to continue to teach modern biology and to use literary classics such as "Hansel and Gretel," *The Canterbury Tales,* and *Romeo and Juliet* (all of which have been challenged in recent years). They should also be prepared—and prepare their teachers—to offer a well-thought-out rationale for teaching such material to anyone who asks. Today, public school educators walk a fine line between course content and attitudes that needlessly offend some students on the one hand, and their professional responsibility to provide an intellectually sound curriculum on the other. This line is fine indeed, but leaders must know where it lies and communicate its location clearly to teachers.

RECOGNIZING AN IDEOLOGICAL CONFLICT.   Recognizing an ideological conflict is not always easy. However, school leaders should be on the alert for three indications that an ideological disagreement is at the root of a conflict. The first is the emotional intensity surrounding the issue. Ideological beliefs are deeply held; because they are closely related to people's ideas about human nature and the universe, they structure the way people perceive reality (Paris & Reynolds, 1983). As a result, when these beliefs are challenged—directly or indirectly—people become distressed. Ideological beliefs are often held as fervently as religious ones; indeed, ideological and religious beliefs are often intertwined, and during an ideological argument people sometimes feel as if everything they believe is under attack.

A second sign to look for is faulty communication patterns. Often, people are unable to respond cogently to statements made from an ideological perspective different from their own. They may completely misinterpret another person's meaning or ignore views with which they do not agree. Or they may respond by calling the people who hold the other ideological position names such as "communist" or "religious nut." They may even express astonishment at the ideas being expressed, making statements such as: "I can't believe you said that," or "No intelligent person could really believe that!" People involved in an ideological conflict often feel as if those on the other side are not really listening, and that everything they say is falling on deaf ears.

A final sign that an argument is basically ideological is that the participants make "strenuous efforts . . . to explain away the inconsistencies, incongruences, and practical failings" of their ideology (Paris & Reynolds, 1983, p. 209). A case study by Ray and Mickelson (1990) provides an excellent example of this phenomenon in education. They studied a business-education task force's attempts to reach agreement on a reform for the local school system. The business representatives—ardent advocates of business conservatism—strongly believed that public schools were turning out inferior graduates and that area employers were dissatisfied with the local labor force. They had not reached this conclusion from their personal experience in the region, however; rather, they had absorbed it while attending national business conferences and reading articles in the national business press about the "education crisis." As developed in these forums, the "crisis in educational quality" was an integral part of a larger ideological attempt to explain economic problems in the United States.

The business representatives on the task force set out to bolster their arguments for reform by surveying local employers. Neither the 11% response rate to the survey nor the fact that only 50% of the employers who responded expressed dissatisfaction with their workers supported their ideological position. Nevertheless, they eventually developed a complex explanation for their survey results that was obviously false, but that was consistent with their ideology. They never abandoned the idea that a large majority of local employers were dissatisfied with the quality of the workforce, even though the results of their own survey raised serious doubts about this belief. Whenever school leaders notice similar behavior or other signs of ideological conflict, they should ask themselves: Is this basically an ideological argument? What ideologies are involved?

OBTAINING INFORMATION ABOUT AN IDEOLOGICAL ISSUE. As soon as school leaders realize they are dealing with an ideological conflict, they should begin seeking information about the underlying ideological position. The obvious starting point is their opponents in the conflict. Two or three of the apparent leaders should be invited to meet in a relaxed atmosphere to discuss their grievances with a few selected school leaders. If possible, at least one of the school leaders should feel some sympathy (if not total agreement) with the opposing view. In such a discussion, really listening and trying to determine the major outlines of the ideology and the most significant areas of conflict are important. Identifying possible points of compromise is also important. In many instances such a discussion is heartening, because school leaders may realize that the gulf between them is not as wide as they had originally feared. In all instances, giving challengers a chance to speak and listening to them attentively communicates the fundamental respect for others without which no solution can be reached.

Obtaining information from other sources is also wise. Usually, such conflicts are not isolated occurrences; often they have already surfaced in other places not far away. The state affiliates of the school boards' association and administrator groups should be able to provide information about other schools or districts where similar conflicts have occurred. Talking to school administrators in those places may be helpful. The information gathered may provide valuable insights into the issue, and suggest the best way to deal with it.

OPENING THE DEMOCRATIC PROCESS. When facing an angry group with loud voices and strong opinions, leaders easily make one of two mistakes. The first is to capitulate to the dissatisfied group. Such a unilateral surrender has nothing to do with democracy, because small dissident groups usually represent the views of a tiny but vocal minority of the general population. Moreover, collapse in the face of opposition sets a dangerous precedent, encouraging numerous dissatisfied groups to cause uproars and exert some pressure, hoping for a collapse favorable to their interests. The second undemocratic response is to "circle the wagons" and stonewall the opposition, hoping that it will just go away. This reaction will probably cause dissatisfaction to spread as more people reach the conclusion that the school leadership is unresponsive.

The best response in an ideological conflict is to open up the democratic process. In his 1993/1994 article "A Tale of Two School Districts," Fritz Detwiler tells how the Adrian School District in Michigan did precisely this when faced with a conservative religious group that stridently opposed the district's participation in a systemic reform project. Unfortunately, Adrian did not enter the reform process in a democratic fashion; top administrators unilaterally decided to become part of the reform initiative without involving teachers, parents, or the general public. However, once an ideological conflict broke out, district leaders did respond democratically.

First, Superintendent Al Meloy determined the numeric strength of his opposition. When he discovered they were less than 8% of community residents, he communicated this fact to the board and the public, supporting his claim with careful documentation. Next, a concerned citizen allied with the district leadership wrote a series of four articles about the challenging group for an area newspaper. These factual articles explained the group's ideology and linked them and their materials to the national organizations with which they were connected. The author did not deny the group's right to challenge the reform project through the political process; of course, it had that right, and he expressed deep respect for it. However, entering the political process *does* mean "enter[ing] into the arena of public discussion and democratic debate" (Detwiler, 1993/1994, p. 27). Everyone who becomes involved in politics and policymaking should expect to see their ideas studied, analyzed, and assessed in public and private debate. The articles gave the public an opportunity to do just this, and as a result, the public began to feel increasingly skeptical about the ideas of the challenging group and its connections with national organizations.

Next, the Adrian district broadened the base of participation in the democratic process. Administrators, school board members, and many teachers held meetings with church and community organizations; they also held open houses in each school building in the district, where they displayed examples of the new curriculum. As a result, the community united behind the school district and its new project. In Adrian, opening up the democratic process led to stronger community support, defusing the ideological conflict.

FINAL POINTS

At one time, education leaders could ignore questions of values and leave ideology out of consideration. That time has ended; as policymaking in the United States becomes more ideological and value laden, the dimension of ideas becomes an increasingly important dimension of the policy environment. School leaders who overlook or underestimate the significance of this dimension find themselves in a poor position to deal with ideological conflicts when they arise or to understand why particular policies are proposed. As the third millennium begins, the intangible and invisible domain of ideas in U.S. education policy is more important than ever.

QUESTIONS AND ACTIVITIES FOR DISCUSSION

1. In class, share the results of your assessments of your own ideologies. Which ideologies are represented in the class? Which are most common? Are any missing? How do you explain the general ideological complexion of the class?
2. Attend a school board or faculty meeting and try to identify all the policy values to which participants refer. Which values were mentioned most frequently? Least? Not at all? How do you explain the policy values of this group?

3. Clip an editorial on education or a letter to the editor about education from a newspaper. Analyze its policy values and ideology, and then write a brief response to it.

4. Identify an occasion when you dealt with an ideological or values conflict in your school. How did you handle it? In retrospect, did you make any mistakes? If so, what might you have done differently?

INTERNET ASSIGNMENT

Using a search engine, locate the Web sites of the Heritage Foundation and the Economic Policy Institute. Analyze these Web sites in order to answer the following questions for each: What policy values are most important to this organization? Which of the ideologies discussed in this chapter is closest to its ideological position?

FOR FURTHER READING

Cigler, A. J., Joslyn, M., & Loomis, B. A. (2003). The Kansas Christian Right and the evolution of Republican politics. In J. C. Green, M. J. Rozell, & C. Wilcox (Eds.), *The Christian Right in American politics*. Washington, D.C.: Georgetown University Press.

> The authors trace the history of the Christian Right in Kansas, from its early days to the peak of its power in the late 1990s when it captured the Kansas Board of Education and raised questions about teaching evolution. An interesting aspect of the article is its depiction of the struggle over this issue that went on *within* the Republican Party.

Darden, E. C. (2007, November). Dealing with the culture wars. *American School Board Journal*, 42–43.

> Writing from an administrative perspective, Darden tells how a band director's choice of a song to play at the Peach Bowl unleashed a firestorm. He provides advice on how to cope with the controversies that are part of the culture wars between competing ideologies.

Gewirtz, S. (2000). Bring the politics back in: A critical analysis of quality discourses in education. *British Journal of Educational Studies, 48,* 352–370.

> The author analyzes the educational discourse of Tony Blair's Labour Party in the United Kingdom, finding that although it seemed to focus on quality, it defined quality in very narrow economic terms, a phenomenon evident in the United States as well.

Heywood, A. (2007). *Political ideologies: An Introduction*. 4th ed. New York: Palgrave Macmillan.

> Heywood provides a highly readable overview of ten ideologies found in the modern world, from anarchism to multiculturalism. For each, he provides a history and a discussion of contemporary examples. His tables contrasting different ideologies are especially helpful.

Perry, L. (2009). Conceptualizing education policy in democratic societies. *Educational Policy* 23 (3), 423–450.

> The author describes a model she has developed for analyzing how democratic education policies are. The model includes three democratic values: equality; cohesion; and freedom. The last of these is further subdivided into choice, participation, and diversity. Perry also discusses some of the conflicts between these values.

PART II

POLICY ACTORS AND THE POLICY PROCESS

6 | THE MAJOR EDUCATION POLICY ACTORS

Focus Questions

▌ Who are the major participants in the policy process at the state level?

▌ Which participants wield the most influence?

▌ How can education leaders identify the major players in their own states and obtain information about them?

▌ How can education leaders follow state-level education policymaking?

THE *DRAMATIS PERSONAE* OF THE POLICY DRAMA

Before exploring the policy process itself, identifying those who are actively involved in it is important. In policy discourse, these individuals and groups are called **policy actors.** Collectively, they make up the *dramatis personae,* or cast of characters, who play major and minor roles in the ongoing drama of policy development, adoption, and implementation. Although policy actors exist at the federal, state, and local levels, this chapter emphasizes state-level actors for two reasons. First, education is a domain that is reserved implicitly to the states by the Tenth Amendment of the U.S. Constitution. Although for generations states delegated much power over education to local governments, since the mid-1970s, the states have taken back much of their constitutional authority over education policy (Mazzoni, 1993). This means that in education, state policy actors are now considerably more important than either federal or local ones. Second, because both political science textbooks and the mass media emphasize policymaking at the federal level, the state level is often poorly known and understood. Especially in a book designed for education leaders such as this one, redressing this imbalance is important.

Because the purpose of this chapter is to identify and introduce the major education policy actors, their activities are not presented in detail here. Rather, their roles are briefly described so readers can develop a general sense of who they are and what they do. In the next five chapters—which present the stages of the policy process in some depth—these actors patterns of behavior and interaction become clearer. A 1980s study of the relative importance of education policy actors and a study of the same issue in the 2000s are referred to throughout the chapter. In the late 1980s, Marshall and her colleagues (1989) studied the education policy process in six states: Arizona,

TABLE 6.1 Number of States in Which Policy Actors Are Important

Policy Actor	States in Which Important
Governor	6
Legislature	6
Business groups	5
Chief state school officer	3
State board of education	3
State department of education	3
Unions/professional groups	3

Source: Based on Louis, et al., (2006) and Louis, et al., (2010). The total number of states studied was seven.

California, Illinois, Pennsylvania, West Virginia, and Wisconsin. As part of their project, they asked 135 state policy actors to assign each of fifteen individuals or groups a score from 1 (lowest) to 7 (highest), reflecting their importance to education policy in their own state. More recently, Louis and her colleagues (2006, 2010) studied the policy process in seven states—Indiana, Mississippi, Missouri, Nebraska, New Mexico, Oregon and Texas—seeking to identify the major education policy actors in each. Table 6.1 summarizes their findings. The differences between the results of these two studies can probably be attributed both to the passage of time and to the fact that different states were investigated.

This chapter is divided into three broad sections. In the first, the major government actors, elected and appointed officials of the three branches of government, are presented. Next, the nongovernment actors are described. These include interest groups, policy planning organizations, and the media. Although these policy actors usually keep a low profile, often they are as important as the more visible government actors. The last section includes practical suggestions for identifying the important government and nongovernment policy actors in a specific setting and obtaining information about them.

GOVERNMENT ACTORS

The Legislative Branch

THE LEGISLATURE: FUNCTION AND STRUCTURE.   Fifty-one legislatures exist in the United States: the U.S. Congress and the fifty state legislatures, all of which exercise similar functions and are organized in similar ways. A major function of every legislature is, of course, the development and passage of **statutes,** one type of law. However, legislatures play other roles as well. For example, before developing bills, legislatures often hold hearings where experts provide testimony on public issues. Periodically, legislatures also review existing laws to determine if they should be continued, amended, or repealed. A major legislative function is approving the government's budget. Occasionally, legislatures establish task forces or appoint commissions to which they delegate the responsibility for studying a policy issue.

They may also establish a special committee to oversee the implementation of a new piece of legislation. Finally, legislatures sometimes exercise an investigatory function (Rosenthal, 2009). The Appendix gives the addresses of the Web sites of the U.S. House and Senate as well as how to find similar information for a given state.

The U.S. Congress and forty-nine of the state legislatures are bicameral; they have two chambers or houses. The single exception is Nebraska, which has a unicameral legislature that, unlike the other legislatures, is nonpartisan. In all the bicameral bodies, the smaller chamber is called the *Senate.* Senates tend to be rather sedate, in part because senators usually serve relatively long terms and can afford to move slowly. The most common name for the larger chamber of a legislature is *House of Representatives;* other names used include *Assembly, General Assembly,* and *House of Delegates.* In contrast to senates, houses tend to be colorful, lively, and partisan. Moreover, because most house members serve two-year terms, they are always running for reelection. Not surprisingly, state legislators do not demographically resemble their constituents. In 2009, 29% were women, about 9% were African American, and a mere 3% were Hispanic. Historically, among state legislators the largest occupational groups were lawyers and farmers; however, legislatures have become more occupationally diverse as they have become more professionalized. Today, a significant number of legislators list their primary occupation as "legislator." Members of the legal profession are still well represented, but businesspeople have largely replaced farmers. The typical legislature also counts a handful of other professionals as members, such as physicians, accountants, and engineers. Significantly underrepresented are educators, clergy, and blue-collar workers (Squire & Moncrief, 2010).

Both senates and houses have officers. The most important officer in a state senate is usually called the *president;* in twenty-eight states, the lieutenant governor serves as the president of the senate by virtue of his office. In the other states, the president is a senator who is either elected by the senate or appointed by another official and then confirmed by the senate. The top officer in the house is the *speaker.* Speakers are elected by the members of the house in an election that is often fierce and filled with conflict, because the speaker wields great power. Usually, the speaker is a veteran leader of the party that holds a majority of the seats in the house. Other important legislative officers include the majority leader, minority leader, and whip in each chamber (Rosenthal, 2009).

Both Congress and state legislatures have numerous *committees* that accomplish most of the actual work of the legislature. Each chamber has a committee to handle proposed legislation in each specific policy domain. Typical committees in a state legislature deal with areas such as highways, prisons, welfare, education, and the justice system. Each chamber also has a committee that determines the level at which new laws will be funded; this committee may be called the *Ways and Means Committee, Appropriations Committee, Finance Committee,* or something similar. The legislative leaders control committee appointments; each party has appointees on every committee, but the majority party usually holds the majority of the votes on all of them (Rosenthal, 2009).

Finally, in most state legislatures, each political party has a *caucus,* which consists of all the legislators affiliated with the party, regardless of the chamber in which they serve. The caucuses are important because they develop the policy agenda that the party pursues in the legislature. Although some caucuses are led by chairpersons who play no other major role in the legislature, in others, one of the legislative officers also chairs the party caucus (Rosenthal, 2009).

LEGISLATIVE STAFF.   State senators and representatives are relatively visible: their names and pictures appear in newspapers and they make frequent public appearances. Much less visible, but almost as important in the policy process, are the men and women who staff their offices. State legislators have not always had staffs. In fact, throughout most of U.S. history, state legislatures have been amateurish bodies dominated by a group of each state's leading "good ol' boys," who were better known for living it up during their brief visits to the state capital than for effective governing. Because state legislatures lacked the resources necessary to function well in the modern world, nothing more could be expected of them. For example, as recently as the early 1960s, the only staff members serving the 240 members of the Massachusetts House were five typists working in a secretarial pool. Because the representatives did not have offices in the state capital, they were forced to conduct official business wherever they could find an empty spot—perhaps on a couch in the lobby, or in a cafeteria across the street from the capital. Their mail and other messages were placed in a set of pigeonholes similar to those once found in college dormitories (Bowman & Kearney, 1986). Massachusetts was not unusual; this was the norm across the country.

Today, most state legislatures have modern office buildings and staffs. What happened? First, in 1962, the U.S. Supreme Court handed down the *Baker v. Carr* one-person–one-vote decision. This ruling forced states to redraw the electoral districts for their legislatures, weakening the power of rural areas and leading to more representative legislatures. Second, in the early 1970s, groups such as the Citizens' Conference on State Legislatures recommended reforms to make state legislatures more modern and efficient. Among the recommended reforms were larger staffs and sufficient office space and equipment for those staffs to do a good job. Third, Reagan's New Federalism gave the states more responsibility for initiating and implementing policy. As a result of these events, state legislatures have become more professionalized. Increasingly, state-level lawmakers receive fair compensation for performing their legislative tasks, work full-time at their legislative jobs, and receive the resources needed to hire competent staffs. However, state legislatures differ considerably in the extent of their professionalization (Bowman & Kearney, 1986; Hamm & Moncrief, 2004; Rosenthal, 2009). Table 6.2 divides the states into three groups based on their legislature's degree of professionalization. The criteria used to determine the degree of professionalization include (1) the number of full-time legislators, (2) the salaries paid to legislators, and (3) the size of the legislative staff (Hamm & Moncrief, 1999; Rosenthal, 2009).

State legislators normally use three types of staff members. *Clerical staff* perform the tasks involved in running any office: answering telephones, creating letters and other documents, preparing mailings, and maintaining calendars. Although sometimes these workers are young and poorly paid, a legislator's clerical staff often wields considerable power. In particular, they control access to the legislator or to her *professional staff members*. The latter are, as their name suggests, people with professional expertise who help with the substantive aspects of legislative work. Usually they have

TABLE 6.2 The Degree of Professionalization of the State Legislatures

Highly Professionalized	Partially Professionalized	Largely Unprofessionalized
California	Alabama	Arkansas
Illinois	Alaska	Georgia
Massachusetts	Arizona	Indiana
New York	Iowa	Kansas
Ohio	Kentucky	Louisiana
Pennsylvania	Maryland	Maine
Wisconsin	Minnesota	Montana
	Mississippi	Nevada
	Missouri	New Hampshire
	Nebraska	New Mexico
	Nevada	North Dakota
	North Carolina	Rhode Island
	Oklahoma	South Carolina
	Oregon	South Dakota
	Texas	Tennessee
	Vermont	Utah
	Washington	Virginia
		West Virginia
		Wyoming

Source: Based on Hamm and Moncrief (2004) and Rosenthal (2009).

college degrees in such fields as political science, sociology, or law. They perform tasks such as screening and filtering all the material that reaches a legislative office and summarizing its important elements for the lawmaker. They also do much of the routine casework with constituents, such as writing letters and making phone calls to help a mayor from the district obtain a grant to repair a bridge, or meeting with a citizens group that opposes the construction of a new prison in their community. In addition, professional staff members review and analyze budgets for busy legislators and prepare succinct reports on major issues for them. Education leaders should not underestimate the power and influence of the professional legislative staff. "Legislative staffs have a major effect on policy making because of their proximity to the legislators and the centers of legislative power and because of their key role in processing and providing the information legislators require," states Patterson (1996, p. 194). Finally, in addition to the clerical and professional staff members who work in their own office, lawmakers usually have access to a *centralized staff agency* that provides services for the entire legislature. Often called a *legislative reference service* or a *legislative research bureau,* this agency performs specialized work such as drafting sample bills, researching legal questions, and providing the background of previous attempts to pass a law. Although staff workers in these agencies are even less visible than office staff, they too are in a position to exercise considerable influence on the policy process (Bowman & Kearney, 2009; Patterson, 1996).

IMPORTANT LEGISLATIVE ACTORS.   Marshall et al. (1989) found that although the legislature as a whole was quite influential in relation to education policy, individual legislators were even more so. In fact, they emerged as the most important actors in the process overall. As Table 6.1 shows, Louis et al. (2006, 2010) made similar findings; in their study, the legislature and governor tied for most influential. Usually the most influential individual legislators are members of an *education committee,* with the committee chair likely to be especially important. Every state legislature has at least one education committee. Four states—Nebraska, Connecticut, Maine, and Massachusetts—have only one. Thirty states have two education committees—one in the House and one in the Senate. Sixteen states have three or four education committees; the third and fourth committees are either joint committees (including both Senate and House members) or special committees for higher education. Regardless of the number of committees or their names, the members of those committees have great influence on state education policy because education committees exercise several important functions. These include developing education laws, reviewing existing legislation, and holding hearings on education policy issues (Rosenthal, 2009). Because education is a major item in every state budget, the members of the finance committee—again, especially the chair—are also influential. A powerful speaker is another individual legislator who may have enormous impact on what kind of education policies are developed. Although legislative staff members ranked far below the legislature in influence, Marshall et al. (1989) found that they ranked slightly above the average. Indeed, they scored higher than the state board of education (SBE), school boards' and administrators' associations, and the federal government. The Marshall et al. (1989) study supports the importance of legislative staff in shaping education policy, and suggests that overlooking them is a serious mistake. However, legislative staff do not appear in Table 6.1.

The Executive Branch

GOVERNORS.   Although Marshall et al. (1989) found that governors had considerably less influence on education policy than the legislature, the later study by Louis et al. (2006, 2010) found that governors and legislatures were equally important. Activist governors who place education high on their policy agendas can have a great impact not only within their own states but nationally as well. Prominent examples since the early 1990s include former Governor Bill Clinton of Arkansas and former Governor George W. Bush of Texas.

The power of the governor's office varies considerably among states. Although as a general rule the strongest governors are found in the Northeast and the weakest in the South, notable exceptions exist. Tennessee, for example, has a strong governor, whereas Vermont has a weak one (Bowman & Kearney, 2009). A governor's power is a function of several factors. The first of these is institutional power—the authority granted the governor by the state constitution and other state laws. The strongest governors are elected to serve a four-year term and can be reelected at least once, have the power to appoint numerous state officials, have considerable control over the state budget, and can veto legislation of which they disapprove. Several other factors can enhance gubernatorial power. A governor elected by a landslide or by a comfortable majority is more powerful than one who just barely won an election or succeeded to office because of a death or resignation. Governors with much previous experience in state government have an advantage over those who are new to state politics. A governor who belongs to the most powerful political party in the state has an advantage over a governor from a minority party. Finally, a governor with an appealing personal style and strong presence is more powerful than one who is drab and lackluster (Beyle, 2001).

Governors often act as "issue catalysts" in state policymaking. An activist governor selects key issues, publicizes them in his speeches, and leads the public and the legislature to focus on them. Increasingly, education policy is one of governors' favorite issue areas. In part, this interest results from the activities of the *National Governors Association* (NGA). Headquartered in Washington, D.C., it had ninety-two staff members in 2011 and conducts research, engages in lobbying, and provides various services to state governments. The first of its research studies focused on public education. Its Center for Best Practices provides information and assistance to governors who wish to develop and implement new policies; one of its five areas of interest is education policy. As an example, starting in 2002, the Center provided help to states as they implemented the federal *No Child Left Behind Act*. The NGA also provides an important forum where governors can discuss education and exchange ideas about possible policy initiatives. In addition, it serves as a clearinghouse for governors and their staffs, providing information about policy in various states (National Governors Association, 2011). The importance of the NGA's influence on governors' education reform agendas is well documented. In the spring of 2011, for example, its Web site offered 13 reports on early childhood and K-12 education policy issues, ranging from "Early Childhood State Policy Infrastructure" to "Common Core State Standards" (National Governors Association, 2011).

STATE BOARDS OF EDUCATION. Although *state boards of education* (SBEs) exercise both quasi-legislative and quasi-judicial functions, they also have an important administrative role and are appointed by the governor in two thirds of the states. Therefore, they have been included in the executive branch.

SBEs first became a part of U.S. school governance in the early 1800s. By 1900, twenty-eight states had them; today, only Wisconsin lacks one. SBEs are second only to legislatures in exercising direct authority over education policy at the state level. The typical SBE has nine or eleven appointed members, most of whom are not professional educators. With few exceptions, SBEs are responsible only for K-12 and vocational education; a board of regents usually exercises similar functions for public higher education. Within a legal framework developed by the legislature, SBEs make education policy in areas other than school finance. Their most important policy tasks include (1) developing and approving the rules and regulations used in implementing education laws enacted by the legislature; (2) developing certification requirements for K-12 teachers and administrators; (3) approving and monitoring educational assessment programs, including state tests; (4) deciding on minimum high school graduation requirements; and (5) determining accreditation standards. In addition, SBEs often serve as the final step in the appeals process for administrative redress cases that arise in K-12 school systems (McCarthy et al., 1993; State boards of education, 2011).

In the 1980s, Marshall et al. (1989) found that SBEs were not among the most influential policy actors in the states studied, but as Table 6.1 shows, Louis et al.

(2006, 2010) found them playing an important role, though not the most important one. A plausible reason for their relative lack of activism is that SBEs often do not have enough resources or staff of their own to act independently of the chief state school officer, the state department of education, and the legislative education committees. Occasionally, however, when granted such resources, they become active in influencing education policy. A case in point is Tennessee, where governance reforms in the mid-1980s stimulated the SBE and its chair to become important players in Nashville (Fowler, 1987).

CHIEF STATE SCHOOL OFFICERS.   Since 1900, all U.S. states have had a *chief state school officer* (CSSO), a public official charged with the supervision of public education. The CSSO is often called the *superintendent of public instruction,* the *state superintendent of schools,* or the *commissioner of education.* Most CSSOs are professional educators with several years of administrative experience. CSSOs are appointed in forty-two states, most often by the SBE, but in seventeen they are appointed by the governor. In the remaining states, the CSSO is popularly elected. The method used for selecting the CSSO reveals a lot about a state's education policy system. CSSOs appointed by the governor are more likely than others to accept the governor's policy agenda and work to advance it. Although they usually have a good working relationship with the governor and his or her office, they may or may not work effectively with the legislature and usually hesitate to resist the governor or take independent initiatives. However, a CSSO appointed by an SBE will probably act independently and may even challenge or resist the governor or the legislature on occasion. Most independent are the few CSSOs who are still popularly elected. However, because they have no built-in connection to any other individual or governing body, they may be so isolated in the state capital that they can accomplish little (NASBE, n.d.).

In a broad sense, the CSSO's job is the general supervision of all public schools in the state. In discharging this responsibility, he or she heads and is assisted by the SDE, as discussed later. Effective CSSOs can have a great impact on education policy; both Marshall et al. (1989) and Louis et al. (2006, 2010) found that they were often major players in the policy process.

STATE DEPARTMENTS OF EDUCATION.   One of the most important education policy actors in any state is the *state department of education* (SDE), sometimes called the *state education agency.* Although the SDE does not appear explicitly in Marshall et al.'s rankings, they combined it with the CSSO in their study. They found that, working with the CSSO at its head, it ranked immediately below the legislature in influence. As Table 6.1 shows, Louis et al. found that the SDE was an important actor in about half of the states they studied. Both studies concur, then, that the SDE can be an important player in the state education policy process.

The SDE is a state bureaucracy headed by the CSSO and headquartered in the state capital, often right downtown near all the legislative and other offices. Although many SDE employees are professional educators, others are not; people with training in fields such as finance, accounting, political science, and economics are often employed by SDEs. Much of the influence of the SDE on education policy grows out of its legally defined role. While new legislation is under consideration, SDE legislative liaisons provide the education committees with data and with their assessments of the probable impact of a proposed policy. After the passage of a new law, it develops the detailed rules and regulations to use during implementation. As the new law goes into effect, the SDE provides assistance to districts and oversees and monitors their degree of compliance. Of course, the SDE is not a neutral machine at the service of the legislature and the CSSO. It is staffed by humans who have their own perspectives on education policy and may or may not agree with new directives. An SDE may ignore or block legislation, or it may opt to dilute it by the way it writes the rules to accompany it. It may monitor district compliance aggressively, loosely, or not at all (Hamann & Lane, 2004; Madsen, 1994).

Very few scholars have studied the inside workings of an SDE; however, in her book *Educational Reform at the State Level,* Jean Madsen (1994) recounts the fascinating tale of how the unnamed SDE in which she worked for three years blocked the implementation of the *Excellence in Education Act* (EEA), which its legislature had passed in 1986. This SDE apparently did not resist for ideological reasons, but rather because the legislature failed to provide it with enough resources to implement the reforms, thereby overwhelming SDE employees with work. Madsen's story underlines the key importance of the SDE in the policy process. She concluded several years later: "Today in this state, the EEA, so promising at the outset, is almost nonexistent" (p. 166). Such is the potential power of an unsupportive SDE.

The Judicial Branch

Just as the U.S. Supreme Court and the lower federal courts play an important policymaking role, so do the fifty *state court systems.* Two types of state court systems exist: two-tiered systems and three-tiered systems. The eleven states with two-tiered systems—trial courts and a supreme court—are either sparsely populated or small in area. The systems of the other thirty-nine states include an intermediate appellate court that hands down the final decision in most cases, thereby lightening the supreme court's workload. At the trial court level, evidence is presented and cases are argued in a courtroom, often before juries. Higher courts take cases only on appeal from lower courts and base their decisions not on factual evidence, but on the correctness of the legal procedures followed in the trial court and the soundness of the judge's legal interpretation. If the judges of a higher court find that insufficient factual evidence was presented, they send the case back to the trial court, or remand it. At all levels of state court systems, judges are former lawyers. Procedures for selecting judges vary among states; they can be either appointed or elected. Even if they are elected, however, state judges usually keep a low public profile; in fact, they have been described as the "least visible" state officials (Beyle, 2001; Jacob, 1996).

Despite their low profile, *judges* are political figures who can exercise considerable influence over education policy. Ultimately, judges interpret the statutes enacted by legislatures and can overturn them. Assuming that judges are somehow isolated from the broader policy process and therefore "above" it is a serious mistake. Both groups and individuals with definite policy agendas often seek to influence the courts. One way to do so is to quietly support the election or appointment of judges favorable to one's cause. Another way is to pay the legal expenses of plaintiffs whose cases are relevant to a specific policy issue. For example, at the federal level, the National Association for the Advancement of Colored People (NAACP) financially supported the parents who brought suit against the Topeka Board of Education in the 1950s, ultimately leading to the U.S. Supreme Court decision that outlawed racial segregation in schools. Similar support is frequently provided at the state level, too. In addition, interested groups can file *amicus curiae* (friend of the court) briefs presenting their position on a key case. These briefs then become part of the official record. In short, the courts are an important policy arena (Jacob, 1996). Since the 1970s, state courts have played a major role in shaping school finance policy by either upholding or over-turning those school finance systems that have been challenged by dissatisfied plain-tiffs. Often the plaintiffs in these cases have been school administrators in districts with financial troubles—an excellent example of education leaders working together to influence policy through the state court systems.

Local Government Actors

This book focuses on state education policy processes and, therefore, on policy actors at the state level. Nonetheless, local officials play a role in this process. Thus, this sec-tion describes that role. Its purpose is *not* to provide an exhaustive discussion of the functions of local boards of education or superintendents, but rather to suggest their roles in the broad sweep of state policy processes.

LOCAL BOARDS OF EDUCATION. *Local school boards* play an important role in forty-nine states; Hawaii is the lone exception. Legally, local boards are agencies of state government; their make-up, how they are selected, and what powers they may exercise are spelled out in state law. Historically, boards of education have played a central role in education policymaking, for state governments traditionally delegated most of their constitutional authority over education to them. However, since the mid-1960s, states have increasingly reclaimed that power and asserted their dominance by en-gaging in policymaking in such areas as setting state curriculum standards, requiring students to pass state tests, and, in many states, gathering data on district performance and publishing it in the form of "state report cards" (Fowler, 2000; Kowalski, 1999).

Nonetheless, boards still play an important role in the policy process in most states. First, they typically develop policies suited to their district within a broader policy framework developed by the legislature or SDE. For example, state law may require public schools to be in session for a minimum of 180 days. Local school boards usually have the authority to determine if their district will exceed the minimum and, if so, by how much. They also may determine the dates when school begins and ends as well as when vacations during the academic year occur. A second important school board task is the implementation of state-mandated policies. In recent years, for in-stance, many state legislatures passed laws establishing state testing programs. Local school boards cannot choose whether their students take these tests. However, they can decide how much emphasis is placed on preparing students for them, if special curriculum materials are purchased to strengthen instruction in areas covered by the tests, and what type of remedial programs are offered to students who fail tests. Local boards of education can greatly influence the success or failure of state policies by the way they implement them.

SUPERINTENDENTS.   As the chief executive officers of local school districts, almost all *superintendents* are appointed by school boards. The average superintendent is in his or her mid-to-late fifties, is a former teacher and administrator, and holds a doctorate. In 2010, almost 25% of superintendents were women, but only 4% were either African American or Hispanic. Moreover, studies show that minority superintendents usually work in districts that are more than 50% minority. A central theme in books and articles about the superintendency is the "crisis" in the position: the average age of superintendents is rising; their average time in office is shorter than it used to be; and fewer educators are interested in the job than were in the past (Brunner & Björk, 2001; Cooper, Fusarelli, & Corella, 2000; Domenech, 2010; Pascopella, 2008).

Many causes for this crisis have been identified, but one is certainly increased pressure from state governments to implement **mandates** that are often unfunded, as well as pressure to participate in accountability systems such as NCLB. As early as 1997, Carter and Cunningham noted that two decades of state-initiated reforms had pushed superintendents into subordinate roles and caused them to feel powerless. At that time these authors argued that implementing state policies was a major task for superintendents. However, they also argued that more superintendents were becoming active in the state-level policymaking process and seeking to give state officials advice about policy development and evaluation. They said: "As superintendents become dissatisfied with the barrage of shifting state and federal mandates that have drained their resources, they find themselves actively involved in trying to influence and shape those mandates" (p. 66). The enactment of the NCLB in early 2002 added enormous pressure from the federal level to the already existing pressure from state capitals.

NEWS STORY FOR ANALYSIS

Stiff Challenge Awaits Grasmick's Successor

BALTIMORE, MD—The greatest challenge the next Maryland state schools superintendent may face is that he or she isn't Nancy S. Grasmick. Grasmick has been such a powerful figure in education for two decades, by virtue of the relationships she built with legislators, board members, and district superintendents, that it will be difficult for anyone who follows to have the same independence, observers say. Grasmick announced this week that she will retire after serving as the state schools superintendent since 1991. The state school board will appoint the next leader of the school system.

Robert C. Embry, president of the Abell Foundation, said the state board will have to first decide what their agenda will be for the coming years. It may be, he said, that Marylanders are happy with the status quo and will not want to embrace a more

radical agenda. "I don't know what the present school board has as its priorities. There are a lot of very controversial issues nationally," he said.

But more importantly, experts also said, the state school board should focus on the next superintendent's personality and background as much as the agenda. Much of Grasmick's capacity to get things done, said Baltimore schools chief Andrés Alonso, has to do with her "history, her political astuteness and quite frankly her personal capacity." Alonso said that state superintendents are removed from what happens in classrooms and don't have much authority, but that Grasmick has been able to gather power from her ability to work collaboratively with district superintendents, teachers and school boards. Grasmick has a deep knowledge of how schools work and of education policy. "What

(Continued)

Stiff Challenge Awaits Grasmick's Successor (*Continued*)

I experienced most at first was a person with the extraordinary knowledge of the work," Alonso said.

Senate President Thomas V. Miller would like to see that in the next superintendent. "We need someone with a great deal of teaching experience and supervisory experience," he said, adding that the next leader also must place children first and draw authority from the assumption that student needs are behind all of their actions.

The change in leadership does offer some advantages, several experts said, including the opportunity for the governor to become more involved in education with a dynamic personality whom he helps choose. Though the governor is not directly involved in hiring the superintendent, Gov. Martin O'Malley has appointed all of the current members of the state school board who will decide on Grasmick's replacement. And it gives the state a chance to shift course if officials choose to do so. Particularly in these poor economic times, the new

leader must work well collaboratively, as Grasmick has not always done. She often butted heads with governors, including O'Malley, who tried to force her to step down early in his first term.

(Adapted from Liz Bowie, "Big Shoes to Fill for Maryland Schools; Stiff Challenge Awaits Grasmick's Successor," *The Baltimore Sun*, 1 April 2011, P. 1A. Reprinted with permission of *The Baltimore Sun*. All rights reserved.)

QUESTIONS

1. Identify all the government policy actors mentioned in this article.
2. The article states both that Grasmick worked well collaboratively and that she did not. Explain this apparent contradiction.
3. Why is it significant that the governor appointed all the members of the state school board?
4. Why was Grasmick able to "butt heads with governors" and get away with it?

NONGOVERNMENTAL POLICY ACTORS

Interest Groups: What They Are and What They Do

An **interest group** is "an association of individuals or organizations . . . that, on the basis of one or more shared concerns, attempts to influence public policy in its favor" (Thomas & Hrebenar, 2004, p. 102). Both the number of interest groups and the intensity of their activities have grown in recent decades; increasingly, their attention is focused at the state level. In a series of studies conducted between 1985 and 2002, political scientists Thomas and Hrebenar identified the types of groups most active in the fifty states. Figure 6.1 summarizes their findings. Interest groups usually retain one or more lobbyists who operate under the euphemistic title *legislative liaison*. Despite their somewhat shady public image, most lobbyists are honest, personable individuals whose jobs consist primarily of (1) establishing the relationships that facilitate their access to governmental policy actors and (2) providing these actors with information

Teachers' unions
State departments of education
School boards' associations
Administrators' associations
Parent-Teacher Associations (PTAs)

FIGURE 6.1 Most active interest groups at the state level about their organization's key issues. Lobbyists' major source of power is their specialized knowledge about a specific policy area. Most of their efforts are aimed at legislators and at officials in the state agencies relevant to their issues. Sometimes such agencies are so powerfully influenced by lobbyists that they become subservient to the industry they are supposed to be regulating. Such agencies are said to have been "captured" (Thomas & Hrebenar, 2004).

Education Interest Groups

Although the levels of their activity and effectiveness vary, the same set of education interest groups can be found in most states. The literature agrees that the *teachers' unions* are by far the most powerful education interest groups, a fact that emerged in the Marshall et al. (1989) study. Political science researchers agree. Indeed, Thomas and Hrebenar (2004) found that teachers' unions were the second-most powerful group at the state level, period. The larger of the two unions is the National Education Association (NEA) with 3.2 million members, fifty-one state affiliates (including Washington, D.C.), and thousands of local chapters. Indeed, the NEA is the largest union in the United States and is a force to be reckoned with in nearly every state (NEA/National Education Association, 2011). The smaller union, the American Federation of Teachers (AFT), has 1.3 million members. Concentrated primarily in large metropolitan areas and affiliated with the American Federation of Labor–Congress of Industrial Organizations (AFL–CIO), the AFT has historically been the NEA's strong rival. Nonetheless, in recent years the two organizations have drawn closer; NEA members rejected a proposed merger in 1999, but the two groups collaborate extensively (AFT: A Union of Professionals, 2011).

The other education groups are significantly weaker than the two unions, largely because of their smaller size. The National School Boards Association (NSBA), with over 90,000 members, and the American Association of School Administrators (AASA), with about 13,000 members, usually maintain a visible presence in the state capitals (AASA/American Association of School Administrators, 2011; NASBE, n.d.). As for the Parent–Teacher Association (PTA), its 5 million members in 25,000 local chapters in all fifty states should give it considerable strength (National PTA, 2011). However, its diverse membership—parents, administrators, teachers, and students—often cannot reach consensus on a policy agenda. The Appendix provides the addresses of the Web sites of nine national education interest groups.

Noneducation Interest Groups

The interest groups that represent business, often collectively called the **business lobby,** are among the most influential policy actors in every state capital. In one study, Hrebenar and Thomas (2004) found several types of business groups active in state politics, including (1) general business organizations, such as chambers of commerce; (2) trade associations, which represent a specific economic sector such as banking or agriculture; (3) manufacturers and their associations; and (4) utility and insurance companies. Interestingly, although their original 1985 study found that the two teachers' unions were the most influential interest groups in state politics, by 2002, the unions had dropped to second place, having been displaced by general business organizations. The exact composition of the business lobby varies among states; in some states, the Farm Bureau is a powerful player; in others, service industries or heavy manufacturing is important. Regardless of the type of business, however, they usually agree on one policy goal: keeping taxes low. Because public schools are a major beneficiary of state tax dollars, this means that the education and business lobbies often find themselves on opposite sides of policy issues in state legislatures. In recent decades, business has developed a keen interest in education policy that extends far beyond reducing its cost. For example, in a study of trends in state politics, Mazzoni (1995) found business leaders and organizations increasingly involved in state-level education reforms; Table 6.1 suggests that this trend has continued.

Although no other general type of interest group is as influential as business, others may wield considerable clout in certain states or in relationship to particular issues. Especially worthy of mention are *ethnic-* and *religious-based interest groups*. Ethnically oriented groups such as the NAACP and La Raza—which represent the interests of African Americans and Hispanics, respectively—do not lobby on most education issues, but may become intensely involved regarding a few policy controversies that touch them closely. Obviously, both are usually concerned about any policy proposal that could increase segregation or that relates to teaching about their racial group in the schools. In addition, Hispanics have a special interest in bilingual education. Similarly, religious interest groups such as the Conference of Catholic Bishops, the Christian Coalition, and the Anti-Defamation League tend to mobilize only when certain key issues are under consideration. Moreover, in recent years, *single-issue ideological groups* such as anti-abortion organizations have grown in influence in many states. In order to avoid unpleasant surprises, education leaders must be aware of those groups in the state that are likely to surface—often with a great show of force—when particular issues are at stake. The Appendix provides the addresses of the Web sites of several general interest groups and business groups.

Policy Networks

Increasingly, groups interested in education policy are becoming part of large, loose national organizations called **policy networks** that coordinate a wide range of efforts to influence policy. The most important education policy network is probably the *Education Commission of the States* (ECS), founded in 1966 by the National Governors' Conference. First proposed by Harvard president James Bryant Conant, on its Web site the ECS describes its mission as "to help state leaders identify, develop, and implement public policy for education" (Education Commission of the States, 2011). Fifty states, the District of Columbia, and three territories belong to the ECS, which is based in Denver and funded by the government and private **foundations.** As a nonpartisan clearinghouse, it is an important source of information on education policy for government officials.

Other policy networks are active in state policy arenas as well. For example, the *Children's Defense Fund*, which states on its Web site that its purpose is to be "[a] strong, effective, independent voice for *all* the children of America" (Children's Defense Fund, n.d.; emphasis in the original), works actively on several educational policy issues that touch upon areas usually reserved to the states, including early childhood education and improving the reading achievement of elementary school children. Thus, policy networks are important actors in the development of education policy at both the federal and state levels.

Policy Planning Organizations

THINK TANKS DEFINED.   Even less visible to the general public than the courts are the *policy-planning organizations.* Popularly called **think tanks,** they emerged in the early twentieth century and greatly expanded in number and activity during the period immediately following World War II. Although some are connected with the government, most are not and thus depend on foundations, corporations, and individuals for financial support. Officially, think tanks gather empirical data about public policy issues and then communicate those findings to governments (Weiss, 1992). However, as they do so, they play a crucial role in defining policy issues. In the process of deciding what problems to study, selecting sources of information about them, and summarizing the results of their research, the staffs of think tanks quietly determine which social problems will be considered public policy issues and how those issues will be conceptualized, both by policymakers and by the general public. Think tanks are arguably the most important actors in the policy process; as political scientist Schattschneider (1960) insisted decades ago, "The definition of the alternatives is the supreme instrument of power" (p. 68).

THINK TANKS AND POLICY ENTREPRENEURS.   In addition to publishing books and holding conferences, think tanks sometimes disseminate their ideas by sponsoring the activities of *policy entrepreneurs.* These individuals are outspoken advocates of a specific policy proposal, such as vouchers or merit pay, who invest much time, energy, and money in working to bring about the policy changes they desire. They tirelessly speak up on their behalf and lobby for them, often playing a key role when a fleeting opportunity presents itself to turn their pet ideas into legislation. Policy entrepreneurs do not always work for think tanks; they may also be government employees, politicians, or academics (Kingdon, 2003). However, entrepreneurs funded by think tanks play an important role in education policy innovations. In a study of thirty-eight states whose legislatures considered adopting school-choice policies between 1987 and 1992, Mintrom (1997) found that the presence of active policy entrepreneurs in a state significantly increased the likelihood that a school-choice policy would be approved. He concluded:

> Policy entrepreneurs play an important role in articulating innovative ideas onto government agendas. They work hard at developing close ties with people through whom they can realize their policy goals and they seek to develop convincing arguments for selling their policy ideas. (p. 765)

The Web addresses of several important think tanks and policy research institutes are included in the Appendix.

The Media

THEIR POLICY ROLE.   The *mass media,* including print and broadcast media, news agencies, online services, and the Internet, not only report on policy issues and some stages of the policy process, but are also important actors in it. A newspaper story, radio or television program, or information offered by an online service should never be considered a neutral presentation of mere facts. All result from an important process of selection and recontextualization that reflects, consciously or unconsciously, a stance on questions such as what constitutes real news and the meaning of that news. Because the media must screen, select, and recontextualize information, they inevitably play a major role in the policy process. Although they can potentially have an impact at several stages of that process, they are most important in **agenda setting:** the process by which issues move onto the short list of public problems to which policymakers devote serious consideration (Graber, 2010).

Editors decide what topics will receive attention in the media, thereby setting the *media agenda*. Often, such media attention leads the general public and political figures to become so concerned about a problem that they insist it be addressed. In such cases, the issue has moved from the media agenda to the *public agenda*. Of course, this procedure is far from automatic. The media may persistently cover a topic that stimulates little interest among the general public and politicians. Or, the public may respond to it with great interest, whereas policymakers prefer to continue to ignore the situation, perhaps because it appears too complex to solve quickly. Although most people first become aware of issues through television and radio coverage, the broadcast media are less important policy actors than the news agencies and newspapers. Indeed, the news agencies and newspapers largely set the agenda for television and radio. To a great extent, they also set it for the online services and the Internet.

THE ORGANIZATION OF THE MEDIA.   The three largest *news agencies* (Associated Press, Reuters, and Agence France Presse) are organized internationally, providing news stories, background information, and pictures to media outlets around the world (*Encyclopedia Britannica Online*, n.d.). *Television channels* and *online services* are usually organized at the national level and therefore focus on national news. Although *newspapers* are increasingly part of large national or international syndicates, they tend to focus on national news (provided by the news agencies) and local news (provided by their own reporters). Radio also has a dual focus: national and local. Media outlets are rarely organized at the *state* level.

This aspect of the structure of the U.S. mass media causes state news coverage to be what Graber (2010) calls "a neglected stepchild" (p. 273); news about politics at the state level is skimpy and shallow. This journalistic inadequacy is intensified by the fact that the U.S. media are also organized around markets that have nothing to do with political units (Graber, 2010). Beyle (2001) identifies three types of state media market structures. In the first, some states are overpowered by the media markets of large metropolitan areas outside the state. For example, New Jersey is dominated by the New York City and Philadelphia media; West Virginia is split by three outside markets—Cincinnati, Pittsburgh, and Washington, D.C. In such states, finding good coverage of events in the state capital can be extremely difficult. A second possibility is fragmentation into several large markets within the state, for example, California, Florida, New York, North Carolina, and Texas fit this pattern. In these places, some coverage of state politics is provided, but none of the markets (except the one including the state capital) offers thorough reporting of it. Finally, some states are dominated by the media market of one large city in the state, such as Denver, Atlanta, and Boston. In this situation, state capital affairs will probably be amply reported *if* the dominant city is also the state capital. Where this is not the case, state politics may take a back seat to the politics of the dominant metropolitan area.

The structure of the U.S. media means that people who are interested in education policy and policymaking may discover that finding out about state-level politics, even in their own states, is difficult. Some ways to solve this problem are suggested in the last section of this chapter.

CASE STUDY

"Stop The Bullies!" The Politics of Accountability

In 1987, the Ohio General Assembly passed H.B. 231, adopting learning outcomes in mathematics, reading, writing, and citizenship; these outcomes then became the basis of Ohio's first proficiency test, a ninth-grade test that students had to pass in order to graduate, starting in 1993. As the years passed, the legislature expanded its testing program, adding fourth-, sixth-, and twelfth-grade tests and including a science section. Increasingly, instruction in Ohio's schools focused on preparing students to take the tests. Educators were not happy about this narrowing of the curriculum, and among themselves they questioned the tests' validity. However, they made few attempts to get this policy changed because they thought the legislature would interpret such efforts as opposition to accountability.

In 1997, the General Assembly unveiled an even more rigorous version of its accountability system. With S.B. 55 it established a district report card system, based almost entirely on test scores. These report cards were to be released to the media each year so that taxpayers could see how effective (or ineffective) their public schools were. S.B. 55 also included a "Fourth Grade Guarantee" that required fourth-grade children who failed the reading section of their tests to be retained, starting in 2001, unless they had an Individualized Education Plan (IEP) or their principal and teacher waived the requirement.

Among themselves, Ohio educators joked sarcastically that soon the fourth-grade population would explode and elementary schools would need to expand their parking lots to accommodate all the teenage students who would be driving to fourth grade. But Ohio parents were not amused, especially when it was revealed that about 42% of fourth graders regularly failed the reading test. Mary O'Brien and Teri Zeigler, mothers in an affluent Columbus suburb, formed a grassroots movement

called "Stop Ohio Proficiency Tests," adopting the slogan, "Stop the Bullies!" The "bullies" were the state's legislators. Over a period of several months, they wrote numerous letters to newspaper editors, appeared on television, gave testimony before the State Board of Education, and held noisy demonstrations on the lawn of the state capitol.

Ohio's political leaders responded quickly. Governor Taft appointed a Commission for Student Success to study the issue and make recommendations in December 2000. Although he urged his fellow Republicans in the legislature to wait for the commission report, several of them introduced bills to amend the policy during the fall of 2000.

Meanwhile, educators began to speak out, too. The Ohio Education Association sponsored thirty-three public forums across the state to discuss problems with the tests. Administrators and their organizations began to criticize both the tests and the district report cards publicly. For example, Joyce Bowersock, an assistant superintendent, complained: "We're punishing 9-year-olds because they're not reading where . . . legislators think they should be reading. I think that's ridiculous." Superintendent David McWilliams said, "I am frustrated with the comparisons between school districts. Districts represent different communities." And John Stanford of the Ohio School Board Association observed that the publication of district report cards hurt some districts' reputations and made it hard for them to pass tax referenda.

In December, the governor's commission recommended reducing the number of tests. In 2001, the General Assembly accepted that recommendation and also greatly weakened the Fourth Grade Guarantee. ■

(Based on About Us, n.d.; Clark, December 16, 2000; Ebbing, September 6, 2000; History of Ohio Proficiency Tests, n.d.; Hunt, Tortora, & Mrozowski, September 3, 2000; OEA Online News, n.d.; Sidoti, September 5, 2000;

(Continued)

"Stop The Bullies!" The Politics of Accountability (Continued)

(Welsh-Huggins, September 5, 2000; Welsh-Huggins, November 30, 2000.)

QUESTIONS

1. Identify all the policy actors in this case study and categorize them, using headings from this chapter.

2. Were the state's educators wise to delay their attack against this accountability system until the parents revolted? Why or why not?

3. Why were the parents so successful in getting the policy changed?

4. Discuss Superintendent McWilliams's statement.

IDENTIFYING AND LEARNING ABOUT POLICY ACTORS

Overall Approach

Effective interaction with policy actors requires knowing who they are, where they can be reached, and who should be contacted about specific issues. This means that school leaders should have a thorough, up-to-date listing of all the key players in their state. Yet, school leaders are extremely busy people and become busier every year. The same is true for their staff, to whom the development of such a list might be delegated. Moreover, because resources are limited, few can afford to travel widely to search for information or to make numerous long-distance telephone calls. Therefore, the following principles should be followed in developing the list:

1. Where possible, existing lists should be used in developing one's own comprehensive directory of policy actors.
2. The least expensive methods of obtaining information should be tried first.
3. As it is developed, the list should be put into a form readily accessible and easily updated. The ideal format is a computer file that can be easily modified and printed out.

In developing the lists of suggestions in the following sections, the author sought to follow the first two of these principles. Recommendations are therefore organized from the closest, cheapest sources to the most distant and possibly expensive. However, in some settings, switching the order of the recommendations in order to follow the general principles may be advisable.

Locating Elected Government Officials

Tables 6.3 and 6.4 list elected officials at the federal and state levels who should be identified and the information one should gather about them. Facts about these policy actors are relatively easy to find; therefore, this process should not be particularly onerous. Places to look for information include

1. *The district office.* Possibly it maintains a current list or has a slightly out-of-date one that could be revised.
2. *The telephone book.* The introductory section may list area politicians with their addresses and phone numbers. It may also provide phone numbers for the state capitol building or statehouse. Additional information is probably

TABLE 6.3 Federal Officials to Identify and Information Needed

Officials	Information Needed
Representative	Address
Both senators	Phone number
	Email address
	Fax number
	Web site and Facebook pages, if any
	Party affiliation
	Length of tenure in office
	Year of next reelection campaign
	Margin of victory in last election
	Known positions on education
	Whether the official serves on an education or finance committee

TABLE 6.4 Elected State Officials to Identify and Information Needed

Officials	Information Needed
Governor	Address
Senator(s) for school district	Phone number
Representative(s) for school district	Email address
Speaker of the House	Fax number
President of the Senate	Web site and Facebook pages, if any
Chair of House Education Committee	Party affiliation
Chair of Senate Education Committee	Length of tenure in office
	Year of next reelection campaign
	Margin of victory in last election
	Known positions on education

available in the white or business pages under the headings "U.S. Government" and "[Name of State], State of."

3. *The public library.* In the reference section, one can find various directories to state government. A librarian may also be able to suggest additional sources on the Internet, on a CD-ROM, in vertical files, and so forth.

4. *The Internet.* A search engine such as Google can be used to locate information.

5. *The League of Women Voters.* The league produces and disseminates factual information about area politicians.

6. *Politicians' offices.* On request, most offices provide citizens with information about the politician's record and policy positions.

7. *Newspapers.* Around election time, most papers carry information on candidates; moreover, when the legislature convenes, usually in January, many

carry special features on state government. Back issues of local newspapers should be available on microfilm in the local library; Lexis-Nexis indexes major newspapers in every state, and provides an electronic version of the text. It is accessible through many university Web sites.

Identifying Appointed Officials and Groups

These policy actors are less visible than elected officials; nonetheless, finding them should not be difficult. Table 6.5 provides a framework for organizing information about them. The following sources are recommended:

1. *The SDE directory.* Most state departments of education publish a directory or handbook for administrators in the state; it is probably also available online. Generally, it includes information on the SDE itself, the CSSO, and the SBE. It may also list major education interest groups with their addresses and phone numbers.
2. *The telephone book for the state capital.* A copy should be in the local library in book, microfiche, or electronic form. Sections to consult include government listings in the introduction, the state government listings in the white or business pages, and listings of "Associations" in the yellow pages.
3. *Organizational headquarters.* On request, most interest groups gladly provide flyers and brochures that provide facts about their group and its policy positions. Most also maintain Web sites and can be found by searching for their name with a search engine.

Identifying Policy Planning and Related Organizations

Because these groups maintain a low public profile, they are the hardest to find. However, checking the sources recommended here over a year or two should facilitate the identification of most of the groups, including national organizations, active in the state. Tables 6.6 and 6.7 help organize information about these groups.

TABLE 6.5 Appointed State Officials to Identify and Information Needed

Officials[a]	Information Needed
Chief state school officer	Address
Members of state board of education	Phone number
	Email address
	Fax number
	Web site or Facebook pages, if any
	Party affiliation, where applicable
	Length of tenure in office
	Who appointed the official
	Year term expires
	Known positions on education

[a] Elected in a few states; use Table 6.4 in those cases.

TABLE 6.6 Groups to Identify and Information Needed

Groups	Information Needed
State administrator associations	Address
State business roundtable	Phone number
State chamber of commerce	Email address
State department of education	Fax number
State Parent-Teacher Association	Web site or Facebook pages, if any
State school board association	Name of current head
State teachers' unions	Name(s) of publication(s)
Other influential groups in state	Number of members or employees
	Known positions on education

TABLE 6.7 Policy Planning and Related Organizations to Identify and Information Needed

Groups and Individuals	Information Needed
Active state or national policy research organizations	Address
	Phone number
Active state or national foundations	Email address
University-based policy research centers	Fax number
	Web site or Facebook pages, if any
Foundation-supported policy entrepreneurs	Party connections
	Ideological tendencies
	Funding sources
	Known positions on education

1. *Recent policy reports.* Policy planning groups develop and disseminate reports on issues that interest them; foundations sponsor research and summaries of it. The documents they issue commonly list those who participated in the project as well as the funders. Because school leaders frequently receive such reports in the mail or at professional meetings, copies are probably available in the district.

2. *Newspapers.* Most papers occasionally publish feature articles on innovative school programs in their area; sometimes these articles reveal information about the foundations and other groups that are backing the project.

3. *Education Week.* This national weekly devoted to education carries articles about think tank and foundation reports, as well as the requests for proposals put out by such groups. This information can be helpful in identifying the organizations

that advocate for specific education policies and that may be behind similar policy movements in a given state.

4. *Internet.* Once the name of a policy planning group has been identified, further information can be obtained by searching the Internet.

LOCATING THE "NEGLECTED STEPCHILD"

School leaders who wish to follow state education policymaking should first assess the quality of the coverage by media outlets in their geographic area. A good time to conduct such an assessment is when the legislature is in session. Coverage should be monitored for several weeks, because some newspapers provide only periodic summaries of legislation enacted and the votes of local lawmakers. Assessing the coverage of any newspapers published in the state capital and of any prestige newspapers published in the state, such as the *New York Times,* the *Philadelphia Inquirer,* or the *Los Angeles Times,* is also important. If some of these provide excellent coverage, their Web versions should be consulted regularly.

If newspaper coverage is inadequate—and this is usually the case—the school leader should identify the interest groups that maintain legislative updates on their Web sites. Most likely to do so are the NSBA state affiliate and the NEA and AFT state affiliates. Checking these updates regularly makes it easy to keep up with what is happening in the state capital.

School leaders should also identify all the legislative hot lines associated with education in the state. These are recorded updates of the status of pertinent bills and can be accessed by dialing a toll-free number; they are often more current than the Web sites and may change from day to day when the legislature is in session. Again, education interest groups based in the state capital are most likely to maintain these. Sometimes the statehouse also has one that provides general information about committee meetings and scheduled hearings.

The "neglected stepchild" syndrome is truly an anachronism in a period of increasing activity at the state level of the federal system. Nonetheless, those who want to follow state education policymaking can do so if they identify and systematically use alternative sources of information. For now, we can only hope the day will soon come when the media recognize the importance of state government and provide more thorough coverage of it.

QUESTIONS AND ACTIVITIES FOR DISCUSSION

1. Using multiple sources, try to determine how interested your governor is in education policy issues. Does he/she strongly advocate any specific education reforms?
2. Find out how the SBE and CSSO are selected in your state. To which of the models discussed in this chapter does your state conform, if any? How does this governance structure affect the relationships among the governor, the SBE, and the CSSO?
3. Identify the most important education and business interest groups in your state. How do they interact?
4. Analyze and evaluate the coverage of state politics in a daily newspaper available in your area.

INTERNET ASSIGNMENT

Find the Web sites of your governor and legislature as well as the Web sites of three interest groups active in your state. Identify the educational issues that are important to each. Are different issues important to different policy actors? Explain any differences and similarities that you find.

FOR FURTHER READING

Edlefson, C. (1994). The substance and politics of education reform: A view from a governor's office. *Planning and Changing, 25*(1/2), 41–55.

Edlefson, who was the educational specialist on Ohio Governor Celeste's staff in the late 1980s, gives the inside story of how Celeste set the agenda for education reform. Her article provides a rare glimpse into the usually hidden workings of the governor's office.

Garda, R. (2011). The politics of education reform: Lessons from New Orleans. *Journal of Law & Education 40*, 57-103.

Long considered a seriously deficient school district, the New Orleans system was radically reformed after Hurricane Katrina, with most of its schools converted into charters. Garda not only tells the interesting story of the politics that emerged from the reform, but also depicts numerous policy actors—including a school board, teachers' union, state legislature, mayor, and governor—struggling with each other and with the reforms.

Gray, V., & Hanson, R. L., (Eds.). (2008). *Politics in the American states.* 9th ed. Washington, D.C.: CQ Press.

This edited book is the standard political science overview of state politics. Its valuable chapters summarize recent developments and new research in every branch of state government and in special policy areas—an indispensable source on politics at the state level.

Hamann, E. T., & Lane, B. The roles of state departments of education as policy intermediaries: Two cases. *Educational Policy 18*, 426-455.

After studying how the SDEs in Maine and Puerto Rico implemented the *No Child Left Behind Act*, Hamann and Lane concluded that in both jurisdictions the demands of the federal law were interpreted in ways that corresponded with local problems as well as with previous patterns of local action. In both instances, the SDEs acted as important mediators between the federal policy and the local implementers.

Madsen, J. (1994). *Educational reform at the state level.* Bristol, PA: Falmer Press.

As a low-ranking administrator in an SDE, Madsen had the opportunity to observe how the agency put up roadblocks during the implementation of the state legislature's education reform act. She provides an interesting and passionately felt description of the power of a state agency.

7 SETTING THE STAGE AND GETTING ON IT: ISSUE DEFINITION AND AGENDA SETTING

Focus Questions

▌ How are policy issues defined?

▌ Why is the definition of an issue important?

▌ What is a policy agenda and how do policy issues get on it?

▌ How can education leaders follow and influence these stages of the policy process?

PERCEPTION AND REALITY IN THE POLICY PROCESS

In an amusing story from his own high school days, scientist Benno Muller-Hill (1988) provides an example of how human perceptions of reality are shaped by others. As part of one of Muller-Hill's high school science classes, the teacher set up a telescope on the school grounds and asked his students to line up to look through it; they were supposed to observe one of the planets and its moons. The first student announced that he could not see the planet; however, after the teacher showed him how to adjust the focus, he stated that he could see it clearly. After him, several other students looked through the instrument and said they could see the planet and its moons. But the boy in line just ahead of Muller-Hill loudly insisted that he saw nothing. The exasperated teacher looked through the telescope himself, and a strange expression came over his face. He had forgotten to remove the cover from the lens! Not a single one of the students had really seen the planet and its moons. For our purposes, whether the students pretended to see the planet and its moons in order to avoid embarrassment (and a poor grade) or whether they actually thought some speck of dust or glint of light on the lens was the planet is irrelevant. The point is that we human beings have a powerful desire to perceive the reality we think we *should* perceive. Breaking free of a definition of reality that those around us accept and expect us to accept is extremely difficult.

This tendency is especially important in the first two stages of the policy process: issue definition and agenda setting. If a policy issue is not well defined, it is not perceived as important. If it is not perceived as important by a large number of people, it never attracts enough attention to reach the policy agenda. If it never reaches the policy agenda, it certainly never becomes formal policy. Important as they are, these two stages of the policy process are relatively unfamiliar to the general public, including school leaders. In part, this is because they occur quietly and out of the glare of media attention. In part, too, it is because high school government classes and even many college courses in political science overlook them entirely, focusing instead on the more visible stages of **policy formulation** and adoption. Yet issue definition and agenda setting are arguably the most important steps in the entire policy process, irreversibly influencing what happens next.

Education leaders who are unaware of these two stages of the policy process often feel blindsided by education policy proposals and changes. To them, new policy ideas seemingly emerge from nowhere and move rapidly into the legislatures or the courts, drawing on a surprising level of support. They often feel that somehow professional educators have been left out of the loop and that no one cares about their ideas or experience. Leaders who wish to be ahead of the game rather than always trying to figure out what the game is must understand these first stages, know how to follow them, and have the skill to influence them.

Chapter 7, then, describes the issue-definition and agenda-setting phases of the policy process. The final section of this chapter presents ways that school leaders can monitor and influence these processes.

ISSUE DEFINITION: SETTING THE STAGE

Defining Issue Definition

Issue definition is a political process that involves transforming a *problem* into an *issue* that the government can address. It is a discursive process, occurring through both written and spoken communication. It also involves developing an attractive image of the issue and associating appealing symbols with it in order to gain public support. Intelligent definition of an issue can increase the likelihood of political support, reduce the likelihood of opposition, and shape the policy debate. It sets the stage for the more visible phases of the process to follow (Anderson, 2003; Baumgartner & Jones, 2009; Liu et al., 2010).

In thinking about issue definition, distinguishing problems from **policy issues** is important (Best, 1989; Stone, 1989). The world is full of problems—difficult situations that render life unpleasant and inconvenient. All educators know that schools abound with problems: school buses sometimes break down, teachers may feel out of sorts, and children's minds are more often filled with fantasies derived from television than with reflections on their lessons. Yet for the most part, educators accept these problems either as an inevitable part of school life or as minor daily annoyances. They do not usually see them as issues requiring government action.

Figure 7.1 lists five common problems in schools. Most educators agree that these are problems, but they probably feel no urgency about dealing with them. In Figure 7.2, however, each of the five problems has been transformed into a policy issue. Unlike the problems, the issues are controversial; they imply an interpretation of the problem, a set of values, and an understanding of the proper role of government. Leaders should understand that any problem can yield several policy issues.

1. Many teachers and principals suffer from low morale.
2. Students are often hard to motivate.
3. Many children change schools during the school year because their families move.
4. Children who spend a lot of time watching television and playing computer games may find school boring.
5. Educational resources are often used unwisely.

FIGURE 7.1   Five common problems in schools

1. Because low morale results from a lack of control over major professional decisions, teachers and principals ought to be empowered through site-based decision making.
2. If students had to maintain a C or higher average in order to obtain a driver's license, their motivation in school would increase.
3. Parents with school-age children should be legally prohibited from moving outside their school attendance zone during the school year.
4. Only educational and motivational media should be available to children younger than 18.
5. If schools had to compete with each other for students, they would use their resources more wisely.

FIGURE 7.2   Five policy issues based on the problems in Figure 7.1

1. If students had to maintain a C or higher average in order to obtain a driver's license, their motivation would increase.
2. If corporal punishment were restored in U.S. schools, we would see a dramatic increase in student motivation.
3. National standards and assessments would motivate students to work harder in school.
4. If teachers taught a curriculum that was more relevant to students and used more hands-on learning activities, motivation problems would decrease.
5. If schools were small enough that students could know their teachers and classmates better, students would be more motivated.

FIGURE 7.3   Five policy issues regarding student motivation

Figure 7.3 lists five of the many issues that could be derived from the second problem noted in Figure 7.1—that of motivating students. During the issue-definition stage, several competing understandings of a single problem are often under discussion simultaneously. Ultimately, however, only two or three are accepted as valid definitions of the problem; the "winners" prevail primarily because of the skill with which their supporters define them.

The Education Policy Planning and Research Community

ITS NATURE AND STRUCTURE.   Although issue definition is an intellectual process and therefore occurs within human minds, minds are found in bodies that must be located somewhere. This means that issue definition must occur in specific places at identifiable times. In the United States, almost all education policy issues are defined within a loosely linked set of institutions that some call the *education policy planning and research community* (EPPRC). Some aspects of agenda setting also occur there. Although these institutions play an important role in the policy process, their public visibility is low. More than 20 years ago, Fred Burke (1990), former commissioner of education in Rhode Island and New Jersey, described this network's issue-definition process as a "para-private" one that is "peculiarly informal, private, diffuse, episodic, and from a public policy point of view, unaccountable" (p. 11). Among the participants, he identified the U.S. Department of Education (USDOE), nonprofit foundations, professors at a few leading universities, and teachers' unions. More recently a study of influences on national educational policy ranked the same policy actors among the top ten most influential organizations (Swanson & Barlage, 2006).

Figure 7.4 depicts the EPPRC and relates it to government and the media. In this diagram, foundations, universities, policy planning groups (think tanks), and the USDOE constitute the core of the EPPRC. Although thousands of foundations, approximately 1,000 policy planning organizations, and many universities are located in the United States, not all of them are important in education policy development

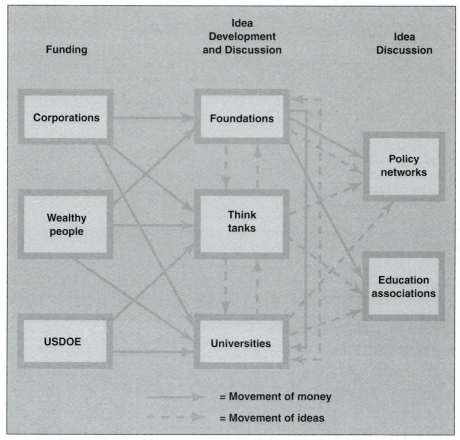

FIGURE 7.4 The education policy planning and research community

(Lagemann & de Forest, 2007; Rich, 2004). Many specialize in other policy areas such as defense or agriculture; many more are not involved in policy development at all. Only a few are major players in education. Figure 7.5 lists eleven foundations that have been especially interested in education; Figure 7.6 lists eight think tanks known for their work in education policy; and Figure 7.7 lists five major universities that work in this area. These five universities form the Consortium for Policy Research in Education (CPRE). Although other foundations, think tanks, and universities participate in education policy development, these twenty-four institutions are unusually important. Most of their names are familiar to school leaders.

Annie E. Casey Foundation
Bill and Melinda Gates Foundation
Carnegie Corporation
Danforth Foundation
Ford Foundation
Heritage Foundation
Lilly Endowment
Pew Charitable Trusts
Rockefeller Foundation
Spencer Foundation
Thomas B. Fordham Foundation

FIGURE 7.5   Some foundations that sponsor educational policy research and initiatives

Harvard University
Stanford University
University of Michigan
University of Pennsylvania
University of Wisconsin–Madison

FIGURE 7.6   Some policy research organizations (think tanks) that study educational policy

American Enterprise Institute
Brookings Institution
Committee for Economic Development
Economic Policy Institute
Heritage Foundation
Hudson Institute
Manhattan Institute
RAND Corporation

FIGURE 7.7   University members of the Consortium for Policy Research in Education (CPRE)

These institutions are by no means monolithic, and they do not all agree. Most foundations and think tanks have an ideological orientation. For example, the Economic Policy Institute is extremely liberal, whereas the Carnegie Corporation, RAND Corporation, and the Committee for Economic Development are liberal. In contrast, the American Enterprise Institute, the Hudson Institute, and the Manhattan Institute are well known for conservative research and publications. The Heritage Foundation is to the right of most the groups listed here, although it is by no means the most conservative U.S. think tank (Lenkowsky & Piereson, 2007; Rich, 2004). This means that, far from cooperating in some type of conspiracy, these organizations actually compete fiercely with each other to have their definitions of education problems accepted by other participants in the issue-definition process.

FUNDING THE EPPRC.   Like all organizations, participants in the EPPRC require substantial financial support to keep their **programs** going. Their funding comes from three major sources: corporations, wealthy individuals, and the government (especially the USDOE). Many think tanks receive much of their financial support from foundations, but ultimately, most foundation money comes from either corporations or wealthy people.

Money can be given to these institutions in several ways. Corporations and wealthy individuals sometimes give outright donations. When the Heritage Foundation was founded in 1973, a wealthy businessman, Joseph Coors of Colorado, provided much of its original funding. Other donors included Richard Mellon Scaife (another wealthy man), the Olin Foundation, and several corporations (Peschek, 1987). Another common way to give money is to contribute to an institution's endowment fund. Because endowment moneys are invested and only their income is available for spending, they provide a stable source of revenue. The Brookings Institution, one of the oldest think tanks in the United States, is heavily endowed; much of its original endowment was provided by steel magnate Andrew Carnegie (McGann, 1995). Many universities are also heavily endowed; Harvard, Yale, and Princeton top the list (National Association of College and University Business Officers and Commonfund Institute, 2011).

Another way to provide money for these institutions is to make grants to them. Grants, of course, are competitive. When the federal government or a foundation plans to give money through a grant program, it first issues a request for proposals (RFP). The RFP usually includes a description of what kind of project is eligible to receive grant money and guidelines for writing the proposal. Institutions and individuals submit their proposals, and a few are selected for funding. Much of the education research conducted by both universities and think tanks is funded this way. CPRE, for example, was founded in 1985 with a five-year grant from the Office of Educational Research and Improvement (OERI), a division of the USDOE. It also receives grant money from several foundations, including the Carnegie Corporation (CPRE, 2007).

Sometimes funding comes in the form of contracts. The RAND Corporation, a California-based think tank, provides a good example. Under federal government contracts, it conducted many of the evaluations of federal education programs in the 1960s and 1970s. Commissioned books and research involve a special kind of contract. For example, a newcomer on the foundation scene, the Bill and Melinda

Gates Foundation, has provided funding for several research projects, including *Getting Traction, Gaining Ground*; *The Silent Epidemic: Perspectives of High School Dropouts*; and *Education Week*'s 2006 study, *Diplomas Count*. In fact, this foundation provides an excellent example of how much influence a foundation can exercise over education policy. Established in 1994, by 2006 the Bill and Melinda Gates Foundation was found to rank third in importance among organizations that influence education policy—right after the U.S. Congress and the USDOE. Moreover, Bill Gates was ranked as the most important *individual* in influencing education policy, ahead of then President Bush and the late Senator Ted Kennedy. His foundation also provided funding for four other organizations ranked in the top ten in influence: Achieve, the Center on Education Policy, the Education Trust, and the NGA (Swanson & Barlage, 2006). Universities, too, receive support from several funding streams: government grants and contracts, gifts from corporations and wealthy individuals, and foundation moneys as well as student tuition and (in some cases) taxes. For all these institutions, obtaining a steady supply of sufficient funding is a constant challenge.

DEVELOPING AND DISCUSSING NEW IDEAS.   The EPPRC provides multiple forums in which new policy ideas can be developed, discussed, and then disseminated to policy planning groups, the media, and policymakers (Swanson & Barlage, 2006). Think tanks and research-oriented universities are the sites of most of this intellectual activity. Think tanks employ researchers and writers who work together to pursue a research and publishing agenda developed by the organization's leadership. In research-oriented universities, professors are hired with the understanding that their job includes scholarship: conducting research and then making presentations, writing articles, and publishing books based on it. In a world where knowledge is an increasingly crucial source of **power,** producing new knowledge is important. The United States is fortunate to have a network of think tanks and universities that produces much of the new knowledge in the world.

NEW IDEAS FROM RESEARCH.   One important source of new ideas is research. Researchers employed by think tanks and universities conduct three broad types of research: basic, applied, and integrative. *Basic research* is the most theoretical and (some would say) the least practical. Yet, as basic researchers point out, much research that was originally pursued for purely intellectual reasons has had important practical applications. One area of basic research that has had considerable impact on education policy is learning theory, an aspect of psychology. For much of the twentieth century, the psychological theory called behaviorism was dominant. University researchers such as B. F. Skinner taught rats to negotiate mazes and press levers for food pellet rewards, demonstrating that some learning is based on a stimulus-response reaction and that rewards and punishments can improve it. Under the influence of this basic research, curriculum policy changed. Schools in the United States adopted "behavioral objectives" and encouraged teachers to use reward systems to manage their classrooms (Ravitch, 1995). However, learning theory has changed considerably since the late 1970s, again, largely because of basic research. Cognitive psychology, today's dominant theory, emphasizes the social nature of learning and the fact that human beings "construct" their own knowledge as they learn. It also suggests that both children and adults learn better by solving open-ended problems with several possible answers than by memorizing facts. Cognitive theory, too, has had considerable impact on curriculum policy; people who advocate portfolio assessments and essay-type examinations reflect this influence (Ravitch, 1995).

Applied research tests theory in real-life settings. Whereas a basic researcher usually works in a carefully controlled laboratory-like environment, an applied researcher may study a school or a classroom to see if a curriculum based on cognitive theory leads to improved learning. A special type of applied research is **evaluation** research, which seeks to assess how well a new education policy or program is working. Although both universities and think tanks enter into contracts to conduct evaluation research, several of the most influential evaluation studies have been done by think tanks. Probably the most famous were the RAND Corporation's evaluations of several federal education programs during the 1970s (Williams & Palmatier, 1992). The findings of evaluation research sometimes lead to major policy changes.

Finally, *integrative research* draws on a wide range of past research studies on a single topic and integrates them into a single work that seeks to describe what the research as a whole says. Examples of integrative research include textbooks, literature reviews, and general overviews of a subject. Diane Ravitch (1995), working under the auspices of the Brookings Institution, wrote *National Standards in American Education: A Citizen's Guide*. In it, she provides a history of curriculum and testing in the United States, a history of the development of the movement for national standards, and a description of the political conflicts surrounding national standards. As the title of her book suggests, it offers a useful overview of the subject for a broad audience.

Although basic, applied, and integrative research provide some new policy ideas, assuming that policymakers immediately accept researchers' findings and translate them into policy, or that they accept all the ideas scholars develop, is naive. On the contrary, policy researchers often lament that policymakers are uninterested in their work and resist applying it. However, studies of policy development over long periods of time—a decade or more—indicate that some research findings do ultimately change people's understanding of policy problems and thus influence policy development (Rich, 2004).

NEW IDEAS FROM IDEOLOGY.   Ideology shapes issue definition at least as much as research does. Most think tanks and foundations adhere to a specific ideological position, and so do many university policy researchers. Their ideology influences their issue definition work in at least two ways. First, their basic beliefs predispose them to analyze policy problems in some ways rather than in others (Lenkowsky & Piereson, 2007; Rich, 2004). For example, both conservatives and liberals are concerned about low school achievement among schoolchildren, but they understand this problem differently. Conservatives are more likely to view low school achievement as the result of individualistic factors, such as broken families and inadequate efforts by both children and their teachers. Therefore, conservative solutions often encourage a return to traditional values and basic education. Because conservatives distrust activist government, they are also more likely to select a policy delivery system based on the market or privatization. Some form of school choice, private tutoring, or economic incentives for parents to stay together might occur to them as ways to solve this problem. In contrast, liberals might define the problem as one caused primarily by the larger society rather than by individual families, children, and teachers. Typical liberal solutions might include improved nutrition for poor children, remedial programs for the schools that serve them, and job training for parents. Because liberals favor active government intervention in social problems, they feel comfortable with these approaches even though they expand government and increase public spending.

Second, ideology helps determine the type of research that is done and the questions that guide it. Foundations award grant money to researchers and writers whose proposed **projects** are consistent with their own ideological positions. Similarly, most think tanks employ people who share their views. Not surprisingly, then, much research and writing are done on those topics that are at the center of current ideological controversy. Not coincidentally, several conservative foundations have funded private voucher programs and sponsored research on them. Also not coincidentally, the liberal Carnegie Corporation and Economic Policy Institute have provided financial support for scholars who have reservations about school choice. As groups that oppose conservative definitions of education issues, they have good reason to gather evidence to use to challenge them (Lenkowsky & Piereson, 2007). Thus, the research and writing the EPPRC produce as it defines policy issues should never be accepted uncritically as purely scientific or impartial. Although some of it conforms to high standards of scholarship, it varies in quality, and all of it must be considered the product of a political process in which ideology plays an important role.

FORUMS FOR DISCUSSION.   Universities and think tanks do more than pay the salaries of researchers and writers, however. They provide a work environment that not only supports research and writing but also stimulates it. Prominent scholars have access to superb libraries, state-of-the-art computer facilities, clerical support, and research assistants. They normally have travel budgets that permit them to attend professional conferences and visit other scholars in their field. Universities and think tanks also sponsor workshops and symposia in order to give them a chance to hear stimulating speakers.

Especially in think tanks, but also in many research universities, a considerable effort is made to maintain a stimulating intellectual environment in which new ideas can be discussed, refined, or explored. "Food is essential to a successful think tank," argued Patrick Ford (1992, p. 35) as he described the breakfasts, luncheons, and dinners that the American Enterprise Institute sponsors to encourage policy scholars to congregate and talk about their work. And Diane Ravitch (1995), who had previously worked at Columbia University, describes her experience working at the Brookings Institution in these glowing terms:

> Brookings is the most pleasant and productive environment in which I have ever worked. Casual conversations—over the lunch table, at the water cooler, or in the frequent luncheon seminars—were invariably stimulating. The facilities, including the library and the computer services, are state of the art. . . . There are no strictures, formal or informal, on what may be said, written, or argued. (p. x)

In such environments, researchers, scholars, writers, and other members of the EPPRC have the opportunity to discuss social problems, develop new ideas for solving them, and define them through thought and conversation.

DISSEMINATING NEW IDEAS.   Of course, foundations, think tanks, and universities have little interest in merely stimulating thinkers to talk among themselves; they reward them for disseminating their new knowledge. Ideas can be communicated in several ways, and the publication of printed materials is one of them. Both professors and think-tank researchers write articles and books in which they make new ideas widely available. Think tanks typically produce several other types of written documents as well, including research reports, policy briefs, and newsletters. Several think-tank scholars also write newspaper columns. Most think tanks also make their publications or other texts available on their Web sites.

Ideas can be spread through the spoken word as well. University professors, foundation representatives, and think-tank researchers often present talks at professional conferences, appear as members of symposium panels, and, when invited, testify before committees of Congress and state legislatures. In addition, they often sponsor events at which new ideas are orally presented to an audience. CPRE sponsors education policy workshops (funded by the Danforth Foundation) for state and local policymakers. The Heritage Foundation sponsors frequent lectures on and debates about policy issues at its Washington, D.C., headquarters. The Education Commission of the States (ECS)—a nonpartisan policy network that serves state governments by acting as a clearinghouse for education policy ideas—holds an annual meeting at which scholars and others present ideas to an audience consisting largely of state officials from across the nation. Many people consider this ECS meeting one of the most important venues for sharing and discussing new policy ideas in education.

Finally, ideas are often spread as scholars move from one institution to another—a frequent occurrence within the EPPRC. For example, conservative scholar Diane Ravitch was a professor at Columbia University's Teachers' College for many years; she then served as assistant secretary for OERI under the first Bush Administration. After Bush's defeat in the 1992 presidential election, she was invited to join the Brookings Institution, where she remained until 2005. Since then she has been a Research Professor of Education at New York University (Diane Ravitch, n.d.; Ravitch, 1995). Liberal scholar Marshall Smith, a major leader in the movement for standards-based reform, has made even more professional moves. After graduating from Harvard University's School of Education, he held several education positions in the Carter Administration. After Reagan became president in 1981, Smith moved to Wisconsin, where he directed the Wisconsin Center for Education Research. Five years later, he became the dean of the School of Education at Stanford. During his years there, Smith was involved with CPRE; he also had close connections with the National Science Foundation. In 1993, he moved back into government, becoming an undersecretary in the USDOE. Since 2001, he has served as the Program Director of Education for the William and Flora Hewlett Foundation (Marshall Smith, n.d.; Vinovskis, 1996). These examples illustrate the close ties between government and the EPPRC. People move back and forth in a fluid fashion, taking their interpretations of society's problems and their solutions with them. As they move from one institution to another, their ideas spread.

THE SPREAD OF A POLICY IDEA: SITE-BASED MANAGEMENT.   Unfortunately, scholars have not often studied how the EPPRC works, but in the early 1990s, Ogawa (1994) analyzed articles, conference presentations, and printed materials from several national education organizations in order to trace the development of the site-based management (SBM) movement. He also interviewed thirty-two people. He traced the basic SBM idea back to a group of individuals who worked at the National Institute of Education in the 1970s, several of whom had ties to Harvard. They saw SBM as a way to improve education in the United States by professionalizing teaching. Al Shanker, then president of the American Federation of Teachers (AFT), was intrigued by the idea and persuaded three AFT locals to negotiate SBM into their contracts in the early 1980s.

In 1985, the president of the Education Commission of the States suggested to the president of the Carnegie Corporation that the foundation should become involved in studying linkages between education and the economy. As part of this project, the Carnegie president established the Carnegie Forum on Education and the Economy, which in turn established the Task Force on Teaching as a Profession. This task force conducted a study of teaching, publishing its findings in a 1986 report entitled *A Nation Prepared.* In the same year, the National Governors Association (NGA) published a report called *Time for Results.* Both reports proposed SBM as a way to professionalize teaching, and both cited the AFT locals who had negotiated SBM as examples.

Next, the Carnegie Forum established a speakers' bureau that provided speakers to present the report to teachers' unions, education organizations, and business groups. It also arranged for local newspapers and television stations to cover these speeches. Ogawa found that these 1986 events constituted a "watershed period" for the movement. After 1986, national education organizations began to hold SBM workshops. In 1988, the NGA used a Carnegie Corporation grant to fund a conference on SBM. By 1990, articles on SBM were appearing frequently in both scholarly and practitioner journals. Most of the authors were connected with CPRE, one of whose members is Harvard. Ogawa (1994) concluded that there is "an unofficial policy environment, one in which entrepreneurs shape and advance policy initiatives" (p. 545). This "unofficial policy environment" is, of course, what this book calls the EPPRC.

ELEMENTS OF SKILLFUL ISSUE DEFINITION.   Several factors influence which policy definitions succeed in moving onto an agenda, but the skill with which the issue has been defined is probably the most important. In the next sections, the elements of good issue definition are described. Throughout this discussion, most of the examples are based on school choice.

Claims.   Claims must be made about a problem in order to transform it into a policy issue. A *claim* is an assertion that grows out of a broader interpretation of the problem, its nature, and its causes. At least one of the claims made about a problem should indicate what has caused it (Best, 1989a, 1989b). For example, the fifth issue in Figure 7.2, "If schools had to compete with each other for students, they would use their resources more wisely," implies two claims: (1) schools do not use their resources as efficiently as they might, and (2) a lack of competition among schools causes their inefficiency.

Evidence.   Descriptive material should be presented as evidence to support at least some of the most important claims made about a problem. The best forms of evidence are dramatic anecdotes, atrocity stories, and statistics—especially big statistics drawn from official sources (Baumann, 1989; Best, 1989c). For example, claims about the outrageous wastefulness of schools could be supported with a vivid description of the Mercedes Benz a school district allegedly provides for its superintendent and with numbers drawn from a major government report on the small percentage of school funds that actually reaches the classroom.

Solution.   A good issue definition includes a realistic solution for the problem it identifies and describes. A realistic solution is both politically feasible and financially affordable (Young, Shepley, Miskel, & Song, 2010). Various forms of school choice have been suggested as ways to introduce more competition into education and encourage greater student achievement and more careful use of funds. Given the current prevalence of conservative ideas and the public's resistance to tax increases, the school-choice solution has broad appeal.

Discourse.   A good issue definition is expressed in powerful language that links the issue to deeply held values, hopes, fears, and aspirations. Emotional words and expressions, including assertions that the issue has a bearing on key national priorities such as military security and economic growth, can further strengthen a definition. So can the use of metaphors to describe the problem, especially metaphors drawn from medicine, family, warfare, or athletics (Brown & Wright, 2011; Cobb & Elder, 1972). Among the reasons for the appeal of school choice to many people is the fact that it lends itself to athletic metaphors of competition and can easily be linked to the American values of freedom and individualism.

Broad Appeal.   A skillfully defined issue is potentially appealing to a wide audience. Issues have broad appeal when they are relatively vague rather than narrowly specific, important to a high percentage of citizens, significant for the future as well as the present, and defined in laymen's terms rather than in technical jargon (Baumann, 1989; Cobb & Elder, 1972). In relation to these requirements, the school-choice issue does not fare as well as it does in relationship to the other criteria. It is a specific issue, primarily important to the parents of school children, a demographic group that has been declining in relative size for several decades. Such terms and phrases as *voucher, interdistrict open enrollment,* and *charter school* have a technical ring to them. This is probably part of the explanation for the relatively slow progress of the school-choice movement since the late 1950s.

CONSTRAINTS ON ISSUE DEFINITION.   Although any problem can provide the basis for defining numerous policy issues, some definitions are more likely than others. Ideas, values, and ideologies are extraordinarily important in issue definition; they shape and restrict the interpretations that people are able or willing to give problems, as well as the solutions they are willing to offer (Liu et al., 2010). Interpretations and solutions that are immediately obvious to people in one society do not even occur to people in another, and vice versa. In the United States, for example, major government intervention in what is considered the private sphere—businesses, churches, families, voluntary organizations, and the like—are rarely considered. In Figure 7.2, the third policy issue ("Parents with school-age children should be legally prohibited from moving outside their school attendance zone during the school year") and the fourth issue ("Only educational and motivational media should be available to children younger than 18") are unthinkable issue definitions in the contemporary United States and in most other democratic countries. They imply a level of government control over private life that most citizens of those countries would find intolerable. Yet, in many totalitarian states today and during certain historical periods in the United States and Western Europe, such issue definitions would be possible.

Another constraint on issue definition in the United States is constitutionality. A large body of case law developed by federal and state courts over more than two centuries has caused some policy areas to resemble unpredictable minefields. As a result, many people hesitate to define issues in certain ways because they fear that policies growing out of such definitions will be ruled unconstitutional. Issue areas of this sort in education include religious activity in schools, race, gender, and censorship.

Finally, issue definition is often constrained by the cyclical movement of popular values and policy mechanisms. In the 1930s, the most popular approach to solving a policy problem was to establish a large government bureaucracy to deal with it by developing regulations. Since the 1980s, issue definitions that offer more bureaucracy or government regulation as a solution have usually been dismissed out of hand. This fact discouraged many people from proposing a wide range of conceivable, but unpopular, issue definitions. Instead, they were likely to propose definitions that interpreted problems as the result of excessive bureaucracy and to suggest solutions such as deregulation, privatization, or market incentives.

PRO–CON DEBATE: IS THERE REALLY AN EDUCATION CRISIS?

YES: No one who is willing to look at the evidence can deny that there is an education crisis in the United States. Since standards were lowered in the "Silly Sixties," student performance on tests such as the SAT and the ACT has plummeted. In almost every international comparison, U.S. students make a poor showing; it is a cause for rejoicing in the education establishment if they rank average rather than dead last. Our schools are not even safe anymore; both children and teachers fear for their lives as gang members roam the halls looking for someone to bully or rob. Many schools even have metal detectors at the entrances these days to check students for weapons as they enter. Finally, school buildings are in a shocking state—they are filthy, with graffiti scrawled everywhere, and basic equipment in disrepair. How can children learn well in such settings? All these problems seriously hamper the ability of the United States to compete effectively in today's global economy.

NO: There is a crisis in the United States today, but it's not an education crisis—it's an economic crisis. Real wages have stagnated for a quarter of a century now; middle-class families have a hard time buying a house and providing college educations for their children; the gap between the rich and the poor is constantly growing. The United States now has a higher rate of child poverty than any other developed country. Often these indicators are hard to see, but we can see more obvious ones. Decades of insufficient tax revenues have led to deferred maintenance, causing our inner cities to decline, becoming shabby crime centers in which few people would willingly live, work, or shop. And much of our once-prized interstate highway system is now pocked with potholes, again because of inadequate public funds for their repair. Of course, all these problems spill over into the schools, which simply reflect the larger society. Government and business leaders prattle about an education crisis, hoping we will not notice the real economic crisis . . . for which *they*, not educators, are responsible. Fix the economy and the schools will improve.

• *What do YOU think?*

THE POLICY AGENDA

No matter how brilliantly an issue has been defined within the EPPRC and no matter how much research university professors can produce in support of a policy change, it may go nowhere, remaining the topic of heated debate in the ivory tower, but never attracting the interest of a politician. In order to have a chance to become an actual policy, an issue must reach the policy agenda, and this occurs neither automatically nor easily. In this section, policy **agenda** is defined and different types of policy agendas are described. Problems involved in getting on the agenda (and staying there) are discussed before this section concludes with some discussion of nondecisions.

Defining Policy Agenda

A *policy agenda* is composed of all those issues under serious discussion in relation to a specific policy domain. In the broadest sense, the education policy agenda includes all issues under discussion at professional conferences, in education journals, among well-informed educators, in the mass media, among the general public, and among government officials (Kingdon, 2003). However, political scientists distinguish several types of policy agendas. Often, an issue appears on one or two agendas, but not all. If an issue is ever to become official policy, it must eventually reach the *governmental policy agenda*.

Types of Policy Agendas

THE SYSTEMIC AGENDA.   The *systemic policy agenda* is broad, consisting of all the issues people outside government are currently discussing. In order to determine the composition of the systemic agenda in education, a school leader might skim the tables of contents of several education journals, glance through some recent issues of *Education Week,* and add to them any education problems that the mass media are currently highlighting.

Within education's systemic agenda, three subagendas can be distinguished. The *professional agenda* consists of those issues under discussion within various interest groups, education policy networks, and education associations as well as among informed professional educators. School leaders frequently encounter these issues when they attend conferences or read current literature in their field. The *media agenda,* in contrast, consists of those education issues that editors and other decision makers in the communications industry have decided to emphasize (Graber, 2010). As most school leaders know, this agenda often bears little resemblance to the professional one. The mass media are businesses that must attract customers in order to survive; therefore, they focus on exciting issues, such as school violence and sex crimes among teachers. Finally, the third subagenda is the *public agenda,* which includes those education issues to which the general public is actually paying attention (Graber, 2010). This agenda is normally shorter than the other two, and may or may not overlap with them. Usually, although not always, the public agenda is greatly influenced by the media agenda. Together, the professional, media, and public agendas make up the systemic agenda.

THE GOVERNMENTAL AGENDA.   The *governmental agenda* consists of "the list of subjects or problems to which governmental officials . . . are paying some serious attention at any given time" (Kingdon, 2003, p. 3). An issue on this agenda is being discussed seriously by government officials or has been scheduled for official action. Obviously, many governmental policy agendas exist in education. The federal government has an agenda, as does each of the fifty states. Moreover, each of these agendas consists of several components, such as bills slated for introduction or legislative action, court cases on the docket or working their way through the system, and decisions pending in regulatory agencies.

How Agendas Relate to Each Other

The most important fact to understand about policy agendas is that access to them is highly competitive. As a result, most issues that have been defined never reach the government, public, or media agenda at all. The reason is simple: the "carrying capacity" of each agenda is severely limited as Hilgartner and Bosk (1988) noted in their classic article on the subject. Members of the general public do not have enough time to inform themselves about every issue, much less discuss them all. Newspapers and Web sites have limited space for text, and television and radio have even more limited broadcasting time for education news. Above all, legislatures, courts, and administrative agencies have tightly limited resources and cannot introduce every conceivable bill, hear every conceivable case, or make a decision on every controversial point. Thus, the relationship among the items on the agenda is competitive; if a new item moves onto an agenda, an older one usually moves off. As items move from one agenda to another, a selection process occurs. Some issues remain on the systemic agenda for a long time and attract considerable attention, eventually winning this competition and reaching a governmental agenda. Most, however, are discussed for a short while and then vanish, losing the competition.

Figure 7.8 represents the policy agendas in schematic form and uses arrows to depict the most common patterns of movement.

Typically, far more education policy issues are on the professional agenda than the other agendas can accommodate. Some issues, however, do move from the professional agenda to the media agenda and spread from there to the general public. Policymakers, who are usually aware of all three systemic subagendas, select from them a few issues they wish to actively support. Other patterns of movement are possible,

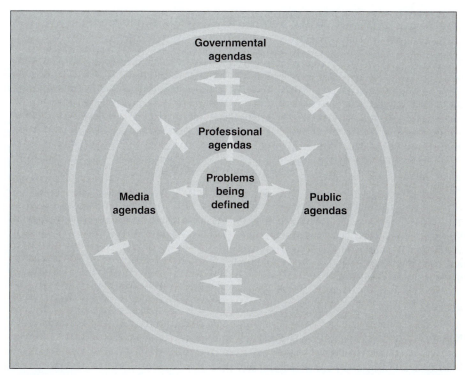

FIGURE 7.8   Policy agendas in relation to each other

however. For example, in the late 1970s, the public in several states became incensed about escalating school taxes, and organized to put tax limitation initiatives on the ballot. This "tax revolt" is an excellent example of a situation in which an issue was both defined and placed on the policy agenda by the general public. In most cases, however, education policy issues follow the path of development suggested in Figure 7.2.

NEWS STORY FOR ANALYSIS

Make Way for Merit Pay!

MADISON, WI—Milwaukee's struggling school district got some good news last week: It will receive $10 million from the federal Teacher Incentive Fund to develop a merit pay system at 16 schools. Paying teachers for performance rather than simply for years of experience and level of education is gaining support across the nation, thanks in large part to pressure from the Obama Administration. The pilot program in Milwaukee seeks to reward teachers and principals for higher student performance. Teachers also could earn more money for taking on difficult assignments and responsibilities, and for teaching in hard-to-staff subjects. The $10 million was part of $442 million for 62 school districts and nonprofits in 27 states to create merit pay programs.

Deborah Kenny, CEO of the successful and innovative Harlem Village Academies charter schools in one of the poorest parts of New York City, summed up the need for change in a *Wall Street Journal* guest

(Continued)

Make Way for Merit Pay! (*Continued*)

column last week: "We need to stop treating teachers like industrial-era workers and start treating them like professionals," she wrote. Kenny lets her teachers choose their own textbooks and design their own courses. But they are then held accountable for how their students perform. So far, the results are promising, with test scores among the best in the nation for math, science and social studies.

Many teachers mistakenly fear that test scores will be the sole determinant of merit. Under most systems being proposed, gains in test scores would be one of several factors. A teacher might get a bonus, for example, for taking on a leadership role in mentoring beginning teachers. In Washington, D. C., the most effective teachers are now eligible to earn almost twice what they used to make, thanks to merit pay.

Private benefactors also are encouraging the trend. Facebook CEO Mark Zuckerberg last week was reportedly donating $100 million to Newark, N.J., schools to support merit pay and expand charter schools. The Bill and Melinda Gates Foundation last year pledged $290 million to pilot programs in four cities that seek to reward the best teachers with more compensation, based on classroom results.

Critics of merit pay are right about one thing: It's not a magic solution to all of the many challenges facing public schools, including broken families, uninvolved parents, unmotivated students, and financial stress. A Vanderbilt study, for example, concluded last week that merit pay offered to middle school math teachers in Nashville didn't lead to higher test scores over three years. But the study's author agreed more research is needed. The study didn't look at whether merit pay will help retain the highest performing teachers. Nor did it explore the likely result of merit pay boosting interest in the teaching profession among young, talented, college students, or its ability to help districts fill high-demand positions. The study did suggest that merit pay does not disrupt the school culture, and teachers in the study thought the goals were attainable.

Virtually every other professional job ties pay to performance. The incredibly important job of teaching should, too, for the sake of all those children in Milwaukee and elsewhere struggling to succeed.

(Adapted by permission of the publisher from editorial "Make Way for Merit Pay: Momentum Is Building for a Performance-based Compensation System that Treats Wisconsin School Teachers Like the Professionals They Are," from the *Wisconsin State Journal*, 26 September 2010. Editorial from the Wisconsin State Journal.)

QUESTIONS

1. List all the members of the education policy planning and research community mentioned in this article.
2. Where on the diagram shown in Figure 7.8 would you place merit pay for teachers? Why?
3. What problem(s) has the teacher merit pay policy issue been designed to address? What other policy issues might be defined to address one or more of these problems?
4. Why is the word *professional* used several times in the article? ■

Getting on the Governmental Policy Agenda

THE STORY OF SCHOOL CHOICE.   Usually, a new idea languishes on the shelf for a long time before it reaches a governmental policy agenda, is acted on, and becomes official policy. School choice is a good example. First seriously proposed in 1962 by Milton Friedman, a professor at the University of Chicago, it was considered an odd professorial type of idea throughout the 1960s. By the early 1970s, however, a few radicals and liberals had become interested in it, even though Friedman was a well-known conservative. Because it was an item on the professional agenda, people such as Christopher Jencks and James Coleman picked up the idea and advocated it as a way to empower poor parents and equalize educational opportunity for their children. In the early 1970s, school choice moved briefly onto a governmental agenda when the federal government funded a choice experiment in Alum Rock, California. This pilot program was generally considered a failure, and choice dropped off the governmental agenda, but remained on the professional agenda. In 1980, conservative Ronald Reagan was elected president. Propelled by the professional agendas of many of the conservative groups that had supported him, he moved choice onto the governmental agenda again by advocating tuition tax credits and vouchers in his speeches. Soon both forms of choice were introduced as bills in Congress . . . and introduced, and introduced, always going down to defeat. By the late 1980s, however, states such as Minnesota and Ohio had not only moved choice onto their governmental policy agendas but also adopted some forms of it as policy. Since then, several states and the District of Columbia have enacted public voucher programs, whereas virtually all of the other states and the District of Columbia have adopted charter school policies. Thus, after languishing on various agendas for thirty years, school choice rapidly moved onto governmental agendas and into official policy during the last decade of the twentieth century (Morken & Formicola, 1999).

PUBLIC OFFICIALS AND AGENDAS.   The story of the movement of school choice from a newly defined policy issue to the professional agenda to various governmental agendas illustrates how many issues finally reach the governmental agenda. Major political leaders—especially the president and governors, but also prominent legislators—often play a central role in agenda setting (Anderson, 2003). Because they frequently give speeches and hold press conferences, they can call attention to an issue and keep attention focused on it. Moreover, because their public appearances are, by definition, media events, they can easily move an issue onto the media agenda. The school-choice issue stayed on the governmental agenda in part because in the spring of 1983, a presidential commission issued *A Nation at Risk,* an official report claiming that education was in a state of crisis. Although this report did not advocate school choice, it gave credibility to the claim that a crisis in education existed. One of the best ways to draw attention to an issue is to associate it with a real or perceived crisis. Therefore, school choice became a favorite item on all the policy agendas because many people saw it as a cheap, but effective, way to deal with that crisis.

OTHER PATHS TO THE AGENDA.   Issues can reach the governmental policy agenda in other ways. Sometimes a *triggering event* occurs, clarifying or dramatizing an issue that has hitherto attracted little attention (Baumgartner & Jones, 2009; Young et al., 2010). Triggering events are especially likely to propel issues related to health and safety onto center stage. In many states, for example, policymakers, school leaders, and education groups know that many school buildings are rundown and need repairs to bring them up to current health and safety codes. This issue has been on their systemic agenda for years. Yet, nothing happens. The reason is clear: Renovating buildings costs money and might necessitate a tax increase, so many politicians would rather think about something else. However, if the roof of a school building collapses and injures fifty children, this catastrophe may act as a triggering event, attracting media attention, causing a public outcry, and almost forcing the state legislature to act. Or again, it may not; if the story about the collapsed roof has to compete with a major national news story for media attention, it may be buried in the back pages of the papers and in brief reports on the 11:00 P.M. news. Especially if education leaders are not ready to act swiftly as soon as a triggering event occurs, the issue may evaporate within a few days and things may continue as before.

Other forces can also put an issue on the systemic or governmental agenda. Interest groups often play a major role, providing information about their issues to key policymakers and mobilizing sustained pressure to draw attention to an issue through letter-writing and lobbying campaigns. Or they may use the same tactics to keep an issue off the agenda (Kingdon, 2003). Policy networks, such as the ECS, the Institute for Educational Leadership, and the Business Roundtable, also play a role. They usually focus on a few education policy issues of major importance to them; then, through their publications, programs, and conferences, they repeatedly reinforce these key issues. This practice tends to narrow the systemic agenda, but it also increases the likelihood that their favorite issues will eventually reach the governmental agenda. Issues sometimes reach the governmental agenda because bureaucrats in state agencies—who have good access to policymakers—point out problems to them (Young et al., 2010). Finally, many policy actors stage events to attract media attention to an issue, hoping to move it onto the media agenda and from there to a governmental agenda. For example, a group of parents of special needs children might converge on the state capital to demonstrate for increased funding for special education.

THE PROBLEM OF THE DISEMPOWERED.   To this point, all the ways discussed to get items on the agenda involve exercising considerable power. Students of the agenda-setting process have long recognized that some people and groups have more influence on the agenda than others. In their seminal study of agenda setting, Cobb and Elder (1972) demonstrated that, where agenda setting is involved, all citizens are definitely not equal: the powerful have more influence on policy agendas than do the disempowered. They argued, however, that disempowered groups sometimes use violence or the threat of violence to draw attention to their issues. For example, students have been known to hold protest marches and sit-ins or even stage food riots to make their concerns known. African Americans used similar strategies in the 1960s to demonstrate their dissatisfaction with the pace of school desegregation. Even so, such demonstrations of power require a level of planning and support that makes them unrealistic tactics except in extreme situations. For the most part, powerless groups have little impact on agenda setting.

Staying on a Policy Agenda

Although gaining access to any of the policy agendas is difficult, dropping off them is extremely easy. Indeed, all policy agendas are marked by great instability; issues that were hot in January may be forgotten by June. Once an issue has faded, reviving interest in it is difficult, because it now seems out of date. Among political scientists this phenomenon is known as the *issue–attention cycle*; in every policy area issues suddenly become the center of enormous attention on several agendas . . . and then, as suddenly, "lurch" out of everyone's thoughts (Baumgartner & Jones, 2009). In part, this instability results from the tendency of the mass media to prefer new ideas to old. In part, too, it results from the tendency of the general public to prefer novelty. However, after several years off the agenda, old ideas may resurface in a slightly different form and with a new name and reach the agenda again. Anyone who has been in education for more than a decade is aware of how cyclical education policy is.

The vagaries of the issue–attention cycle mean that advocates of particular policy changes must work hard to keep their ideas on the agenda once they get there. Informal clusters of advocates develop around some issues, providing ongoing support for a new policy idea (Hilgartner & Bosk, 1988). The "policy entrepreneurs" associated with such communities churn out fresh material on the issue, develop new approaches to it, and may even develop new terminology in the attempt to keep the issue ever new and attractive. Communities of operatives developed around education issues such as school choice, inclusion (which, in a slightly different form, used to be called *mainstreaming*), and national standards. Such ongoing support keeps an item on the agenda for long periods of time, enhancing the likelihood that it will eventually lead to official policy.

Nondecisions

As noted earlier, the *failure to act* on certain problems is a dimension of policy just as surely as an official action is. The technical term for such failures is *nondecisions.* Most nondecisions occur, not in the legislatures, courts, or executive offices, but rather during the problem-definition and agenda-setting stages of the policy process. Often, being able to identify just exactly where nondecisions occurred is important, because they provide important clues to how official policies and official policy rhetoric should be interpreted.

In many states, school finance equalization is an enduring nondecision that has occurred between the systemic and governmental policy agendas. About twenty years ago, in his yearlong study of state politics in Kansas, Burdett Loomis (1994) learned that the related issues of equalizing school funding and reforming the property tax were important items on the systemic agenda. In fact, for many years Kansas educators and various state interest groups had discussed these issues and pressured the governor and the legislature to change the taxation and school finance systems. Almost everyone in Kansas politics considered them outdated and unjust. Yet, year after year, nothing happened. Governmental policy actors simply refused to move property tax and school finance reform onto their agendas because they knew that dealing with these issues in a serious manner would be controversial. They also recognized that any meaningful solution would cost money. Kansas is not the only state in which school finance reform has been a nondecision. In fact, this is why in several states, education leaders and parents finally formed organizations to challenge school funding systems in the courts. School finance reform is still a nondecision in many places, suggesting how unwilling contemporary lawmakers are to increase taxes or redistribute them.

SCHOOL LEADERS AND THE EARLY STAGES OF THE POLICY PROCESS

Following the Early Stages

By definition, the first stage of the policy process is never covered by the mass media. Also by definition, many aspects of agenda setting are not covered either, which makes following issue definition and agenda setting challenging for school leaders. It is not impossible, but it does require using specialized sources. Three of these are especially important.

American School Administrator
American School Boards Journal
Educational Leadership
NASSP Bulletin
The Phi Delta Kappan
Principal

FIGURE 7.9   Some leading journals published by educational associations

Most accessible to education leaders are the journals of professional educational associations. Figure 7.9 lists several of the more important ones. Most of them carry regular reports on research as well as book reviews. Leaders interested in issue definition should scan these regularly, paying special attention to those publications produced by major foundations and think tanks. Articles that present new or unusual ideas are probably based on current issue definition discussions. Those that deal with the current crop of hot ideas are drawn from various agendas. A regular reader of these journal features therefore develops a good sense of what is going on at both stages.

A second valuable resource is *Education Week,* an education newspaper published throughout the year by Editorial Projects in Education in Washington, D.C.; its Web version is called *Education Week on the Web* and includes searchable archives. Although it covers all aspects of the education policy process, its coverage of the first two stages is particularly helpful. For example, *Education Week* usually runs articles about major foundation grants and think-tank reports on education, permitting outsiders to follow the ongoing definition of issues within the EPPRC. These articles often provide information about related Web pages, making it easy to access details on the Internet. Just scanning the headlines of the articles each week suggests which issues are on the professional and governmental agendas. The ECS annual meeting is covered in detail, providing valuable information about which issues government officials are discussing. *Education Week* also publishes summaries of the sessions and workshops at the annual conferences of the major education associations. These summaries make identifying which issues are now on this portion of the professional agenda possible.

Finally, the Internet makes following both issue definition and agenda setting easy. The USDOE, several major think tanks, and all major education associations have Web sites that offer much information. The materials available include position papers, publication lists, reports on meetings and conferences, and speeches by organization leaders. As more Web sites are developed and as existing ones are refined, the EPPRC activities will become increasingly visible to those who wish to track them.

Influencing the Early Stages

INFLUENCING NATIONAL ISSUE DEFINITION.   At the outset, school leaders should recognize that national issue definition is the least accessible stage of the policy process and therefore the most difficult to influence. Significantly, Burke (1990) called the process and the institutions involved in it "para-private." This means that most of the discussions, debates, and meetings within the EPPRC are closed to the general public and thus to almost all education leaders. Even so, there are some ways to influence the process, even at the national level. One of the simplest is to respond to new issue definitions in writing. Publications put out by think tanks, foundations, and universities are easy to identify, and a reference librarian can quickly locate the addresses of these institutions. This means that education leaders who have concerns about a new policy idea and would like to react to it from a practitioner's perspective can do so by writing a letter to one or more of the people actively involved in defining that issue. Because the policy actors within the EPPRC, unlike elected politicians, are not accustomed to receiving letters from constituents, they would certainly notice one that critiqued their ideas. The Internet provides another channel for written responses. The USDOE, think tanks, foundations, and education associations do not usually provide elaborate feedback mechanisms such as chat rooms and bulletin boards with their Web sites. However, they often give email addresses to use to convey questions and comments, so school leaders could use them to convey their opinion of an educational idea the organization advocates.

CHALLENGING NATIONAL DEFINITIONS LOCALLY.   Although influencing issue definition at the national level is difficult for ordinary educators, they should find challenging a nationally defined issue locally easier. Ray and Mickelson (1990) did a case study of a group of local business leaders who sought to reform a southern school district. Thoroughly imbued with the claims of the national business community about the failures of public education, these businesspeople established a task force to study ways to make the district more "competitive." Their preferred solution to the school system's alleged failure was to establish a central vocational high school where all students who did not plan to go to college could "be socialized as productive workers" (p. 127). However, as the task force continued to meet, school leaders presented more and more counterevidence to undermine the business community's claims. For example, they invited experts to address the group about successful local school programs and also about the social conditions that caused many children to fail. At one important meeting, a central office administrator presented evidence that many local business people were actually satisfied with the schools, and then shifted to the theme of "the widening gap between 'the haves and have-nots'" (p. 129). In short, school leaders repeatedly grabbed the issue away from the business leaders and redefined it. As Ray and Mickelson summarize their behavior:

> Throughout the final stages of the Task Force deliberations business leaders kept inserting remarks about the need for centralized vocational education. The ranking school district official, however, forcefully finessed each attempt by first reiterating the social and curricular drawbacks of centralized vocational education, and by consistently repeating the shortcomings of a particular population of students. The numbers of low income youngsters were expanding, he insisted, "it's going to get worse!" (p. 130)

Ultimately, the education leaders' redefinition of the issue prevailed. The final report of the task force said much about poverty and recommended more early childhood education programs rather than a centralized vocational high school. School leaders throughout the country should remember that the fact that an issue has been defined at the national level does not mean that it is final or beyond question. This case study suggests that those who understand issue definition and can use discourse skillfully can often reshape an issue when it surfaces locally.

INFLUENCING AGENDA SETTING: BASIC PREREQUISITES.   Because agenda setting occurs in more visible and more accessible arenas than issue definition does, it is easier to influence. Usually, affecting agenda setting involves either (1) getting an issue moved from the systemic agenda to the governmental one, or (2) keeping an issue on the systemic agenda off the governmental one. Effectiveness at this stage of the policy process requires developing one's power sufficiently to be able to exercise impact.

Three power resources are especially important. The first is knowledge. Education leaders who wish to affect agenda setting must systematically work to be well-informed about new trends in education policy at the state and national levels. This means keeping up with professional reading and attending professional conferences. Only by following the unfolding issues in these forums can one gather enough information to know which policy issues are most likely to reach a governmental agenda in the near future. The second essential power resource is allies. No principal, district office administrator, or superintendent should even consider working alone on such efforts. Effective action requires having allies in four arenas: in professional associations, at the SDE, among government officials, and among colleagues in school leadership. Such networks do not just happen; they must be developed over time and in a systematic and reflective way. Part of Chapter 8 discusses how to develop relationships with various policy actors. Most of the recommendations made there are also relevant for influencing agenda setting. Finally, one must build enough organizational effectiveness to be able to respond quickly to events in agenda-setting arenas. Kingdon (2003) argues that windows of opportunity for moving an issue onto the governmental agenda open suddenly; they close quickly, too. This means that anyone who wants to influence this stage of the policy process must be prepared to act and to act fast.

ATTRACTING ATTENTION TO AN ISSUE.   Drawing the attention of the media, the general public, and policymakers to a policy issue is the most important method of influencing agenda setting (Hilgartner & Bosk, 1988; Kingdon, 2003). This method can be used at both the national and state levels. It can also work effectively at the district level when a superintendent wants to motivate a school board to take needed steps to solve a problem. Many techniques can be used to attract attention; Figure 7.10 lists several. Except for the most urgent situations, education leaders should avoid demonstrations and rallies and select one of the less dramatic techniques. An essential dimension of attracting attention today is obtaining media coverage; therefore, all special events designed to capture attention for an issue should be planned to include a public relations component from the start. Leaders should make sure the media receive notice of the event and accurate information about the issue. They should also plan ways to facilitate media attendance and provide opportunities for reporters to interview visiting experts, panelists, and guest speakers. A sequence of carefully planned activities may be needed to focus attention on an issue and persuade key players to give it serious consideration.

- Invite an expert to give a talk about it.
- Sponsor a workshop on it.
- Hold a mini-conference on it.
- Put out a press release explaining how the issue affects local schools.
- Ask the PTA or teachers' union to discuss it at a meeting.
- Present a multimedia program about it to civic organizations.
- Put it on the agenda for a faculty retreat.
- Send an article about it to legislators.

FIGURE 7.10 Ways to attract attention to a policy issue

REDUCING ATTENTION TO AN ISSUE. Sometimes leaders do not want to attract attention to an issue. Instead, they wish to reduce the amount of attention it is already receiving in order to keep it from reaching a governmental policy agenda. The most effective way to achieve this goal is to persuade policymakers that solving the policy issue or adopting the solutions advocated by proponents would be prohibitively expensive. The first step required in using this approach is a careful and realistic cost analysis. (Chapter 9 includes a method for determining the total cost of a policy.) Then, some of the methods listed in Figure 7.10 can be used to draw attention to the potential costs. Other, similar strategies should also be considered. A realistic estimate of the extent to which the policy would expand government bureaucracy might be carried out, or a lawyer could be asked to specify those aspects of the policy idea that might open the door for litigation. Key segments of the electorate most likely to oppose the policy idea (and vote against policymakers who support it) could be identified. These negative analyses must be *realistic;* unsubstantiated and exaggerated claims look like scare tactics and may backfire. Of course, appropriate publicity for these analyses must be included as a key element of this strategy.

FINAL POINTS

Issue definition and agenda setting are the least visible stages of the policy process. Moreover, they are the stages that scholars in political science and the politics of education have studied least. As a result, these are the stages that educational leaders will find it most difficult to influence . . . or even to track. Even so, a leader who keeps informed and develops an extensive network of contacts in his or her state may at times find opportunities to impact even issue definition or agenda setting.

QUESTIONS AND ACTIVITIES FOR DISCUSSION

1. Do some research to determine how the problem of high school dropouts has been defined. Identify the claims made about this problem and the evidence used in support of the claims. Then suggest how this problem definition might be challenged.

2. Select a current education problem definition. Identify the claims made about it and the evidence used to support them. Then suggest how the issue could be redefined.
3. Identify a nondecision in your district or state. In your opinion, why has it remained a nondecision? What does this nondecision reveal about the constraints on education policymaking in your environment?
4. By skimming recent issues of publications put out by business and education groups, develop a list of the education issues on the professional policy agenda. Then, by skimming several recent local newspapers, develop a list of the education policy issues on the media agenda. Compare the two agendas. What differences do you notice? How do you explain them?

INTERNET ASSIGNMENT

Locate the Web sites of five organizations listed in Figures 7.5 and 7.6. Analyze them to determine the ideological orientation of each, and be prepared to discuss them in class.

FOR FURTHER READING

Berliner, D. C., & Biddle, B. J. (1995). *The manufactured crisis*. Reading, MA: Addison-Wesley.
    In this well-documented book, the authors argue that the education crisis of the 1980s and 1990s was fabricated for political reasons. After challenging the evidence for the education crisis, they offer a redefinition of the education problems in the United States.
Dye, T. R. (2002). *Who's running America? The Bush restoration*. 7th ed. Upper Saddle River, NJ: Prentice Hall.
    Dye presents a detailed picture of the leading individuals and institutions in U.S. society early in the twenty-first century. Although the entire book is relevant to issue definition and agenda setting, chapters 4 and 9 are especially pertinent.
Feulner, E. J. (2000). The Heritage Foundation. In J. G. McGann & R. K. Weaver (Eds.), *Think tanks & civil societies*. New Brunswick, NJ: Transaction Publishers.
    In this book chapter, the president of the Heritage Foundation discusses the history, funding, and work of his conservative think tank. He also explains how his organization's marketing of its publications influences think tanks generally.
Liu, X., Lindquist, E., Vedlitz, A., & Vincent, K. (2010). Understanding local policymaking: Policy elites' perceptions of local agenda setting and alternative policy selection. *Policy Studies Journal 38*, 69-90.
    Although agenda setting has been extensively studied at the national level, little research has been done at the local level; these authors seek to begin to close that gap. They found that local government officials and interest groups had a great deal of influence while local media had little. Local agenda setting is, however, greatly constrained by budgetary limitations.
Young, T. V., Shepley, T. V., Miskel, C., & Song, M. (2010). Understanding agenda setting in state educational policy. *Education Policy Analysis Archives 18* (15). Available at epaa.asu .edu/ojs/article/view/771.
    Comparing the rise of reading policy to the public agenda in California, Michigan, and Texas, the authors found that public feedback, student test scores, and a belief that schools were failing all played an important role. So did activist governors. They offer advice to educators who wish to influence state agenda setting.

8

GETTING THE WORDS AND THE MONEY: POLICY FORMULATION AND POLICY ADOPTION

Focus Questions

▍ In what government arenas are policies expressed in words and adopted?

▍ Why are some policies mandated but not funded?

▍ How can school leaders influence policy formulation and adoption?

THE HIGH-VISIBILITY STAGES OF THE POLICY PROCESS

Although the first two stages of the policy process occur so quietly that they are almost invisible to the general public, the third and fourth stages—formulation and adoption—occur in more visible arenas. Indeed, when most people hear the word *politics,* this is one of the two political processes that they think of. The other, of course, is elections. Policy formulation and adoption constitute the heart of most government and political science courses and attract ongoing attention from the media. They are the parts of the policy process about which school leaders feel best informed and that they are most likely to seek to influence. However, even familiar territory can conceal unexpected surprises.

During policy formulation and adoption, three major processes occur. First, and in many ways most important, the policy is expressed in written language, taking the form of a statute, an administrative rule, or a court decision. This process is never easy, because words have a range of meanings and can be interpreted in several ways. People who formulate policy language are acutely aware of the fact that such details as the choice of *may* rather than *must* or the definition of *day* affect a law's range of possible interpretations. It also affects the level of support available for the policy in the legislature and its chances of being adopted at all. During both policy formulation and policy adoption, mighty battles are often fought over word choice, the inclusion of a phrase, and punctuation marks. Although these battles may appear trivial to the un-initiated, they are not; major policy issues can hang on a preposition or a semicolon.

When a legislature formulates a policy, wording is not the only issue at stake; because legislatures control the government's purse strings, funding is equally important. Neither the U.S. Congress nor the fifty state legislatures are required to fund all the policies for which they adopt official wording. Alas, school leaders of today are all too familiar with the unfunded mandate. Legislators often have much to gain by voting for popular legislation—it gives them something to brag about when they make speeches back home. They have little to gain by generously funding such legislation; generous funding implies an eventual tax increase, which is unpopular with voters. As a result, they tend to take the easy way out: adopting policy language, but failing to adopt appropriate funding to support it. This means that in legislatures, policy formulation and adoption are always battles fought on two fronts: words and money.

Finally, a policy as formulated in words must be adopted. In a legislature, this means that a majority of both houses must vote for it and that the executive must sign it. Policy language is often adopted in two arenas other than legislatures: administrative agencies and courts. Administrative agencies write **rules** that guide the implementation of statutes; agencies write operating procedures indicating which panels, committees, or officials must approve their rules. In the courts, the majority of a group of judges sitting in a given court must approve a particular written decision. Sometimes a judicial decision must move through a series of courts, being scrutinized by several panels of judges in succession as an appeals process plays out before the final wording of the decision is determined.

In this chapter, the policy formulation and adoption processes in three arenas—legislatures, administrative agencies, and courts—are presented in detail. After the process in each arena is described, ways that school leaders can follow and influence the process are discussed.

POLICY FORMULATION AND ADOPTION IN LEGISLATURES

A Conservative Process

In a videotape developed to teach school leaders how to influence state legislatures, former Ohio State Representative Mike Fox begins by emphasizing that the legislative process was designed to be conservative. By *conservative,* he does not mean that it is ideologically conservative, but that it was deliberately constructed to make passing laws difficult. Because the Founding Fathers feared governments that could change policies speedily, they created a slow and cumbersome system (Ohio State University [OSU], 1991). Both the U.S. Congress and the fifty state legislatures still use the complex process developed in the eighteenth century; in all of them, a bill must cross numerous barriers to be enacted into law. Lorch (1987) counted eighteen such barriers, or *battles,* as he called them, in the Colorado legislature, observing, "It is jungle warfare" (p. 240). The Colorado legislature is typical, not unique. As a result of this complicated system, the large majority of bills introduced in legislatures in the United States never become laws at all. For example, in the 109th Congress (in session from 2005 to 2007) 10,703 bills and resolutions were introduced, but only 417 (4%) were eventually enacted into law (Oleszek, 2007).

In the following discussion, procedures common to most of the fifty-one U.S. legislatures are emphasized; the federal and state levels are combined to avoid repetitiveness. On occasion, however, distinctive features of one of the levels or of some state legislatures are pointed out.

Legislative Proposals and Where They Come From

The policy ideas developed and discussed in the first two stages of the policy process usually become *legislative proposals* before they become bills, then statutes, and finally official policy. A legislative proposal is a serious recommendation for a policy change in the current or next legislative session; it can be considered the first step in policy formulation. Usually in written form, it might appear in a governor's memo to her staff, in an interest group's current legislative program, or on a U.S. senator's list of new laws to sponsor in this session of Congress. Not yet a formal bill, it has nonetheless moved well beyond the systemic policy agenda and is on the verge of being drafted into legal language. Such proposals can come to a legislature from several sources. Obviously, legislators are frequently the originators of legislative proposals that may fulfill a campaign promise, meet constituents' needs, or further a cherished policy goal (Anderson, 2003; Rosenthal, 2009).

However, assuming that only legislators develop proposals is a mistake. One of the most common sources of proposals is the chief executive—the president at the federal level and the governor at the state level. Chief executives and their staffs usually develop several policy proposals for introduction in each session of the legislature. Naturally, legislators are acutely aware of the proposals originating in the White House or governor's mansion; because of their powerful backer, they are likely to give them careful consideration (Hamm & Moncrief, 2008; Rosenthal, 2009). Administrative agencies are another common source of proposals. Most often, they propose new laws to plug loopholes in already-existing laws; their role in policy implementation places them in an excellent position to know what "bugs" exist in the original law and how best to eliminate them. For example, after three years of working under a law establishing statewide proficiency testing in order to comply with the *No Child Left Behind Act*, a state department of education (SDE) may realize that the testing dates should be changed from early March to early April. The SDE may therefore propose such a change in the legislation in order to improve the current law.

Interest groups are a third common source of legislative proposals. Most interest groups have a long list of policy changes they would like to see; when they judge that the time is ripe, they develop them into legislative proposals. Most teachers' unions, for instance, have ideas about how their state's collective-bargaining law could be strengthened and how teacher compensation could be improved. Year after year, they develop corresponding legislative proposals, hoping to advance their long-range goals (Rosenthal, 2009). Among the types of interest groups most likely to initiate education policy proposals are teacher organizations, administrator and school board organizations, and business groups. Increasingly, foundations and think tanks are also active at this stage of the policy process, often operating in national and state legislatures through "policy entrepreneurs" who usually advocate a specific policy change such as merit pay or improved reading curricula (Young et al., 2010).

There is a major difference between legislators who develop proposals and everyone else, however. A legislator can develop a proposal, get it drafted as a bill, and introduce it directly into his or her house of the legislature. Chief executives, administrative agencies, and representatives of interest groups can develop a legislative proposal and get it drafted as a bill, but they cannot introduce it directly into the legislature. They must persuade two legislators—one in each house—to "sponsor" their bill by introducing it and shepherding it through the legislative process. Naturally, they usually have allies in the legislature who work closely with them and often "carry" their bills, as legislators would express it.

In a study of twenty Minnesota education issues that surfaced between 1971 and 1991 and eventually became state law, Mazzoni (1993) identified the originators of the initial policy proposals. Tables 8.1 and 8.2 summarize his findings. As Table 8.1 shows, although proposals were put forth by a single individual or by a single type of policy actor about one third of the time, proposals were usually developed by a coalition

TABLE 8.1 Originators of Twenty Minnesota Education Policy Proposals, 1971–1991

Originator	Percentage of the Twenty Proposals
Legislator(s)	15
Interest group(s)	15
Governor + interest group(s)	15
State department of education	10
Legislator(s) + interest group(s)	10
Governor + legislator(s)	10
Governor	5
Governor + state department of finance	5
Interest group(s) + legislator(s)	5
State department of education + legislator(s)	5
Legislator(s) + state department of education + interest group(s)	5

Source: Based on Mazzoni (1993).

TABLE 8.2 Cumulative Involvement of Various Policy Actors in Policy Proposals in Mazzoni Study

Actor	Percentage of Initiatives in Which Involved
Legislators	50
Governor	35
Interest groups	35
Education	10
Noneducation	45*
State department of education	20

*One noneducation group acted in alliance with an education group regarding one initiative.

of actors. Given the legislative system's bias against change, this practice is smart strategically, guaranteeing that the proposal enters the process with broad support. Table 8.2 summarizes the relative frequency of the involvement of each type of actor. In it, although the central importance of the legislature and its individual members emerges clearly, it is also clear that the governor and interest groups play major roles in initiating proposals. Education leaders may find it sobering that education interest groups were relatively unimportant; even more sobering is that both instances of education interest group influence involved teachers' groups. The noneducation groups were almost all either business groups or policy entrepreneurs representing members of the policy planning and research community; often, they worked in alliance with each other. The SDE, although significantly less involved than the other actors, was more involved than many people might expect. School leaders should never underestimate its potential importance in legislative policy making.

How Bills Are Drafted

The second stage in policy formulation is the transformation of a legislative proposal into a **bill,** or proposed law. Legislative proposals are expressed in the language of laypeople, but bills introduced into a legislature must fit a specific format and be expressed in legal discourse. Writing a bill is a technical process, and few people, even among lawyers and legislators, know how to do it. Therefore, legislatures usually have a legislative drafting office staffed by lawyers who have the special technical skills required for drafting legislation. Legislators submit written versions of their proposals to this office, which edits them into correctly drafted bills. As part of this task, lawyers check the federal or state law code to determine how existing legislation would be affected if the new law were enacted. This used to be a time-consuming process; today, however, the entire law code for the federal government and each state is computerized. Lawyers can search their legal database rapidly, locating all related statutes and identifying the sections that might be affected (Anderson, 2003; Hamm & Moncrief, 2008).

People and organizations who frequently submit legislation usually have their own legislative drafting office or a specialized staff lawyer to transform proposals into bills. The president and most governors have drafting offices; administrative agencies and interest groups typically use the services of a lawyer they employ for this purpose. Groups without a lawyer on staff often submit their proposal to the legislators who have agreed to sponsor it, and they in turn submit it to the legislature's own drafting office.

Bills must conform to a specific format. Figure 8.1 summarizes the fundamental components of a bill. Although many bills are popularly referred to by their number

1. Title
2. Text that enacts the legislation
3. Definitions of key terms
4. Effective date
5. List of portions of existing legal code potentially affected

FIGURE 8.1 Major components of a correctly drafted bill

(e.g., H.B. 70) or by a nickname (e.g., "the Grab 'Em by the Keys Bill"), or by an acronym (e.g., KERA), they all have an official title. For example, the title assigned to the 2002 reauthorization of the *Elementary and Secondary Education Act* was the *No Child Left Behind Act*. Although the text of the legislation is obviously crucial, and is the focus of the "jungle warfare" of the legislative process, definitions and the effective date are also important and may give rise to much debate before a bill is finally formulated and adopted.

How Bills Move Through a Legislature

Most school leaders are familiar with the distinction between the formal and the informal organization. The *formal organization* consists of the official structure and power relationships, including the communication system, rules, and procedures of the organization; the *informal organization* is the actual human culture that has grown up within that structure (Rosenthal, 2009). As most people realize, actual power relationships are not necessarily identical to those depicted in a formal organizational chart; and actual practice does not necessarily conform to the official policy manual. In this respect, U.S. legislatures are no different from other organizations; they have both a formal and an informal face. In this section, the *formal procedures* that must be followed in order for a bill to become a law are described. In the next section, we discuss the *informal political practices* that have arisen around the formal procedures. Understanding both is important. Figure 8.2 depicts the formal procedures followed in a typical American legislature; the procedures followed in Congress and in forty-nine of the state legislatures resemble it, differing in only minor ways. (The exception is the Nebraska legislature, which has only one house.) The procedure described next is a generic procedure; any specific legislature in the United States conforms to its overall outline, but differs from it in unimportant ways.

Every bill must be sponsored by a member of the house of the legislature in which it is to be introduced. This *sponsor* introduces the bill by submitting it to an official, often called a *secretary* or *clerk*, who is responsible for handling new bills. This person assigns it an identifying number, which consists of two parts: (1) letters that indicate the house in which it was introduced, and (2) numerals that indicate its order among the bills introduced during this session. In the U.S. Congress, House bills receive the letters "H.R." and Senate bills, the letter "S." (*Congress A to Z*, 1999). Various lettering systems are used in the states. For example, in Colorado, House bills are labeled "H.B.," whereas Senate bills receive the prefix "S.B." (Colorado General Assembly, 2011). The secretary or clerk also sees that the bill is printed and that copies are distributed to every member of the house.

Next, the bill moves to a committee, often called the *Reference Committee*, that assigns it to an appropriate standing committee for hearings, debate, possible revision, and a decision on whether it should proceed. If the standing committee votes favorably on it—or "reports it out," to use legislative jargon—the bill moves to yet another procedural committee, often called the *Rules Committee*. This committee schedules it for a debate on the floor of the house and a vote of the whole house. During this debate, the bill may be amended (Rosenthal, 2009).

If the whole house passes the bill, one of four things can happen. In the unlikely event that the *companion bill* (a similar bill that has been simultaneously

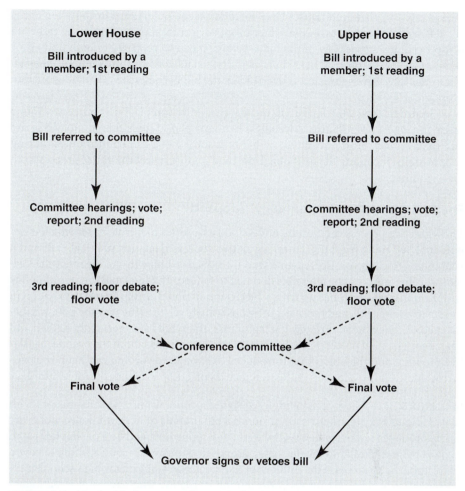

FIGURE 8.2   The legislative process in a typical state legislature

Source: Based on Hamm & Moncrief, 2008, and Squire & Moncrief, 2010.
Solid arrows indicate required action for all bills that become laws; broken arrows indicate action for bills when the two houses disagree.

progressing through the other house) also passed in a form identical to the final form of the bill in this house, then it passes directly to the chief executive—the president or governor. If no companion bill was introduced, then the bill is sent to the other house to go through the same process there. If a companion bill produced in the other house differs from this bill, even by as little as one word or one punctuation mark, then those differences must be resolved. Most often, this is accomplished through informal negotiation. Increasingly, however, both bills go to a *Conference Committee,* which includes equal numbers of members from each house. This committee's task is to resolve the conflicts to produce a single, mutually agreeable version. If the Conference Committee succeeds, the revised bill returns to each house for a final vote (Rosenthal, 2009).

Assuming that both houses have voted to accept an identical formulation of the bill, it is sent to the chief executive who can approve or disapprove—*veto*—it. If the bill is approved, it becomes law. If the bill is vetoed, it can be returned to both houses for an *override* vote—approval by a supermajority, usually of two thirds, in both houses. If the chief executive's decision is overridden, the bill becomes law. Overrides are rare (Rosenthal, 2009).

In order to become law, a bill must successfully complete this process within a single session of a legislature, normally a two-year period. Bills that do not do so are said to have *died*. However, the same bill or a similar one can be introduced during later sessions, including the next one. If so, then it must repeat the entire process from the beginning.

The Politics of Getting a Policy Adopted

The legislative process can best be understood as a series of hurdles over which every potential law must leap; therefore, legislative success demands political skill and a willingness to compromise. Anyone who introduces a bill with the idea that the current wording must not be altered is doomed to failure. The informal process of **policy adoption** involves negotiating with a succession of policy actors in order to get them to vote to adopt a bill, and those negotiations usually relate to the way the policy is formulated. As they move through the legislature, then, bills are repeatedly revised and amended. The final product usually differs considerably from both the original legislative proposal and the bill as first introduced. Although rewording can happen at numerous points, the following discussion focuses on a few particularly crucial hurdles.

SPONSORSHIP.   The person with a legislative proposal must select sponsors with care. Although any legislator can introduce a bill into his or her own house, not every legislator makes a good sponsor. Obviously, the sponsor should be a person known to support policies similar to the one being proposed. A business group wishing to have a bill introduced to increase the number of math courses required for high school graduation will probably look for sponsors among legislators who have supported higher academic standards in the past. Among this group, they will focus their attention on legislators who meet certain criteria. The ideal sponsor is a member of the majority party and of the standing committee to which the bill is most likely to be assigned. He or she has a good working relationship with the members of that committee and also with key officials in the house, such as the speaker or senate president, the majority leader, and the chair of the Appropriations Committee. Such a legislator is well suited to shepherd the bill through the legislative process, making the compromises necessary to obtain favorable votes. Of course, the sponsor may insist on changing the formulation of the proposal somewhat as a condition of sponsoring it; this may be the point at which the first reformulation occurs (Rosenthal, 2009).

REFERENCE COMMITTEE.   After introduction, a bill is always sent to a committee or to a leader of the house, who decides to which standing committee it will be assigned. This is an important decision, because bills undergo their most important revisions in committee; in fact, most die there. This decision is so crucial that legislative policy actors do not leave it to chance; formally or informally, the leadership of the house always decides where a bill is sent. If the leaders strongly oppose a bill, they send it to one of those convenient committees known as "killer" or "death" committees, not to be heard of again. A lesser degree of opposition may be expressed by keeping a bill in Reference Committee for an unusually long time; after all, the later it is sent to a standing committee, the more likely it is to die at the end of a session. Or it may be sent to a standing committee whose composition is such that it is either allowed to die there or is revised extensively before being reported out. Support by the leaders, however, is suggested when a bill emerges rapidly from the Reference Committee and is assigned to a committee whose majority is likely to look favorably on it (Rosenthal, 2009).

STANDING COMMITTEE.   Many possible fates—mostly bad—await the flood of bills that surges onto the agenda of the typical Standing Committee of a U.S. legislature. An unlucky bill may be *laid on the table* (i.e., delayed), amended beyond recognition, indefinitely postponed, or sent to another committee. Bills that have a brighter future are scheduled for hearings. These are meetings, normally open to the public, at which experts on the substantive content of the bill testify before the members of the standing committee, providing them with information and answering their questions. Hearings may be held in or near the capitol building or out in the field, in which case they are called *field hearings*. After the hearings end, the committee usually revises and amends the bill extensively, using information obtained from expert testimony. The thoroughgoing nature of this reformulation is suggested by the nickname given to it in Washington, D.C.: *mark-up,* in reference to the extensive editing marks that now appear on the printed bill. If a majority of the committee votes to approve the marked-up bill, it is reported out, moving on to the next step (Oleszek, 2007).

RULES COMMITTEE.   A novice might imagine that the rest of the process is smooth sailing for any bill that, triumphant over dozens of lesser bills, finally manages to receive a majority vote from a Standing Committee. Not so. Although its prospects of becoming law are far brighter than when it entered the Standing Committee, it must now face another procedural hurdle: either the Rules Committee or an individual officer charged with the functions of a rules committee. The Rules Committee has been called the traffic cop of the legislature because it regulates the flow of legislation to the floor for debate and voting (Oleszek, 2007). In doing so, it decides on a "rule" for each bill, determining its priority among other bills scheduled to go to the floor of the full legislature, how long it can be debated, and the extent to which it can be amended. Supporters of the bill hope—and work—for a high priority ranking, a short debate, and limited possibilities for amendment, whereas opponents lobby for the opposite. Many bills meet their doom in the Rules Committee, either because they are scheduled late on the legislature's docket or because, during a long floor debate, they are amended beyond recognition. Nonetheless, most bills that the Rules Committee sends to the full legislature for a vote are passed. Passage should not be confused with enactment, however (Lowi, Ginsberg, & Shepsle, 2007; Oleszek, 2007).

CONFERENCE COMMITTEE.   The last major hurdle many bills must cross is the Conference Committee. Obviously, even if identical bills were originally introduced in each house of the legislature, by the time they emerge from their respective houses months later, they are no longer the same. Yet, in order to become a law, identical bills must be approved by both houses. Often this task can be accomplished informally, but controversial or major legislation frequently must go to a conference committee whose task is to work out disagreements. In the 108th Congress, 7% of the bills went to Conference Committee (Oleszek, 2007). State legislatures also use conference committees to resolve conflicts, and they have become increasingly important (Rosenthal, 2009).

Composed of members from both houses, the Conference Committee tries to negotiate a version of the bill that is acceptable to both houses. Although full meetings of the Conference Committee are open to the public at the federal level and in many states, in actual practice much of the hard bargaining is done in private. Unfortunately, both in Washington, D.C., and in state capitals, this bargaining process often degenerates into a power struggle between the two houses, with conferees from each determined to make a point with members of the other house (Oleszek, 2007). Many bills die in Conference Committee, not because of substantive differences between the two houses, but because of power politics. No doubt this is why one U.S. senator stated in 1966:

> I have been in this body long enough to beware of the chairman of a committee who says in an enticing voice, "Let me take the amendment to conference," because I think that is frequently the parliamentary equivalent of saying, "Let me take the child into the tower and I will strangle him to death." (R. F. Fenno, Jr., *The Power of the Purse* [Boston: Little, Brown, 1966], p. 610, as cited in Oleszek, 1996, p. 275)

There is no reason to believe that this understanding of the Conference Committee has changed since then. The bill that does pass a conference committee has an excellent chance of becoming law. True, it must return to both houses for a majority vote and go on to the chief executive for approval, but those steps are rarely fatal. The bill that emerges from a conference committee belongs to that select group of bills that jumped all the major hurdles; it is now in the home stretch of an arduous marathon. However, it may not be funded.

Obtaining Funding

Because the wording of a law and its funding are determined by separate legislation in U.S. lawmaking, the battle for any new policy must be fought on two fronts: words and money. For example, in her case study of the reauthorization of the *Dropout Prevention and Reentry Act* in 1989–1990, Martin (1994) recounts the complex legislative struggles required to obtain congressional approval of the extension of the wording of the law for two more years. Yet, even after the reauthorization bill was signed into law on March 6, 1990, she frequently received frantic phone messages from a woman who directed a dropout program at a technical college in Milwaukee. The messages were always the same: "What about the funding?" (p. 78). This educator anxiously reminded Martin—herself a political science professor—that although "it was fine that the program had been reauthorized . . . it meant nothing if appropriations were not forthcoming" (p. 78). The battle for dollars was still to be fought and, as usual, it was a tougher battle than the battle for words. Advocates of a new policy must simultaneously work for the wording they want and fight to see that money will be available for the project. The struggle for dollars occurs during the budget and appropriations process, described next.

THE BUDGET PROCESS.   The government's budget for the next fiscal period is included in one of the most important laws passed during any legislative session. At the most superficial level, a *budget* is a detailed statement of how much revenue the government expects to receive and how it plans to spend that revenue. At a deeper level, it is a statement of the overall policy direction of the government, revealing the policy choices it has made and its true policy priorities. School leaders who want to know what their state's policy toward K–12 education really is should read its laws and its budgets simultaneously to determine if the government is "putting its money where its mouth is." Legislators frequently pass laws but fail to fund them, which is why the advocates of a policy must be vigilant during the budgeting and appropriations processes; if they are not, the law they fought to get adopted may be reduced to empty words. These processes cannot be brushed aside as boring procedures of interest primarily to accountants and tax lawyers; the financial decision making of a legislature is especially important, because many laws are meaningless if they are not funded during the budget process (Rubin, 2006).

The Federal Budget Process.   The federal budget is adopted annually through a process that gives both the president and Congress important roles. Although developing a budget proposal for submission to the legislative branch is the chief executive's responsibility, most of the actual work is carried out by the Office of Management and Budget (OMB), one of the fourteen offices and permanent agencies that make up the Executive Office and to which the chief executive delegates management tasks. As the first step in the process, OMB economists estimate the probable economic climate and federal tax revenues for the next two years. Using these estimates as well as the current budget as their framework, they sketch out a preliminary budget. This tentative budget helps them develop guidelines for budget requests, which they send to all federal agencies and departments. After the departments and agencies send back their budget requests for the next fiscal year—using OMB guidelines to do so—the OMB bargains, negotiates, and argues with agency representatives until everyone agrees on a reasonable amount of money for each agency. Then the OMB, working closely with the president and his staff, develops the final budget proposal (Oleszek, 2007; Rubin, 2006).

Current federal law requires the president to send his budget proposal to Congress on the first Monday in February, known as *Budget Day*. The law also stipulates a series of deadlines for Congress, which Table 8.3 summarizes. The budget proposal goes to several specialized committees in Congress that work on various portions of it. First, it goes to the budget committees of both houses, which develop a concurrent budget resolution establishing the total amount of federal expenditures, the amount of revenue needed, and the projected amount of federal debt or surplus for the coming fiscal year. After this resolution is adopted by both houses, the House Ways and Means Committee and the Senate Finance Committee begin to work on the revenue side of the budget, while the appropriations committees in both houses focus on the expenditure side. Ultimately, of course, everyone must agree and all the numbers must add up. The complex procedure used to reach these objectives

TABLE 8.3 Important Deadlines in the Federal Budget Process

Date	Deadline to Meet
First Monday in February	President submits budget proposal to Congress
Mid-March	Congressional committees send cost estimate to budget committees
April 1–15	Congressional budget committees are supposed to complete budget resolution
June 15	Congress must pass budget reconciliation bill (if necessary)
June 30	Appropriations bills must be adopted
October 1	Beginning of federal fiscal year

Source: Based on T. J. Lowi and B. Ginsberg (1994), *American Government* (brief 3rd ed.), p. 161; from *American Government: Freedom and Power,* 5th ed., by Theodore J. Lowi and Benjamin Ginsberg (1994); and on W. J. Oleszek (2007), *Congressional procedures and the policy process,* 6th ed., p. 59.

in a cantankerous organization such as the U.S. Congress is called, appropriately enough, *reconciliation*. It involves much coalition building; many deals are made, and some of the fiercest battles fought in Congress are waged. Ultimately, however, a budget emerges, although in some years it is late. Of course, this budget differs substantially from the proposal submitted by the president and the OMB, but usually its basic framework remains (Oleszek, 2007; Rubin, 2006).

Education leaders must understand that this **budget process** is playing out simultaneously with the process of policy formulation and adoption described previously. This means that people working for the adoption of a new policy through legislation must follow and try to influence both processes at the same time. Usually, they have carefully thought-out strategies for each. An attempt to obtain funding for a new education policy might start by seeking to persuade the U.S. Department of Education (USDOE) or an agency within it to include money for the new policy in its initial budget request in hopes that it will ultimately appear in the president's proposal. Even if it does not appear in his proposal, all is not lost; appropriations committees can be lobbied to allocate funds to it. Appropriations committees, however, are notoriously stingy, regarding themselves as stern "guardians of the Treasury" (Martin, 1994, p. 78). Usually composed of powerful legislators from safe districts, these committees have an adversarial relationship with the rest of Congress and cultivate a reputation for stinginess. This means that getting the funding one wants is usually harder than getting the words (Martin, 1994).

Even so, it can be done. Continuing funding for the *Dropout Prevention and Reentry Act* was not even included in the president's budget proposal for fiscal year 1991, and congressional novice Martin began working on funding for the policy late. Experts in Congress warned her that there were "nearly insurmountable odds against funding for [the] program" (p. 79). Nonetheless, she and other staff members built a broad-based, bipartisan coalition of support for funding both inside Congress and out, and (after a dramatic defeat in the Senate Appropriations Committee) managed to get funding through an amendment added on the Senate floor. Another well-orchestrated strategy helped the amendment survive the deliberations of the Conference Committee, and the program for dropout prevention was funded. In her final analysis, Martin suggests that their success was the fruit of a well-orchestrated grassroots effort to influence the appropriations process. Her case study illustrates not only the difficulty of the fight for funding, but also the fact that the federal budget process can be influenced relatively easily.

Budgeting at the State Level.   Like the federal government, each state government adopts a budget to guide its financial activities. There are some differences, however, between the federal budget process and its counterparts in the fifty state capitals. Most important, state governments cannot engage in deficit spending; the revenue and expenditure sides of their budgets must balance. Another difference is that, although the federal government adopts its budget annually, not all states do; some adopt biennial budgets. Finally, unlike the president, most governors have the legal power to use a line-item veto to eliminate spending approved by the legislature (Rosenthal, 2009; Rubin, 2006).

The budget process also differs among states; the procedures used can be arranged on a continuum, ranging from a top-down, gubernatorially dominated process, to a bottom-up, legislatively dominated one (Rubin, 2006). Maryland uses a top-down approach, possibly the most top-down in the country. In that state, the legislature is not permitted under the Maryland constitution either to add funds to the budget proposed by the governor or to switch money from one section of his or her budget to another; all it can do is eliminate funding from the governor's budget proposal. The legislature is not absolutely powerless in relationship to the governor, but it does have to rely heavily on persuasion if it wishes to see any of its priorities in the budget proposal (Rosenthal, 2009). At the opposite end of the continuum is Texas, whose budget process centers in the legislature. Although the governor has the power to set a ceiling on state expenditures, the legislature takes the lead in developing the budget. This decentralized process permits interest groups to play a large role and exercise considerable influence on the outcome (Rubin, 2006). Because of the fiscal constraints since the early 1980s, the trend in state budgeting is toward a top-down process in which the governor plays a central role. Although this approach is less broadly participative than the bottom-up approach, controlling expenditures and keeping taxes down is easier (Rubin, 2006).

Obtaining funding for a state policy is more difficult than obtaining the enactment of the legislation that authorizes the policy. In the states, as in Washington, D.C., unfunded mandates have proliferated in recent decades. Part of the problem is the cost-conscious appropriations committees, which often look with jaundiced eyes at any program that is going to cost public money. Their attitude was beautifully captured by a politically experienced Midwesterner who, as early as 1981, claimed this about education politics in his state:

> They can have a nice time in house education and in senate education talking about textbook selection, competency-based education, and a lot of other things like that. Not much is going to happen on those things. It's the people who control the money who are calling the shots up and down the line. (Rosenthal, 1981, p. 291)

In the state capitals, then, obtaining money for new education ideas is difficult. This means that advocates for policy change must always incorporate into their strategies not only plans for getting the wording that they want, but also detailed plans for getting adequate funding approved.

POLICY FORMULATION AND ADOPTION IN ADMINISTRATIVE AGENCIES

Rule Making

WHY RULES ARE NEEDED. Because U.S. legislatures write vague laws, administrative agencies must fill in the details by developing rules, regulations, and policy guidelines (Kerwin & Furlong, 2011). Figure 8.3 contains most of the text of a 1994 Tennessee education law designed to establish coordinated children's services. Although the Tennessee General Assembly clearly mandated cooperation between the SDE and the Department of Mental Health and Retardation (two administrative

---

49–6–6101. Improvement and coordination of services.—The state departments of education and mental health and mental retardation shall take the following actions to improve and coordinate services for behavioral/emotionally disordered children. Any policy change required as a result of these actions will be presented to the state board of education for review and approval:

   (1)   Delineation of each state and local agency's responsibilities;

   (2)   Development of joint agency planning and training, especially between Tennessee's state and local agencies of mental health, mental retardation, and education;

   (3)   Development of a systematic process for securing funding for a continuum of related service options;

   (4)   Development of a definition of the target population;

   (5)   Development of ongoing needs-assessment process that addresses:

      (A)   The complex and diverse needs of the children and their families; and

      (B)   The resources of schools, mental health/mental retardation providers, and public/private agencies;

   (6)   Prepare an inventory of a continuum of existing services and options, known private or public agencies, and families;

   (7)   Development of an interagency agreement on the principles to be included in a plan of care as they relate to intervention and/or treatment goals. The plan of care shall have:

      (A)   Child involvement if developmentally appropriate;

      (B)   Measurable outcomes;

      (C)   Identification of agency or agencies that shall monitor the plan of care;

      (D)   Family involvement; and

      (E)   Sensitivity to unique cultural needs; and

   (8)   Development of interagency training plan in the area of truancy prevention. [Acts 1994, ch.985, § 4.]

FIGURE 8.3 A Tennessee education law

agencies), it also granted them considerable authority to define and shape their efforts. In doing so, they must formulate numerous documents, identifying the responsibilities of several agencies, spelling out a funding process, defining their target population, and so on. If approved by the SBE, these texts become rules and have the force of law (Kerwin & Furlong, 2011).

Administrative rules serve three different functions. First, and perhaps most important, they may fill in gaps in the law that lawmakers either did not recognize or left to the experts working in government agencies. A second possible function of rules is defining the key terms in a law or in the body of laws governing a specific domain. For example, SDEs often develop official definitions of such terms as *teacher, school,* and *secondary education.* Finally, administrative agencies also write the rules that define their own internal procedures, including procedures for writing rules (Anderson, 2003; Kerwin & Furlong, 2011). Figure 8.4 contains several rules from the section of the *Oregon Administrative Rules, 2002 Compilation* that covers district improvement plans. These rules spell out in detail how districts are to develop their plans and various procedures to follow in relationship to them, filling in gaps in the legislature's statute.

HOW RULES ARE WRITTEN.   In formulating rules, agencies usually follow a three-step procedure: (1) gathering information, (2) providing for public participation, and (3) submitting their proposed rules to a designated individual or panel for approval. Agency workers consult several sources of information as they prepare to make rules.

Assessment and Evaluation
581-022-0606
District Improvement Plan
Each district shall:
(1)   Identify school and district needs for improvement of student achievement at the district and school levels by conducting self-evaluations that include a review of test results and other evaluative information (e.g., at a minimum demographics, other student performance data, student access to and utilization of educational opportunities and staff characteristics.)
(2)   Based on the self-evaluation described in section (1) of this rule, develop and implement a written improvement plan for the district and each school to include, where appropriate, plans for:
(a)   Continuous short-term and long-term staff development;
(b)   Programs and policies to achieve a safe educational environment; and
(c)   Local efficiencies and efforts to make better use of resources.
(3)   Revise and update the district improvement plan on a biennial basis.
(4)   Annually review and report test results and progress on the district improvement plan to the community.
(5)   Maintain copies of the school and district improvement plans as a public record.
(6)   Submit the district improvement plan to the Department of Education when requested.
Stat Auth.: ORS 326.051
Stats.Implemented: ORS 326.051

FIGURE 8.4   Some administrative rules governing education in Oregon

For example, they may study rules developed in other states with similar legislation, read research reports about the implementation of similar policies elsewhere, and discuss possible rules informally with people in the field (Kerwin & Furlong, 2011). Public participation in rule making is a widely shared, but not always honored, ideal. At a minimum, most agencies publish some kind of notice to inform interested parties about when specific rules will be developed and to solicit some form of participation. This participation can take various forms: the agency may invite written comments on its proposed rules, hold public hearings during which interested parties can raise questions about them, establish an advisory committee to help with the initial formulation of the rules, or even negotiate the rules with the major interest groups concerned. Although private individuals may participate in these activities, the most frequent participants are interest groups, business representatives, and leaders of organizations affected by the rules. In education, teachers' unions, the major administrator and school board groups, business associations, and activist education administrators are often involved (Kerwin & Furlong, 2011; Madsen, 1994).

Although administrative agencies often have considerable leeway in formulating rules, the rules must be approved by someone external to the formulation process. Often, as in the example from Tennessee, education rules are adopted by a vote of the SBE, or a special committee of high-ranking officials who review new rules may have to approve them. Like all laws, administrative rules are subject to judicial review and so can be challenged in the courts; indeed, litigation over rules is common. Thus, although administrative agencies have broad discretion in formulating and adopting rules, there are important checks on their power (Kerwin & Furlong, 2011).

WHY ADMINISTRATIVE RULE MAKING IS HELPFUL.   Because administrative agencies (including SDEs) and their rule-making function evolved between 1887 and 1917 as part of the Progressive Era, they reflect progressive reformers' faith in expert "scientific" knowledge and in governmental bodies that are supposedly above politics and partisan conflict (Kagan, 1986; Sabatier, 1975). As the twentieth century unfolded, agencies became increasingly powerful and promulgated more rules, provoking attacks from both liberals and conservatives (Hall, 1988). Among the most common criticisms were complaints that the agencies and their rule making were undemocratic (e.g., Lowi, 1979) and accusations of inefficiency and rigidity (e.g., Wilson, 1989). No doubt, many of these criticisms were valid, and most contemporary school leaders could cite numerous examples of "formalistic compliance, paperwork, and . . . meaningless legal procedures" (Kagan, 1986, p. 65). Even so, policy formulation and adoption by administrative agencies has a positive dimension as well as a negative one. Many agency employees formerly worked in the business or profession they now regulate; for example, both the USDOE and SDEs employ numerous former teachers, school administrators, and college professors. Because of their familiarity with education, these workers are better able to develop the details of education policy than are legislators, most of whom have never worked in a school. Thus, agency rule making provides an arena in which professional expertise can shape policy. When those who currently work in schools and school districts are permitted to participate in a meaningful way, the influence of professional expertise is amplified (Kerwin & Furlong, 2011).

Administrative rule making serves two other important functions as well. First, it can facilitate a more responsive and flexible implementation of new policies. If legislatures wrote detailed laws, amending them in necessary ways might take years, and faulty programs could continue indefinitely even though everyone recognized their flaws. Because changing rules is easier than changing laws, an SDE that establishes a new testing program or new teacher certification standards can revise its rules and clarify its policy guidelines as problems emerge during implementation. Finally, delegating some policymaking authority to agencies lightens legislatures' workload. Because all U.S. legislatures are overburdened with bills and other business, shifting detailed policy formulation to agencies such as the USDOE and the SDEs streamlines the legislative process, making it more efficient. Despite widespread criticism of government bureaucracy, then, administrative agencies will probably continue to play a role in policy formulation and adoption for the foreseeable future. In fact, the importance of SDEs in policy development has increased considerably since 1980.

FEDERAL RULE MAKING.   In 1946, Congress passed the *Administrative Procedures Act,* standardizing the rule-making procedures of federal agencies. This law requires agencies to base rules on information about a policy area and to give the public notice of their intention to write rules. It also requires them to permit public participation in rule making, although this participation can take several forms, ranging from submitting written comments to holding hearings (Kerwin & Furlong, 2011).

As with other federal agencies, the USDOE publishes notices of its intention to write rules in the *Federal Register,* a volume of which is published in paperback form on most weekdays of the year. The *Federal Register,* also available on the Internet at archives.gov/federal-register/index.html, publishes announcements of the USDOE's intention to develop rules, identifies the sections of the law for which rules will be made, and summarizes the general thrust of the proposed rules. Some form of public participation is always solicited; most commonly, interested parties are invited to submit letters with their comments by a specific deadline. On occasion, however, broader participation is possible. For example, on January 18, 2002, the USDOE invited written feedback in the form of "advice and recommendations" for rules to accompany the *No Child Left Behind Act* of 2002, which reauthorized the *Elementary and Secondary Education Act* of 1965. It invited several specific categories of stakeholders, including parents, teachers, and administrators, to submit comments (*Federal Register,* January 14, 2002). Six weeks later, the DOE announced it had received comments from 100 individuals and groups and published information about the time and location of five public meetings of a group that would review the proposed regulations. It also indicated that four regional meetings would be held throughout the country to give a broad audience a chance to offer feedback (*Federal Register,* February 28, 2002). Although the USDOE is not required to use the comments that it solicits in writing new rules, it often does so. The final rules, as adopted by the USDOE, are published in the *Federal Register,* along with an analysis of the comments received from the public and an explanation of how the comments were used or why they were not. The final version of the rules is also available in the *Code of Federal Regulations* (CFR), a multivolume collection that fills many shelves and is also available on the Internet at gpoaccess.gov/cfr; most education rules appear in the three volumes that cover Title 34, although a few appear under other headings.

Rule Making in the States

As might be expected, the procedures used to develop rules and regulations vary among states. However, the writing of rules for education policy is typically the responsibility of the SDE; often, the SBE adopts them formally. In her inside story of three years as an employee in the SDE of an unidentified state, Madsen (1994) devotes much of a chapter to the development of rules to accompany the state's 1985 *Excellence in Education Act*. In her SDE, she observed a variety of procedures for rule making. For example, the director of certification unilaterally developed the regulations for the Career Ladder Program and prepared a handbook for school districts to use as they implemented the program. "He made most decisions regarding career ladder policies in isolation," Madsen later wrote, concluding: "This director greatly influenced how programs were interpreted" (p. 50). The commissioner of education also decided many rules unilaterally.

Nonetheless, some rules were formulated with the participation of the education community. The law itself required advisory committees to participate in formulating some rules, and the commissioner established several advisory committees not required by the law. The number of members of each committee ranged from fifteen to thirty; the SDE selected them with care, seeking to balance them by region and district size as well as by professional education position, including teachers, administrators, teacher educators, union representatives, legislators, and parents. Committees convened monthly, holding daylong meetings with lunch provided by the SDE. The commissioner attended most of these sessions, and SDE officials were always present. The rules formulated by the committees were sent to the SBE for discussion and approval or rejection. Finally, public hearings on the rules were held at several sites around the state so that people could comment on them. Those rules that provoked numerous complaints were then revised.

In Madsen's view, the SDE dominated the process of rule formulation; indeed, she describes the committees as "little more than rubber stamps" (p. 103). Nonetheless, at least some of the rules were developed in a way that could lead to potentially meaningful participation by educators and others.

POLICY FORMULATION AND ADOPTION IN THE COURTS

Judges as Policy Actors

A black-robed justice, seated at an elevated desk and routinely addressed as "Your Honor," provokes awed respect from most people. Indeed, the purpose of this traditional symbolism is to provoke awe and enhance the authority of judges, who must deal with many difficult and even dangerous people in the course of their work. Awe and respect should not obscure objective reality, however; judges are important policy actors in the U.S. political system (Baum, 2010; Hall; 2008; Lowi et al., 2007; O'Brien, 2005). For those who did not already understand this, the presidential election of 2000 made it abundantly clear.

Nor are judges apolitical actors. Although insulated from the crassest aspects of the political hurly-burly by mechanisms such as appointment or low-visibility elections, long terms, and the secrecy of their deliberations in their chambers, judges are political figures just as much as members of Congress or governors are. Most have ties with one of the major political parties (otherwise they would never have become judges), and in most cases their ideological orientations are well known in legal circles. Their appointment or election to office usually comes about because more visible policy actors hope that as judges they will make the right kind of decisions, however they may define *right* (Abraham, 1998). Of course, sometimes they surprise those who appoint them by developing an independent streak after they begin to hand down decisions on the bench. Nonetheless, the political stance of judges, regardless of whether they change their views, is important, because a court "is more than a judicial agency—it is also a major lawmaking body" (Lowi & Ginsberg, 1994, p. 189).

When judges make decisions about the cases they hear, they are playing the crucial policy role of interpreting the laws passed by a legislature or the rules developed by an administrative agency. They write their interpretations in the form of *opinions,* the most important of which are collected and published in one type of law book, establishing *precedents* for future legal interpretations by other judges and lawyers. Judges' written opinions constitute **case law,** and are part of the law just as legislation is. In addition, judges can use their power of *judicial review* to invalidate the laws passed by a legislature or the rules written by an agency if they consider them unconstitutional (Abraham, 1998; Baum, 2010; Lowi et al., 2007).

Although some courts behave in a restrained manner, showing great deference to precedent and the legislature, others are known for their activism and play a leading role in shaping the direction of policy (Baum, 2010). At the federal level, the Warren Court of the 1950s and 1960s was activist, outlawing school segregation in 1954 and blazing new trails in other areas concerning civil rights (Kirp, 1986; Tyack, 1986). State court systems are often even more activist than federal courts, taking the lead in pressuring other branches of government to act. In New Jersey, for example, one Supreme Court justice publicly affirmed that he and his colleagues deliberately wrote decisions in such a way as to prod the legislature to move in specific policy directions, including reforming the school finance system (Porter, 1982). In fact, the New Jersey Supreme Court is well known among school finance experts as the court that overturned its state's school finance system in *Robinson v. Cahill I* and then, in a series of cases numbered like horror films and their sequels, rejected plan after plan developed by the state legislature in *Robinson v. Cahill II–VI* ("Unfulfilled Promises," 1991). New Jersey is not alone; school finance equalization has been and still is a major issue facing many state courts. Clearly, then, school leaders can never afford to overlook the importance of judges in formulating and adopting education policy. Ultimately, many education policy questions are decided by judges, not legislatures. And, sooner or later, most school administrators will find themselves dealing with a court.

Taking Cases to Court

Unlike the other two branches of government, the judiciary is reactive rather than proactive. Even if judges believe a piece of legislation is unconstitutional or that the legal rights of a segment of the population are being violated, they do not announce this fact publicly or search out aggrieved citizens to challenge the law in court. Instead, they must wait for someone to pursue a judicial remedy for unjust treatment (Baum, 2010).

Legal principles govern who can bring suit in a court. A citizen who believes in the abstract that a law is being violated or that a statute or practice is unconstitutional is not enough; only those individuals or groups who have actually been injured in some way have what is called *standing* and can bring a court challenge. This injury may be physical, psychological, or economic, but plaintiffs must be able to demonstrate actual damage in order to successfully seek remedy through the justice system. In addition, a real *controversy* must exist and an *adversary* must be named as the defendant in the case (Alexander & Alexander, 2008). For example, parents who believe their child's school progress has been hampered by racial discrimination cannot simply file a general complaint; they must also identify individuals or groups they hold responsible—perhaps a superintendent and school board—and these individuals or groups must disagree with them. If the defendants agree with their charges and offer a settlement, no controversy exists and therefore no case exists, even though the plaintiffs might like to take it to court in order to publicize their point. This means that abstract, hypothetical, or theoretical cases are not tried in U.S. courts; if such cases are filed, they are dismissed at an early stage of the process (Baum, 2010; Lowi et al., 2007).

Organizations can, however, advance specific causes by bringing *test cases* to court as part of a broader strategy for causing policy change. Usually such groups conclude—often with good reason—that they have little chance of obtaining the policy changes they seek from the legislative branch. Therefore, they turn to the courts and, over a period of years, bring many cases into the court system in an attempt to change policy gradually. One decision that such groups (and all litigants) must make is in which court system—federal or state—they will seek redress. Because the two systems have somewhat different jurisdictions, this decision is often clear-cut; some suits, however, potentially fall under both jurisdictions and a choice must be made. Although state court decisions are binding only within a single state, decisions in state court systems are widely read and often have a broad impact. Decisions handed down in other states may, for example, encourage a legislature to take action because it fears a lawsuit. Decisions reached in federal courts are binding on all the states served by an appellate court, or, in the case of the U.S. Supreme Court, on the entire nation.

How Judges Formulate and Adopt Policy

In the *trial courts* at the lowest level of both the state and federal court systems, a single judge hears the evidence in a case. In the kinds of cases that most often change education policy, usually no jury is present. Nonetheless, as trial court judges weigh evidence and seek to apply the law to individual cases, they do not act in total isolation. They are supposed to follow the precedents laid down by other judges in similar cases, and they realize that their decisions may be appealed to higher courts where other justices evaluate the accuracy of their findings. Thus, their concern for their professional reputation, if nothing else, encourages trial court judges to avoid eccentric and implausible rulings (Hall, 2008; Lowi et al., 2007).

Above the trial court level, a panel of judges hears each case. In the *U.S. Supreme Court,* this panel has nine members; in many *state supreme courts,* seven; and in most *appellate courts,* three. This makes procedures for reaching consensus necessary. Although the secrecy of judges' deliberations means that few citizens ever observe this policy formulation and adoption process, the general practices followed are well known.

Courts with several members have a *chief justice* who chairs their closed meetings and facilitates decision making. After hearing several cases, the justices hold a *conference* in which they discuss these cases and argue about them. Such meetings are often tumultuous; a California Supreme Court justice once commented: "[Conference] is . . . like a battleground where opposing philosophies meet in hand-to-hand combat" (Abraham, 1998, p. 214). Periodically, tentative votes are taken on the decisions. When a clear majority position seems to have emerged on a particular case, a final vote is taken and the outcome is recorded. Then the chief justice assigns a member of the majority to write an *opinion,* stating the decision and the court's reasons for it. The first draft of the opinion is circulated among the other justices for comments and suggestions. The members of the court may negotiate with each other over the inclusion or exclusion of specific points, phrases, and reasoning. Judges who disagree with the majority can write a *dissenting opinion* (O'Brien, 2005). This procedure can take a long time. For example, the Warren Court took more than one year to decide and draft an opinion in the *Brown v. Board of Education* (1954) school segregation case because the chief justice wanted a unanimous decision and a single opinion for this controversial issue. After having reached a number of decisions, a higher court announces them to the public on a designated date often called *Opinion Day.* At that time, the authors of the opinions read them—or summaries of them—aloud to the audience assembled in the courtroom. Later, these opinions are published in law books called *reporters* and become part of the case law consulted by attorneys and judges (O'Brien, 2005).

Examples of Education Policymaking by Judges

IN STATE COURTS.   State court judges have played an important role in education policymaking since the earliest days of the nineteenth-century Common School Movement. In a study of the history of judicial lawmaking in education, Tyack (1986) found that 90% of nineteenth-century state courts' decisions about education dealt with school finance and governance. For example, in 1882, an Illinois court found the state compulsory attendance law constitutional; in 1886, an Indiana court upheld school boards' power to require the teaching of a specific curriculum. In other important cases, courts upheld the authority of states to use tax money to support public education and the power of school boards to go into debt to fund building construction (Alexander, 1998). Of course, court decisions handed down in one state are not binding in other states; even so, Tyack (1986) concluded that legal precedents set in states that established school systems early strongly influenced what other states did.

In the twenty-first century, state courts are still making important decisions on school finance policy. Table 8.4 summarizes the state court cases challenging the constitutionality of school finance systems litigated between 1971 and 2007. It illustrates vividly how a judicial decision in one state can encourage people in other states to file similar suits; in fact, challenges have been brought in almost every state. What the table does not show is that the overturning of finance systems in a few states encouraged state legislatures across the country to adjust their own school finance formulas either to head off litigation or to place themselves in a stronger position if they were sued.

IN FEDERAL COURTS.   Only seven education cases reached the U.S. Supreme Court during the entire nineteenth century (Tyack, 1986), but after World War I, federal

TABLE 8.4 Summary of School Finance Litigation by State, 1971–2007

Successful Litigation	Unsuccessful Litigation	No or Dormant Litigation
Alaska	Alabama	Delaware
Arizona	Colorado	Hawaii
Arkansas	Florida	Indiana
California	Georgia	Iowa
Connecticut	Illinois	Mississippi
Idaho	Louisiana	Nevada
Kansas	Maine	Utah
Kentucky	Michigan	
Maryland	Minnesota	
Massachusetts	Nebraska	
Missouri	Oklahoma	
Montana	Oregon	
New Hampshire	Pennsylvania	
New Jersey	Rhode Island	
New Mexico	South Dakota	
New York	Virginia	
North Carolina	Wisconsin	
North Dakota		
Ohio		
South Carolina		
Tennessee		
Texas		
Vermont		
Washington		
West Virginia		
Wyoming		

Source: Based on information available on the Access: Education Finance Litigation, School Funding Policy and Advocacy Web site, "State by State." Retrieved January 27, 2007, from schoolfunding.info/states/state_by_state.php3.

judges began to play an important role in education policy. For example, in 1923, the high court struck down a Nebraska law prohibiting the use of any language other than English for instruction in grades K–8; two years later, it declared unconstitutional an Oregon statute that required all children to attend public schools. These two decisions foreshadowed the education policy role the federal courts would play throughout much of the twentieth century: protector of the rights of teachers, students, and various minorities. This role was greatly enhanced by the 1954 *Brown v. Board of Education* decision, which "sparked a revolution in the role of American courts" (Jensen, 1985, p. 18). Over the next two decades, the federal courts shaped education policy actively, championing civil rights and equality under the law, but creating considerable controversy as well (Kalodner, 1990; Kirp, 1986).

Like the state court systems, the federal courts often make decisions that have a ripple effect, influencing the behavior of the legislative branch. A good example is provided by a 1971 case, *Pennsylvania Association for Retarded Children v. Commonwealth,* in which a coalition of parents brought suit against Pennsylvania in federal district court, alleging that the state had failed to fulfill its legal obligation to provide public education for handicapped children. After a single day of testimony in court, the state conceded and signed a consent agreement in which it affirmed that in Pennsylvania, mentally handicapped children between ages six and twenty-one had a legal right to "a free and appropriate public education" (Jensen, 1985, p. 29). During the next three years, 899 bills related to the rights of handicapped children were introduced in state legislatures, and more than 200 passed. Moreover, the U.S. Congress also reacted, passing relevant legislation in 1973 and 1974, and P.L. 94–142, the *Education for All Handicapped Children Act* of 1976 (Jensen, 1985). Thus, judges shape education policy not only directly by their decisions, but also indirectly by stimulating legislative action.

INFLUENCING POLICY FORMULATION AND ADOPTION

General Principles

KNOW THE PROCESS.   Any school leader who wishes to influence education policy must understand the policy process; otherwise, he or she makes foolish mistakes and wastes valuable resources. For example, those who are ignorant of the legislative process often contact their congressional representative just as the bill is going to the floor for a final debate and vote. Although some bills are stopped or altered at that time, it is not the best point of intervention. Rather, the earlier one can intervene, the more likely one is to be effective. Likewise, the legal codes are full of laws whose advocates worked earnestly to obtain the passage of the language they wanted, but did not realize that fighting for funding was also necessary. The first part of this chapter provides a thorough overview of the process and contains enough information to permit intelligent thinking about it. School leaders should not expect to fully grasp the process from reading this book, however; they should anticipate a period of learning, and this book and others provide useful resources for them to return to when they are unsure of what is going to happen next.

FOLLOW GOVERNMENT ACTIVITY.   As the earlier parts of this chapter make clear, the policy formulation and adoption processes operate within a time frame that includes numerous official deadlines. This means that often those who wish to influence these processes must not only be aware of what is happening, but must also respond in a timely manner. Of course, all government bodies publish official records of their schedules and actions; these are usually available on the Internet; however, many school leaders find using the resources of their professional organizations the easiest way to monitor legislative activity because these cover only education policy.

Organizations such as the American Association of School Administrators (AASA), National Association of Secondary School Principals (NASSP), and National Association of Elementary School Principals (NAESP) as well as their state affiliates provide three important resources to facilitate keeping informed about policy events. First, they publish information about government activities, especially in the legislative branch. Often, in addition to a monthly magazine, they put out a weekly legislative update while Congress or the state legislature is in session. Although they may not send the update to all members, they will usually add any member to their listserv on request. An advantage of these updates is that they include only legislation relevant to education and highlight especially key issues, often explaining them in some depth. If a major case is moving through the courts, such updates often include information about that as well. A second service associations usually offer is a Web site, part of which is devoted to the organization's legislative agenda, to major bills introduced into the legislature, and to other policy events. Finally, professional associations usually have a government relations office with one or more staff members. These experts are usually more than willing to provide additional information to members who have been unable to obtain enough detail from other sources.

WORK WITH OTHERS.   No reader of this book needs to be told that school administrators are busy people with little time to spare. Influencing policy formulation and adoption is an essential part of education leadership, but it does not have to be done alone, and indeed, should not be, because "lone rangers" are rarely effective in politics. In large school districts, a district office administrator often has the responsibility for developing and maintaining liaisons with government officials at the local, state, and federal levels. Such a government relations officer plans and coordinates the policy activities of the whole district. Naturally, administrators employed in such districts should establish a good working relationship with this individual, communicating their major policy concerns to him or her and using this district resource as much as possible.

Smaller districts usually cannot afford to employ a government relations specialist; nonetheless, working together to influence policy is important in these districts, too. Superintendents, central office supervisors, and principals should strive to create a professional climate in which everyone is aware of major trends in state and national education policy and understands that on occasion, becoming active is necessary. Much of the day-to-day monitoring of policy developments can be delegated to those who are most directly concerned. For example, in many districts, the vocational education programs are funded largely with federal money. As with all federal programs, vocational education laws must be reauthorized and re-funded periodically; in addition, the regulations governing it frequently change. These are important policy issues for such districts, and should be followed closely. However, superintendents and principals need not assume the major responsibility for doing so; rather, the person who supervises vocational education and the teachers who work in the program could do the daily tracking and contact federal officials as necessary, working within general guidelines determined by the district. In this and other ways, school leaders should try to build a broad base of policy awareness and involvement among their colleagues.

SET PRIORITIES.   In any given year, dozens of bills related to education are introduced in Congress and in state legislatures, many regulations are written or revised, and several relevant court decisions are handed down. No single education leader, school, or district can have an impact on all of them. Setting clear priorities for one's activity and learning to ignore issues of lesser importance are therefore essential. Priority setting can take many forms. For example, in a large metropolitan district, the government relations office may have a written list of priorities developed with the central office staff and divided into three categories labeled First Tier Policy Priorities, Second Tier Policy Priorities, and Third Tier Policy Priorities. At the other extreme, in a small rural district the superintendent may carry her list in her head: "First, protect district funding. Second, expand the vocational agriculture program. Third, obtain more realistic school lunch regulations." The form of the list and the process of developing it may vary, but priorities should be developed and respected. Otherwise, attempts to influence policy will be scattered, diffuse, and ineffective.

Influencing Legislatures and Agencies

THREE APPROACHES.   There are three general approaches to influencing policy formulation and adoption: government relations, working through professional organizations, and "lobbying." These approaches are complementary rather than mutually exclusive. Skillful education leaders use all three, building a strong foundation of solid relationships with other public officials, participating in and networking through professional organizations, and "lobbying" by contacting officials about specific bills or rules as necessary. Many school leaders make the mistake of neglecting the first two components; then, whenever they become good and angry about a proposed policy change, they aggressively "lobby" legislators or agency administrators who are strangers to them, hoping somehow to influence them. This approach is worse than ineffective; it antagonizes those it is intended to sway (Turner, 1995). This is why "most legislators view educators as whiners who show up only when they want something— usually more money" (Turner, 1995, p. 1). Educators must, then, learn a better way to relate to public officials. In this section, the three approaches that together constitute a better way are detailed. Before beginning a discussion of each, a concrete illustration or vignette of how this approach might be used in real life is presented.

GOVERNMENT RELATIONS.   This is the indispensable foundation on which the other two approaches are built, and becomes clearer in the following sections.

   Vignette I: Making the Case for Technology.   Elementary school principal Keisha Vernon believed strongly in the importance of building positive relationships with the community, and she interpreted the community as including local and state government officials as well as the congressman who represented the district. She sent all of them copies of the school newsletter and invitations to special school events, such as graduation and the December holiday pageant.

   Over the years, Keisha had come to know most of these people by sight, and they knew her. However, a somewhat closer relationship had developed between Keisha and Cynthia Hernandez, the woman who represented the area in the lower house of the state legislature. Keisha and Cynthia belonged to the same chapter of the Soroptimist Club, and sometimes they sat together at club dinners. Keisha once arranged for Cynthia to participate in a panel discussion about the new state graduation requirements and occasionally sent her representative an article from a professional journal about social justice, one of Keisha's special concerns.

One evening at Soroptimist Club, everyone at the table where Keisha and Cynthia were sitting began to talk about the sad state of education in the United States today. Keisha tried hard to be unbiased, but also to defend schools against some of the more unreasonable criticisms. At one point in the conversation, Cynthia exclaimed, "I don't know why I'm talking so much! You know, I don't have kids of my own, and I haven't been in an elementary school since the day I finished sixth grade!" The words popped out of Keisha's mouth before she could stop them: "Why don't you come visit my school, then?"

Two weeks later, she was surprised when Cynthia called to schedule an appointment to visit her school. On the morning of the visit, Keisha took her on a tour of the building and grounds, introduced her to teachers and staff, and presented her with a giant greeting card one of the first-grade classes had made for her. Over coffee in Keisha's office, Cynthia asked, "Keisha, do kindergartners and first graders really need computer education?" "Oh, yes!" the principal replied. She went on to explain why young children need to learn about computers, how computers can support classroom instruction in basic subjects, and the importance of thorough professional development for primary grade teachers. Cynthia asked a few questions and accepted a copy of a special issue of *Principal* devoted entirely to computer education.

Several months later, Keisha noticed in a legislative update from the state affiliate of the NAESP that Cynthia was cosponsoring a bill to fund more computers for grades K–3; it included a strong professional development component. Keisha quickly wrote a short note thanking her for sponsoring such important legislation. Two years later, after the bill had finally become law, Cynthia laughingly told Keisha at a Soroptimist meeting: "That law should be named the *Hernandez-Vernon Act* because of the way I picked your brain about computers that day!"

Influence Through Building Relationships.   President Lyndon Johnson, one of the most skillful politicians of the twentieth century, was fond of saying, "The time to make friends is before you need them" (Turner, 1995, p. 1). Yet far too many school leaders neglect this fundamental principle of politics, contacting government officials only when they have a complaint or want money. Above all, legislators, officials in administrative agencies, and judges are human, and like all humans, they feel suspicious of people who approach them only when they need something, and tend to trust those who show an ongoing interest in them. Thus, the indispensable foundation of all policy influence is building relationships. Education leaders must broaden their understanding of the school community beyond students, teachers, parents, the school board, and district taxpayers to include those government officials who potentially have direct influence on education in their school or district (Turner, 1995; Wiget, 1995). Figure 8.5 lists the major officials to include in this expanded concept of the school community.

Relationships are built through regular, two-way communication. The easiest and least time-consuming way to open communication channels with government officials is to send them the district or school directory and place them on the mailing

- Mayor*
- City council member*
- County executive*
- County commissioner*
- Representative and senator in state legislature
- Congressional representative
- Selected officials in state department of education
- Selected officials in federal agencies
- Local judges
- Appellate and Supreme Court justices who live in the area

FIGURE 8.5 Officials to consider including in a government relations program

Provide information to them:

- The district or school directory
- The district or school newsletter
- The district's legislative agenda
- Newspaper clippings about special school or district programs and events

Receive communication from them:

- At town hall meetings
- At legislative hearings
- At political receptions and dinners
- At their speaking engagements in the area

Involve them in schools:

- Arrange a school visit
- Invite them to attend a special school or district function
- Invite them to a school open house
- Invite them to speak to faculty, the district leadership team, the school board retreat, a class, and so forth
- Ask them to present awards to students at graduation or an awards ceremony

FIGURE 8.6 Ways to communicate with public officials and involve them in schools

list or listserv to receive the newsletter and other communications designed for a general audience. In the first letter or e-mail sent to an official, the school leader should include a short letter of introduction. Other ways to build these relationships include extending appropriate invitations. Figure 8.6 summarizes ways to communicate with public officials and to involve them in school activities. Readers should note that good communication includes a willingness to receive messages as well as to send them; therefore, Figure 8.6 also includes suggestions for making oneself available to listen to government officials. School leaders should either attend these meetings or send an appropriate representative to report back on what was said and how the audience responded. Approaching the official before or after the affair to introduce oneself and one's professional affiliation is appropriate. A school leader might also express appreciation for the official's presence and willingness to receive feedback (if willingness has been apparent) at such events.

School leaders usually have numerous opportunities to listen to SDE officials and other administrative agency workers at the meetings and workshops they sponsor. Educators should perceive these occasions not just as times to learn about how the rules have changed and all the new paperwork, but also as opportunities to build positive relationships with agency administrators and to gain a better understanding of their perspective.

Over time, relationship building can bear much fruit. A chance to influence policy directly may result, as it did for Keisha Vernon. Obviously, too, legislators with questions about education issues or practices are likely to contact school leaders who are known to them rather than strangers. Similarly, when SDE department heads or federal agency administrators are establishing a task force to study a problem or an advisory committee to work on new rules, they usually invite school leaders with whom they are already acquainted to participate. Even judges, deliberating over a tricky decision in an education case, recall communication from and contacts with those education leaders who included them in their government relations programs; they have no reason to think of the many schools and districts that did not.

Another, more subtle result often becomes apparent over time. School leaders gradually find themselves dealing with government officials who understand schools better than before, express more sympathy for the work of educators, and recognize that both schools and children have changed since their own days in the classroom. A good government relations program educates those politicians involved. As Turner (1995) says: "Legislators will make laws with you or without you. They will make better ones with you. If they don't get information about education from you, they'll get it from someone else" (p. 2).

The politicians are not the only ones who become more educated, however. An even more subtle result—but possibly the most important one—is that school leaders who implement a government relations program learn a great deal about the policy process and those involved in it. They shed naive and uninformed popular attitudes such as, "All politicians are crooks" and "You can't fight City Hall." They gain an increased appreciation of (and skill at) the policymaking game. Their respect for the political process grows, and they begin to model informed, active, and responsible citizenship for the entire school community. For all these reasons, a good government relations program represents a sound investment of money and time.

Working Through Professional Organizations

Vignette II: Working for Higher Mathematics Standards.
After nine years as a high school mathematics teacher, Bruce Jensen was selected to serve as the mathematics supervisor for his large suburban district. Bruce was delighted with this opportunity

to make a broader impact on mathematics education because he had identified several serious problems during his years in the classroom. His concerns included the small number of mathematics courses required for elementary teaching certification, the high percentage of people without certification teaching high school math classes, and the emphasis on rote learning in his state's mathematics curriculum. He recognized that these problems could not be addressed at the school or district level. In fact, he had reached the conclusion that the best way to solve them would be for his state to officially adopt the mathematics standards developed by the National Council of Teachers of Mathematics (NCTM).

Bruce believed that as a professional mathematics educator, he had an obligation to work for this policy change, but he hesitated to do so through his school district. Although the NCTM standards were not inconsistent with his district's legislative agenda, they were not mentioned in it, either. Moreover, some school board members had recently expressed opposition to national standards. Deciding that pursuing his commitment through district channels would be ineffective and possibly unethical, Bruce turned to one of his professional organizations, the state Council of Teachers of Mathematics (CTM). He volunteered to serve on the CTM's Government Relations Committee. Because Bruce's district was known for its effective government relations program, and especially because he had gained a certain amount of experience in it, the state CTM leaders gladly appointed him to the committee.

During the next three years, Bruce became a leader in this group. He arranged training workshops for the committee and helped draft its first legislative proposal. He spearheaded a letter-writing campaign and visited numerous members of the state legislature and SDE officials. In the third year, he was invited to testify before the House Education Committee. Bruce did not hide the fact that he was a mathematics supervisor in his district, but he always clearly stated that he was working with the state CTM and representing its positions, not those of his employer.

With the passage of the *No Child Left Behind Act*, Bruce's state adopted standards for mathematics, but they were not fully compatible with the NCTM standards. Therefore, Bruce is still fighting for curriculum policy changes in his state, but he does not feel that he has wasted his time over the last several years. He now realizes that a broad effort to educate policymakers must precede a change of such magnitude. He also understands that policy victories usually go to the persistent. Right now, Bruce believes that the education of his state's policymakers is almost complete, and he looks forward to the day when they finally revise the current mathematics standards to make them consistent with the NCTM standards.

Professional Organizations—a Powerful Resource.   There are many reasons for joining one or more professional organizations. For school leaders who wish to influence the policy process, such memberships are essential. Selecting the best organizations with which to affiliate is an important decision that requires careful analysis and reflection. Table 8.5 presents some of the major education organizations active in the United States; it is a representative, rather than all-inclusive, list. It divides education organizations into three broad categories: (1) specialized administrator groups,

TABLE 8.5 Representative Professional Education Organizations

Administrator and Related Organizations	Subject-Matter Organizations	General Organizations
American Association of School Administrators (AASA)	American Vocational Association (AVA)	Association for Supervision and Curriculum Development (ASCD)
National Association of Elementary School Principals (NAESP)	Council for Exceptional Children (CEC)	Delta Kappa Gamma
	International Reading Association (IRA)	Kappa Delta Pi
National Association of School Business Officials (NASBO)	National Association for the Education of Young Children (NAEYC)	National Education Association (NEA)*
National Association of Secondary School Principals (NASSP)	National Association of School Counselors	Phi Delta Kappa
		Pi Lambda Theta
National School Boards Association (NSBA)	National Council for the Social Studies (NCSS)	
National School Public Relations Association (NSPRA)	National Council of Teachers of English (NCTE)	
	National Council of Teachers of Mathematics (NCTM)	
	National Science Teachers Association (NSTA)	

*In some states.

(2) subject-matter groups, and (3) general associations. All school leaders should affiliate with the specialized administrator group most appropriate for their school role. In addition, they should consider joining one or two other groups. For instance, as with Bruce Jensen in vignette II, they may continue to have a strong interest in the subject they taught and wish to remain involved in shaping its development. Joining a subject-matter group is one way to do this. Belonging to one of the general associations also has advantages because they accept a variety of professional educators as members and concern themselves with a wide spectrum of policy issues. For example, the Association for Supervision and Curriculum Development (ASCD) welcomes all types of educators as members, including administrators, teachers, and professors in colleges of education. Similarly, the Greek letter societies—which are education honoraries—accept a wider segment of the education community than do the specialized administrator and subject-matter organizations. Such groups provide a venue for meeting and working with a variety of education professionals. Although in some states the National Education Association (NEA) refuses membership to administrators, in others (especially in the South) it welcomes them. In these inclusive states, the NEA may be the most effective general education group at work, especially because it also accepts college professors. (The American Federation of Teachers is not

mentioned here because administrators are not permitted to join it.) Thus, in deciding which groups to join, school leaders must weigh numerous factors, including their professional responsibilities, interests, and the nature of each group's recruitment and activity in their own state. There is no single best choice.

The benefits professional organizations provide school leaders who wish to influence policymaking are numerous. First, they offer a rich source of information and expertise. As discussed in Chapter 7, most organizations publish journals, and in many of them policy developments are regularly featured. Many of these organizations also retain lobbyists who work in Washington, D.C., and in the state capitals; some even have full-fledged government relations offices. The most active groups put out a steady stream of useful policy updates in printed or electronic newsletters, on the Internet, and on telephone hot lines. They usually sponsor informative policy sessions at their state and national conferences. As noted in Chapter 6, the regular print and broadcast media cover education news intermittently, especially at the state level; therefore, school leaders find these information sources indispensable if they wish to influence education policy.

Moreover, professional organizations provide a valuable forum in which administrators can meet other people who share their policy interests and discuss them. Such interactions clarify and solidify policy positions. They also break down feelings of isolation, sometimes leading to joint action either within the organization or outside it. Many professional organizations have official legislative agendas that they try to advance in each session of Congress or the state legislature. Like Bruce Jensen, some school leaders find or help develop an agenda compatible with their own views. Others may discover that they must work outside the organization, usually because working within it would split that group. Even so, they may locate allies within the organization and use them to build a new network. In several states, for example, challenges to school finance systems have been brought by coalitions of school superintendents who originally met through the state AASA affiliate. Learning that many other school leaders shared their frustrations about the ongoing financial crisis, they worked together to try to bring about a solution through the courts. Although they considered it wise to work outside their AASA affiliate, that group provided the original basis for their organizing efforts.

Lobbying

Vignette III: Avoiding a Financial Loss.   Superintendent Harry Levinson was answering e-mail when business manager Suzanne Matsuo rushed in.

"Have you seen this, Harry?" she demanded, shoving a "Legislative Alert" published by the state affiliate of the National Association of School Business Officials (NASBO) into his hands.

Harry looked at it. She had circled one item in bright red; it concerned companion bills introduced into both houses of the state legislature the previous week. One of its provisions would reduce the state subsidy for students transported by bus by increasing the minimum distance for which the state would reimburse districts from 1.5 to 2 miles.

"How much will we lose?" Harry asked.

"We figure about $63,000," Suzanne replied. "But the real problem is that almost all the kids affected live in San Pedro. We'll have to transport them no matter what."

San Pedro was a mining town, located halfway up a mountain, and accessible only by a steep and narrow road with many sharp curves. San Pedro had operated its own school system for decades, but after several mine closures had brought the district to the brink of financial disaster, the state had consolidated it with Harry's district.

"How far is it to San Pedro?" he asked Suzanne.

"I had Ted check the bus routes—he says 1.7 miles for the elementary kids and 1.9 miles for the high schoolers."

Harry groaned. "Well, the good news is that this bill has just been introduced. We have plenty of time to get it amended."

That afternoon Harry developed a lobbying plan. He would write a letter to the representative from his district asking him to urge an amendment to the bill. Because his state senator served on the Senate Education Committee, Harry decided to pay a personal visit to her local office. During the twenty minutes he spent with Senator Blackstone, he described the San Pedro situation to her and presented a one-page financial fact sheet that Suzanne had put together the day before. Senator Blackstone said she would do what she could. Harry also called two SDE people with whom he had an especially good working relationship as well as several area superintendents, asking for their support.

In May, when the heavily amended bill narrowly squeaked through the legislature, it contained the provision that districts with hardship cases could apply for a waiver of the two-mile requirement. Although this was not exactly what Harry had hoped for, he was glad that the new law recognized exceptional cases. The next year, his district applied for and received a waiver for San Pedro.

CASE STUDY

The Gadfly

As he moved into the last decade of his professional career in a Midwestern state, Superintendent Jack Donato became increasingly disgruntled about education policy trends. Although he was comfortably ensconced in a district with several booming shopping malls and no financial woes, all around him he saw school systems on the verge of bankruptcy and increasing poverty among schoolchildren. Yet, at both the national and state levels, politicians were blaming educators and developing policies to reward high test scores and punish low ones.

Jack launched his first attack about seven years before his retirement, when the state legislature passed an education reform act establishing an interdistrict open enrollment program to improve schools through competition. He worked with the regional section of the state superintendents' association to create workshops on the new law, inviting legislators, SDE representatives, and out-of-state critics of open enrollment to speak to school administrators about it. Next, he persuaded another superintendent to file suit against the state with him; they challenged the portion of the law that required every district to send demographic data about students and their test scores to the SDE, alleging a violation of privacy rights. In the state capital, these activities earned Jack the nickname "The Gadfly," but Jack didn't care.

Although he lost his court case, Jack continued his crusade. In order to raise questions about the way political and business leaders defined education problems, he and his district sponsored a lecture series, inviting nationally prominent figures to speak about alternative perspectives on public education and its problems.

During the year before he retired, Jack was distributing information about the legislature's proposed voucher plan to his teachers and urging them to let legislators know their opinion of it. Of course, the teachers were well aware of Jack's strong opposition. When The Gadfly retired, the legislature was still considering vouchers, but Jack believed that he had fought the good fight.

QUESTIONS

1. What aspects of Jack's personal and professional situation permitted him to take strong stands? Describe a more subtle campaign that a differently situated leader might have waged.

2. Describe Jack's use of coalitions and allies as well as his attempts to influence all three policy formulation and adoption arenas.

3. To what extent did Jack choose the best stage of the policy process for his interventions? How might he have sought to influence the policy process at an earlier stage?

4. What legal and ethical questions might be raised about Jack's activities? ■

[*Note:* Jack Donato is based on a retired superintendent with whom the author is personally acquainted.]

When to "Lobby."   Readers have probably noticed that the word *lobby* has been enclosed in quotation marks up to this point. That is because under both federal law and many state laws, public officials who contact legislators or agency workers in an official capacity about issues that affect their work directly are not **lobbying,** technically speaking; they are performing a fundamental part of their job responsibility. For most other people, however, *lobbying* means contacting an executive or legislative branch official, orally or in writing, about the formulation, adoption, or modification of a statute or rule (deKieffer, 2007). School leaders must be prepared to contact officials as their job requires. In vignette III, for example, Harry Levinson was going to either lose part of the district's state funding or endanger children's lives by requiring them to walk on a treacherous road. This issue clearly related to the best interests of the district and his students; he was right to contact legislators and agency officials as part of his responsibility as superintendent.

Issues are not always so clear-cut, however. The line between a personal conviction and the best interests of children is sometimes blurred. "Lobbying" can easily shade over into real lobbying, which is covered by detailed laws. Before contacting political figures about a specific bill or rule, therefore, school leaders should ask themselves a series of questions and answer them with brutal frankness. Figure 8.7

- Does this issue clearly relate to my job responsibilities or is my interest in this issue really a matter of personal taste or commitment?
- Would the school board see contacting this official about this issue as clearly a part of my job? would parents? would area newspaper editors? would the teachers' union?
- How long would explaining to someone how this action relates to my job take me?

FIGURE 8.7   Questions for reflection before "lobbying" government officials summarizes some questions that might be asked. If a leader has any doubts about the answers, he or she should move with caution and consider working through a professional organization with registered lobbyists. Another possibility, of course, is for the district to retain its own lobbyist. Regardless of the course of action chosen, school leaders must understand that lobbying is a heavily regulated political activity, requiring registration and the filing of detailed paperwork. School leaders who become active in contacting officials about specific rules and laws should therefore be absolutely sure that they understand the most current federal and state regulations governing lobbying. As Wiget (1995) warns: "No matter how honest we are, no matter how pure our motives or how solid our principles, there are rules to be followed—particularly regarding lobbying" (p. 37).

Written Communication.   Three of the most effective ways to "lobby" public officials are written communication, telephone calls, and personal visits. Written communication is discussed here, and telephone calls and personal visits later in the chapter.

Although writing a letter is the most traditional method of contacting a government official, it is still one of the most effective, especially as made easier by faxes and e-mail. The most effective letter is a unique, original one—that is, the only one exactly like it that the official receives. It should be signed by hand and printed on letterhead. Letters that meet this description are likely to be read, although not by the official. The staffs of government officials usually read them before entering them in a log, noting the issues they addressed and the positions of their authors. A summary of correspondence is eventually given to the official. Such letters are often answered, too, although the answer is almost certain to be computer generated.

Members of the U.S. Congress and state legislatures have long had e-mail addresses that are readily available to the public, usually on a Web site maintained by the legislative body of which they are part. Not surprisingly, then, e-mail has supplanted much of the "snail mail" that legislators used to receive. E-mail can be an effective way to communicate with policy actors if certain considerations are kept in mind. An e-mail message should be brief—even briefer than a letter—and the message should not include an attachment. Because computer viruses often travel in attachments, many legislative staff members routinely delete any e-mail correspondence that includes one. Even though the message is an electronic one, the sender's address should be included; legislators always want to be able to distinguish constituents from non-constituents. Finally, the e-mail should be sent to only *one* address; a message addressed to a long list of recipients is ineffective.

Mass-produced correspondence, such as when fifty people all send the same letter to an official, is less effective. Usually it is not read; it is *weighed* (deKieffer, 2007), meaning that producing fifty or sixty such letters and getting different people to sign them is a waste of time and money. Generating several hundred or several thousand, however, might have an impact—at least that many letters would weigh a significant amount. Figures 8.8 and 8.9 detail the norms that govern letters, including e-mail, to legislators.

Professional educators should keep in mind one additional rule: Send only letters whose spelling and grammar are flawless; the reasons are obvious. Special norms

U.S. Senators

Address: The Honorable Jack R. Clemmons
             U.S. Senate
             [Office number and building]
             Washington, D.C. 20510
Salutation: Dear Senator Clemmons:

State Senators

Address: The Honorable Stanley Cernak
             State Senator
             State Capitol
             City, State ZIP
Salutation: Dear Senator Cernak:

U.S. Representatives

Address: The Honorable Bernice Cohn
             U.S. House of Representatives
             [Office number and building]
             Washington, D.C. 20515
Salutation: Dear Representative Cohn:

State Representatives

Address: The Honorable Iris Wong
             State Representative
             State Capitol
             City, State ZIP
Salutation: Dear Representative Wong:

FIGURE 8.8   How to address legislators

- Include your name and address on the envelope and in the letter.
- Deal with one issue or bill.
- Keep letters short; one page is ideal.
- Identify the legislation by number in the first paragraph.
- Clearly state your position and give your reasons for it, drawing on your expertise and experience.
- Ask the legislator to support your position.
- Be pleasant, polite, and constructive.
- Sign your name by hand.
- Write a letter of appreciation if the legislator does support your position.

FIGURE 8.9   Tips for effective letters to legislators

also cover written communication to agencies in response to their calls for comments on proposed rules. Usually, these are provided in the official notice of the proposed rule making. They should be followed to the letter; otherwise, agency officials will probably disqualify them.

Telephone Calls.   Especially when time is short, the most effective way to contact a legislator is by telephone. Calls can be directed either to the legislator's office in the capital or to his or her district office. Needless to say, busy legislators rarely answer their office telephones; a secretary or receptionist handles that task. Because members of legislative staffs often specialize in specific policy areas, callers should

- Before calling, prepare a short written outline of the points you want to make.
- Identify yourself and where you live at the beginning of the call.
- State what issue concerns you; identify the issue by bill number as well as a brief description.
- Tell your own position and explain your reasons for holding it.
- Ask for the legislator's support.
- Be pleasant, polite, and constructive.
- Follow up with a letter if time permits.

FIGURE 8.10   Tips for telephoning legislators

indicate why they are calling so that they can be referred to the right person. The tips in Figure 8.10 are helpful in preparing for and structuring a telephone call. As with letters, calls should be brief—no more than five to ten minutes (Bootel, 1995; deKieffer, 2007; Wiget, 1995).

The telephone is often the best way for a school leader to contact an agency administrator. Although agency administrators do not answer their own telephones either, they are often willing to return a call. As with legislators, callers should be prepared either to give the number of the rule they wish to discuss or to identify the area where they are having problems. Contacting agency workers with questions, requests for clarification, and complaints about new policies or rules is appropriate. Offering to help develop new rules in your area of expertise is also appropriate. Often they value honest input that can help them plan the implementation of a new policy (Bootel, 1995).

Personal Visits.   Sometimes talking with a legislator face to face is advisable; such a personal visit can be extremely effective. An appointment must always be arranged well in advance, and it is wise to plan to visit early in a session of the legislature rather than later when calendars are packed and days are full. Appointments can be arranged with the legislator's secretary. Staff members may ask about the purpose of the visit; their questions should be answered fully and accurately.

A typical appointment with a legislator lasts only about fifteen minutes; therefore, to get the most value from a visit, it should be carefully planned, which means knowing exactly what must be said and being ready to say it. Educators should prepare a brief outline of major points to make. Many people also put together information to leave with the lawmaker. Frequently, these include a fact sheet that summarizes their position and the reasons for it.

Educators must arrive punctually for an appointment with a legislator. Sometimes, however, the legislator is not able to keep the appointment personally and arranges for a staff member to handle it. Naturally, this is disappointing, but school leaders should not interpret it as either an insult or an indication of a lack of interest. Rather, this is one of the ways in which legislators manage the heavy demands on their time and the unpredictability of legislative work. A visitor should talk to the legislative staff member sitting in for the legislator just as he would speak to the legislator—after all, the staff member is the one who will report on this conversation to the legislator. Whether meeting with the legislator or a staff member, taking notes is always appropriate. As with letters and telephone calls, the tone of the visit should be polite and constructive.

After a visit, education leaders should write letters thanking the legislator and any staff members involved in scheduling the appointment and holding the meeting. The letter should also briefly recall pertinent facts from the conversation. This is often a suitable time to send information items, especially if the legislator or a staff member expressed an interest in having them (Bootel, 1995; deKieffer, 2007; Wiget, 1995).

Special Comments on Influencing the Judiciary.   Attempting to influence the policy formulation and adoption process of the court systems raises some delicate issues that do not arise in relation to the other two branches of government. Although school leaders should include judges in their government relations programs, they must also understand that they should never "lobby" a judge. The professional norms of those who sit on the bench dictate that they should reach decisions through the impartial application of the law, precedent, and legal reasoning (Abraham, 1998). Therefore, they regard any attempts by laypeople to sway them in one direction or the other as an insulting violation of their judicial prerogatives. Although school leaders may frequently encounter judges at civic and political functions, they should carefully avoid bringing up any education cases pending in their courts. Should a judge raise the issue, school leaders should speak carefully, letting the judge set the parameters of the conversation.

This does not mean, however, that one cannot express views about an important case. The formal and institutionalized method for expressing an opinion to a panel of judges is the *brief amicus curiae,* or friend of the court brief. This is "a partisan brief filed by an outside individual . . . or group who is not a litigant . . . but is vitally interested in a decision favorable to the side it espouses" (Abraham, 1998, p. 259). Such a document typically presents an argument couched in legal terms in support of its position. There are important limits on the use of the brief amicus curiae. Individuals and groups who wish to submit such a brief must file applications with the relevant court, and permission to file a brief amicus curiae is not always granted. Education leaders who are considering this route should seek advice and legal counsel from one or more professional organizations.

DANGER—BEWARE!   Influencing the policy process is not an activity for the naive or the uninformed. People who become involved in political activity of any sort must be aware of several possible legal pitfalls, as discussed here.

Partisan Activity.   Many school leaders belong to a political party or at least feel strong sympathy for one. They should understand, however, that in their capacity as professional education leaders, their behavior must be carefully nonpartisan. Relationships must be built with all relevant policy players, regardless of their party affiliation or ideological orientation. Invitations must be extended to officials representing a variety of views, not just the ones with whom school officials agree. Education leaders must avoid favoring one party or party faction over another, or even appearing to do so. Many states have laws governing partisan activity by public officials (Wiget, 1995). This is an area where knowing the rules and playing by them is important.

Campaign Contributions.   Sooner or later, most school leaders are approached for a campaign contribution. Needless to say, school funds must never be donated for political purposes, which means that all contributions must come from the individual's own resources, and professional educators rarely have abundant funds. Also, contributing to one campaign often means feeling obligated to contribute to others. Unfortunately, there is no single, universal, hard-and-fast rule; politics is rarely that simple. Nonetheless, the following advice should be helpful.

All aspiring and new education leaders should try to decide how they will respond to requests for contributions before they are asked. Their two major considerations should be the law and local professional norms. Their professional organization can provide information about federal and state laws; it may even publish a brochure summarizing legal guidelines. Aspiring and new leaders should also ask practicing administrators in their district what the local norms are. These may be even more restrictive than the law. For example, although in one state contributing up to $100 to each campaign may be legal; in one school district everyone may have quietly decided not to make any contributions at all. In an adjacent district, the practice may be to give a token sum—$5, perhaps—to everyone who asks. A special situation arises when a new or aspiring leader learns that local professional norms violate the law. In such a case, he or she should first make sure, by consulting outside sources, that the practice in question is actually illegal. If outside sources confirm that it is, hard choices must be made.

Gifts.   Gifts to politicians, like campaign contributions, are heavily regulated by both federal and state law. Even taking a legislator to lunch at an inexpensive restaurant or offering a small gift such as a book, poster, or decorative mug may violate the law, or may have to be reported to a special agency. Law in this area changes rapidly, so school leaders who want to give gifts must know the law and follow it, updating their information annually.

FINAL POINTS

Hopefully, the previous few paragraphs were not so disconcerting that some education leaders are now inclined to avoid interacting with government officials. School leaders cannot stay away from the policy formulation and adoption processes. As public officials, part of their responsibility is to work to obtain the best possible policies for schools. As education leaders, part of their responsibility is to model effective citizenship in a democracy. One reason that education policies are often unrealistic or even harmful is that too many school leaders avoid politics. Yet, to eschew politics is to become the victim of politics and to see ineffective policy after ineffective policy visited on the schools by people who know little about them or the children they serve. Influencing policy formulation is hard and often risky work, but it is part of the work of anyone who wants to be an education leader.

QUESTIONS AND ACTIVITIES FOR DISCUSSION

1. Identify three organizations in your state that provide information about the activities of the state legislature. Access their Web sites and discuss your findings with your class.
2. Contact the SDE in your state and ask what provisions, if any, it makes for the participation of educators in rule making. Discuss your findings with your class.
3. Find a copy of the legislation that governs lobbying and gifts to politicians in your state. What activities are permitted? Forbidden?
4. Develop a plan for building better relations between your school district or building and appropriate area government officials.

INTERNET ASSIGNMENT

Search the Internet for Web sites maintained by the legislative, executive, and judicial branches of your state's government. Then, evaluate them by assessing them in terms of these criteria: (1) user-friendly design; (2) up-to-date information; (3) accurate and complete information; and (4) provision of information about how to contact government officials.

FOR FURTHER READING

Jennings, J. (2010/2011). The policy and politics of rewriting the nation's main education law. *Phi Delta Kappan 92*(4), 44–49.

Jennings, the head of the influential Center on Education Policy, discusses the major controversies surrounding the rewriting of the *No Child Left Behind Act* and reviews the positions of various Washington, D.C., policy actors on the revisions. His article provides interesting insights into federal education politics.

Lewis, J., Jongsma, K. S., & Berger, A. (2005). *Educators on the frontline*. Newark, DE: International Reading Association.

The authors provide a handbook of strategies that educators who want to influence the policy process could use to guide their advocacy efforts. The sample letters, articles, and press releases are especially valuable.

Oleszek, W. J. (2007). *Congressional procedures and the policy process,* 7th ed. Washington, D.C.: CQ Press.

The author Provides an inside picture of how the U.S. Congress does its work, from the budget process to how conflicts are resolved. Although he describes the functioning of Congress, much of his information can also be applied to state legislatures.

Rosenthal, A. (2004). *Heavy lifting: The job of the American legislature.* Washington, D.C.: CQ Press.

Rosenthal provides a detailed and interesting description of the work of state legislatures. Based to a great extent on the author's research, the book covers theories of what state legislators should do, as well as a picture of the tasks and challenges of contemporary legislatures.

Squire, P., & Moncrief, G. (2010). *State legislatures today.* Boston, MA: Longman.

This very readable book provides a lot of information about contemporary state legislatures that is not readily accessible to non-political scientists, including the impact of term limits, the special characteristics of elections to state legislatures, and the work performed by state legislators.

9

LOOKING AT POLICIES: POLICY INSTRUMENTS AND COST EFFECTIVENESS

Focus Questions

▮ How can leaders anticipate what kind of politics will develop around a new policy?

▮ How can they select the best instrument for achieving a policy goal?

▮ How can they determine the true costs of a policy?

LEARNING TO ANALYZE PUBLIC POLICIES

Just knowing about policy development, formulation, and adoption or about the roles of various policy actors is not enough for school leaders: they should also know how to take policies apart and scrutinize them closely as well. This analytical process can yield clues about how well a policy will work and predict with some accuracy who will support and oppose it. School leaders need this skill for two reasons. First, as administrators, they must develop policies themselves. Principals are responsible for adopting policies that permit their schools to operate as positive learning environments for children. Superintendents must draft policy proposals on many subjects and recommend them to the school board. Dress codes, tardiness, test scores, unruly behavior in the cafeteria—in these areas and more, administrators often find themselves formulating policies. Yet, unless they are familiar with the forms that policies can take, they probably address all problems with the same type of policy—a rule with a penalty attached. Sometimes a rule with a penalty attached is the best policy, but not always. When leaders understand several policy options, they can choose among them, matching the policy to the problem and its context. Second, education leaders today often find themselves implementing policies developed by others. Chapter 10 discusses implementation in depth, but the first step toward skillful implementation is understanding the structure of the policy. How likely is this policy to work? How will various stakeholders react? What problems are most likely to arise? What will it really cost? These are questions that policy analysis can help answer.

This chapter, then, presents three lenses through which school leaders can examine policies critically, both their own and others'. Although these analytical approaches are different, they are complementary. Each brings a slightly different aspect of policy structure into focus. Together they constitute a powerful instrument for examining education policies closely. Unlike the other chapters, the exercises in this one are provided after each major section to permit readers to apply each framework to concrete examples immediately.

LOWI'S TECHNIQUES OF CONTROL

In a classic 1964 article, Theodore Lowi advanced the thesis that there are three basic types of policies: *distributive, regulatory,* and *redistributive,* and that each generates a distinctive political arena. Thirty years later, he and Benjamin Ginsberg (1994) slightly refined the original thesis, calling the policy types *techniques of control* and renaming *distributive policy* as *promotional policy.* This discussion draws ideas from both the 1964 and 1994 writings, but retains the 1964 terminology because it is so widely used (see, e.g., Kraft & Furlong, 2007).

Distributive Policies

DISTRIBUTIVE DEFINED. *Distributive policies* bestow gifts on citizens, and these gifts may be goods, services, or special privileges. Although the idea of a government giving gifts may seem strange to some, this practice is actually an old one. In ancient times, kings used gifts to win the loyalty of their followers and build their power. In the Anglo–Saxon epic *Beowulf,* synonyms for *king* include *ring-giver* and *dispenser of treasure* (Abrams et al., 1962). Although contemporary governments do not bestow jewelry on their citizens, they have other ways to distribute wealth and privileges. Lowi and Ginsberg distinguish three: (1) subsidies, (2) contracts, and (3) nonregulatory licenses.

SUBSIDIES. A *subsidy* may consist of "cash, goods, services, or land" (Lowi & Ginsberg, 1994, p. 389). For example, both the federal and state governments subsidize the building and repair of roads (Kraft & Furlong, 2007). A county government that needs to fill the potholes in some of its roads usually applies to a higher level of government for a subsidy. If the application succeeds, county officials are overjoyed. They brag to county residents about this proof of their effectiveness and even erect signs at construction sites, proclaiming how much money they received for the project.

CONTRACTS. *Contracts* are another form of distributive policy. Under a contract, a private firm agrees to provide a product or service to the government in exchange for a specific amount of money. Lowi and Ginsberg (1994) argue that many policies commonly called *privatization* are actually forms of government contracting. Current proposals to privatize education functions such as transportation, custodial services, and management fall into this category. Although the businesses that enter into contracts with school districts must perform work in exchange for their gift, nonetheless, the school district is bestowing on them a privilege with a substantial cash value attached.

NONREGULATORY LICENSING. "A license is a privilege granted by government to do something that it otherwise considers to be illegal" (Lowi & Ginsberg, 1994, p. 391). *Licenses* can be obtained by paying a fee without having to meet many requirements. For example, in most states, people who have reached a certain age can obtain a hunting license with little difficulty. All licenses allow license holders to perform activities for which they could otherwise be charged with a legal violation. Through them, the government distributes privileges that those who do not hold licenses lack. Currently, nonregulatory licenses are rarely used in education.

DISTRIBUTION AS CONTROL.   In ancient times, chieftains bestowed jewelry and land on their followers to keep them loyal, but they usually did not seek to control their behavior in other ways. Today, of course, governments have broad public purposes in mind when they use distributive policies (Kraft & Furlong, 2007). They use them to influence behavior. For example, the federal school lunch and milk program, first established in 1946, is distributive. Although some children qualify for "free" or "reduced" meals based on family need, all students (and school staff as well) receive subsidized meals from the government. Since its inception, this program has served to improve child nutrition, especially among the poor, but probably among the middle class as well. At the state level, governments often provide flat grants based on enrollment to subsidize school services such as transportation and testing. Their distributions encourage districts to provide these services to children; otherwise, they might not. Figure 9.1 lists some typical distributive policies used in education; this list suggests the many ways that distributive policies can shape behavior.

DISTRIBUTIVE POLITICS.   A return to the metaphor of the ancient king clarifies the nature of the political arena generated by distributive politics. Rulers of long ago needed the support of their vassals in battle; they also wanted to discourage them from revolting.

Subsidies

- Many professional development programs
- State subsidies for school transportation
- State programs for upgrading computer technology in schools
- State programs supporting capital outlay
- School lunch and milk program
- State or federal block grants
- Flat grants as part of school funding
- Some foundation formulas used to allocate state funds to districts

Contracts

- State or district contracts with textbook companies
- State or district contracts with testing companies
- Contracting out transportation, custodial, or cafeteria services
- Contracts for designing and constructing school facilities

Nonregulatory licenses

- Parking permits issued to students
- Parking permits issued to staff
- Library cards issued to community users of a school library

FIGURE 9.1   Examples of distributive policies in education

Distributing gifts was an excellent way to achieve these goals. As long as a ruler was both generous and fair, his followers were likely to remain uninterested in challenging his power. Wise distribution practices encouraged followers to focus on nurturing their relationship with the king, not on paying attention to his other followers. Among themselves, followers tended to practice mutual noninterference. The wise distribution of gifts also made inciting a rebellion difficult for the occasional malcontent, because contented followers usually calculated what they would gain from joining a rebellion and decided the costs would outweigh the benefits. Of course, rulers did not always distribute gifts wisely. In that case, their gift-giving policy became redistributive rather than distributive, and redistributive politics generates a different political game.

In contemporary U.S. politics, distributive policies create a political arena similar to that of the wise king. When the government is distributing "gifts"—such as grants for remedial education or school transportation money—potential recipients focus their attention on the relevant government agency, largely ignoring each other. If the agency is skillful in its distribution, the political arena is stable and conflicts are rare. Of course, skillful distribution requires constant concern for "equality, consistency, impartiality, uniformity, precedent, and moderation" (Schattschneider, 1935, p. 88). Politicians like pork barrel policies precisely because they are distributive, providing them with an opportunity to reduce conflict among their constituents . . . and discourage potential challengers in the next election.

Regulatory Policies

REGULATORY DEFINED. *Regulatory policies* are formalized rules expressed in general terms and applied to large groups of people (Kraft & Furlong, 2007). They either reduce or expand the alternatives available to those regulated. Rules imply enforcement by the government and penalties for those who break them. Although regulatory policies appeared early in history, Lowi and Ginsberg (1994) argue that not until the nineteenth century did governments rely heavily on them. The reason is clear: Until recently, government's ability to enforce rules was limited. The communication and information revolutions changed this, however.

TYPES OF REGULATORY POLICIES. Most regulatory policies take the form of laws or administrative rules that explicitly require or prohibit certain behaviors. A special type of regulatory policy is *regulatory licensing*. A regulatory license makes practicing a profession illegal until people have met specific requirements set by the government. For example, teachers' and administrators' licenses are regulatory licenses.

Educators often feel that they are swimming through a sea of regulations. As Figure 9.2 suggests, they have good reason to feel that way. From the day that they enter a teacher education program that leads to a regulatory license, professional educators deal with government regulations. Many federal grant programs involve such heavy regulation of recipients that Lowi and Ginsberg (1994) categorize them as regulatory rather than distributive. State governments seem to have a strong preference for regulatory policies. They use rules and laws to prescribe how many days a year schools must be in session, what subjects they must teach, how school buildings must be constructed, under what conditions a teacher can be dismissed, and so on. At the local level, school

Regulatory licenses

- Teacher certification
- Administrator certification

Laws, rules, regulations, and guidelines

- Graduation requirements
- State or district curriculum frameworks
- State or district textbook adoptions
- State or district rules regarding school day, week, and year
- Dress codes
- Fire and safety codes
- Compulsory attendance requirements
- School discipline codes
- Federal or state grants with detailed guidelines
- Required criminal record checks
- Prescribed teacher evaluation procedures
- Some foundation formulas used to allocate state funds to districts

FIGURE 9.2   Examples of regulatory policies in education

boards and educators follow in the footsteps of higher levels of government. Smoking policies, dress codes, disciplinary handbooks, and teachers' classroom rules are all regulatory policies.

REGULATORY POLITICS.   Regulatory policies create a political arena different from that generated by distributive ones. Several social groups with conflicting interests are usually concerned about regulatory policies. For example, if a state legislature is proposing to increase the length of the school year, several groups will be interested in this legislation. Teacher and administrator groups will be concerned about the possibility that their members will be expected to work more days without a commensurate pay increase. School board groups will fear that the longer school year will generate additional expenses, which will fall on them rather than on the state. Some business groups will favor the legislation as a way to raise standards and possibly reduce their on-the-job training requirements. People in the tourist industry, however, may oppose the bill, because they depend on the cheap summer labor of young people. Parent groups will probably be split, with some favoring more schooling (and supervised care) for their children and others concerned about lost opportunities for family trips. No single regulatory policy will please all these groups. In such an arena, the political actors pay a great deal of attention to each other, both competing and seeking to find allies. This arena is unstable and filled with conflict. Coalitions form quickly and fall apart quickly; participants bargain and negotiate. These conflicts, however, are largely nonideological, with most participants willing to concede points in order to make a deal.

Redistributive Policies

REDISTRIBUTIVE DEFINED.   A *redistributive policy* is one that shifts resources or power from one social group to another. By doing so, the government "seek[s] to control conduct . . . indirectly by altering the conditions of conduct or manipulating the environment" (Lowi & Ginsberg, 1994, p. 397). The policy goal may be economic, such as shifting income to the middle class in order to stimulate consumer buying; it may also be social or political, such as providing a modest income to the unemployed in order to keep social unrest from becoming a problem.

TYPES OF REDISTRIBUTIVE POLICIES.   Redistributive policies fall into two broad categories: those that shift economic resources and those that shift power. The government usually shifts material resources by manipulating taxation or the monetary system. A good example of such a policy is Social Security, which is not a form of insurance or old-age annuity, but a redistribution of income through taxation. The federal government deducts a special tax from the paychecks of most U.S. workers and channels this money to Social Security to pay benefits to the elderly, the disabled, and some children. Thus, Social Security taxes "redistribute wealth from higher to lower income people and from . . . workers to . . . retirees" (Lowi & Ginsberg, 1994, p. 401). Redistributive policies may also shift power, usually by granting new rights to a large social group. Redistributive policies are often used in education. Figure 9.3 lists major past and present redistributive policies.

Obviously, these are the hot topics of education policy. Redistributive policies of the 1960s and 1970s shifted resources and power from dominant social groups to groups that had been, or felt they had been, oppressed. Among the major beneficiaries were African Americans, residents of the South and inner cities, the poor, women, and those with handicaps. As one would expect, these redistributive policies sparked much controversy and were subjected to much criticism. Today, most redistributive education policies shift power within the education establishment. Vouchers reallocate the power to assign pupils (and state funds) to schools, removing it from school

- Affirmative action programs
- Desegregation
- Education for All Handicapped Children Act
- Privatization of school management
- Privatization of teaching special subjects
- School finance systems based on power equalizing
- School finance systems based on full state funding
- Site-based management
- Title I (remedial programs for the poor)
- Title IX (gender equity)
- Vouchers

FIGURE 9.3   Examples of redistributive policies in education administrators and giving it to parents. Site-based management moves power from the school board and district office to the school site. Reagan's New Federalism shifted much authority over education from the federal to the state level. As redistributive policies, they have generated conflict and intense ideological debates.

REDISTRIBUTIVE POLITICS.   Redistributive policies are usually controversial and "cut closer than any others along class lines" (Lowi, 1964, p. 707); therefore, they generate a political arena marked by intense conflict. Precisely because of this conflict, the groups involved—usually large associations—typically form two stable coalitions and face off against each other. They are unlikely to negotiate or "cut deals" because each is convinced that it alone is right. The attitudes and discourse of the participants in this arena are deeply ideological. In a redistributive political arena, the government often plays the role of mediator and umpire. In the 1960s, for instance, the Civil Rights Movement and the laws that it pressured Congress to pass created a redistributive political arena. The National Association for the Advancement of Colored People and its allies stood on one side, calling for equal rights and dignity for African Americans. On the other side White southerners and many northerners as well spoke with equal passion for preserving states' rights and their traditions. This conflict frequently erupted into violence. Meanwhile, behind the scenes, government officials tried to find ways to convince both groups to accept legalistic approaches to resolving the conflict. Although most redistributive policies do not spark violence, all redistributive political arenas are marked by sharp divisions and ideological intensity.

Do Lowi's Categories Overlap?

When one tries to apply Lowi's categories to specific policies, they seem to overlap. For example, what seems at first to be a purely distributive policy, such as the school lunch and milk program, reveals aspects of regulation and redistribution when analyzed thoughtfully. The rules controlling lunch content have the effect of regulating the cafeteria staff's behavior. Also, providing subsidized lunches to schoolchildren redistributes public money to farmers; indeed, this was one of the original purposes of the policy. Lowi (1964; Lowi & Ginsberg, 1994) anticipates this criticism, arguing that these categories should be understood as describing the short term, rather than the long term. Because most citizens and politicians think and act in the short term, the categories describe short-term perceptions of policies. In the long term, all policies are both regulatory and redistributive.

Using Lowi's Categories in School Leadership

ANTICIPATING POLITICAL SITUATIONS.   Lowi's basic policy types provide a way to anticipate the political environment that develops around a policy both when it is under consideration and after its adoption. Moreover, the relationship between the techniques of control and their political arenas suggests ways to manage policy change at the local level. Lowi's framework can also make developing strategies for influencing the policy process easier. In this section, each of these uses of Lowi's categories is considered in turn.

MANAGING POLICY CHANGE.   Analyzing policy ideas using Lowi's techniques of control can help leaders at the district level plan several policy changes over a period of years. Generally, one should not introduce too many policies of the same type simultaneously, especially if the changes are redistributive. The following example clarifies this principle.

Imagine a school board, a superintendent, and a central office team who, after much discussion and argument, agree that numerous policy changes must be made over the next few years, including the following:

1. Requiring teachers to submit lesson plans to their principal;
2. Using a large reserve fund to repair buildings;
3. Adopting a uniform dress code for students;
4. Reducing class size to fifteen in grades K–3;
5. Implementing a pay-to-play policy for the athletic programs;
6. Applying for a grant to support a dropout prevention program;
7. Applying for foundation funding for a preschool program;
8. Providing a day of release time each year for teachers to attend a technology workshop;
9. Moving to an intradistrict open enrollment plan; and
10. Requiring more frequent evaluations of teachers whose students have low scores on the state proficiency test.

Using Lowi's categories to analyze these policies makes it clear that numbers 2, 6, 7, and 8 are distributive; numbers 1, 3, and 10 are regulatory; and numbers 4, 5, and 9 are redistributive. In planning how to introduce these changes over a period of a few years, district leaders should reflect about the political arenas they will generate and especially about which people and groups they will activate. For instance, implementing changes 4 and 5 simultaneously would probably arouse middle school and secondary teachers, coaches, and the parents of secondary students. They might well form an alliance, making common cause around the issue of unfair treatment of secondary schools. Such a coalition, fired by redistributive politics, might create a volatile situation that leaders could not handle. Less dramatically, but with equal potential for political harm, trying to put regulatory policies numbers 1 and 10 in place at once could so activate the teachers' union that it might be able to build unprecedented power among angry teachers. At first, no political risks might seem to be attached to putting several distributive policies in place at once. This perception is mistaken, however. The fact that distributive policies are often referred to as *pork* and *patronage* suggests why. Excessive use of such policies appears weak at best and corrupt at worst. This situation, too, is one to avoid.

In general, then, wise education leaders should plan a gradual introduction of several changes, taking care to use a judicious mix of policy types. Above all, they should avoid (1) making too many policy changes of the same type close together, (2) making too many policy changes that activate the same individuals and groups at about the same time, and (3) making a combination of changes that activate too many people and groups in the policy arena at the same time.

PLANNING INFLUENCE STRATEGIES.   As suggested in Chapter 8, education leaders should play an active role in policy adoption and formulation, contributing their professional knowledge and bringing their influence to bear on those issues that concern them. However, because different policies generate different political configurations, leaders must select appropriate strategies. Lowi's categories suggest ways to do this.

As an illustration, let us imagine a superintendent who feels strongly about three bills the state legislature is considering and wishes to support them. The bills are the following:

1. *Computers for Our Schools Bill.* This bill proposes that $500 million in unexpected tax revenues be used to upgrade computer systems in schools across the state. Funds will be allocated proportionally on the basis of enrollment. Districts will be able to use them to rewire old buildings and purchase up-to-date hardware and software.
2. *H.B. 203.* This bill would modify teacher certification requirements, mandating more field experience and exposure to diverse educational contexts. It would also assess prospective teachers' knowledge of content areas using a nationally standardized test.
3. *A Bill to Expand Education Choices for Families.* This proposal would establish a statewide open enrollment program. Parents would be able to apply to enroll their children in any public school in the state; each child's share of state foundation moneys would be sent to the receiving district. Schools could not discriminate on the basis of race, gender, handicap, or native language.

As a first step in planning to influence politicians, the superintendent should analyze these bills by applying Lowi's categories to them. Such an analysis suggests that the *Computers for Our Schools Bill* is basically a distributive policy, H.B. 203 is regulatory, and *A Bill to Expand Education Choices for Families* is redistributive. Unless there are complicating factors in state politics, each bill will generate a different sort of political arena, and the superintendent should strategize accordingly.

Strategies for Distributive Arenas. Distributive policies generate stable arenas in which little conflict exists; the recipients of "gifts" focus most of their attention on the distributor rather than on each other. During the policy formulation phase, therefore, the superintendent should focus on communicating to lawmakers information about how the bill as introduced would affect his district. If necessary, the superintendent should suggest ways to amend the bill to help his district more. No conflict within the K–12 education community should arise over this bill. Any opposition will come from other state-level players, such as the board of regents or the prison system, who may perceive the bill as redistributive. The superintendent might, therefore, indicate to the bill's sponsors his willingness to help obtain passage by contacting those legislators most likely to be influenced by the other groups. After passage, the superintendent should focus on seeing that the rules written by the state department of education (SDE) are fair to his district. He should also work to develop and maintain a good relationship with those in the state agency who administer the program.

Strategies for Regulatory Arenas. H.B. 203, however, is a regulatory policy. It will probably generate a competitive but pragmatic political arena in which most major players are connected with K–12 education. Therefore, the superintendent should first tentatively identify these competitors and their probable positions. Hypothetically, one would expect the teachers' unions, subject-matter associations, administrators' groups, and teachers' colleges to be most interested in this policy. Each will have a different agenda but be willing to enter coalitions and negotiate. A good second step would be for the superintendent to contact his professional association to gather information about its position and discuss his views with the lobbyists who will work on this bill. He might offer to help the association in its efforts to see that the final law reflects administrators' concerns. The superintendent should expect that as the bill is being formulated and adopted as official policy, deals will be cut and alliances will form and fall apart. He should not waste his time by castigating people for selling out. He should understand that this is a pragmatic arena, not an ideological one; in it, unyielding positions are out of place. Nor should the superintendent lose interest after the bill is passed. The groups that worked to influence the law will compete to influence its accompanying rules. Only after rules have been formally adopted should he and his allies relax their vigilance.

Strategies for Redistributive Arenas.   *A Bill to Expand Education Choices for Families* is a redistributive policy, which would reallocate the power to decide which districts and schools children attend from public officials to parents. It would also reallocate some state foundation funds to those districts that, for whatever reason, can attract students from outside their boundaries. This proposal will probably generate an intensely ideological arena in which two opposing sides will emerge. As a first step toward participating in this arena, the superintendent should identify who is most likely to join each side. The supportive side will probably include districts that expect to gain students, parents who are interested in transferring their children, businesses, and conservative groups. On the opposing side, one would expect to see those districts that fear they would lose students, associations that represent cities' interests in the state capital, and liberal groups. The African American community may be split, with those who live in inner cities supporting the bill and others opposing it. Districts that anticipate no major impact from the policy—large rural districts, for instance—will probably remain uninvolved.

Such an analysis would suggest to the superintendent where he is most likely to find individuals and groups who share his position. They might consider forming an ad hoc umbrella organization, combining all supporters of the bill. Such an organization would magnify the power of supporters and provide a vehicle within which people from diverse backgrounds could work together. He should realize that building a strong coalition will require much ideological work such as developing appropriate slogans, flyers, news releases, and speeches. The superintendent should understand, too, that ideological battles are often won by the side whose discourse most resonates with the public. Finally, he should recognize that getting this policy adopted may require a campaign of several years, during which supporters must educate legislators and the public, build an effective organization, and raise funds to support their efforts. Long-term persistence is often the key to passing redistributive policies.

EXERCISES ON THE TECHNIQUES OF CONTROL

1. Identify each of the following policies as distributive, regulatory, or redistributive.
   a. A federal preschool program for poor children.
   b. A school board policy detailing the procedure for expelling students.
   c. A legal requirement that minority teachers be hired to staff an inner-city dropout prevention program.

   d. A bill to require all children in grades K–6 to study the dangers of drugs.
   e. A law requiring the development of state content standards in all major subjects, grades K–12.
   f. A bill to require a certification procedure for teachers' aides.
   g. A state program that gives high schools $100 for each student enrolled in driver's education.
   h. A state law that grants school districts funds to provide a mentoring program for first-year teachers.
   i. A federal court decision requiring girls' athletic programs to be funded equally with boys' athletic programs.
   j. A school board's plan to contract with an educational management company to operate five schools in the district.
2. For policies a, d, f, and h, describe the political arena that each policy will probably generate. Identify probable supporters and opponents as well as the nature of the conflicts that will ensue.
3. For policies c, e, g, and j, decide whether you support or oppose each policy; then, outline a strategy for influencing the policy process in the direction you prefer.
4. Do any of the policies in question 1 have the characteristics of more than one technique of control? If so, which? How would these mixed characteristics affect the politics surrounding the policy?

MCDONNELL AND ELMORE'S POLICY INSTRUMENTS

McDonnell and Elmore (1987) argued that four "alternative policy instruments, or . . . mechanisms [exist] that translate substantive policy goals . . . into concrete actions" (p. 134). Those four instruments are *mandates,* **inducements, capacity building,** and **system changing.** Seven years later, McDonnell (1994) added a fifth instrument to the framework: **hortatory policy,** or *persuasion.* Although Lowi's three techniques of control are based on the impact of policies on society, McDonnell and Elmore developed their framework of policy instruments by considering "the conditions under which these instruments are most likely to produce their intended effects" (McDonnell & Elmore, 1987, p. 133). Lowi's categories can be understood as a wide-angle lens for looking at policies, bringing the whole society into view. McDonnell and Elmore's typology resembles a close-up lens, permitting a detailed view of how a particular policy type functions. This section first discusses each policy instrument. Table 9.1 summarizes the highlights of this discussion. Next, the use of multiple policy instruments by five states is discussed. Finally, this section explores ways that school leaders can use McDonnell and Elmore's ideas.

Mandates

A *mandate* is a "rule governing the actions of individuals and agencies" (McDonnell & Elmore, 1987, p. 138). It usually consists of two components: (1) language that spells out required behavior for all people in a specified social group, and (2) a prescribed penalty for those who fail to comply. These components may take the form of a statute, an administrative rule, a court decision, a school board policy, or a school or classroom rule. A good example of a mandate is a compulsory school attendance law. Such

TABLE 9.1 McDonnell and Elmore's Policy Instruments

Policy Instrument	Components	Best Context	Costs	Major Drawback
Mandates	1. Language requiring behavior 2. Penalty	1. Uniform behavior desirable 2. Strong support	1. Enforcement 2. Compliance 3. Avoidance	Adversarial relationships
Inducements	1. Short-term transfer of resources 2. Guidelines	Diverse behavior desirable	Oversight	Excessive diversity
Capacity Building	1. Long-term investment 2. Guidelines	Existing institutions unable to respond	1. Investment 2. Administration	Intangibility of short-term results
System change	Shift of authority	Existing institutions unwilling to respond	Countering resistance	Unpredictable results
Hortatory Policy	1. Information 2. Symbols, images 3. Appeal to values	Target population most likely to act on information	Disseminating information	Danger of manipulation

Source: Based on L. M. McDonnell and R. F. Elmore (1987), "Getting the Job Done: Alternative Policy Instruments," *Educational Evaluation and Policy Analysis, 9,* pp. 137, 141; McDonnell (1994).

a statute requires the parents of children between certain ages to send their children to school or arrange for their home schooling. Most school districts have district-level administrators—who used to be called *truant officers* but now have more pleasant titles—who monitor attendance figures and check up on children who are not attending school. They usually start by issuing a warning to the parents but, if necessary, can take them to court where a judge may impose a fine.

Mandates are appropriate policy instruments only in certain situations. A mandate functions best when one wants to encourage all members of a group to behave in the same way and when the mandate can be enforced. Mandates also require strong political support. Compulsory attendance laws meet both criteria; almost all people, both average citizens and political leaders, believe that children should be educated, and school attendance can be enforced easily. However, like all policy instruments, mandates imply costs. These include the cost of enforcing a mandate, the cost of complying with it, and the cost of avoiding compliance. School districts must pay the administrators who enforce attendance and provide them with offices, clerical help, and automobiles. The families incur costs, too. School attendance entails expenditures for items such as suitable clothing, required fees, and necessary materials. The family also loses the domestic labor or supplementary income that older children could provide. Noncompliance involves costs as well. Tactics to elude the truant officer, such as frequent moving and time spent persuading friends and relatives to cover for the family, impose a toll.

The ideal result of a mandate is widespread, uniform behavior of a socially desirable sort. Compulsory attendance laws have led to a society in which almost everyone has received some education. Less desirable results may also occur. Mandates may encourage uniform behavior in a situation where diversity would be preferable. Finally, mandates usually create an adversarial relationship between the enforcing agency and those who do not wish to comply. The comic antics of children playing hooky as they try to avoid a pursuing truant officer are a frequent theme in popular culture; they illustrate in amusing fashion the hostile relationships that can develop around a mandate.

Inducements

An *inducement* is a "transfer of money [or in-kind grants] to individuals or agencies in return for the production of goods or services" (McDonnell & Elmore, 1987, pp. 137–138). Inducements consist of two components: (1) the money, services, or in-kind materials to be transferred; and (2) guidelines that spell out how they are to be used. These guidelines may be broad, as with block grants, or detailed, as with categorical grants. Most often, the language in which an inducement is formulated appears in a statute or administrative rule. Theoretically, however, it could also be included in a school board policy or in school or classroom rules. A good example of the use of inducements in education is Title I of the *Elementary and Secondary Education Act* of 1965. Passed as part of President Johnson's War on Poverty, Title I has evolved through numerous mutations, changing its name from Title I to Chapter 1 and back again. For decades, it offered federal grant moneys to public and private schools in exchange for their provision of remedial education services. The guidelines changed over the years, but they always required schools or districts (or both) to serve a certain percentage of poor children in order to qualify for grants (Spring, 2005).

Inducements are appropriate only in certain situations, however. First, because accepting inducements is voluntary, leaders should not use them to encourage a behavior so desirable that everyone should display it. For example, inducements would be a poor policy instrument to use in implementing compulsory school attendance. The most appropriate contexts in which to use inducements are those in which diverse behavior is desirable or at least acceptable. Second, inducements work best when large numbers of potential implementers are willing to implement the policy but currently lack the resources to do so. Finally, because adopting inducements does not require strong political support, they are the ideal policy instrument for situations in which it may be difficult to pass a mandate, a system change, or a capacity building program. Title I represents an appropriate use of inducements. Its main purpose was to provide educational support for poor children; however, because many schools and districts have few poor children, diverse behavior in the area of remedial education for the underprivileged was acceptable. Moreover, public school professionals were generally willing to provide such remedial services but could not afford to hire additional teachers without financial assistance. Finally, because the passage of Title I in 1965 was hotly contested, those who formulated the bill believed that Congress was more likely to approve inducements than mandates.

Naturally, inducements entail costs. Money must be provided to fund grants or provide in-kind contributions such as teaching materials and testing services. Oversight is required to make sure that guidelines are followed, and this cannot be provided free of charge. Moreover, grant recipients are usually expected to contribute some of their own resources to a project—at a minimum, space, utilities, and administrative overhead. Sometimes they must provide matching funds. Title I has been a costly program, with the federal government providing grant money and local districts contributing classroom space, furnishings, materials, supervision, and other tangible and intangible goods.

The ideal result of inducements is diverse behavior in policy domains where diversity is acceptable. Because school districts and schools serve different populations and must therefore meet different needs, inducements offer an opportunity to develop flexible and responsive programs tailored to local situations. Excessive diversity can pose problems, however. Inducements should be used to advance broad, coherent policy goals; otherwise, a patchwork quilt of unrelated and contradictory programs may evolve.

Capacity Building

Capacity building can be defined as "the transfer of money for the purpose of investment in material, intellectual, or human resources" (McDonnell & Elmore, 1987, p. 134). The word *investment* indicates the major difference between inducements and capacity building. The latter policy instrument is designed to bring about a major, permanent change in the functional ability of an individual or an organization. Therefore, it represents a long-term investment whose full impact will not be apparent for years. A major component of capacity building is a large sum of money that is transferred to the implementing agency as a grant or as an appropriation of earmarked funds; a second major component is guidelines for how the money is to be spent. In their study of how five states had brought about education reform, Louis et al. (2006) found that all five had used capacity building as part of their efforts. In their interviews school and district leaders mentioned support in the form of funding for new positions to help implement the reforms, providing a retreat for principals, funding regional service centers, and offering professional development programs. Often the state government's capacity building efforts meant the difference between successful implementation of reforms and failure. As one rural school district leader said: "We literally could not have done it without them" (p. 33).

Capacity building is well suited to situations in which the currently employed staff and existing institutions cannot carry out desired policies because they are incapable of doing so. This incapacity may result from insufficient training, a lack of appropriate experience, inadequate equipment, or some combination of these. The ideal result of capacity building is people and institutions capable of implementing desirable new programs and policies. However, capacity building has a major drawback. Precisely because it is expensive and yields results only in the long term, its political—and therefore its financial—support may evaporate before sufficient capacity has been built. Not surprisingly, Louis et al. (2006) found that leaders in every state studied considered that the reform initiatives they had implemented were underfunded. Complained one assistant superintendent: "Mainly they're tying our hands right now. They're not providing us the ability to generate the resources that we need" (p. 35).

System Change

System change is a policy instrument that "transfer[s] . . . official authority among individuals and agencies" (McDonnell & Elmore, 1987, p. 139). Its central component is a statute, administrative rule, or board policy that weakens or eliminates the authority of an official or agency over a specific decision-making area while simultaneously shifting that authority to different individuals or agencies. As a secondary effect, a system change may reallocate resources; however, in a true system change, the shift of resources follows the shift of authority. Voucher plans offer a good example of system change. In their much discussed and still important book *Politics, Markets, and America's Schools,* Chubb and Moe (1990) recommended vouchers, which they called *scholarships.* Under their plan, state governments would shift the authority to decide which schools children attend from state and local officials to parents. After parents choose schools, the state government allocates funds, in the form of scholarships, to schools on the basis of enrollment. Thus, parents individually select their own child's school; collectively, acting through market mechanisms, they also determine how much state funding each school receives.

System change is an appropriate policy instrument when new behavior is needed but the currently employed staff and existing institutions are unresponsive to demands for change. Chubb and Moe (1990) explained at length their view that public schools, as institutions, could not provide high-quality education to children in the United States. Therefore, they argued, an institutional change was needed. They considered vouchers the best way to improve education because they believed vouchers would stimulate competition among schools. Advocates of system changes often believe their policy reform will save money, leading to greater efficiency in the use of resources. However, a high, though intangible, cost is associated with system change. People who stand to lose power and resources (and perhaps their jobs) through a system change will not stand idly by while it occurs. They will probably mount resistance to the proposed change, and if change comes anyway, they may work to sabotage it. Such resistance can entail costs in both morale and lowered productivity. In 1990, Chubb and Moe anticipated strong opposition to their plan from professional educators. Since then, reactions in states where voucher legislation has been proposed have confirmed their expectations. However, the debate that developed around *Politics, Markets, and America's Schools* probably opened the door for less radical forms of system change, such as interdistrict open enrollment and charter schools.

The ideal result of a system change is a revolutionized institution able and willing to meet the new demands placed on it. The major drawback is its unpredictability. The individuals or agencies to whom authority has been shifted may be as unable to meet new demands as the previous ones were. Unforeseen consequences may also arise, causing problems equal to or worse than those that existed under the older system. Voucher opponents base their central arguments on this unpredictability. They claim that parents will not be able to choose schools well, and that competition will lead to educational winners and losers by causing resegregation and the development of "dumping-ground schools."

Hortatory Policy, or Persuasion

Hortatory, or *persuasive, policies* "send a signal that particular goals and actions are considered a high priority by government" (McDonnell, 1994, p. 398). Because they are intended to persuade, hortatory policies are primarily discursive, using symbolism and imagery to appeal to values in order to encourage citizens to act on them. The major components of hortatory policies are written, spoken, or graphic texts that communicate information and suggest that people should behave in a certain way. Common examples in schools include campaigns to encourage children to recycle trash and "Just say no" drug education programs. Simply providing information to the public may play a hortatory role. Many states release district-by-district or school-by-school test results to the media as a way of persuading educators to take the tests seriously and, if necessary, change their curriculum. A good example of a proposed hortatory education policy at the national level is provided by the Clinton Administration's proposed voluntary national tests to assess fourth-grade reading and eighth-grade mathematics. Because the tests were to be completely voluntary, some questioned their usefulness. These objections overlooked their potentially persuasive nature, however. The test scores would have permitted comparisons of states, districts, and schools, making it possible for some parents to compare their own child's results to average results in other places (Lawton, 1997). Such information, if widely disseminated, could have persuaded some educators to alter their teaching to make a better showing. As Lyle Jones, a North Carolina psychology professor, observed, "The pressures to teach what is being tested are bound to be very large . . . particularly . . . where teachers and principals know the results will be published" (Hoff, 1997, p. 34).

Hortatory policies are appropriate when the desired change can be linked readily with symbols and information and when people are likely to act on new information. They are especially suitable as the first step in a long sequence of policies designed to change behavior gradually. Often, when political support is weak, a hortatory policy is the only one with a chance of being adopted. President Clinton's voluntary national tests meet these three criteria. Linking the rhetoric of education excellence to test scores is easy, and educators do tend to modify their practice in response to tests. Even though this hortatory policy was never officially adopted, it influenced the debate surrounding standards based accountability (SBA) reforms. In less than a decade, a national SBA program would be enacted, with the passage of NCLB. Finally, considerable opposition to national tests existed then and, in fact, still does. Under NCLB the states are expected to develop or select their own tests. Mandatory national tests are still not politically feasible in the United States.

The major cost of a hortatory policy is the dissemination of information. Hortatory policies usually involve public relations techniques such as posters, radio and television commercials, and printed flyers, all of which are expensive. Moreover, distributing such materials is costly, too. The ideal result of a hortatory policy is successfully persuading the targeted population to act differently. The major drawback of hortatory policies is the ease with which persuasion can slip into propaganda and other forms of manipulation. Those who adopt hortatory policies should bear in mind the principles for the ethical use of discourse discussed in Chapter 2.

The Use of Policy Instruments in the States

As part of a larger study of how state governments shape what happens in schools, Louis and her colleagues (2006) investigated the use of McDonnell and Elmore's policy instruments in five states—Mississippi, Missouri, New Mexico, Oregon, and Texas. Using interviews with state and district leaders as well as state Web sites, they analyzed their data to determine how often each instrument was mentioned as having been important in state reform initiatives. They identified (or looked for) only the four instruments originally described by McDonnell and Elmore: mandates, system change, capacity building, and inducements. Their findings are summarized in Table 9.2.

TABLE 9.2 Frequency with Which Policy Instruments Were Used in Five States

		Instruments		
States	**Mandates**	**System Change**	**Capacity Building**	**Inducements**
Mississippi	4	1	4	5
Missouri	3	1	3	0
New Mexico	3	4	3	4
Oregon	5	5	1	0
Texas	11	5	4	4
Totals	**26**	**16**	**15**	**13**

Source: Based on findings reported in Louis et al., 2006.

Several interesting facts emerge from this table. One is that the states differed significantly in which instruments they preferred. Although all the states used mandates, Texas utilized this instrument more heavily than any other state. Two states did not use inducements at all, but this was the most popular policy instrument in Mississippi. New Mexico and Oregon relied to a considerable extent on system change, whereas this instrument was rarely used in Mississippi and Missouri. The research team concluded that each state's choice of instruments was shaped both by national forces and by the "state's policy culture" as well as by its "previous educational policy actions" (p. 37).

Another interesting finding is that, although mandates were the most popular instrument, system change and capacity building were used more extensively than one might have expected. One possible explanation is that the study focused on *reform initiatives*; it may be that reform policies use these two instruments more than other types of policies do. It is also possible that education leaders are more aware of the range of policy instruments open to them than they used to be.

Using McDonnell and Elmore's Ideas in School Leadership

DIVERSIFYING POLICY INSTRUMENTS.   As Table 9.2 suggests, mandates are the most popular policy instrument. At times a mandate is the perfect instrument to select; nonetheless, mandates are probably overused in education, not only at the state level but also by superintendents, school boards, and principals. They are probably popular because they seem simple and straightforward. Louis et al. (2006) found, however, that a heavy use of mandates "may generate lower levels of trust in school districts and more uncertainty about how best to respond" (p. 40). This means that all school leaders should give serious consideration to using a range of policy instruments rather than relying too heavily on mandates.

McDonnell and Elmore's theories about policy instruments provide a way to conceptualize policy alternatives and also suggest criteria for assessing their probable effectiveness. For illustrative purposes, let us imagine a superintendent who discovers the reading levels in several primary classes are much too low. In reflecting on this problem, she immediately thinks of several possible mandates. She could require all primary teachers to submit detailed reading lesson plans to their principals, increase the hours of required reading instruction, or mandate a new phonics program. McDonnell and Elmore's framework suggests, however, that such an approach would be inappropriate. In the first place, she does not need to change the behavior of all the primary teachers, but only some. Moreover, the costs of requiring principals, who usually have little free time, to check more lesson plans may be high, including both neglect of other important duties, as well as lowered morale. Finally, this approach may not even achieve the desired policy goal. After all, if some teachers simply do not know how to teach reading well, requiring all teachers to submit lesson plans, teach more reading, and use phonics workbooks will not address the cause of the problem.

Deeper reflection on this problem, using McDonnell and Elmore's framework, suggests that capacity building would be a more appropriate instrument. The superintendent could identify individual teachers with problems and require them to spend several in-service days at special workshops on reading pedagogy. She could ask the language arts supervisor to locate several recent articles on effective reading instruction and use them in discussion groups with weak reading teachers. She could purchase a set of DVDs on reading and urge these teachers to look at them several times and use them to change their instruction. This approach should build capacity in the teachers. As a side effect, it would probably also exercise a hortatory impact on other primary teachers. Noting their colleagues' supplementary duties, many would no doubt decide to devote a little extra attention to reading instruction if only to avoid extra activities next year.

COMBINING POLICY INSTRUMENTS IN SCHOOL LEADERSHIP. McDonnell and Elmore's framework suggests ways that education leaders can combine policy instruments for maximum impact. The effective combination of several instruments depends on *coherence:* all instruments must be used to achieve the same broad policy goal. Failure to keep this principle in mind leads to a confusing set of policies that undercut each other.

As an illustration, let us imagine a middle school principal who wishes that his building looked cleaner and more attractive. At the moment, the school's halls are littered, the floors near eating areas are stained, and graffiti covers desk tops as well as the booths in student restrooms. His first reaction to this mess might be to crack down by announcing several new, punitive mandates. Any child caught littering, spilling food, or defacing school property might automatically be given a detention. Deeper reflection should suggest problems with this approach. It would have to be enforced by faculty and staff, so it would probably increase hostility between teachers and students—always undesirable. Moreover, it would pose enforcement problems. Although youngsters often commit the relatively minor offenses of littering and spilling food in the presence of adults, the more serious offense of damaging school property is usually committed privately. Therefore, vigorous enforcement could lead to a blatantly unfair situation in which minor infractions were punished and major ones were not. Of course, middle school students would be quick to perceive this injustice and point it out.

A more effective approach would be to combine policy instruments in a long-term strategy. This strategy might begin with several hortatory policies. For example, the first day of school, the principal might declare this year Make Our School Beautiful Year. A special assembly program and posters and banners in the halls could be used to reinforce this message. Littering, careless spills, and petty vandalism could be identified as some of the barriers to a beautiful school while focusing on the positive theme. Next, the principal might use inducements. Middle school youngsters are unlikely to relish writing grant proposals, but they do enjoy contests. Each month, classes could submit a plan for beautifying some part of the building. The winning class could be given free time to carry out its proposal, a pizza party on its completion, and publicity to celebrate its achievement. The principal should not overlook capacity building, either. He should seriously consider the possibility that the custodial staff or its equipment is inadequate. Are enough trash cans placed in the halls? Are they located in the most crucial places? Do the custodians need training on how to organize their work or remove spills and graffiti? All these possibilities should be explored.

After three or four months, the principal might issue some mandates; by this time, support for them should be stronger than it would have been with a sudden crackdown. Of course, ideally, the penalties for violation should advance the broader policy goal. Instead of sitting in a detention hall for thirty minutes, children caught littering might pick up trash in the restrooms. Those caught writing on walls might be given a bottle of household cleanser and told to remove their own graffiti and others'. Most children would perceive a certain fairness in such penalties, reducing resentment and adversarial attitudes.

With a carefully planned combination of several policy instruments, all aimed at improving his school's appearance, the principal will probably have a more attractive building at the end of the year than he had at the beginning. Possibly even more important, he will have sensitized his pupils to an important environmental issue and improved school climate. In schools, the simultaneous use of several instruments can increase the likelihood of a successful policy implementation.

EXERCISES ON THE POLICY INSTRUMENTS

1. Write three brief policies designed to reach each of the following goals. For each goal use three different instruments.
   a. Improve district test scores.
   b. Expand the use of computers in schools across the state.
   c. Increase the number of young women enrolled in engineering programs.
   d. Reduce student tardiness in a high school.
   e. Encourage students in the district to become more interested in mathematics.
2. For two of the policy goals in question 1, develop a long-term set of coherent policies designed to reach the central objective over five years.
3. Analyze part of a school handbook or a board policy manual. Describe its use of the five policy instruments.
4. Analyze the *No Child Left Behind Act* (or the most recent version of ESEA) to determine which policy instruments are used the most in it, which are used the least, and which are not used at all.

COST ANALYSIS AND COST-EFFECTIVENESS ANALYSIS

Thinking About Costs

School leaders feel daily pressure to use school funds wisely. Yet, the best way to use resources is not always clear. In *Cost-Effectiveness Analysis,* Levin and McEwan (2001) describe a 1987 study of four approaches to raising students' scores on mathematics achievement tests: (1) adding an hour to the school day, (2) computer-assisted instruction, (3) cross-age and adult tutoring, and (4) reducing class size. Although the tutoring program was more expensive than the other alternatives, it was also far more effective. In fact, when costs were divided by effects to obtain a cost-effectiveness ratio, researchers found that the tutoring programs were almost ten times more effective than adding an hour to the school day. This illustration points to a serious issue. Many school leaders adopt new policies without realistically analyzing either their cost or their cost-effectiveness. This can lead to wasted time and money as well as poor educational results. Therefore, leaders need ways to analyze costs in order to choose wisely among educational alternatives (Clemons & McBeth, 2009).

In this section, both **cost analysis** and **cost-effectiveness analysis** are presented as tools for educators. In thinking about both types of analysis, one must understand the terms *cost* and *benefit* (Dunn, 2004). Many people think *cost* is synonymous with *expenditure,* but this is untrue. Costs are closely related to benefits. A *benefit* is "anything you gain by undertaking a particular course of action" (Coplin & O'Leary, 1981, p. 129). A *cost* is "anything you must give up in order to obtain those benefits" (Coplin & O'Leary, 1981, p. 129). Costs therefore include both expenditures and those potential benefits lost by following a course of action. For example, if a room in a school is transformed into a student lounge, the costs include not only expenditures for fresh paint and new furniture, but also the lost opportunity to use the room for something else, or an *opportunity cost.* Both costs and benefits may be either tangible or intangible. A *tangible* cost or benefit can be quantified. Higher test scores and lower dropout rates are examples of tangible benefits. Examples of tangible costs include the number of dollars spent or hours worked on a project. *Intangible* costs include teacher burnout and lower student morale; stronger community support is an intangible benefit. In thinking through the potential costs and benefits of a policy, considering both the tangible and the intangible ones is essential (Dunn, 2004).

Cost Analysis

LEVIN AND MCEWAN'S INGREDIENTS METHOD.   Levin and McEwan (2001) recommend a system for estimating the tangible costs of a policy or program. It requires calculating the expenditures and opportunity costs involved in providing five ingredients: personnel, facilities, equipment and materials, client inputs, and miscellaneous inputs. Each of these ingredients is explained next.

Personnel includes all people who will work on the program, full time and part time, paid employees and volunteers. The cost of the services of each should be expressed in dollars. For paid employees, this figure should be based on their salary plus fringe benefits. For part-time workers, a percentage of this is calculated. Volunteer work should be assigned a price comparable to what the work would cost in the marketplace.

Facilities include all space used to house the program, such as offices and classrooms. The price assigned could be the cost of an actual lease or mortgage or what it would cost to lease a similar facility. Facilities are normally stocked with *equipment and materials,* which include necessary office machinery, audiovisual equipment, and furniture. To calculate annual costs, actual prices should be divided by the number of years of anticipated use. Thus, the annual cost of a $500 microscope that should last five years is $100.

Required client inputs should never be forgotten. This ingredient reflects costs imposed on the participants or their parents. If additional transportation is required, its cost should be estimated; driving time for parents should not be overlooked. Other required client costs include books, materials, or clothing that must be purchased and food donated for special events. *Miscellaneous inputs* do not easily fall into the other four categories. They include utilities, maintenance, administrative overhead, and added insurance costs.

THE INGREDIENTS METHOD APPLIED.   Tables 9.3 and 9.4 analyze the costs and expenditures involved in setting up a new computer laboratory in a middle school. In this hypothetical case, the school serves grades five through eight and enrolls

TABLE 9.3 Cost Analysis of a Computer Laboratory

Ingredients	Total Annualized Costs	Total Costs, First Year	Costs to School District	Costs to Other Government Agencies	Private Contributions	Required Client Costs
Personnel						
Media specialist	$47,350.00	$47,350.00	$47,350.00			
District technical support (5%)	1,906.50	1,906.50	1,906.50			
2 parent volunteers (5 hrs/week)	3,751.20	3,751.20			$3,751.20	
5 student assistants (5 hrs/week)	4,635.00	4,635.00			4,635.00	
Facilities						
800 ft^2 classroom	3,600.00	3,600.00	3,600.00			
Materials and Equipment						
30 PCs	7,200.00	36,000.00	10,000.00	$20,000.00 (State grant)	6,000.00 (Local business)	
5 printers	299.95	1,499.75	1,499.75			
20 inkjet cartridges	280.00	280.00	280.00			
10 tables	200.00	2,000.00	2,000.00			
30 student chairs	225.00	2,250.00	2,250.00			
1 teacher desk	12.50	250.00	250.00			
1 teacher chair	5.00	100.00	100.00			
1 metal file cabinet	6.25	125.00	125.00			
252 reams paper	998.00	998.00	998.00			

Client Inputs					
350 workbooks	3,500.00	3,500.00			$3,500.00
3500 diskettes	900.00	900.00			900.00
Miscellaneous					
Administrative overhead	3,665.40	3,665.40			
Maintenance	2,000.00	2,000.00			
Utilities	500.00	500.00			
Added insurance	250.00	250.00			
Total	$81,284.80	$115,560.85	$76,774.65	$20,000.00	$14,386.20	$4,400.00

TABLE 9.4 Analysis of District Expenditures

Ingredients	Total First-year Expenditures	Total Annual Expenditures After First Year
Personnel		
Media Specialist	$47,350.00	$47,350.00
Materials and Equipment		
PCs	10,000.00	
Printers	1,499.75	
Inkjet refills	280.00	280.00
Tables	2,000.00	
Student chairs	2,250.00	
Teacher desk	250.00	
Teacher chair	100.00	
File cabinet	125.00	
Paper	998.00	998.00
Miscellaneous		
Utilities	500.00	500.00
Added insurance	250.00	250.00
Total	**$65,602.75**	**$49,378.00**

700 children. The staff includes a principal, an assistant principal, twenty-eight teachers, two secretaries, five cafeteria workers, and three custodians. The school already has one computer lab, and seventh and eighth grade students are required to take two hours of computer science in the lab each week. The district leadership wishes to take advantage of a state technology grant to create a second laboratory, permitting the 350 fifth and sixth graders to take two hours of computer science each week also. An empty classroom currently storing district audiovisual equipment would be used for space. A new media specialist would be hired to operate the laboratory and teach the classes.

In making calculations, the following procedures were used. Most personnel costs are based on the annual salary plus 23% in fringe benefits. The cost of parent volunteers is based on the salary of teachers' aides; the cost of student assistants is calculated at minimum wage with no fringe benefits. The PCs and printers were annualized over five years; student furniture, over ten years; and teacher furniture, over twenty years. Administrative overhead, maintenance, and utilities were calculated on the assumption that the lab would absorb 2% of the overall costs of the school.

The usefulness of such a cost analysis is apparent. First, and perhaps most important for the pressured administrator, it reduces the chance of unanticipated expenditures. Such a procedure makes it easy to conceptualize exactly what the financial impact of a new project is likely to be, and permits decision makers to plan accordingly.

A second advantage is that it makes it easy to see ways to save money. For example, perhaps appropriate furniture is available elsewhere in the district, or could be purchased at a lower cost from a business that is closing. Finally, cost analysis can also alert leaders to potential problems. This computer lab adds to the workload of the district's technical support staff as well as to that of the building's administrators, secretaries, and custodians. If they have some spare time during the day, this should not matter. However, if their workloads have been increased at other times, reevaluating them may be necessary. If additional responsibilities are repeatedly added to certain positions, eventually more employees will be needed. Failure to recognize this situation and intervene early can lead to morale problems. Another potential problem is the imposed student costs. Under this plan, each fifth and sixth grade student would have to pay an additional $15 in fees. In some districts, this would be an unrealistic burden for families. School and district leaders should reflect carefully on the wisdom of imposing such a requirement.

ANALYZING TANGIBLE AND INTANGIBLE COSTS AND BENEFITS. As a supplement to Levin and McEwan's (2001) ingredients method, leaders should also carry out the analysis of both tangible and intangible costs and benefits recommended by Dunn (2004). Table 9.5 presents such a cost–benefit analysis of the computer lab. The meaning of this type of analysis must be interpreted within its context. In many districts, these intangible costs must be taken seriously. If rapid staff turnover is a problem and a parent group has recently complained about high fees, these costs should weigh heavily in leaders' thinking. However, if school leaders see no indicators of staff dissatisfaction and fees are low, leaders may not need to feel particularly concerned about these intangible costs. Benefits must also be understood in context. Improving public image and raising scores on accreditation reviews are not important issues everywhere. Such an analysis should be related to a specific context in order to answer this key question: Do the potential

TABLE 9.5 Potential Costs and Benefits of the Computer Lab

	Tangible	Intangible
Costs	$76,774.65	1. Excessive workloads for some staff 2. Burnout among some staff 3. Parent resentment of fees
Benefits	1. Higher level of student computer literacy 2. Improved scores on accreditation reviews 3. More team planning time for fifth and sixth grade teachers	1. Improved public image 2. Higher morale among fifth and sixth grade teachers

benefits of adopting this policy outweigh the potential costs? Only if the answer is in the affirmative should the policy be adopted. As Coplin and O'Leary (1981) warn: "A project should be undertaken only if its benefits are at least equal to its costs" (p. 130).

Cost-Effectiveness Analysis

THINKING ABOUT EFFECTIVENESS.   No policy, even a low-cost one, should be adopted if it is unlikely to be *effective,* and an existing policy should be changed or dropped if it is proved *ineffective.* An *effective policy* is one that leads to the intended outcomes, such as higher reading achievement scores, better attendance, or increased parent involvement. *Cost-effectiveness analysis* is a systematic way to compare alternative methods for reaching the same goal in terms of cost and effectiveness. The most desirable alternative is the one that costs the least while also reaching the policy goal. In the absence of a cost-effectiveness analysis, leaders often make the mistake of selecting the least expensive policy or program. If a policy is ineffective, it is too costly, even if its cost is low (Clemons & McBeth, 2009).

STEPS IN COST-EFFECTIVENESS ANALYSIS.   Levin and McEwan (2001) outline several steps for a good cost-effectiveness analysis. The first and most important step is to accurately identify one's *true policy objective.* This is often harder than one might think. For example, consider a school board and superintendent who face a common problem: they must cut the budget. Too often, they hastily identify their policy objective as cutting the budget, whereas their real objective should be cutting the budget in the way that least reduces the effectiveness of the educational program. Starting with the wrong objective, they limit their ability to see all the alternatives and their true costs. The result is typically the selection of an ineffective policy, such as closing small schools.

The next step is to select an appropriate measure of the effectiveness of the available alternatives. This might be the number of dollars saved, results of a school climate assessment, or a dropout rate. After that, all alternatives should be identified, ideally in a group brainstorming session in which no ideas are rejected as outlandish. Such a session may yield creative alternatives with much potential for enhancing the quality of education. For example, at least three cost-saving alternatives to closing a small school may exist: (1) sharing teachers and administrators among small schools; (2) sharing resources with a nearby community college; and (3) leasing empty space in the school building to groups such as senior citizens' organizations.

After all the viable alternatives have been specified, a thorough cost analysis of each should be carried out. This analysis should consider both tangible and intangible costs. When small schools are closed, the savings are not always as great as anticipated, as they are partially offset by increased transportation costs. Moreover, consolidating schools often discourages parent involvement, reducing the number of volunteer hours available and the number of in-kind contributions. Over the long term, a district that has closed several small schools may lose financially as bond issues fail, opposed by resentful citizens in the areas that lost schools.

Next, the effectiveness of each alternative should be considered carefully. A staff member should locate research on each, taking care that the research selected relates to the effectiveness measures chosen earlier. The research on many widely adopted policies contains surprises. For example, the research literature raises serious doubts about the educational effectiveness of closing small schools. School consolidation seems to jeopardize student learning, faculty morale, school climate, and participation in extracurricular activities (Levin & McEwan, 2001). In considering closing a school, these intangible costs should be weighed carefully. Only after comparing the costs and effectiveness of each alternative carefully should choices be made. The best choice is not necessarily either the cheapest alternative or the most effective one; rather, cost must be balanced against effectiveness, keeping in mind the context in which the policy must be implemented.

FINAL POINTS

In recent years, many have stressed that school leaders must reflect before acting. Reflection and thoughtful analyses are especially important when one is developing policies or implementing policies adopted by others. Making policy mistakes is easy. As demonstrated in Chapter 10, most policy implementations fail primarily because those in charge of developing the policy or planning the implementation did not think enough about their decisions. The three types of analysis presented in this chapter—Lowi's techniques of control, McDonnell and Elmore's policy instruments, and the analysis of costs and effectiveness—are useful tools for guiding reflection. Education leaders who use them intelligently will find that they can smooth both policy change and policy implementation.

EXERCISES ON COST ANALYSIS AND COST-EFFECTIVENESS ANALYSIS

1. A Midwestern state legislature passed a law requiring all school districts to gather data on seventy-eight demographic, financial, and educational variables, enter them in a special computer program, and send them electronically to the SDE each spring. Legislators bragged to the newspapers that this bill had a $0 "fiscal note." However, local school leaders did not believe this plan would cost *them* nothing. Using Levin's ingredients method, calculate a reasonable cost for compliance for a district with 5,000 students.

2. A Southern school board is considering a policy that would require every third grade student who fails the state reading test to repeat the third grade. Children who fail the test during their second year in third grade would be promoted to fourth grade, however. Assume that the district has 2,000 third graders each year, that 10% fail the test each year, and that every student who fails third grade eventually completes the twelfth grade in this district. Assume also that the district spends an average of $5,000 of local money on each student annually. Do a cost analysis of the cost to the district during the first twenty years of implementing such a policy.

3. A large New York district with an enrollment of 25,000 has the lowest scores on the state's Regents' examinations. The school board wants to raise the scores over the next two years. Using cost analysis and cost-effectiveness analysis, develop and evaluate two possible plans for reaching this goal and make a recommendation to the board.

4. A large suburban district in the West is receiving $2.5 million in new revenues each year because of taxes generated by a new power plant. The school board is considering

the following ways of using the money to improve student learning: (1) raising teachers' salaries, (2) reducing average class size K–12 from 25 to 21, (3) adding a half-day kindergarten program for four year olds to the existing full-day program for five year olds, and (4) establishing a merit pay plan for teachers, awarding significant pay raises to those whose classes score in the top 25% on a standardized achievement test. Using the research literature, which alternative would you recommend as the most cost-effective plan for improving student learning?

INTERNET ASSIGNMENT

Find your state legislature's Web site and use it to locate the texts of three recent education laws. Analyze these laws to determine which policy instruments were used. Compare your findings to Table 9.2.

FOR FURTHER READING

Chrispeels, J. H. (1997). Educational policy implementation in a shifting political climate: The California experience. *American Educational Research Journal, 34,* 453–481.

Chrispeels analyzes ten years of curriculum reform legislation in California to determine which policy instruments were used. Her findings suggest that using multiple instruments to achieve the same goal improves the quality of policy implementation.

Grubb, W. N. (2009/2010). Correcting the money myth: Re-thinking school resources. *Phi Delta Kappan, 94*(4), 51–55.

Although Grubb does not address cost-benefit analysis directly, he offers some thoughtful insights into how money is used and misused in schools. He also suggests forms of capacity building that could lead to a wiser use of resources.

McDonnell, L. M. (2009). Repositioning politics in education's circle of knowledge. *Educational Researcher, 38,* 417–427.

McDonnell argues that although it is important to study how the political process shapes policies, it is equally important to investigate how adopted policies shape politics. She believes that such research would enhance our understanding of democracy and education.

Pruslow, J. T. (2001, November). What do we spend to educate a child? The student resource allocation model. *School Business Affairs,* 33–36.

Pruslow, an educational cost analysis specialist, describes a method for determining educational costs for individual students based on Levin's ingredients approach. He suggests that this method can be used for analyzing the costs of proposed instructional changes.

Youngs, P. (2001). District and state policy influences on professional development and school capacity. *Educational Policy, 15,* 278–301.

Youngs presents a useful concept of school capacity and analyzes research to determine how state and district leaders can build capacity at the school level. He also uses his findings to suggest types of professional development that build school capacity.

10

POLICY IMPLEMENTATION: GETTING PEOPLE TO CARRY OUT A POLICY

Focus Questions

▌ Why is implementing new policies difficult?

▌ What does research tell us about successful and unsuccessful implementation?

▌ How can a school leader plan a policy implementation that increases the likelihood of success?

▌ What courses of action are open to school leaders who are expected to implement a policy that they or important stakeholders oppose?

THE SURPRISING DIFFICULTY OF IMPLEMENTATION

In *Presidential Power,* Richard Neustadt (1960) tells how President Truman chortled about the transition from military to government leadership that General Eisenhower would have to make when he took office. "'He'll sit here,' Truman would remark (tapping his desk . . .), 'and he'll say, "Do this! Do that!" *And nothing will happen.* Poor Ike—it won't be a bit like the army'" (p. 9). As an experienced political leader, Truman knew that the mere fact that a president, legislature, or court has promulgated a policy does not mean that people will immediately execute their orders; in fact, many official policies are never implemented at all, and many others are implemented only partially or incorrectly. Implementation can never be taken for granted. As with the other stages of the policy process, school leaders in charge of implementing a policy must think about what they are doing and plan carefully.

Of all the stages of the policy process, implementation is the one with which education leaders can least avoid involvement. Conceivably, they could work for years without contacting a member of the state legislature or paying attention to issue definition or agenda setting, but they cannot work for even one year in a leadership position without being required to implement a policy. Indeed, to a great extent, their jobs can be summarized in two words: *policy implementation.* A new attendance policy adopted by the school board, an interdistrict open enrollment law passed by the legislature, or federal grant money for vocational education—all are policies that others have chosen but education leaders must implement. Today, especially, with education policy changes emanating from most state legislatures with amazing speed, school leaders must be prepared to guide districts, schools, and teachers through the often difficult task of changing to meet new expectations.

This chapter, then, explores policy implementation. Many policies are easy to implement. New regulations that involve only minor changes and can be enforced easily pose few problems (Murphy, 1990). Therefore, this chapter concentrates on more difficult implementation situations in which redistributive, capacity-building, or system-changing policies are involved. It also discusses the issues involved in implementing complex policies that require significant changes in pedagogy or the expansion of a program from a few sites to many. The first part of the chapter presents the research on implementation from the early 1970s until today, and discusses the implications of this body of research for school leaders. The next section provides practical guidelines for implementing a policy. The final section addresses a dilemma that school leaders face more and more often: having to implement an unpopular policy or one that they find objectionable.

THE RESEARCH ON IMPLEMENTATION

Defining Implementation

Implementation is "organizational activities directed toward the carrying out of an adopted policy by administrative bureaucracies at the national, state, and local levels." (Clemons & McBeth, 2009, p. 79). The major actors in the implementation arena are the *implementers. Formal implementers* are government officials who have the legal authority to see that a new policy is put into effect. In education, the formal implementers are often administrators who work in the U.S. Department of Education (USDOE) or in a state department of education (SDE). However, if a local school board adopts a new policy, the formal implementers are the superintendent and possibly other central office administrators. *Intermediaries* are implementers to whom the formal implementers delegate the responsibility to help with implementation. They are all the people and groups who operate between the formal implementers and the point at which the policy has an impact on the target population, usually students. When the USDOE implements a policy, the intermediaries include SDEs, school boards, district administrators, and—preeminently—classroom teachers. During the implementation of a policy that originated at the state level, the professional employees of local districts (both administrators and teachers) are the intermediaries. Locally developed policies are implemented by intermediaries such as building principals and teachers.

Successful implementation depends on developing and maintaining both the *will* and the *capacity* of the intermediaries. The individuals and agencies who must cooperate in order to implement a policy must have reasons for doing so—in other words, they must be willing. Motivation can be encouraged in many ways, but formal implementers should never take it for granted. Moreover, motivation, although necessary for good implementation, is not sufficient. All the will in the world cannot overcome lack of capacity or inability to do what the policy requires. As with will, formal implementers must constantly keep in mind the capacity of the intermediaries (McLaughlin, 1987; Spillane, Reiser, & Reimer, 2002).

A Rapidly Growing Field

In the preface to their 1971 case study *Implementing Organizational Innovations*, authors Gross, Giacquinta, and Bernstein observed that "the implementation phase of the process of planned organizational change . . . has received little attention in the social science and educational literature" (p. v). However, more than forty years later, in the preface to the fourth edition of *The New Meaning of Educational Change*, Fullan (2007) could assert: "[T]he knowledge base of change is becoming more profound and accessible, and . . . it is absolutely indispensable to leading [school reform]" (p. xiii). In the intervening decades, then, researchers produced much new knowledge about how to implement policies in education settings. Today we can say, without exaggeration, that of all the stages of the policy process, implementation is the second best understood, after policy evaluation.

This implementation research grew out of practical concerns. In the 1950s and 1960s, the federal government provided new funding for numerous education reforms, such as revised science curricula and compensatory education for disadvantaged children. Naturally, federal officials wanted to know if these millions of dollars were achieving the intended results. Therefore, they commissioned quantitative evaluations of the programs. The results were surprising. Many of the statistical findings were so puzzling that researchers decided to observe what was actually going on at the program sites—in other words, they wanted to study them using qualitative research methods. They found that their statistical results were peculiar because many federal programs were nonevents. Nothing had changed because nothing was happening. This discovery stimulated research on implementation itself (Firestone & Corbett, 1988).

The implementation research can be divided into three generations. The first generation began to appear in print in the early 1970s; the second, in the late 1970s; and the third, about 1990. As with the generations of a family, who are born at different times but continue to live side by side for decades, all three generations of implementation research are very much alive today.

First-Generation Research—The Difficulty of Implementation

OVERVIEW. First-generation implementation research focuses on the difficulty— in some cases the impossibility—of policy implementation. Researchers attribute the extreme difficulty of implementation to various causes. For example, after synthesizing several studies of Title I of the *Elementary and Secondary Education Act* of 1965 (ESEA), Jerome Murphy (1971) concluded that politics and federal bureaucracy hindered the implementation of compensatory education programs. He found that the USDOE was woefully understaffed and, even if it had employed enough personnel to oversee implementation, agency workers probably would not have supported the goals of compensatory education for ideological reasons. His major conclusion was pessimistic: "The federal system . . . not only permits but encourages the evasion and dilution of federal reform, making it nearly impossible for the federal administrator to impose program priorities" (p. 35).

Other first-generation studies focused on cultural barriers rather than political ones. In his influential book *The Culture of the School and the Problem of Change,* first published in 1971 and reissued in 1996, Seymour Sarason argued that most education reforms fail because reformers do not take school culture into account. They devise new policies as if they will be implemented in a vacuum rather than in an institutional setting with more than a century of cultural traditions. One of Sarason's examples of misguided reform was the New Math of the 1950s and 1960s. Developed in universities (whose institutional culture differs markedly from that of schools), the New Math curricula were inconsistent with many of the most fundamental features of school life. The failure of this reform was predictable. Sarason's thesis inspired many later researchers to study how culture interacts with implementation efforts, posing difficulties.

IN-DEPTH LOOK AT A TYPICAL STUDY.   In the late 1960s, Gross et al. (1971) conducted a yearlong case study of an attempt to introduce a policy change in an elementary school located in the slums of a New England city. The reform required teachers to modify their pedagogy and classroom role. They were supposed to stop running teacher-centered classrooms and become "catalytic role models." "Catalytic" teachers "assisted children to learn according to *their* interests throughout the day in self-contained classrooms" (Gross et al., 1971, p. 12). Children's activities were supposed to include lots of "fun" learning kits and games.

Before they began their fieldwork, the researchers expected that the major barrier to implementation would be teacher opposition. On the contrary, however, all the teachers at Cambire School (a pseudonym) supported the innovation because it was consistent with the open education movement, whose ideals they espoused. Nonetheless, by the end of the year, the teachers had lost their enthusiasm for the change. Almost all had reverted to their former teaching methods. One commented in a May interview:

> I have to admit . . . I am failing to make as much effort as I was in the past because of my doubts about the assumptions and values . . . and also the effect of this thing on the kids when you let them go. (Gross et al., 1971, p. 120)

In their analysis of the situation, the researchers identified five barriers to effective implementation. The first four caused the last one to develop. They were:

1. The teachers never really understood the change.
2. The teachers did not know how to use the new pedagogy.
3. The materials needed to establish open classrooms were not available.
4. The culture and institutional organization of the school were not consistent with the requirements of the new policy.
5. The teachers became discouraged and lost their motivation to implement.

Gross et al. (1971) concluded their book with a call for more research; over the next decades, hundreds of researchers responded.

LESSONS FROM THE FIRST GENERATION.   The major lesson that first-generation research teaches is that implementation is difficult. Before the early studies of implementation appeared, many people assumed—like Truman's caricature of Ike—that when people receive authoritative policy directives, they naturally follow them. Nothing could be further from the truth. The fact that a government body has come up with a new policy does not mean that it will be followed. The implementers may not want to follow it, or they may not be able to. Moreover, change is hard and the status quo is comfortable. Policies are implemented only if the formal implementers and the intermediaries are willing and able to work hard to put them in place.

First-generation research also suggests why policy implementations often fail. Indeed, the 1971 account of Cambire School contains in embryonic form all the major reasons that later studies confirmed. First, implementers frequently do not understand what they are supposed to do. Too often, education policy changes are introduced at a short in-service session at the beginning of the school year. A pep talk by a consultant precedes the distribution of glossy materials to a room full of apprehensive teachers and principals. This approach leaves the intermediary implementers confused. At Cambire School, teachers had no idea what a "catalytic" teacher was supposed to do because they had never observed one teach. Not surprisingly, then, they were unable to behave "catalytically."

A second problem revealed by the first generation of implementation research is that intermediary implementers often lack the knowledge and skills necessary to implement a policy. The effective operation of an open classroom does not happen by chance. It requires a high level of planning and organizational ability; yet, no one thought to teach these skills to the Cambire teachers.

Finally, first-generation implementation research underscores the critical importance of resources in implementation. The two key resources are materials and time. At Cambire, teachers lacked the abundant materials essential for running an open classroom. The problem was twofold: they did not have enough materials, and the materials they did have were of poor quality. Although the formal implementer had explicitly recognized the key role of materials during the planning process, he never made them available. Gross et al. (1971) does not explain why, but the most likely reason is that teaching materials—especially games and kits—are expensive. Probably the true cost of the program had not been calculated before implementation began.

Time is as important as are materials, and it, too, is a cost factor, as pointed out in Chapter 9. At Cambire, teachers were asked to take on many new tasks simultaneously. They were also required to do a great deal of additional paperwork. The effect was to increase greatly the length of their workday without increasing their salaries. Not surprisingly, then, by the third month of implementation, many of them were visibly "exhausted and short tempered" (Gross et al., 1971, p. 180). Fatigue and overwork undercut their motivation—the intangible cost of basing an implementation on the assumption that teachers will work extra hours to compensate for insufficient personnel.

The lessons from the first generation of implementation research have been available since the early 1970s. Researchers would like to be able to report that policymakers and implementers have learned them so well that they no longer repeat the errors of the past. Sad to say, this is not the case. In education, many contemporary policy implementations—perhaps most—continue to make the same mistakes that were made at Cambire School in the late 1960s, which is why the first generation of research is still relevant today.

Second-Generation Research—Analyses of Failure and Success

OVERVIEW.   Second-generation research studies both successful and unsuccessful implementations, attempting to determine why some policies are fully implemented and others are not. The best known early research of this type was the Rand Change Agent Study, whose principal investigators were Paul Berman and Milbrey McLaughlin. In 1973, under contract with the U.S. Office of Education (USOE), Rand researchers began a multiyear investigation of the implementation of 293 federal projects in eighteen states. Like first-generation researchers, the Rand team drew a largely negative conclusion: "In most cases, the innovations funded by federal seed money had not taken root" (Berman & McLaughlin, 1978, p. 12). Even so, they did find some success stories among the 293 projects. In the official report to the USOE, Berman and McLaughlin sought to explain these differences among the projects. They decided that successful implementation was not a mechanical process of following recipes from a policy "cookbook"; rather, a process of "mutual adaptation" had occurred in the successful projects. Mutual adaptation involved changes in both the implementers' behavior and in the details of the policy design, which was modified to fit local circumstances (McLaughlin, 1976). The Rand Change Agent Study clearly found that implementation, although difficult, was possible. Soon, other implementation researchers began to report similar findings.

First-generation studies suggested that the education policies put in place during the War on Poverty were failures that had made little impact on schools. However, in 1980, Kirst and Jung challenged this view. Thirteen years after the passage of the ESEA, they conducted research on the implementation of Title I compensatory education programs. They discovered that by the late 1970s, substantial implementation had, in fact, occurred. They concluded that short-term implementation studies magnify the proportion of failures, and argued that researchers should study a policy implementation over the course of a decade. Several years later, Peterson, Rabe, and Wong (1986) further refined Kirst and Jung's thesis. They suggested that implementing Title I took a long time because it was a redistributive policy. Although its early implementation was tumultuous, the quality of Title I implementation improved significantly as the policy matured. They argued that because redistributive policies are complex, they are eventually implemented only if those who direct the programs are highly skilled (Peterson et al., 1986).

In 1990, Joseph Murphy reported on the implementation of a different set of education policies: the reforms of the 1980s, such as increased graduation requirements. Many policy scholars, drawing largely on first-generation implementation research, predicted the failure of these reforms. Yet, after analyzing a large body of research, Murphy (1990) concluded that they had been implemented quickly and were already influencing schools in the United States. He understood this success as the result of the design of the policies. Most important, the policies of the 1980s were regulatory; therefore, they were easier to implement than the policies of the 1960s and 1970s had been. Moreover, they built on existing school structures and "emphasized quantitative increases" (Murphy, 1990, p. 35). These landmark studies and many similar ones conducted during the 1980s and 1990s laid a solid foundation for increased understanding of policy implementation.

IN-DEPTH LOOK AT A TYPICAL STUDY.   In the late 1970s and early 1980s, Huberman and Miles (1984) conducted a USDOE-funded three-year study of the implementation of various "school improvements." Although their study looked at 146 schools, they selected twelve schools for in-depth, comparative case studies. Their book *Innovation Up Close: How School Improvement Works* (1984) reports their findings from these twelve sites. The schools were located "in rural, urban, and suburban settings in 10 states from Maine to California" (p. 1), and they achieved a range of results. Huberman and Miles concluded that two of the implementations were extremely successful, two were miserable failures, and the rest fell somewhere in between. They were not content, however, with merely chronicling success rates; rather, they described their purpose in writing the book as "to show just *what happened* in the course of these school improvement efforts, to explain *why* it happened, and to suggest the *implications* for changes . . . elsewhere" (p. vi, emphasis in original).

Consistent with the findings of the first-generation research, Huberman and Miles discovered that implementation, especially early implementation, was difficult. Common problems reported by teachers were similar to those observed fifteen years earlier at Cambire School. At the sites where implementation succeeded, however, this painful early period ended eventually. After teachers mastered the components of the change, they felt proud and self-confident. At the unsuccessful sites, feelings were quite different; discouragement and burnout were often reported. At the conclusion of the implementation period, the policy change had been institutionalized at the five most successful sites. It was there to stay. At the other schools, various scenarios had played out. Turnover in the project's leadership, the loss of administrative support, and budget crises were among the factors contributing to the demise or declining importance of the failed policies.

In their book, Huberman and Miles (1984) divided the twelve schools they studied in-depth into four "families": (1) highly successful implementations, (2) relatively successful implementations, (3) relatively unsuccessful implementations, and (4) unsuccessful implementations. The story of what happened in each family is illuminating.

Both *highly successful* implementations had been initiated by central office administrators who were deeply committed to the new program. Both projects were ambitious ones requiring substantial change in teachers' classroom practice. However, although much change was demanded, the new policy fit well into the district and was consistent with its philosophy. Although the central office administrators who advocated the innovation pressured principals and teachers to implement it, they offered strong assistance in the form of materials, training, and consultants throughout implementation. The researchers commented about these two schools: "Local administrators used muscle along with tutoring and tenderness" (Huberman & Miles, 1984, p. 277).

The four *relatively successful* schools followed a different path. Because the new policies addressed well-recognized problems in these districts, a crusading atmosphere developed among the teachers. They were strongly committed to making the programs work in order to solve the problems they had identified. Both central office support and leaders' preparation for implementation were adequate, but the real key to the success of these projects was the willingness of many teachers to work long hours to master new skills. Although district administrators exerted little pressure and also provided little assistance, the teachers in the schools helped each other a great deal. As time passed, however, many teachers experienced burnout and opted to weaken the innovations.

The four *relatively unsuccessful* schools adopted modest policy changes that demanded little of them. Their district leaders, who had been supportive at first, quickly lost interest after implementation began. They offered little assistance, and when principals and teachers approached them with requests for permission to downsize their projects even further, they readily agreed. "The administrators 'helped' most by granting latitude to make changes," Huberman and Miles (1984) observed (p. 265). The result, however, was that the policy changes were never truly implemented.

The researchers considered two projects pitiful *failures*. In both instances, district-level administrators launched policy changes as part of broader strategies for personal career development. Their programs were poorly designed, and these leaders were never really interested in implementation. They neither prepared carefully for implementation nor offered assistance to principals and teachers. Considerable resistance to both policies developed; the building principals spearheaded it. Before long, implementation ground to a halt. Huberman and Miles (1984) did not criticize the uncooperative principals, however. They concluded: "In a sense, these two 'failures' can be seen as a successful effort by users to protect their schools against poorly conceived ideas" (p. 269).

LESSONS FROM THE SECOND GENERATION.   Like first-generation implementation research, the research of the second generation suggests that implementation is difficult. Many policies—perhaps most—are never really implemented. Among those policies that are not implemented, a watered-down version is often put in place. Sometimes nothing changes at all. This means that the people responsible for an implementation can never take it for granted that those under them will put a policy into effect simply because they are supposed to.

Unlike first-generation research, however, the research of the second generation suggests that implementation is possible. Although in successful implementations a process of "mutual adaptation" occurs, which changes both the design of the policy and the behavior of the implementers, the core and the spirit of the new policy do take effect (McLaughlin, 1976). Success requires hard work and pressure. It may cause some implementers to burn out. But success can and does happen. Most important, second-generation research suggests why some implementations succeed whereas others fail. Using carefully constructed quantitative and qualitative research designs, second-generation researchers have teased out many of the common characteristics of strong and weak implementation. As a result, making concrete recommendations to school leaders about how to plan and carry out a policy implementation is now possible.

Third-Generation Research—Implementing Complex Policies

OVERVIEW.   Beginning about 1990, proposed educational reforms became considerably more ambitious than they had been in the 1960s, 1970s, and 1980s (Honig, 2006). It is relatively easy to implement such reforms as increasing the number of mathematics courses needed for high school graduation, mandating that teachers participate in more professional development, or requiring students to take state proficiency tests. The compensatory education reforms of the 1960s and 1970s were hard to implement because they were redistributive policies. However, the *substance* of those reforms was not complex. For example, Title I of ESEA required special Title I teachers to provide extra reading instruction to poor children who were having trouble learning to read. It did *not* require the reading teachers to use a reading pedagogy with which they were unfamiliar. The Title I teachers taught reading in the same way the regular classroom teachers did, and—in many cases—in the same way that they themselves had been taught to read decades earlier.

Many of the reforms proposed since 1990 have, however, demanded that schools adopt new and unfamiliar approaches to teaching. For example, in 1991, New American Schools (NAS), a nonprofit corporation, was founded as part of America 2000, a school reform initiative launched by President George H. W. Bush. Through a national competition, NAS selected eleven school reform designs to be implemented, mostly in urban school districts. For various reasons, only nine of these designs were ultimately tried in school settings. Most of them demanded significant changes in curriculum and pedagogy (Bodilly, 1998). One of them—the Audrey Cohen College System of Education—expected "traditional subject areas and important skills [to be absorbed] by action-oriented dimensions" (Bodilly, 1998, p. 122). Another— Expeditionary Learning—called for instruction based on "expeditions"—"long-term, in-depth investigations of themes or topics that engage students in the classroom and in the wider world through authentic projects, fieldwork, and service" (Bodilly, 1998, p. 136). Clearly, such reforms required teachers, building administrators, and district supervisors to alter their practice in fundamental ways.

Moreover, NAS added an additional dimension of complexity to its project. Initially, the school reform designs were implemented in just 147 schools in ten geographic areas, but the overall plan included a "scale-up strategy"—expansion to 557 schools by 1997; 685 schools by 1998; and more than 1,000 by 2000. Not surprisingly, a RAND evaluation of the first two years of the scale-up phase found that scaling up was a complex process, and that many of the schools were not truly implementing their school reform designs (Bodilly, 1998).

This experience and others similar to it have led implementation research in new directions. Much of the recent scholarship on implementation has focused on two questions: How can teachers and administrators learn to implement programs that require a major change in their professional practice? And how can a successful reform be expanded from a few sites to many? This section first describes the research on how educators can learn new ways to work; then it discusses some of the issues involved in scaling up.

Implementers as Learners

OVERVIEW.   As early as 1971, Gross et al. found that the teachers at Cambire School did not understand how to act as "catalytic" teachers in their classrooms. Later researchers also often discovered that implementers were confused about exactly what they were supposed to do and how they were supposed to do it. However, it was not until the 1990s that implementation researchers began to focus on this problem and to seek to determine why so many teachers and administrators could not understand the increasingly complex reforms they were expected to implement. Using a theoretical framework drawn from cognitive psychology, they began to study implementers as learners who frequently tried hard to master a new approach to teaching but never fully grasped the changes they were expected to make (Coburn, 2001; Little, 2003; Spillane, 1998, 1999, 2000; Spillane & Callahan, 2000; Spillane et al., 2002).

Research on human cognition suggests that "new information is always interpreted in light of what is already understood" (Spillane et al., 2002, p. 394). Humans use their previous experiences and learning to develop *schemas*—conceptual structures that they use to interpret new information as well as to predict what is likely to happen in a new situation. Therefore, when faced with a new situation, people naturally draw on their already formed schemas to interpret it. As they do so, they are likely to seize on aspects of the new situation that resemble their past experiences and to overlook aspects of it which do not readily fit into their preexisting schemas. They are especially likely to focus on superficial or concrete aspects of the new experience, while overlooking its deeper and less obvious components (Spillane, 2000).

Anyone who has traveled or lived abroad has experienced dramatically how applying preexisting schemas in a new context can lead to misunderstandings and confusion. For example, an American who dines in a restaurant in Paris for the first time naturally anticipates that a French restaurant will function like an American one; and, indeed, in some respects it does. She sees tables, chairs, and menus as well as waiters and waitresses serving the restaurant's patrons. However, she may not understand that the waiter will not take an order until she signals to him that she is ready by closing the menu, or that diners at the other tables expect conversation to be in a very low voice, or that it is normal in French restaurants for pet dogs to lie quietly at their owners' feet while they eat, or that the waiter will ask for an appraisal of the quality of the cooking at the end of the meal. The American's lack of knowledge of the French schema for dining in a restaurant will probably lead to some awkward moments and perhaps to frowns or glares from the other patrons. Of course, if she is perceptive, and especially if experienced Americans or French friends provide her with some effective teaching, she eventually learns the French schema for dining in a restaurant and applies it appropriately in French contexts.

Similarly, when teachers and administrators encounter a new approach to education—perhaps a new way to teach reading—they naturally seek to understand it in terms of their past experiences. As a result, they see the new method as more similar to the reading pedagogy with which they are familiar than it really is. For example, in a study of the implementation of a reading program in California, Coburn (2001) found that groups of teachers who had different past experiences with teaching reading used a mandated reading series quite differently. One group felt that because the series did not introduce new phonics skills before each story as they were accustomed to doing, it "did not fit" (Coburn, 2001, p. 155). Therefore, they continued using the old series with which they were familiar rather than the new one. However, two teachers who had learned to teach reading as part of interdisciplinary thematic units drew on the textbook series as a source of stories for their units. Some other teachers, who liked to stress decoding skills, used the supplementary phonics readers that were part of the series, but not the main textbook. There were also teachers who felt so comfortable with the new series that they used it without difficulty. These variations in practice are precisely what cognitive psychologists would predict. Implementers interpret a new policy in terms of their past experience . . . unless those who are leading the implementation effort work very hard to help them learn new schemas.

Much of the implementation research based on cognitive theory has also explored the circumstances under which implementers learn best. Although many American schools are still based on the old "egg crate" model, in which teachers practice their profession in almost complete isolation from each other, recent research suggests that implementers are best able to grasp new policies when they can discuss them with other implementers. The conversations in department meetings, at the teachers' lunch table, or in the faculty lounge can provide important opportunities for teachers to grapple with new programs and interpret their meaning together (Cobb, McClain, Lamberg, & Dean, 2003; Coburn & Stein, 2006; Little, 2003; Spillane, 1999). As Coburn and Stein (2006) argue, policy/makers should not only issue documents outlining the changes in educational practice that they believe are needed, they should also provide the infrastructure necessary for teachers to learn collectively how to implement the changes. In short, they must "support the development of communities of practice focused on teaching and learning" (Coburn & Stein, 2006, p. 42). Moreover, recent research also suggests that implementers perform best when they are receiving messages about new policies from multiple sources in the environment, and not just from their school district or the state department of education. As a matter of fact, Coburn (2005) found that policy messages from such "nonsystem actors" as preservice teacher education programs, graduate-level university courses, professional development programs offered by independent providers, and the mass media exercised *more* influence on teachers who were implementing a new reading program than did messages from within the school system. Her findings are consistent with Spillane's (1999) earlier discovery that teachers who were doing the best job of implementing new mathematics curricula were situated in "enactment zones" that included both people and materials from multiple sources.

IN-DEPTH LOOK AT A TYPICAL STUDY.   The great majority of the studies of implementers as learners look at *teachers* as learners. However, because this book is aimed primarily at an audience of practicing and aspiring administrators, a study that includes *administrators* as learners has been selected. Spillane (2000) investigated the implementation of a new mathematics program in nine Michigan districts, focusing on how well "district leaders" understood the reform. He defined *district leaders* as central office administrators, curriculum specialists, and lead mathematics teachers. The mathematics reform that they were supposed to be implementing was based on recommendations of the National Council of Teachers of Mathematics (NCTM) and required a major shift in mathematics pedagogy. Traditionally, school mathematics in the United States has concentrated on teaching children procedures for obtaining the correct answers to mathematical problems. In contrast, the NCTM-sponsored reform advocated teaching "the mathematical ideas and concepts that undergird mathematical procedures" (Spillane, 2000, p. 144). In this approach to mathematics, correct answers and procedures are not as important as discussing and communicating mathematical reasoning—in other words, talking or writing about various possible approaches to solving a mathematical problem.

Using interviews of eighty program implementers, Spillane and his team sought to determine how well they understood the requirements of this new approach to teaching mathematics. As cognitive theory predicts, they found in their interviews that most of the implementers focused on the two aspects of the reform that were most similar to their previous practice, or at least that they *thought* were most similar. These aspects were "hands-on mathematics" and "problem solving." The district leaders had very little to say about "mathematics as communication" and "mathematics as reasoning." Moreover, as cognitive theory predicts, the two aspects of the reform that they mentioned most were also more concrete than the two aspects of it that they tended to ignore. In addition, the great majority of these district leaders did not really understand the two aspects of the reform they focused on; instead, they interpreted "hands-on activities" and "problem solving" in terms of the sorts of learning activities and materials with which they were already familiar. They found it difficult to grasp the underlying purpose of the changes; instead, they "shifted the focus of the mathematics reforms to a reconfigured means to a familiar end" (p. 154). Spillane concluded,

> Although district leaders in this study understood the mathematics reforms as representing change for their existing mathematics program, and they pursued the enactment of these ideas, their understandings of the reforms tended to miss the full import of reformers' proposals. (p. 169)

As a result, he recommended that those who would like to bring about a major reform in classroom practice should bear in mind that the leaders of the implementation effort as well as the teachers in their classrooms must learn to understand the deep meaning of the reform, and this new learning may require considerable time and effort on the part of everyone involved.

Scaling Up

OVERVIEW.   Although implementing a major educational reform in one school or in a few schools is difficult, expanding the reform to a large number of sites is even harder. Since the late 1990s, many implementation researchers have focused on this problem. *Scaling up* is usually defined as "the deliberate expansion to many settings of an *externally-developed* school-restructuring design that previously has been used successfully in one or a small number of school settings" (Stringfield & Datnow, 1998, p. 271, emphasis added). In fact, virtually all of the scaling up research investigated the expansion of externally developed reforms. Table 10.1 suggests why: since the early

TABLE 10.1 The Scaling Up of Reform Designs

Reform Design	Number of Schools Using
Accelerated Schools	1300+*
Achievement Via Individual Determination	700+*
Coalition of Essential Schools	1000+*
Comer School Development Program	500+*
Core Knowledge Schools	800+*
New American Schools	2000+*
NSF's Local Systemic Change Initiative	4000+**
Success for All	1600+*

*In 2002.

**In 2005.

Source: Based on data from Datnow, Hubbard, & Mehan (2002, p. 1) and from Weiss & Pasley (2006, p. 2).

1990s, a large number of education reform designs have been developed by groups external to public education, such as universities and foundations, and by the turn of the twenty-first century, many of them were being implemented at hundreds or even thousands of school sites. But if a large school district or a state department of education developed an innovative reform, piloted it, and then expanded the model, it too would be engaged in scaling up. To date, however, either such bodies have developed no major reform models, or those models are not represented in the literature. Therefore, this section discusses only the scaling up of externally developed school reform designs.

Scaling up is a challenging process. For example, in a study of forty NAS schools, Bodilly (1998) found great variation in the quality of implementation. Only about half of the schools were truly implementing their reform designs; the others were either not implementing them at all or implementing them at a low level. Interestingly, however, some reform designs had been scaled up more effectively than others. Schools that adopted Expeditionary Learning or Roots and Wings were implementing their designs very successfully. However, a study of the impact of professional development on the scaling up of the National Science Foundation's Local Systemic Change Initiative discovered that most districts found it difficult to institutionalize new pedagogies in secondary science and mathematics. In fact, after five years of implementation, the institutionalization of the reforms was seen as "likely" in only 17% of the projects (Weiss & Paley, 2006).

Implementation researchers identified several reasons for the difficulty of scaling up. When a reform design is expanded, implementers encounter both internal and external challenges. Internal challenges occur within the school site itself. The most important of these has already been described in detail: both teachers and administrators find it difficult to learn new ways to teach and lead schools (Steiner, 2000; Weiss & Paley, 2006). Another problem at school sites is structural. The schedules, configuration of space, and tracking system are often incompatible with reform designs (Weiss & Paley, 2006). Finally, the culture of most schools does not support the type of collaboration among teachers that many reforms require (Coburn, 2003; Datnow et al., 1998; Weiss & Paley, 2006).

External challenges also threaten efforts to scale up. First, many states have testing programs that are not aligned with most externally developed reform models. As a result, teachers and administrators who implement such reform designs are often caught in the middle, between pressures to raise test scores and pressures to implement a program that is incompatible with the tests (Datnow et al., 1998). A related challenge is public pressure for results. In general, neither the general public nor the mass media understand that meaningful reform takes time, and that authentic improvements in education may take five or ten years, or even longer (Weiss & Paley, 2006). Finally, resource issues pose a major challenge. A school that is implementing a significant pedagogical change is resource hungry. Among other things, it needs appropriate materials, ongoing professional development, and a program facilitator. More often than not, the funds for these crucial forms of support either are not available throughout the long process of implementation, or are never available at all (Steiner, 2000; Weiss & Paley, 2006). Scaling up educational reforms is, then, a challenging process that demands resources, skills, and conditions that are not always present in American schools and school districts.

IN-DEPTH LOOK AT A TYPICAL STUDY.   As indicated previously, Roots and Wings is a comprehensive school reform model that has scaled up relatively well (Bodilly, 1998). Therefore, this section describes a study of the scaling up of Success for All (SFA), the reading component of Roots and Wings. Developed at Johns Hopkins University by Robert Slavin and others, SFA was first implemented in a school in Maryland in 1987. Since then, it has scaled up dramatically; by 2000, it was being used in more than 1600 schools in forty-eight states, as well as in five other countries (Datnow et al., 2002). SFA is a highly prescriptive school reform model; it includes materials that teachers must use, lesson plans, and tests. Implementing schools are also required to have a full-time SFA facilitator. The SFA Foundation, which is now in charge of SFA programs, provides abundant support for implementing schools, including ongoing professional development.

One important component of the SFA reform model is its national reform network. Cooper, Slavin, and Madden (1998) studied the impact of participation in this network on the scaling up of SFA. The national network offered implementers a national conference on SFA that they could attend, as well as local SFA activities in which they could participate. Using surveys from 225 SFA elementary schools across the country and intensive case studies of twenty SFA schools, they concluded that active participation in the network enhanced the scaling up of SFA. For example, implementers who were active in the network activities were more likely than nonparticipants to be using such components of the SFA model as grade-level meetings, regular assessments, and the parent involvement program. The local networks were especially effective at building capacity both for implementing teachers and principals and for the SFA facilitators. They also provided professional development, which more than 70% of the facilitators and principals surveyed considered a key element in their implementation effort. Cooper, Slavin, and Madden (1998) concluded that their reform network was a crucial component of the scale up of the SFA model, writing: "the ultimate purpose of networking is to equip educators with a vision, the tools, and the support to make fundamental changes in their schools and, ultimately, in the lives of their students" (p. 406). The rest of this chapter draws on first-, second-, and third-generation research to suggest how to implement a new education policy, as well as what to avoid.

LESSONS FROM THE THIRD GENERATION.   The third generation of implementation research deepens and extends our understanding of aspects of implementation that first- and second-generation researchers first identified. Perhaps most important of all, it contributes important information about implementers as *learners*. Earlier research revealed that teachers and administrators did not always understand the policies they were expected to implement, but many first- and second-generation studies also implied that grassroots implementers were simply resistant, entrenched in the status quo, or incompetent. While resistance, entrenchment in the status quo, and sheer incompetence can certainly be found in public schools, the research on implementers as learners suggests ways to increase the likelihood that teachers and principals will fully grasp the nature of the changes required of them. Of course, as indicated by second-generation research, ongoing professional development is essential; however, that professional development should be shaped by an understanding of cognitive psychology. Implementers should be shown how the proposed reform resembles their current practice, as well as how it differs from it. Ideally, workshops and seminars should also model the new pedagogy that the implementers are expected to learn. Because new beliefs, norms, and practices cannot be learned overnight, reformers should plan to provide extensive and ongoing professional development over a long period of time.

Third-generation research also suggests the key importance of providing a strong social infrastructure for implementation. Historically, both teaching and building administration have been constructed as individualistic professions to be practiced largely in isolation. A "sink-or-swim" attitude prevailed; teachers and principals either succeeded or failed on their own. Mentors, coaches, and support networks were unheard of. In contrast to the individualistic norms of American public education, third-generation research indicates that people who are implementing new policies or participating in the scaling up of a policy need strong social support. They need opportunities to discuss new ideas among themselves; they need opportunities to observe other educators who are already implementing the policy; they need assistance from facilitators and mentors. They also benefit from access to a support network. The development of such an infrastructure is costly. It implies providing teachers and principals with such amenities as joint planning periods, additional time for professional development, and funds to attend relevant conferences and workshops. Such resources are not always easy to find, but they are probably part of the inherent cost of bringing about meaningful change in American education.

HOW TO IMPLEMENT A NEW POLICY

Implementing policies is one of school leaders' most important tasks. Moreover, as previous sections make clear, central office staff and principals play a crucial role in the implementation process; without their support, implementations are likely to fail. This section, then, presents some general guidelines for implementing new policies. It describes the process chronologically, starting with mobilization for implementation, and moves on to implementation proper, concluding with the institutionalization of the new policy. A fundamental assumption is that the school leaders and other major implementers either support or accept the policy. The final section addresses a more challenging situation: dealing with a policy that the leaders or other major implementers oppose.

Mobilizing for Implementation

Mobilization is probably the most crucial step in policy implementation; serious errors here almost always doom a project to failure. This section is thus unusually long in relation to the other two sections, reflecting the author's conviction that investing time and energy in mobilization is important. Therefore, leaders who hope to bring about a lasting change should pay careful attention to each step of mobilization: policy adoption, planning, and the gathering of resources. They should also understand that mobilization is not a short phase; Huberman and Miles (1984) found that mobilization typically lasted fourteen to seventeen months.

ADOPTING A NEW POLICY.   Many readers are undoubtedly surprised by this heading. After all, much of Chapter 8 dealt with policy adoption. Although many new policies are adopted outside school districts and then passed down to them for implementation, new policies are often adopted at the district or even building level. For example, a central office staff may decide to recommend to the school board that the district's junior high schools be transformed into middle schools, or a principal and the faculty may decide to establish a peer tutoring program. Other policies are initiated at the state or federal level, but are voluntary for schools and districts. Most policies based on inducements fall into this category. For example, a school or district might apply to its SDE for a grant to improve its graduation rate. In all such cases, a local adoption process must occur, and it should be more than a decision by a small group of people who have the authority to impose their ideas on others. A misguided or faulty adoption process undermines the entire implementation. In fact, poor approaches to policy adoption are a common cause of implementation failure. Therefore, school leaders who are considering adopting a policy should be sure that they can answer three key questions in the affirmative. If they cannot, they should alter or abandon their plans for policy change. The remainder of this discussion is organized around these key questions.

Motives for Adopting a New Policy.   The first, and most important, question is: Do we have good reasons for adopting a new policy? The research on implementation suggests that there are both good and bad reasons for adopting policies. The worst reason for adopting a policy is that a few leaders want to build their reputations as innovators in order to advance their careers. Typically, when a policy is adopted as part of a career-building scheme, the key leaders receive job offers in the middle of implementation and leave. When that happens, the implementation falls apart, leaving disillusionment in its wake. Even when the hoped-for jobs never materialize, such implementations are usually poorly planned and consist of more image than substance (Berman & McLaughlin, 1978; Fullan, 2001). Another poor reason to adopt a new policy is the belief that it will enhance the district's reputation as a progressive, cutting-edge system. Innovation for the sake of innovation frequently fails because the implementers sense (accurately) that the new policy is just this year's fad, and as a result, they never take it seriously. Innovation for the sake of innovation also creates an atmosphere of skepticism about all change (Fullan, 2001). Experts believe that not attempting any policy change is better than adopting a new policy for either of these poor reasons.

There are only two good reasons for adopting a new policy (Berman & McLaughlin, 1978). The first is that it helps solve a bona fide, well-recognized problem (Fullan, 2007). For example, district leaders might choose to change from junior highs to middle schools in order to address the growing alienation of preadolescents. If they are able to articulate this genuine problem clearly and explain how the proposed policy change addresses it, they should find that building support for adopting the new policy is relatively easy. Such support improves the likelihood of a successful implementation. The second strong reason for adopting a new policy is to build the capacity of the implementers so they can eventually introduce other changes (Fullan, 2007). For instance, a superintendent may decide that in order to encourage the development of stronger leadership skills among teachers, the district should introduce site-based decision making. The hope is that after some experience with decision making, the faculty will develop the capacity for handling other changes, such as working in teams and mentoring beginning teachers.

- Is the proposed policy consistent with the school's or district's vision statement or philosophy?
- Is it consistent with the school's or district's assessed needs?
- Is it consistent with the school's or district's priorities?
- Is it consistent with the level of available and potentially available resources?
- Is it consistent with the values of the community?
- Does evidence exist that it has been effective with student populations such as the school's or district's in terms of:
  —age?
  —racial or ethnic background?
  —gender composition?
  —socioeconomic class?
  —English language proficiency?
  —life experience?

FIGURE 10.1 Determining whether a policy is appropriate for a specific context

Appropriateness of the New Policy.   The second question leaders should consider before adopting a new policy is: Is this policy appropriate for our school or district? Finding new ideas about how to do things in schools is not hard. Every education journal, every education conference, and many politicians' speeches abound with suggestions. What is hard is determining which of these many possible policy changes are suitable for the specific context within which one works (Fullan, 2007).

Figure 10.1 lists the major issues that should be considered. Although all are important, two merit special emphasis. Some education leaders develop plans for policy changes as if they worked in a social vacuum. Learning about an exciting program that achieved dramatic success in New York or San Francisco, they rush to put it into place in another setting—perhaps in a rural Southwestern community or a small New England town. Of course, sometimes such transplanted policies work well. However, often they do not, attracting the anger of the community, whose values have been ignored. Mirel (1994) recounts the story of such an attempted implementation in Illinois. The Bensenville School District was awarded a $1.5 million grant to develop and implement a "break-the-mold" New American School. However, the controversy that erupted from the teachers' union and the community revealed, a little tardily, that Bensenville was not interested in breaking any molds, which ultimately led to the withdrawal of funding.

Another common mistake is adopting a policy that does not match the resource level of a school or district. Analyzing the resources needed to implement a new policy, to continue it over the long term, and to scale it up is essential. As pointed out in Chapter 9, the resources needed are not just monetary. Issues such as the availability of extra time, volunteer workers, and space must also be considered. When policies are adopted that do not match the resource level of the organization, one of two things usually happens. If the mismatch is very large, the implementation fails from the outset. Prestine and McGreal (1997) describe a case of this sort. Teachers in four schools were told to implement authentic assessment. However, this new policy was not appropriate to their situation. Although there were numerous problems, a major one was that the teachers' classes were already overloaded; they averaged 130 students each. They did not have enough time in the day to prepare for classes, teach all day, and implement authentic assessment for that many students. As a result, the large majority of them never put this reform into effect.

Alternatively, in such implementations all goes well as long as the extra resources provided by a grant are available. As soon as the extra funding ends, however, so does the new policy. The implementers are left with a sense of futility and are likely to develop a reluctance to invest time and energy in future changes.

In trying to determine whether a policy is appropriate for their own setting, school leaders should consult several sources. An Educational Resources Information Center (ERIC) search may uncover articles and other reports on what has happened in places where the new policy has been tried. The SDE and professional associations may have useful information. Visiting schools and districts similar to one's own where the policy is already in place is especially helpful. By exploring these avenues, leaders should be able to gather enough information to determine whether a new policy is appropriate for their own setting.

Adequate Support.   The third question leaders should ask themselves is: Does the policy we are considering have sufficient support among key stakeholders? Policy implementations are as political as policy formulation and adoption in a legislative arena; this means that a policy can be derailed by unwilling stakeholders as quickly as it can be killed in a hostile committee. Therefore, assessing the level of support the proposed policy enjoys is important (Berman & McLaughlin, 1978; Fullan, 2007). Above all, considering the level of support among the major implementers is essential. If members of a central office staff advocate adopting a new policy, they must make sure that the principals and teachers who must implement the new policy accept it. Principals play an unusually important role in implementation; ideally, they should strongly support any new policy they must implement. The support of teachers is not quite as crucial, because they often fall in line behind a principal who is convinced of the value of change. Even so, they are likely to resist any new policy to which they strongly object even if their principal supports it. Therefore, ensuring that the new policy is at least acceptable to most of them is important. Berman and McLaughlin (1978) found that top-down implementations "generally met with indifference or resistance at the school level" (p. 15).

However, if educators at the building level are the primary advocates of a change, assessing support is even more important for them than it is for central office staff. They must be especially certain that the central office and school board solidly backs their plans. Research suggests that implementing a policy change in the face of opposition from high-level management is almost impossible. Such policy adoptions usually remain "isolated . . . within the district" (Berman & McLaughlin, 1978, p. 15), receiving little assistance from central office staff. They are also likely to be among the first victims in a round of budget cuts. Depending on the details of the proposed policy, obtaining the support of other stakeholders, such as parents, social service agencies, unions, and students, may also be necessary.

In determining the level of support, leaders should not merely guess. The adoption process should include an ongoing dialog with all the groups and individuals who will be asked to play a role in implementation or who could derail it. Some may have to be persuaded. Many will not be willing to accept the exact change proposed, but may suggest modifications of it; such negotiations are an important component of the adoption process. Leaders should put aside any notions that they know best and listen carefully to what other stakeholders say. As Fullan (2001) observes, "[A]ssume that one of the main purposes of . . . implementation is to *exchange your reality* of what should be through interaction with implementers" (p. 108). Not until the proposed policy change has gone through this transformative process should leaders move to adopt it officially.

NEWS STORY FOR ANALYSIS

Iroquois Superintendent Warns Race to Top Grant May Be Too Low

BUFFALO, NY—The Iroquois School District's portion of a federal grant will probably be too low to cover the costs of implementing the changes it requires, the interim superintendent said Wednesday at the school board meeting. Superintendent Bruce Fraser called the $48,000 available to the Iroquois district a "disappointing allocation" of the $700 million statewide pool from the Race to the Top program sponsored by the federal government in an effort to increase educational standards nationwide.

He said the money would be paid out over a four-year period as the district implements new evaluation procedures and measures of performance for teachers and administrators. "We will be forced to put in place 95 percent of this new reform agenda anyway," the interim superintendent said. "We'll have to be really resourceful to do it for less than the $48,000 we'll be given." He said the district is expected to form a network team for data analysis, curriculum and instructional purposes so that performance evaluation can be conducted. Among options being considered, he said, is collaborating with neighboring districts to share the costs of the three full-time individuals who will have to be hired to fulfill the grant requirements.

Board member Charles Specht expressed concern that when the grant expires, taxpayers will be forced to foot the bill. "If we're going to be hard-pressed to do all this at $48,000, after four years we'll be going backwards. Is the Legislature looking at the burden this could place on school districts?" Specht asked. Fraser said he would spend Thursday and today with superintendents from all over Western New York to brainstorm ways to tackle Race to the Top's costly mandates. The deadline for final commitments from school districts is Nov. 8, he said, with implementation required by June 2011.

(Adapted by permission of the publisher from E. Werbitsky, "Iroquois Superintendent Warns Race to Top Grant May Be Too Low," from the *Buffalo [New York] News*, 15 October 2010.)

QUESTIONS

1. Good implementation depends on the will and capacity of the implementers. To what extent do you believe that the will and capacity to implement this federal mandate are present in the Iroquois School District?
2. Using the questions about policy appropriateness in Figure 10.1, identify several ways in which this new policy is inappropriate for the Iroquois School District.
3. To what extent is board member Charles Specht's concern about the policy justified?
4. What problems do you think will arise during the implementation of this policy? ■

PLANNING FOR IMPLEMENTATION.   After making the decision to implement a new policy, leaders must plan the implementation. Although *planning* is essential, the research somewhat paradoxically suggests that leaders can also overplan (Fullan, 2007; Louis & Miles, 1990). Because detailed, long-range plans almost always represent the ideas of one person or a small group, such rigid plans are not likely to succeed. This does not imply, however, that leaders should embark on a policy implementation with a casual "Let's just see what happens" attitude; rather, they should engage in what Louis and Miles (1990) call *evolutionary planning*. By all means, they should have a plan, especially for the crucial first weeks of implementation, but they should be prepared to revise it as experience suggests needed changes. As the project evolves, they should modify their plan, adapting it in response not only to experience but also to changes in the environment, such as altered levels of resources or shifting political configurations.

   Who Should Participate in Planning?   There are two schools of thought concerning who should take part in planning a policy implementation. One approach is to form a large steering committee that represents all the stakeholders interested in the project. Such a committee should include administrators, teachers, parents, support staff, community representatives, officials from local government, and possibly students and social service workers. The other approach is to form a smaller steering committee, composed of a few people who have volunteered to work on the project and who are strongly committed to it. Both types of planning groups can succeed; however, the large, broad-based steering committee is most effective in settings where the stakeholders share a general consensus about education policy and work together harmoniously. In contexts with a history of conflict, the smaller committee will probably work best.

   Regardless of which form is chosen, eventually it *must* include representatives of two key stakeholder groups: building principals and teachers. Because they are the grassroots implementers, their input is essential (Fullan, 2007). If they are unrepresented in the initial planning group, they should be added later as plans become more concrete. More than any other participants, they understand both the opportunities and potential difficulties the policy change brings with it. If representatives of the school board and community are not included in the initial planning group, then systematic channels of communication between the planners and those two groups must be established at the start and maintained throughout. Otherwise, the steering committee appears to be acting secretively (Louis & Miles, 1990).

   Planning by Forward Mapping.   The group in charge of planning should try to anticipate all the major prerequisites for beginning the implementation. This is not easy to do. Putting most new policies into practice requires first mustering a broad range of resources, such as materials, equipment, trainers, consultants, and suitable spaces. The exact nature of what is essential to the project is not always obvious during planning. Yet the absence of some resources in the early weeks of implementation can prove fatal. Therefore, school leaders are wise to anticipate as much as possible.

   One technique for identifying implementation needs ahead of time is *forward mapping* (Weimer & Vining, 2004). The first step in forward mapping is developing a written scenario that describes what the new policy will look like when fully implemented. A scenario could be produced by the planning group as a whole, or one member could write it and then present it to the larger group for critique. Once the participants reach agreement on the scenario, they use it as the basis for developing practical questions about it. Table 10.2 presents a short scenario that describes a fully implemented site-based decision-making policy and lists some of the questions it might generate. These questions are then used by the group to develop a plan, which should be a general outline rather than a detailed blueprint. A sample, based on the scenario and questions in Table 10.2, appears in Figure 10.2. A tentative draft of the plan should be presented to all building principals and a representative sample of the teachers who will be involved in implementation. Because they are the grassroots implementers, they know the real context for implementation better than anyone else and are able to offer realistic advice. After their suggestions are used to revise the plan, it should provide a useful guide for the next (and final) stage of mobilization. It may also provide some clues for things that must be done during implementation itself.

TABLE 10.2 A Scenario With Practical Questions

Scenario	Practical Questions
Principal * (1) Smith *checks her watch* (2) and then calls the *regular* (3) meeting of her school council to order. Almost all the *representatives* (4) are present, seated around a large *conference table* (5). "The meeting of the Maple Grove Elementary School Council is *called to order,*" (6) she announces. "The first *agenda* (7) item is the minutes of the last meeting. They were distributed to you last week. Do I hear a motion to approve them?" "*So move,*" (8) responds a teacher. This motion is seconded promptly and passed unanimously, but the meeting bogs down on the next agenda item, a change in planning periods. The upper- and lower-grade teachers *disagree on this issue and spend the better part of an hour discussing it, sometimes heatedly* (9). At length, however, *they reach a compromise* (10) that all can accept. At this point, they decide to hold another meeting to discuss the rest of the agenda and vote to adjourn.	1. Should principals chair the councils? 2. When will these meetings be held? Will representatives need release time for them? 3. How often should meetings be held? Is there a potential conflict with the master contract? 4. What groups should be represented, and how should representatives be selected? 5. Do all schools have a room of the right size for council meetings, and furniture appropriate for participative decision making? 6. How has the principal learned to use parliamentary procedure? 7. How much extra clerical time and materials will be required to prepare for meetings? 8. How have the teachers learned parliamentary procedure? 9. How have the teachers learned to be assertive and manage conflict? 10. How have the teachers learned to negotiate their differences?

*Portions that have triggered questions are italicized.

Planning for Governance Issues

1. Discuss parameters with superintendent.
2. Discuss parameters with school board president.
3. Based on (1) and (2), convene a governance committee.
4. Governance committee develops recommended governance document detailing: council composition, meeting frequency, chairmanship, (s)election processes, and so forth.

Planning for Staff Development Issues

1. Identify possible trainers in parliamentary procedure, assertiveness, conflict resolution, negotiating, and so forth.
2. Schedule preimplementation training sessions.
3. Discuss times for later training sessions.

Planning for Improving the Setting

1. Check available rooms and furniture in each building.
2. Discuss meeting times with superintendent and both contract managers.
3. Are release time or common planning periods or both possible?
4. Discuss clerical implications with clerical supervisors and selected secretaries.
5. Increase budget for clerical supplies as needed.

FIGURE 10.2   Plans for implementing site-based decision making

TABLE 10.3 Implementation Problems Identified by Principals

Major Problems*	Other Problems*
Teacher time and energy	Lack of skills among staff
Money	Slow progress
Arranging staff development	Disagreement over goals
Ongoing communication	Maintaining interest
Limitations of facilities	Overambitious project
Teacher morale/resistance	Unexpected crises
	Competition with other new projects

*Problems are arranged in order of importance, with the most important first.
Source: Based on Louis and Miles (1990).

GATHERING RESOURCES FOR IMPLEMENTATION.   The third aspect of mobilizing for policy implementation is *gathering resources.* As Table 10.3 indicates, many of the problems in implementation are caused by insufficient resources. In fact, of all the major problems that principals in Louis and Miles's (1990) study mentioned, fully two-thirds of them (lack of time, lack of money, inadequate staff development, and poor facilities) and one minor problem (lack of skills) related to resources. Moreover, several of the other problems were probably caused or made worse by resource shortages. A frequent cause of implementation failure is the lack of or unwise allocation of resources (Fullan, 2007; Louis & Miles, 1990; Miles & Huberman, 1984). This means that leaders who wish to bring about genuine policy changes must analyze carefully what resources are necessary and obtain them both before and during implementation.

Money.   Money is important because it can be used to obtain other resources (Fullan, 2007). Many policy implementations are supported by grants obtained from the government or a private foundation. Needless to say, grant opportunities should be explored fully. However, other sources of money may also be available. For example, by reallocating portions of the school or district budget, implementers may be able to free up funds. Area businesses should not be overlooked, either; some of them, especially those with a partner relationship with the school or district, may be willing to contribute funds.

Although a certain amount of money is essential, many education leaders overestimate the importance of abundant fiscal resources (Berman & McLaughlin, 1978). Even more crucial than the total budget available is how money is spent. The research suggests that the best use of one's money is to pay for ongoing assistance for the implementers and to hire a facilitator to direct the project. Providing modest salary supplements or stipends for a lot of people involved is wasteful (Louis & Miles, 1990).

Time.   Time is another crucial resource (Fullan, 2007; Louis & Miles, 1990; Stecher et al., 2008). Inevitably, all policy changes make great demands on the time of everyone involved. In part, this is because performing new behaviors is more time-consuming than acting in routine ways. Therefore, expecting that the implementers will spend additional hours each week working on the change project is reasonable. What is not reasonable, however, is expecting that they will work twelve- to fifteen-hour days or devote weekends and vacation periods to it. Excessive demands of this sort are a sure recipe for failure. Therefore, when leaders muster resources, they must take steps to ensure more hours of work for the project than they can expect teachers and principals to add to their already full workdays.

This can be done in several ways. One is to provide some release time for key implementers. Employing part-time or substitute teachers is one approach. Another is to explore some of the innovative forms of scheduling that can be used to free teachers for team meetings or planning sessions. School leaders should try to avoid wasting the precious time of highly skilled employees on tasks that minimum-wage workers could easily perform. Teachers and principals should not be asked to set up meeting rooms, make coffee, stuff envelopes, meet consultants at the airport, or perform similar routine chores. Ideally, some funds are used to hire less-skilled people to perform such tasks, or volunteer workers (if available) can be used. Solving the time problem is always a challenge, but a combination of realism and creativity enables leaders to do so.

Personnel.   Although few policy implementations can afford to hire large staffs, certain personnel are necessary in order to achieve even a modest change (Stecher et al., 2008). One important personnel decision is the selection of a project director or coordinator. In their study of policy change in large urban high schools, Louis and Miles (1990) found that a major predictor of success was the presence of someone who had assumed major responsibility for the project. This person performed such essential tasks as monitoring progress, handling communication, and taking the initiative to solve problems. Louis and Miles recommend that the project director work at least half time on coordinating the implementation. Even where a half-time position is not feasible, specifically designating a director and providing at least some release time for him or her is advisable. Other personnel are necessary to provide training and other forms of assistance to the implementers (Fullan, 2007). The SDE, professional organizations, and universities are useful sources of people who can lead workshops or act as consultants. Because such people often have full calendars, contacting them early about a date for them to work with the implementers is wise. Training is necessary just before implementation begins and also throughout the process, so more than one date will have to be scheduled.

Space.   In Louis and Miles's 1990 study, two thirds of the principals who responded to their survey identified "constraints of the school's physical plant" (p. 146) as either a major or a minor problem during implementation. Such constraints can take many forms: not enough classrooms; classrooms that are too small; substandard maintenance practices; and, in some cases, no space at all. At one high school, for example, the policy change involved hiring nine new counselors . . . but not enough space was available for them to have offices! These findings suggest that education leaders in charge of overseeing a policy implementation should not deem space issues too trivial to talk about. Inadequate or inappropriate space can seriously undermine the quality of an implementation. In assessing space needs, school leaders should have someone—preferably someone who will be a grassroots implementer of the project—visit each building involved to assess space needs. If possible, visiting a site in which a similar policy has been implemented successfully and noting how space is used is also helpful. The checklist in Figure 10.3 can be used to assess how appropriate the existing space is for the project and to determine how it should be altered.

Equipment and Materials.   At Cambire School, the implementation of a new teaching methodology failed in part because of the lack of materials (Gross et al., 1971). Policy changes often depend heavily on the availability of specific machines

_____   1.   Classrooms are large enough for new teaching methods.
_____   2.   Classrooms/offices have sufficient storage space for new equipment or materials.
_____   3.   Classrooms/offices are wired for modern technology.
_____   4.   Adequate office space can be provided.
_____   5.   Secure storage areas for new equipment can be provided.
_____   6.   Facilities are adequately maintained.

FIGURE 10.3   Checklist for assessing space needs

and materials (Fullan, 2007; Stecher et al., 2008). For example, a policy that includes a computer-assisted instruction component requires the use of computers. In fact, it probably requires a large number of computers, some of which will probably have to be rented, purchased, or borrowed from other programs. Sometimes the materials required by a new program are less apparent. A hands-on science curriculum may obviously require the gathering of wire, batteries, test tubes, and chemicals for experiments. However, the fact that each week students must use two or three photocopies of the lab sheets may escape some leaders. This program feature means that, in addition to the materials for experiments and projects, extra paper and copier ink must be ordered. Nor should extra wear and tear on copying machines be overlooked. Skillful implementers make sure they order additional cases of paper and ink cartridges and provide extra funds for copier maintenance. Otherwise, the project could come to a halt in midyear when teachers can no longer reproduce the lab sheets.

Implementation Proper

Implementation itself should begin only after a solid foundation has been laid during the mobilization period. Implementing a new policy at a logical point in time, usually at the beginning of the school year or a semester, is best. This section considers implementation from two perspectives, the first of which is chronological. Implementation researchers usually identify two stages in the process, *early* and *late,* and each of these is described. Then, several crosscutting themes relevant to both the early and late stages are discussed.

Stages of Implementation

EARLY IMPLEMENTATION.   In their comparative study of twelve implementations in education, Huberman and Miles (1984) found that the early months of implementation are invariably rough. Although solid preparation during mobilization does permit things to run somewhat more smoothly than they would otherwise, even well-prepared projects encounter serious problems. The reason for this difficulty is that the grassroots implementers must learn to act in new ways. Even if they have been well trained, they have not yet had to actually perform the new behaviors day in and day out. Because they are learning, the implementers—usually classroom teachers—probably feel overloaded, tired, anxious, and confused. They make many mistakes and wonder if they are failing. They may feel demoralized and depressed. Said one teacher in Huberman and Miles's (1984) study: "I got into it. I fell down and I had to pick myself up. That happened a lot of times. I'm just beginning to walk" (p. 73). Huberman and Miles found, however, that several factors helped teachers surmount their earliest difficulties and begin to experience some success. Not surprisingly, two of these were rooted in the mobilization stage: "the general degree of preparedness . . . [and] the provision of resources and materials" (p. 88). Also helpful was making ongoing in-service training available throughout early implementation and offering other assistance.

Unfortunately, there are also some negative ways to "help" teachers survive this trying period. In some districts, school leaders responded to complaints by agreeing to downsize the magnitude of the required policy change. These modifications in the adopted policy were not true mutual adaptations, but rather what Huberman and Miles dubbed *midgetizing*. By making the policy change smaller, leaders also made it less meaningful and worthwhile. Huberman and Miles comment: "Such 'midgetizing' eliminated most of the potential headaches but also threw out most of the potential rewards" (p. 88). They conclude that a smooth early implementation is actually "a bad sign" (p. 273). Although a rough start does not necessarily predict ultimate success, a smooth one does predict one type of failure—the failure that comes when a genuine change is transformed "into a modest, sometimes trivial, enterprise" (p. 273). Three factors stand out as predictors of ultimate success: (1) a rough start, (2) pressure by leaders to continue trying the new approach, and (3) ongoing assistance of various kinds. In short, the key to surviving early implementation with both the policy change and the implementers intact is a judicious combination of pressure and support.

LATE IMPLEMENTATION.   Not surprisingly, the nature of *late implementation* depends on the extent to which early implementation has been successful. In this case, *success* means making a genuine change in an education policy. As noted earlier, many implementations fail. Therefore, two scenarios are sketched here: (1) late implementation in failed projects, and (2) late implementation in midgetized and successful projects.

When a policy implementation fails, negative feelings are left in its wake; the onset of these feelings and the behavior that usually accompanies them signal the beginning of late implementation. Typically, failed implementations are characterized by much disappointment and discouragement. Burnout is often apparent. The implementers scale back their personal investments of time and energy at this point. Many revert to their earlier practices—if, indeed, they ever abandoned them. One common cause of negativism is the withdrawal of funding for the policy change; other causes include resentment of a poorly designed project and anger at leaders. In many ways, things gradually return to the status quo, except in one important respect: The next time the leaders suggest implementing a new policy, they may be met with cynicism, the usual legacy of a failed implementation (Gross et al., 1971; Huberman & Miles, 1984; Louis & Miles, 1990).

Midgetized implementations often enter the late implementation stage after five or six months; truly successful ones usually do not mature to this stage until about eighteen months have elapsed. However, in both situations, similar phenomena are apparent. The implementers now feel comfortable with the new policy and confident in their ability to use the new behaviors it requires. They also feel in control and proud of their accomplishments. During this stage, they usually begin to refine the project and debug it. Some ineffective components may be eliminated and more effective ones substituted. Implementers may write a manual describing some of the routines they developed. They may adapt the policy for a different student population, or they may begin to use some of its features in other parts of the curriculum (Huberman & Miles, 1984). One should not think, however, that by this point all problems have been solved. Problems are less frequent and less severe than during early implementation, but they still exist. Nor should one expect otherwise. Thus, late implementation is not a time for school leaders to relax and congratulate themselves, even if their project has been successful. There are still problems that they must face.

Most of all, they must resolve some critical issues if their policy is to endure or be institutionalized.

CROSS-CUTTING THEMES.   Most studies identify three components that run through successful implementations from beginning to end: (1) monitoring and feedback, (2) ongoing assistance, and (3) coping with problems. We discuss each in turn next.

Monitoring and Feedback.

In education, the sink-or-swim approach is an old tradition. Far too often, new teachers are shown the way to their classrooms and then left on their own to struggle to survive. Similarly, new principals are sometimes handed the keys to a building and told, "It's all yours now." Not surprisingly, then, many school leaders adopt this method when they find themselves in charge of an implementation (Louis & Miles, 1990). Although probably not an effective way to induct new educators, it is definitely not an effective way to manage a policy implementation.

Successful implementations depend on continuous *monitoring and feedback.* Someone, ideally a program facilitator or a project director, should be responsible for keeping a close watch on the implementation process. This leader's monitoring task should include frequent visits to the site(s) involved and frequent conversations with implementing teachers. He or she should also regularly communicate what is learned to the central office and building administrators. In addition, a good project director coordinates actions to resolve problems. For example, the director might invite a consultant in to work with several teachers who are experiencing the same difficulty (Fullan, 2007; Louis & Miles, 1990).

Although the project director should manage the daily details of monitoring the project, school administrators should not remain detached from the implementation. The research indicates the importance of pressure from above in successful policy changes. This means that principals and central office leaders should not only stay well informed about the course of the project, but should also be visible at the sites where implementation is occurring. Their presence, questions about progress, and encouraging words communicate an important message to the implementers about the seriousness of their efforts (McLaughlin, 1987).

There is a final reason for involving administrators. Principals and central office leaders should be actively engaged in the evolutionary planning process that characterizes good implementations (Fullan, 2007; Louis & Miles, 1990). Evolutionary planning requires flexibility and an experimental attitude, but it also depends on accurate knowledge about what is going on. Such knowledge cannot be gained by sitting at a desk; it can be obtained only by listening closely to the implementers and visiting them in the field. Only leaders who are in touch with the implementation are able to revise old methods and develop new ones, making needed changes as the process unfolds. Their ability to respond to the dilemmas that emerge as the abstract policy confronts the concrete setting of the implementation helps guarantee that mutual adaptation occurs, rather than either midgetization or failure.

Ongoing Assistance.

Although pressure is essential in successful implementation, so is support, and probably the most important form of support is *assistance* (Berman & McLaughlin, 1978; Fullan, 2007; Louis & Miles, 1990; Stecher et al., 2008). An in-service program the week before the project begins is definitely not sufficient.

People who are struggling to learn new ways of working need help, and that help should be well planned and carefully targeted to the local situation. It should also continue throughout implementation—during the mobilization period; through the entire implementation, early and late; and until the completion of institutionalization. The only way leaders can know when help is needed and what kind it should be is by monitoring the project and gathering regular feedback, as described earlier. As soon as the grassroots implementers begin to flounder or get confused, school leaders at either the building or district level should make sure that they receive assistance. This help can take many forms; Figure 10.4 lists some of the most widely used. There is no single best type of help; however, what is essential is that the assistance be relevant to the problems the implementers are experiencing.

Problem Coping. Multiple problems are inherent in every policy implementation. According to Louis and Miles (1990), they can be divided into three categories: (1) program related, (2) people related, and (3) setting related. Table 10.4 summarizes the most common problems of each type. Research suggests that program related problems are the easiest to solve, whereas those that are setting related are the most difficult. However, the ultimate success of every implementation depends on how well its leaders can identify and cope with problems of each type.

There are two general approaches to implementation problems. One is to consider them unwelcome intruders in an otherwise idyllic world and refuse to see them (much less deal with them) until they mushroom into crisis proportions. The other is to recognize that problems are not unexpected intruders, but a normal part of the process. This realization encourages skillful leaders to scan the implementation environment actively in order to detect problems in their earliest stages by speaking with the key implementers every day and welcoming open and honest discussion in meetings.

Pre–start-up training
Follow-up sessions
External consultants
Internal consultants
External trainers
Internal trainers
Visits to other sites
Off-site conferences
Regular meetings with other implementers
Printed materials
Easing of schedules
Teaching aides
Demonstrations
Chances to exchange materials and tips
Workshops
Formative evaluations
A sympathetic ear

FIGURE 10.4   Seventeen types of assistance for implementers

TABLE 10.4 Most Common Implementation Problems by Category

Program Related	People Related	Setting Related
Weak coordination	Unresponsive target population	Competition from other organizations
Delays	Lack of skills	Outside pressures
Conflicts	Negative attitudes	Unexpected emergencies
Lack of planning	Resistance	Powerlessness regarding key decisions
Contradictory goals	Skepticism	Physical environment
		Insufficient resources

Source: Based on Louis and Miles (1990).

TABLE 10.5 Methods for Coping With Implementation Problems

Technical	Political	Cultural
Break the project up into smaller parts	Create a representative task force to deal with problems	Have frequent discussion of project at meetings
Create task forces to work on problem areas	Mandate staff participation	Have frequent informal discussions with implementers
Phase in implementation gradually	Use incentives to encourage participation	Work to increase consensus on goals
Train staff to train other staff	Transfer unsupportive staff	Publicize the project
Tailor training to staff needs	Insulate implementation from community pressures	Work to improve organizational climate
		Use motivational techniques (e.g., slogans, T-shirts.)

Source: Based on Louis and Miles (1990).

As soon as they detect new problems, they begin to work to resolve them. They do not procrastinate or waste time looking for someone to blame; nor do they eliminate problems by midgetizing their project (Fullan, 2007; Louis & Miles, 1990). Leaders can find many ways to cope well with implementation problems. Table 10.5 lists several ways to cope, divided into three broad categories.

Technical strategies involve analyzing the problem area carefully and targeting the necessary resources to it. *Political* strategies involve mobilizing power to encourage people to act in desired ways. *Cultural* strategies "focus on the shared beliefs, values, and symbols that are the key to the problem" (Louis & Miles, 1990, p. 272). Of the three, technical approaches are usually the most effective; political and cultural methods typically achieve moderate success. Good education leaders thoughtfully use a mixture of all three.

Institutionalization

The final stage of implementation is *institutionalization*, "the period during which an innovation is incorporated into the organization" (Gross et al., 1971, p. 17). A policy has been fully institutionalized when it has been seamlessly integrated into the routine practices of the school or district. No longer perceived as new or special, it has become "the way we do things around here." Institutionalization does not occur because it is the natural product of implementation. It occurs because advocates of the new policy—most commonly district and building administrators—work deliberately to modify the formal rules and procedures of the organization in order to accommodate the policy change permanently. As with the other stages of implementation, it requires both thought and planning. Figure 10.5 provides a checklist for institutionalization. It can be used to assess the extent to which a policy has already been institutionalized, and it can serve as a planning guide, suggesting the next steps in the institutionalization process.

Although *institutionalization* is usually described as the third phase of implementation and is the subject of the final discussion in this section, it often overlaps with late implementation in practice. Skillful leaders of a project should be alert throughout late implementation for opportunities to accomplish any aspect of institutionalization. For example, if the district's procedures for evaluating teachers come up for routine review, they should try to get them modified to make them more consistent with the new policy. Institutionalization is rarely accomplished all at once; it is usually a piecemeal process. If advocates of the policy are alert, early in the implementation they identify all areas of the organization's routine procedures that do not support their project. Therefore, as late implementation begins, they are ready to watch for opportunities to institutionalize their new policy a little at a time. They know when any of the inconsistent routine procedures are scheduled for review, and read meeting agendas carefully to find other openings for needed changes.

While all the issues in Figure 10.5 are important, the last one is especially crucial. Many policy innovations are made with temporary funding, often referred to as *soft money*. As long as major components of the new policy are supported by such funds, it

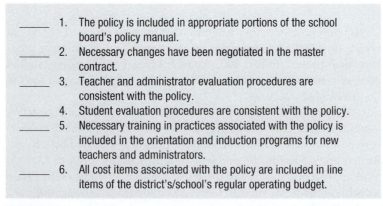

_____	1. The policy is included in appropriate portions of the school board's policy manual.
_____	2. Necessary changes have been negotiated in the master contract.
_____	3. Teacher and administrator evaluation procedures are consistent with the policy.
_____	4. Student evaluation procedures are consistent with the policy.
_____	5. Necessary training in practices associated with the policy is included in the orientation and induction programs for new teachers and administrators.
_____	6. All cost items associated with the policy are included in line items of the district's/school's regular operating budget.

FIGURE 10.5   Checklist for assessing degree of policy institutionalization

is vulnerable. Extra money may be available for special materials, supplementary staff, and release time during periods of financial prosperity. However, few things are more certain than this: As soon as the business cycle turns downward, those special funds will be cut. This means that policy advocates must work conscientiously to move every essential component of their innovation from soft money to a line item in the regular budget of the organization. This is not easy, because as a policy change moves through late implementation, competitors from within the organization will probably surface, hoping to capture some extra dollars as the project comes to an end. The struggle to move the policy into the regular budget will probably be as difficult as any other part of implementation. Even so, only when it has been incorporated into the regular budget does the new policy have a chance to be fully institutionalized and, therefore, fully implemented (Fullan, 2007; Huberman & Miles, 1984).

IMPLEMENTING UNPOPULAR POLICIES

Throughout the previous section we assume that no major groups of implementers, including the school leaders themselves, opposed the policy being implemented. Of course, this assumption is not always valid. Often, policy changes are imposed by high-level administrators or those outside the school organization. In these cases, large numbers of implementers—sometimes most or virtually all of them—may oppose the new policy. Dealing with opposition and resistance is one of the greatest challenges school leaders face. The challenge is compounded when the leaders themselves have serious reservations about the required change. Although no easy answers are ever found in these situations, this section explores the problem, explaining why opposition occurs and suggesting some ways to deal with it, as well as with open and covert resistance. It also discusses occasions when school leaders feel that they too must take the path of resistance.

Why Some Policies Are Unpopular

SELF-INTEREST.   Implementers are unlikely to support policies that they perceive as contrary to their own self-interest (McDonnell, 1991). In particular, they will almost certainly oppose changes that appear to threaten their job security, chances for promotion, or status in the workplace. For example, if a state legislature mandates site-based management throughout the state, central office administrators will probably not feel enthusiastic about it (Malen & Ogawa, 1988). They will suspect that as decision-making authority is devolved to school sites, their jobs will become unnecessary. No one should be surprised, then, if they resist implementing the policy, even though their resistance may not be open. Another aspect of self-interest that often becomes important is the desire to maintain current compensation and working conditions. Readers may recall that in Prestine and McGreal's (1997) study, an outside organization insisted that teachers implement authentic assessment. Although authentic assessment requires considerably more time than traditional assessment, no one proposed raising the teachers' salaries or reducing class size. In effect, the teachers were asked to accept a longer workday without a commensurate salary increase. Not surprisingly, Prestine and McGreal found that teachers were skeptical of the value of the new policy and that "both across and within these schools, authentic assessment never achieved anything close to systemic implementation" (p. 390).

PROFESSIONAL VALUES.   Educators are also likely to oppose implementing policies that conflict with their basic professional values (McDonnell, 1991). Grace (1995), an English researcher, described such a situation in the United Kingdom. During the 1980s, a number of government reforms changed the roles of both head-teachers (principals) and teachers. Previously, head-teachers had been expected to exercise pedagogic and moral leadership in their schools; however, government policy reforms altered their mission dramatically. By the end of the 1980s, they were expected to work as managers in a competitive market environment, publicizing their schools' scores on examinations. Although some head-teachers made this transition easily and even welcomed it, others experienced considerable difficulty, because they disagreed in fundamental ways with the reform. Many of them dealt with the contradiction between their own understanding of their profession and the demands of new policies by downplaying those aspects of the reforms with which they disagreed. However, a few resisted openly, primarily by voicing their disapproval and completely ignoring some aspects of the reforms. For example, a primary school head-teacher stated, "One has to fight harder and harder to maintain one's professionalism as more and more is imposed from above. As a staff we resist 'jumping through hoops' and fix our own priorities within the parameters of the national curriculum" (Grace, 1995, pp. 104–105). Although the resistance of school leaders was usually relatively discreet, teachers in Great Britain sometimes acted more forcefully. For instance, in 1983, primary teachers boycotted a new government test. The British experience demonstrates that many educators are deeply attached to professional values and are unwilling to surrender them lightly. McDonnell (1991) argues that in the United States, such value conflicts, whether recognized or not, are at the root of many incomplete or failed policy implementations.

Issues Surrounding Resistance

EXIT, VOICE, AND DISLOYALTY.   Weimer and Vining (2004), drawing on Albert Hirschman's classic *Exit, Voice, and Loyalty* (1970), argue that three responses are possible when asked to implement a policy with which one disagrees: (1) exit (leaving the organization), (2) voice (speaking up about problems), and (3) disloyalty (quietly or openly failing to conform to the policy). Of course, a single individual may combine these approaches. For example, a middle school principal who disagrees with a new district policy that creates excessive paperwork for teachers may first use voice. He may speak out at the superintendent's regular meetings with principals and schedule an appointment to discuss the issue with the immediate superior, the middle school supervisor. If these approaches fail, three courses of action are open to the principal.

The first is simply *compliance.* He may decide that the issue is not important enough to try exit or disloyalty, and implement the new policy as well as possible, perhaps sympathizing openly with the teachers, but explaining to them that this is just the way things are. However, if the value conflict is very intense, there are two other options to consider. Various forms of *exit* are also possible. The principal may decide that this is a good time to retire or to initiate a search for a job in another district. Other types of exit include returning to classroom teaching or moving into a central office job that does not require implementing the new policy. If exit is not a feasible or desirable option, the principal may choose among various forms of *disloyalty*. Although Weimer and Vining's (2004) term *sabotage* conjures up images of spies and terrorists, there are many less dramatic ways to sabotage a policy. The principal may prioritize the new paperwork and indicate to the teachers that they are required to fill out only some of the forms. He may simplify or streamline the forms without obtaining district approval, or may ignore various shortcuts devised by the teachers, all of which constitute *token compliance* (Bardach, 1977). Another approach is to have the teachers do all the paperwork, but give them extra time to complete it, perhaps letting them use vacation periods to work on their already late reports, known as *delayed compliance* (Bardach, 1977). Outright sabotage includes fabricating the required reports, or "losing" all of the necessary forms and directions. Obviously, all types of disloyalty are risky, and some are unethical. Nonetheless, some people choose these courses of action when faced with implementing a policy they strongly oppose.

CASE STUDY

The Reform That Went Awry

In the mid-1980s, Tennessee set out to change its curriculum policy for elementary schools. Committees dominated by college professors, SDE officials, and representatives of wealthy city districts developed the new policy, called the *Basic Skills First Program* (BSF).

The committees devised a comprehensive system for monitoring student progress in the basic skills. The mathematics and reading components alone included seven manuals, 112 tests, 180 individual student charts, and fifteen pages of class record sheets for each grade. Teachers' record-keeping work was supposed to be facilitated by computers. However, the state provided only one computer per school, and it arrived five months after implementation began. The SDE did offer computer training, however: a two-hour session for one representative from each school. This person was supposed to go back and teach the others how to enter the data in the special software developed for BSF.

The state's teachers, who enjoyed making jokes about the program's acronym, did not enjoy the prospect of doing the many extra hours of paperwork that full compliance would require. In fact, because many of them had neither planning periods nor duty-free lunch periods, they deeply resented the state's new demands on their time. Eventually, most decided not even to do the BSF record keeping. They had divided the number

of teachers in the state by the number of monitors for the program and figured out that at most they would be monitored once every three years. Moreover, they had detected a distinctly cool attitude toward BSF among their principals and superintendents as well.

In Nashville, SDE officials and politicians knew that the BSF implementation was not going as it should, but blamed the traditionalism of Tennessee teachers. They did not think to blame themselves.

[*Source:* Based on Fowler (1985).]

QUESTIONS

1. Identify the errors that the Tennessee SDE made during the adoption stage of this policy.
2. How could the SDE have modified its approach to increase the chances of a successful implementation of BSF?
3. Using the premise that successful implementation requires creating and sustaining the will and the capacity of the implementers, analyze the weaknesses of this implementation effort.
4. Describe the forms of resistance Tennessee educators used, and explain the role school administrators played in this resistance. ▪

COPING WITH RESISTANCE.   Although the strategies of opposition described previously were attributed to a principal, during an implementation any or all of the implementers in a school district or SDE may use them, from the chief state school officer down. In fact, because much resistance is covert, school leaders should suspect its presence any time that one thing after another just "happens" to go wrong with an implementation. School leaders, then, must be prepared for resistance and should have devised some ways to head it off or minimize its impact. One reason that it is essential to involve representatives of all the major implementers in the adoption process is that this approach reduces the likelihood of widespread resistance. However, even if a policy has been adopted through a participative process, some resistance may occur.

The first strategy to use with strong opponents of the policy is *persuasion.* Attempts at persuasion should be preceded by some nonjudgmental listening to opponents as they voice their objections; after all, they may be right about all or part of what they object to (Fullan, 2007). If they do not appear to have valid objections, school leaders should analyze their objections to determine the root of the problem. More often than not, opponents believe either that their self-interest is threatened or that the policy change is inconsistent with their values. They may have objections on both counts. It is possible that they do not fully understand the policy change, so their objections are partially or totally unfounded. In this case, the implementation leaders should provide them with more information, helping them see that they really have no legitimate grounds for opposition. If attempts at persuasion are successful, then leaders should be sure to maintain good channels of communication with these people throughout implementation to detect other misunderstandings early.

Another possible approach is to modify the policy to meet some objections. Although leaders must be careful not to midgetize the policy change (Huberman & Miles, 1984), all policy implementations involve some mutual adaptation between the policy and the setting (Stecher et al., 2008). Modifications to meet the legitimate objections of some implementers may be part of the necessary mutual adaptation. Leaders should certainly be ready to consider this possibility, especially if it will reduce resistance considerably.

Finally, moving strong opponents out of the implementation or excluding them from the outset is often possible. This can be accomplished in several ways. Unhappy teachers and principals can be transferred to schools or grade levels not included in the policy change. Administrators who object can be moved into positions that are not crucial to the implementation, perhaps being promoted or assigned to another administrative position. If a group or office important to the implementation is a problem, supervision of the process often can be assigned to another, more supportive group. Sometimes creating a special steering committee to assume an oversight role may be necessary. When these methods are used, however, they must be used in a limited fashion and with respect for the law, the master contract, and the right of all individuals to hold dissenting views. Overuse of these approaches or a heavy-handed application of them can cause the people who are moved to appear as martyrs, thereby actually increasing opposition to the policy change.

CHOOSING TO RESIST.   Fullan (2007) argues that a leader who critically assesses a new program may decide that it does not meet a real need, is not a high priority, or is not supported by adequate resources. She may also decide that it is not consistent with her professional values or personal ethics. At times a leader's most responsible course of action may therefore be to reject an innovation (Fullan, 2007). Clearly, though, her decision to resist implementing a policy with which she disagrees is not one to be taken lightly. After all, resistance can lead to the loss of both one's job and one's professional reputation. It may irreparably damage the organization. It may take a heavy toll on family, friendships, and health. Nonetheless, it is sometimes necessary.

Probably the first question that a school leader contemplating resistance should ask is: Is this objectionable policy just a symbolic one? Symbolic policies are adopted for purely political, rather than substantive, reasons. Legislatures sometimes adopt them in order to please a noisy constituency and encourage it to stop pressuring them. Presidents, governors, and other prominent leaders may push for a policy that they think will be popular and sound good in the publicity for their next campaign. The fact that the policy has been adopted formally does not necessarily mean that anyone cares much about its implementation. The implementation of symbolic policies is often *pro forma*—poorly planned, underfunded, and understaffed. This means that implementation almost always fails anyway. Thus, wise leaders consider this possibility when faced with an objectionable policy. If it is symbolic, resistance will probably be widespread and individual acts of opposition will go unnoticed. Risks will be low, and leaders may find the best course of action is a quiet failure to comply. Symbolic policies are usually forgotten quickly, and within two or three years no one even notices that noncompliance occurred.

If, however, the evidence suggests that the new policy was motivated by substantive reasons, resistance becomes more serious, especially if the degree of compliance is monitored aggressively. In this case, leaders contemplating resistance must think through their own motives. The best motive for resistance is commitment to a professional, philosophical, or religious principle, especially one that relates directly to the best interests of students. Issues of self-interest must be analyzed carefully to determine if there is a bona fide conflict of interest and if perhaps the best interests of students do not outweigh one's personal self-interest. The worst reasons for resistance are dislike for the proponents of the policy, the desire to settle an old score, or a scheme to damage the career of one of the implementation leaders. Resistance arising from such questionable motives will probably backfire, damaging both the resister and the organization.

Finally, anyone considering resistance should think through the probable outcome. The basic question is: Will resistance force the abandonment or major amendment of the policy? Sometimes it will. Huberman and Miles (1984) write of a principal who blocked the implementation of a poorly conceived and pedagogically unsound curriculum change in his school. Far from considering the principal's actions wrong, they observe that although the implementation failed, the principal was successful in protecting his school from a potential policy disaster. However, many times, opposition changes nothing; the power balance is such that the implementation rolls right over all resistance. In such cases, resisting to make a point and defend an important principle may still be right; engaging in quiet token compliance while conserving one's strength for even more important battles may be even wiser. Principled resistance to implementation should always be the fruit of much reflection and soul-searching. Leaders should be prepared to lose their jobs because of it.

FINAL POINTS

Implementation is an important part of the work of all school leaders and one they often dread. They have good reason to dread it—the implementation of any new policy is hard work at best and an embarrassing failure at worst. However, today, there is no good reason for failure in policy implementation. This is one of the best researched stages of the policy process; the standard errors are well known; workable approaches have been identified and field tested. This means that as leaders begin to plan for the implementation of any new policy, they can and should have the confidence that comes from knowing they are entering a well-mapped territory. Today, there is no excuse for failure; a good knowledge base, combined with thought and planning, leads to success in this difficult endeavor.

QUESTIONS AND ACTIVITIES FOR DISCUSSION

1. Reflect on the implementations in which you have been involved. Which went smoothly? Why? What errors were apparent in those that encountered serious difficulty?
2. Assume that you work in an SDE and that next year you will be involved in implementing a statewide voucher plan. Using a scenario and forward mapping, develop a tentative plan for this implementation.
3. Assume that you are going to lead the implementation of merit pay for teachers in your district. Identify the necessary resources and develop a plan for gathering them.
4. Select one of these policies: merit pay for teachers, vouchers, tying school funding to student test scores, or detracking. Be prepared to discuss the value conflicts that some educators might feel when implementing this policy and the types of resistance they might try.

INTERNET ASSIGNMENT

Using Google or another search engine, do a search of the Internet for implementation and No Child Left Behind Act, or a recent federal education law. Explore several of the sites you located and be prepared to report to your class on what you found.

FOR FURTHER READING

Berman, P., & McLaughlin, M. W. (1976). Implementation of educational innovation. *Educational Forum, 40,* 345–370.

A shortened version of the major findings of the Rand Change Agent Study, this article provides a good introduction to this influential early investigation of policy implementation in education.

Casto, H. G., & Sipple, J. W. (2011). Who and what influences school leaders' decisions: An institutional analysis of the implementation of universal prekindergarten. *Educational Policy, 25,* 134-166.

In this study of the implementation of prekindergarten programs in five districts in rural New York, the authors found that the implementers were far more influenced by local forces and norms than by the state's regulatory policies and national opinion. They discuss the implications of their findings for policy implementation in rural districts.

Jacob, B. (2001). Implementing standards: The California mathematics textbook debacle. *Phi Delta Kappan, 83,* 264–272.

Jacob describes in fascinating detail the heavy-handed, top-down manner in which California implemented a part of its new "standards-aligned" mathematics curriculum. His story reveals the impact of politics and ideology on a statewide policy implementation.

Stecher, B. M., Epstein, S., Hamilton, L. S., March, J. A., Robyn, A., McCombs, J. S., Russell, J., & Naftel, S. (2008). *Pain and gain: Implementing No Child Left Behind in Three States, 2004-2006.* Santa Monica, CA: RAND.

This study of the implementation of NCLB found that the three states under analysis had developed different approaches to implementing the federal law. Attitudes toward NCLB were more favorable in Georgia than in California or Pennsylvania.

Weinbaum, E. H., & Supovitz, J. A. (2010). Planning ahead: Make program implementation more predictable. *Phi Delta Kappan 91*(7), 68-71.

Drawing on a CPRE study of implementation of school-improvement programs, the authors argue that it is possible to predict at what points in an implementation the implementers will deviate from the original design of the program. They suggest ways to increase the "fidelity" of program implementation.

11

POLICY EVALUATION: DETERMINING IF THE POLICY WORKS

Focus Questions

▎ Why should education leaders be knowledgeable about policy evaluation?

▎ How can one tell if a proposed or completed evaluation is of high quality?

▎ Why are evaluations always political?

▎ How can a leader facilitate the evaluation process?

A NERVOUS-MAKING TOPIC

Evaluation is an integral part of the professional lives of all educators. Teachers regularly evaluate students; principals regularly evaluate teachers; and, increasingly, administrators themselves are subjected to regular evaluation. Broader forms of institutional evaluation are also common. Accrediting teams visit schools and districts, observing, interviewing, and collecting data. Many states have established *indicator systems* in order to gather information from school districts in dozens of performance areas, analyzing and comparing these figures, and then issuing official reports on their findings. In some cases, state departments of education (SDEs) even use evaluation results to categorize districts, perhaps labeling them *excellent, effective,* or *deficient* and attaching rewards and sanctions to those labels. Under the provisions of the *No Child Left Behind Act* (NCLB), extensive testing is required, with penalties for districts that appear to underperform. An age of accountability such as our own is inevitably an age of evaluation.

Not surprisingly, then, policies are often evaluated, too. In an ideal world, not only would all policies be thoroughly and fairly evaluated; but policymakers would also act on evaluation findings, modifying or terminating policies on that basis. Of course, our world is far from ideal. As a result, many policies are never evaluated at all; some are evaluated poorly; and, although some others are evaluated carefully, no one ever acts on the findings. However, sometimes the final stage of the policy process unfolds as it should: after an appropriate length of time, the new policy is evaluated carefully and then is maintained as it is, is changed, or is terminated.

Like every other stage of the policy process, evaluation is difficult, in large part because it is political; the major reason is that it threatens people. Stufflebeam (1983), a leader in education evaluation from the 1960s through the 1980s, observed that

Michael Scriven, another leader in education evaluation, "once said that 'evaluation is nervous making,' and it is. I have often been reminded of the biblical warning to 'Judge not, lest ye be judged'" (p. 140). This means that school leaders cannot take a smooth, problem-free policy evaluation for granted any more than they can take a smooth, problem-free implementation for granted. Yet, neither can effective leaders avoid or ignore policy evaluation. Stufflebeam continues:

> We cannot make our programs better unless we know where they are weak and strong. . . . We cannot plan effectively if we are unaware of options and their relative merits; and we cannot convince our constituents that we have done good work and deserve continued support unless we can show them evidence that we have done what we promised and produced beneficial results. For these and other reasons, public servants must subject their work to competent evaluation. (p. 140)

As public servants, then, education leaders must expect to be active participants in policy evaluation. Sometimes they must provide leadership while a school or district policy is undergoing evaluation. On other occasions, they may be required to plan and implement an evaluation themselves. In either case, they must know how and why policies are evaluated.

This chapter provides a knowledge base about some of the fundamental issues in policy evaluation and offers recommendations about making key decisions regarding it. It does not, however, provide detailed directions for designing and executing an evaluation. Many books are available on this subject, some of which are suggested at the end of this chapter. Instead, this chapter offers background for understanding the general principles of evaluation and the choices that must be made as evaluations are carried out. In order to accomplish these goals, some definitions and a brief history of education policy evaluation are provided first, followed by discussions of the general characteristics of policy evaluations, the politics of evaluation, and ways to facilitate a meaningful evaluation. The last section discusses acting on the findings of an evaluation.

DEFINITIONS ASSOCIATED WITH POLICY EVALUATION

As with any specialized field, policy evaluation has developed its own language, and its practitioners use professional terminology that may not be familiar to outsiders. This section defines four key terms: (1) *evaluation,* (2) *project,* (3) *program,* and (4) *stakeholder.*

Evaluation is "the systematic investigation of the quality of programs, projects . . . or any of their components . . . for purposes of decision making . . . leading to improvement and/or accountability. . . ." (Yarbrough, Shulha, Hopson, & Caruthers, 2011, p. xxv). A policy evaluation is a type of applied research in which the practices and rigorous standards of all research are used in a specific setting for a practical purpose: determining to what extent a policy is reaching its goals.

Policies are often first put into effect through *projects.* For example, when the federal government adopted compensatory education as a national policy, it funded short-term Head Start and Title I projects in many school districts. When projects are institutionalized, they become *programs.* Thus, most districts have an ongoing reading program or professional development program that reflects their fundamental policies in these areas. These programs are often based on earlier projects.

In any evaluation, there are a number of *stakeholders*—these are all those individuals or groups "who have a legitimate interest in or are served in some meaningful way by the program . . ." (Yarbrough et al., 2011, p. 23). In a school system, major stakeholders generally include teachers, administrators, support staff, students, parents, the teachers' union and other unions, school board members, and any important interest groups.

A BRIEF HISTORY OF EDUCATIONAL POLICY EVALUATION

Early Evaluation

A good policy evaluation "is a systematic evaluation that tries to determine cause-and-effect relationships and rigorously measures the results of policy" (Anderson, 2003, p. 260). Because the phrase "systematic evaluation" has a contemporary ring to it, assuming that educational evaluation is a recent phenomenon would be natural. This is not true, however. In the United States, educational evaluation can be traced to pre–Civil War Boston, where Horace Mann and the board of education gathered examination data in order to compare schools. In the 1880s, the first large-scale educational evaluation was conducted by Joseph Rice, who used test scores from many districts to evaluate spelling instruction. Because Rice found that children who spent 200 minutes a week on spelling drills scored no better than those who spent only ten minutes, the teaching of spelling changed across the country. The development of standardized testing during the first quarter of the twentieth century made evaluating schools and districts by comparing test scores even easier. In the 1930s, educational evaluation as we know it began to come into its own when Ralph Tyler, then a professor at Ohio State, directed the Eight-Year Study, a comparative evaluation of the college performance of graduates of progressive and traditional high schools. Tyler's idea that educational programs should be evaluated in terms of their objectives was widely influential, encouraging most of the evaluators who followed him to adopt the same perspective (Madaus, Stufflebeam, & Scriven, 1983; Popham, 1988).

The War on Poverty

The passage of the *Elementary and Secondary Education Act* of 1965 (ESEA) was a watershed event in educational evaluation. Because this law represented an unprecedented outlay of federal funds for education, some lawmakers, including Senator Robert Kennedy, insisted that it contain language mandating evaluation. As a result, Titles I and III of the ESEA required that every program funded under their provisions be evaluated; reports of the findings were to be sent to the federal government. Because of the ESEA, educational evaluation became a growth industry. Several people who eventually made major reputations in policy evaluation, such as Michael Scriven and Robert Stake, actually switched from other fields in order to participate in this unusual opportunity to develop and refine the evaluation of education policies.

Over the next decade, thousands of evaluations were conducted by enthusiastic recruits to the field. Soon their enthusiasm waned, however, for their results were disappointing. When their findings were not contradictory, they were negative. As indicated in Chapter 10, one result was that education researchers began to look more closely at implementation; another was that people began to take a closer look at evaluation. Early Title I evaluations had used standardized test scores as indicators of program success; experience quickly revealed that these tests inadequately measured the progress of disadvantaged children. The situation became so serious that in 1971, the education honorary Phi Delta Kappa (PDK) established a national committee to study educational evaluation. Concluding that the field was in crisis, the committee recommended that new evaluation methods be developed (Madaus et al., 1983; Popham, 1988).

The Professionalization of Evaluation

About 1973, evaluation began to mature as a field and to emerge as a distinctive profession within education. One sign that the discipline was coming of age was the establishment of several professional journals, including *Educational Evaluation and Policy Analysis* and *Evaluation Review*. Another was the publication of numerous books, including textbooks, on evaluation. Many universities began to offer courses in evaluation, and a few even established graduate concentrations in it. Moreover, the federal government and several major universities established centers to conduct research and development in policy evaluation. The existence of these forums for discussion facilitated the exchange of research findings and the development of new approaches to evaluation, as recommended by PDK. During the next fifteen years, numerous evaluation "models" were developed and tested in the field. By 1983, Madaus et al. were able to include chapters in their book *Evaluation Models* on ten different models, including Stufflebeam's CIPP Model, Provus's Discrepancy Evaluation Model, and Eisner's Connoisseurship Model. At the end of the decade, Popham (1988) observed:

> Although devout kitten-lovers may be offended by the notion, there is substantial truth embodied in the adage that "there is more than one way to skin a cat." Similarly, there is more than one way to conduct a defensible educational evaluation. (p. 21)

Today, education leaders who want to know how well a policy works are in a very different situation from that of their predecessors in the 1960s and early 1970s. Policy evaluation is a well-established field with numerous professional practitioners and a wealth of experience. Whether the policy in question is a national one or confined to a single school building, it is possible to determine with a fair degree of accuracy how well it is accomplishing its objectives. Increasingly, SDEs routinely collect data for use in assessing the performance of the state as a whole, of districts, and even of individual schools. Increasingly, too, education administrators are expected to have some practical knowledge of evaluation and to be able to use it. Educational policy evaluation has clearly moved out of universities and policy centers and into the daily lives of practicing educators.

CHARACTERISTICS OF POLICY EVALUATIONS

The Evaluation Process

Whether a large national organization evaluates a policy in fifty states or a building principal evaluates a program in a single school does not matter: All policy evaluations follow the same general procedures. These are briefly summarized in this section

1. Determine the goals of the policy
2. Select indicators
3. Select or develop data-collection instruments
4. Collect data
5. Analyze and summarize data
6. Write evaluation report
7. Respond to evaluators'recommendations

FIGURE 11.1   Basic steps in the policy evaluation process

and in Figure 11.1. The first step is to determine as precisely as possible the *goals* or *objectives* of the policy. After all, as Ralph Tyler pointed out in the early 1940s, it is legitimate to evaluate a policy only in relationship to the goals that it is supposed to achieve (Madaus et al., 1983). As an example, if the objectives of a district's new award system are to improve student attendance and morale, then evaluators should assess only the extent to which those two goals have been attained. The impact of the policy on other aspects of school activity, such as test scores, is irrelevant. Since whether objectives have been reached is usually not readily apparent, evaluators must next select *indicators,* which are measurements or signs that a goal has been reached. In evaluating the award system, for example, comparative attendance figures for five years and scores on a school climate survey administered at the beginning of each year of implementation might be selected as indicators.

The third step in conducting an evaluation is to select or develop *data collection instruments.* In assessing the award system, evaluators might develop a form to use for recording data from district attendance records for the previous five years. They might also select a commercially available survey of school climate to administer to all students. Next, the evaluators *gather data.* In studying the award system, someone must locate attendance records and transfer relevant information from them to the form prepared for that purpose. Someone must also administer the school climate survey each time it is given. After the data are collected, they must be analyzed. Numeric data (such as test scores) are usually analyzed statistically; means, ranges, and frequencies are calculated and used to determine if any differences are statistically significant. Such findings are often summarized in the form of graphs, trend lines, and tables. Verbal data (such as interview transcripts) are usually analyzed by identifying recurrent themes in the entire set of transcripts and coding them so that all the occur- rences of each theme can be located. Computer programs are available for analyzing both numeric and verbal data.

After the data are analyzed carefully, the evaluators *write a report,* presenting their findings and making recommendations based on them. For instance, an evalu- ation of the awards system discussed throughout this section might reveal that atten- dance has improved since the awards policy was implemented but that student morale has not. The evaluators might, then, recommend that the awards be continued, but that another approach be tried for raising morale. After district leaders receive the report, they should use it to either modify the policy or **terminate** it (Anderson, 2003; Brainard, 1996; Holden & Zimmerman, 2009).

Criteria for Judging Evaluations

Although evaluations are designed to judge the effectiveness of policies, they can be evaluated themselves. In fact, education leaders must know how to assess the quality of a proposed or completed evaluation. If they have contracted for an evaluation to be implemented, they must know if the recommended research design is sound. If they are using a completed evaluation, they must be able to determine how seriously to take it. In 1975, to meet the need for recognized criteria for evaluation, twelve research associations established a joint committee, assigning it the task of developing standards for assessing educational evaluations; the result of its work was published as a book in 1981. It was revised in the early 1990s, with the second edition appearing in 1994. The most recent edition of the joint committee's book appeared in 2011 under the title, *The Program Evaluation Standards: A Guide for Evaluators and Evaluation Users.* The thirty standards are grouped under five broad categories, which serve as general criteria: (1) *utility,* (2) *feasibility,* (3) *propriety,* (4) *accuracy,* and (5) *evaluation accountability* (Yarbrough et al., 2011).

This section, drawing heavily on *The Program Evaluation Standards,* discusses each of these five criteria (Yarbrough et al., 2011).

UTILITY.   In order to be useful, an evaluation must be conducted by an individual or team well qualified to do evaluations. Qualified people include consultants who work for evaluation firms, college professors, and workers in district or SDE research offices; however, regardless of where an evaluator works, her individual credentials should be scrutinized carefully.

The usefulness of an evaluation also depends to a great extent on stakeholder identification and the collection of meaningful data. Early in the study, a good evaluator identifies all the stakeholders, the people and groups involved in the program under study or those who might be affected by the outcome of the evaluation. Representative stakeholders should be interviewed so that their needs can be identified at the outset and addressed throughout the evaluation process. Moreover, data sources that are relevant to their needs should be selected. All data gathered should relate to the major purposes of the evaluation; information sources should not be used just because they are convenient or inexpensive, but only if they help answer questions important to the stakeholders.

Interim and final evaluation reports should also be useful. They should be written in clear language that the stakeholders can understand and should avoid overly technical words and incomprehensible statistics. If necessary, different versions should be prepared, expressed in the various languages of the stakeholders. For example, a version designed for central office administrators might include more technical words and graphs than a version aimed at a parent group. All reports for all audiences should include adequate information about the policy under study and the general design of the evaluation. The major findings should be clearly related to practical situations, and all recommendations should be specific rather than general. Finally, reports should not be excessively long and should include an executive summary at the beginning (Posavac, 2011; Yarbrough et al., 2011).

FEASIBILITY.   The second criterion is *feasibility;* the evaluation must be doable without imposing unreasonable strains on the school or school district. An important aspect of feasibility is *practicality*. The evaluation should be designed so that it can be completed within the required time frame and implemented without unduly disturbing the professional responsibilities of the educators involved. An evaluation that requires that learning grind to a halt for two weeks so that interviews can be conducted or tests administered is not practical. Another dimension of feasibility is political. As suggested at the beginning of this chapter, evaluations are "nervous making"; nervous people are likely to try to block portions of the study in order to protect themselves or their jobs. This means that evaluations are always political. A good evaluation does not ignore this fact; rather, the evaluation is planned with this in mind. One way to minimize the political controversy that often erupts around an evaluation is for the evaluators to meet with all the interest groups and stakeholders during the planning process to discuss their concerns and hear their suggestions. During the evaluation, leaders must also avoid favoring, or appearing to favor, one group over another in interviewing, observing, collecting data, and so on. Moreover, evaluators with good political skills are careful to maintain communication with all stakeholders throughout the process so that no one has any unpleasant surprises when the final report is issued. Finally, a feasible evaluation is financially responsible. It has a definite budget, which is sufficient to carry out the study but is not perceived as exorbitant in the environment for which it was designed (Yarbrough et al., 2011).

PROPRIETY.   Issues of propriety are legal and ethical; a good evaluation must conform to accepted norms for research. First, evaluators selected should not be in a conflict of interest situation regarding the study. They should not have a personal, professional, or financial interest in the outcome of the evaluation, nor should they be close friends of any of the people who commission the evaluation. Next, a written contract should be signed between the evaluator(s) and the organization commissioning the study, spelling out the purposes of the research, what it is to entail, and when it is to be completed. Evaluators should respect the rights of human subjects as they conduct their work, maintain appropriate confidentiality, and inform each participant of the purposes of the research. Moreover, they should be careful to treat everyone courteously and to solicit a range of opinions, not allowing themselves to be blinded by an individual's status in the organization or by his or her race, gender, or age. The final report should disclose fully the findings of the evaluation, even if evaluators include the discovery of financial fraud or other questionable behavior (Kapp & Anderson, 2010; Yarbrough et al., 2011).

ACCURACY.   It is important for an evaluation to be accurate. In order to produce an accurate report, evaluators must first study the context in which the policy has been implemented, familiarizing themselves with its cultural and socioeconomic characteristics. In their report, they should provide enough detail about their sources of information that readers can determine the value of their information and thus of the conclusions based on it. Data collection should be systematic rather than haphazard, drawing on a range of sources. In the report, evaluators should explain exactly how they reached their conclusions and specify the data on which each conclusion is based (Kapp & Anderson, 2010).

Evaluation Accountability

Finally, evaluators should conduct evaluations in such a way that they can be held accountable for them. First, they should fully document the procedures they used in designing and carrying out the evaluation. Moreover, they should thoughtfully assess their work both as they perform it and after it is completed. Such accountability practices may lead to better evaluations in the future (Yarbrough et al., 2011).

CASE STUDY

A Laughable Evaluation

Several years ago Spruce Valley School District, a suburban system located in the Northwest, had a serious problem with bullying, especially in its six middle schools. Many parents complained and several negative articles appeared in the local newspapers. Things came to a head one spring when three middle school students who had been victimized by bullies attempted suicide. Fortunately, none of these unhappy young people succeeded. At that point Superintendent Scott Jablonski decided that something had to be done. He recommended that the school board hire six new guidance counselors with expertise in psychological counseling and place one in each middle school. The board responded favorably; six competent counselors were hired; and the bullying problem was resolved. Or, at least, Jablonski and the board rarely received complaints about it.

This year, however, the state slashed school funding because of weak tax revenues; and the Spruce Valley District faced serious budget problems. The board suggested that one way to reduce personnel costs would be to eliminate the six extra guidance counselors. Jablonski was appalled; he considered the way he had reduced bullying to be one of his greatest success stories. Needing ammunition to persuade the board to change its mind, he called the six middle school principals to see if any of them had statistics that demonstrated how bullying had declined in their schools; only two had usable data. As he reflected

on the importance today of "data-driven decision making," Jablonski decided on another approach; he developed a survey about the effectiveness of the counselors and the decline of bullying and asked the middle school supervisor to administer it to teachers at each middle school. This she did, distributing the surveys in faculty meetings, stressing the importance of supporting the counselors, and waiting for each teacher to turn in the survey.

Jablonski was thrilled with the results; 92% of the teachers thought the program was a success and should be continued. He wrote up a report on the survey findings, entitled it "Evaluation of Spruce Valley's Anti-Bullying Program," and distributed it at the next board meeting. To his consternation, however, one of the board members burst out laughing after he read it and commented: "This isn't worth the paper it's written on!"

QUESTIONS

1. Identify five mistakes Jablonski made in trying to produce a credible evaluation of the anti-bullying program.
2. Assess Jablonski's "evaluation," using the five criteria developed by the Joint Committee on Program Evaluation Standards.
3. Develop an outline for a low-cost, feasible, yet credible evaluation plan for the anti-bullying program. ■

Purposes of Evaluations

SUMMATIVE EVALUATION.   Policy evaluations can serve at least four purposes. Many are *summative;* they assess the quality of a policy that has been in force for some time, especially when it has reached a critical juncture in its history. For example, many federal policies are evaluated just before they are due to be reauthorized. A negative evaluation could mean the end of the policy because Congress might vote not to reauthorize funding for it. Alternatively, negative findings might mean that the policy would be re-funded, but only with the condition that major changes be made in it. The primary purpose of summative evaluation, then, is to hold the implementers of a policy accountable, which is why the stakes are high when summative evaluations are conducted and why external evaluators are usually used. However, although summative evaluation was popular in the 1960s and 1970s, more recently, formative evaluation has been preferred (Holden & Zimmerman, 2009).

FORMATIVE EVALUATION.   The purpose of a formative policy evaluation is to enable the implementers of a policy to make necessary changes throughout the life of a policy in order to improve it. As a result, formative evaluation is an ongoing and recurrent process. Although the evaluators write formal reports only at predetermined intervals, data are usually collected regularly. Because a formative evaluation is designed to help implementers make good decisions about what they are doing, it is not as threatening as a summative evaluation. Also, because the stakes are not as high, internal evaluators are sometimes used for a formative evaluation (Holden & Zimmerman, 2009).

PSEUDO-EVALUATIONS.   Unfortunately, policy evaluations are not always conducted in good faith. Often, what appears on the surface to be a bona fide evaluation is actually what has been called a *pseudo-evaluation* (Stufflebeam & Webster, 1983). Pseudo-evaluations are of two types. The first is *"the politically controlled study"* (p. 25, emphasis added). Such an evaluation is politically motivated; its purpose is usually communicated, directly or indirectly, to the evaluators, who must then decide if their ethical standards permit them to continue with the project. In such a pseudo-evaluation, the data collection and dissemination of the final report are carefully controlled to create the desired impression of the policy. The desired conclusions about the policy may be either negative or positive, but they do not reflect the truth about the policy's success or failure. Instead, they give a predetermined outcome that those who commissioned the evaluation sought for political reasons.

The second type of pseudo-evaluation is *the public relations evaluation.* Its purpose is to "create a positive public image for a school district, program, or process" (Stufflebeam & Webster, 1983, p. 26). As with politically inspired pseudo-evaluations, those who commission a public relations study usually clearly indicate what the findings must be. In this case, the conclusions in the final report not only must be positive, but also must add luster to the public image that has already been created. In order to bring about this result, the commissioners of the evaluation carefully shape and select the data that they make available to the researchers, limiting where they can go, to whom they may talk, and what questions they may ask. Needless to say, either commissioning or participating in a pseudo-evaluation is unethical.

Methodologies Used in Policy Evaluation

QUANTITATIVE METHODOLOGIES.   *Quantitative research designs* involve the collection and statistical analysis of numeric data. Many types of numeric data are available in schools and school districts. Figure 11.2 lists some of the most common. Quantitative policy evaluations are sometimes based on experimental or

- Transcripts of interviews
- Transcripts of focus group discussions
- Notes on observations
- Open-ended surveys
- Personal statements
- Diaries
- Minutes from meetings
- Official reports
- Legal documents
- Books and materials
- Photographs

FIGURE 11.2 Examples of quantitative educational data

quasi-experimental designs that investigate the statistical differences between a group that participated in a program and a group that did not. For example, evaluations of Head Start compared children who participated in the preschool program to those who did not, seeking to determine if Head Start graduates scored higher on achievement tests and were less likely to repeat grades. However, many quantitative evaluation designs are not experimental. Some use quantitative data to determine if specific objectives have been achieved, and others use surveys to assess attitudes or opinions. Quantitative evaluations have several advantages, perhaps the most important of which is the high level of credibility of a well-constructed quantitative study. Most Americans respect findings that are presented in statistical terms or depicted in graphs. A second major advantage is that quantitative evaluations can often be carried out relatively quickly and at a relatively low cost. The major disadvantage of a quantitative evaluation is that because of its tight structure and precise research questions, it is not well suited for discovering unexpected facts about the policy under study (Anderson, 2003; Brainard, 1996).

QUALITATIVE METHODOLOGIES.   Although almost all early policy evaluations were quantitative, in recent decades *qualitative approaches* have been popular (Kapp & Anderson, 2010). Qualitative research designs involve the collection of verbal or pictorial data. Many types of such data are available in schools and school districts or can easily be generated by a researcher. Figure 11.3 lists some of the most commonly used. Qualitative research designs often involve collecting several types of data and comparing them, a process called *triangulation*. For example, a qualitative evaluation team assessing a dropout prevention project might interview students and teachers, observe classes, and analyze books and other materials associated with the program. Like quantitative evaluations, qualitative evaluations have certain advantages. When the policy under consideration is very new or is a pilot project, a qualitative study can yield valuable insights into how the policy works. Moreover, qualitative evaluations sometimes make unexpected findings that quantitative ones miss; for example, in the late 1960s, qualitative evaluations determined that some federal education policies were not being implemented at all. The major disadvantage of qualitative evaluations is that they are

- Test scores
- Retention rates
- Attendance figures
- Dropout rates
- Per-pupil expenditure
- Teachers' salaries
- Teacher–pupil ratios
- Percentage of students on free and reduced lunch
- Enrollment figures
- Percentage of teachers with master's degrees

FIGURE 11.3   Types of qualitative data

more time-consuming than quantitative ones and therefore more costly. In addition, because most people trust numbers more than apparently subjective findings based on interviews and observations, qualitative evaluations are less credible than quantitative ones (Brainard, 1996; Kapp & Anderson, 2010; Yarbrough et al., 2011).

HOLISTIC EVALUATIONS.   The choice between quantitative and qualitative evaluation is not an either–or one, however. Designing evaluations that include elements of both is possible; these are sometimes called *holistic evaluations.* For example, many case studies draw on both numeric and verbal data. An evaluation of the implementation of middle schools across a state might include in-depth case studies of several schools and analyze numeric data such as test scores, attitude assessments, and attendance rates as well as verbal data such as interviews, observations in classrooms, and open-ended surveys. Such an evaluation permits the use of multiple indicators of several types, and provides a rich understanding of the challenges involved in making the transition from junior highs to middle schools, as well as its relative success. The major advantage of the holistic evaluation is implied by its name; it provides a holistic view of what is happening. This means that the findings are often more valid than the findings of a study that uses only qualitative or only quantitative data. The major drawback is the time and cost required for the collection and analysis of qualitative data. No one best type of evaluation exists; the choice of methodology depends on the purpose of the study and the nature of the questions asked (Brainard, 1996; Yarbrough et al., 2011).

Indicators

As an essential step in any evaluation process, the evaluators must define the *indicators* they use to determine to what extent the policy is achieving its objectives. The exact definition of *indicator* is disputed by practitioners within the field, but a typical one is: "An indicator is an individual or a composite statistic that relates to a basic construct in education and is useful in a policy context" (Shavelson et al., 1987, cited in Nuttall, 1994, p. 18). This definition, of course, excludes qualitative evaluations. Nuttall suggests that indicators can be qualitative, but that even so, they must be quantified to a certain degree in order to be meaningful. For example, in a qualitative evaluation of a school-to-work program, one indicator of success might be that the majority of participants interviewed stated that because of the program, they had obtained a job. The purpose of all indicators, quantitative and qualitative, is to provide reliable information about the quality of a policy so that well-informed decisions can be made about it.

In designing an evaluation, selecting indicators for each policy objective and, if possible, using more than one indicator in relation to each is important. For example, in determining if a new mathematics program increased students' competence in mathematics, evaluators might use three indicators: (1) student scores on a multiple-choice test; (2) student scores on an open-ended problem-solving test; and (3) interviews with selected students in which their mathematical thought processes are discussed (Joint Committee, 1994). By using these three indicators, evaluators obtain a detailed, in-depth picture of the impact of the program. Using just one of them—the multiple-choice test, for example—does not provide complete information, and is therefore less valuable.

Careful thought must be given to the selection of indicators because of the potentially pathological effects of inappropriate ones. Continuing with the previous example, the use of multiple-choice test scores in isolation would probably have a detrimental effect on teachers' pedagogy as they implemented the mathematics curriculum. Multiple-choice examinations encourage a broad but superficial coverage of content as well as an emphasis on facts. Teachers teach differently when they know that measures of problem-solving and thinking ability will also be examined. Sometimes the indicators selected actually encourage educators to stop serving the population for which a policy was designed. One danger of simple reward systems that give schools or individuals extra money if their test scores are high is that they motivate principals and teachers to find ways to remove those students whose scores are most likely to be low. Another danger is cheating. For example, the 2011 testing scandal in the Atlanta Public School System, which involved test tampering by numerous teachers and principals, suggests what can happen when scores on high-stakes tests are one of the few indicators used to assess educational effectiveness (Samuels, 2011).

The way to avoid setting up an unintended pathological dynamic in which misguided indicators drive a program is to use several types of indicators and to provide appropriate oversight (Joint Committee, 1994).

FACILITATING MEANINGFUL POLICY EVALUATIONS

No educator can exercise a leadership role for long without having to deal with an evaluation. It may be an evaluation that the state, federal government, or a private foundation requires as one of the conditions for accepting their money. It may be an evaluation of a locally initiated policy, requested by the school board or central office staff, or it may be a more limited study that addresses questions of interest only within a single building or a high school department. Regardless of how broad or limited its scope, it poses characteristic challenges to those who must play leadership roles during its course. The leader's responsibility is simultaneously to facilitate a useful evaluation and to provide ongoing guidance for the overall educational program—no easy task. Moreover, the leader's environment is probably more turbulent than usual because evaluations threaten the status quo, and thus "program officials will be alert to the possible political consequences of evaluation" (Anderson, 2003, p. 263). This section, then, offers practical guidance for making this challenging job easier. After a discussion of the politics of evaluation, it suggests ways to reduce the conflicts that often surround the evaluation process and provide a setting in which a useful evaluation can be implemented.

The Politics of Evaluation

WHY EVALUATION IS POLITICAL.   The inherently political nature of policy evaluation has long been recognized. As Weiss, nationally known for her evaluation work, observed in 1973: "The politics of program survival is an ancient and important art" (Weiss, 1988, p. 49). Fifteen years later, she affirmed that statement, saying: "I find that I still agree with almost everything I wrote then" (p. 66). Nor is the political nature of evaluation likely to evaporate in the foreseeable future since an evaluation may put many people's "program, influence, or careers . . . in jeopardy" (Anderson, 2003, p. 263).

Evaluations are political for three reasons. First, the programs and projects that they assess are the products of the political process. Second, evaluation reports influence what happens in the political arena, often affecting whether a policy is continued and how much funding it receives. Finally, the careers, professional reputations, and educational benefits of many individuals depend on the outcome of any evaluation (Anderson, 2003). This means that politics—often politics of the crassest sort—surround every evaluation. Wise education leaders will not deny the political aspects of the process, hoping they do not emerge in their setting; instead, they anticipate and plan for them.

THE PLAYERS IN THE EVALUATION ARENA.   Planning for the politics of evaluation requires understanding who the players in this arena are and what motivates them. Many years ago Nakamura and Smallwood (1980) provided an insightful analysis of the interests of the major actors in the evaluation arena: the *policymakers,* the *policy implementers,* the *clients,* and the *evaluators.* Their perceptions are still relevant today.

The Policymakers.   Usually, the policymakers are those who have requested the evaluation and will use it to make important decisions about the future of the policy. Although they are most likely to be members of a school board, state legislature, or Congress, they may also include bureaucrats in an SDE. At one level, policymakers want good information that they can use either to improve the policy in question or to terminate it. However, being motivated by a mixture of values, they are also driven by self-interest: They want to keep their current positions. This means that they must win their next election or, in the case of bureaucrats, help their bosses win their next election. Therefore, policymakers are not necessarily interested in seeing that a technically excellent evaluation is carried out, but rather in guaranteeing that the program is maintained if it is popular with their constituents and cut if it is not (Nakamura & Smallwood, 1980; Posavac, 2011).

The Policy Implementers.   The policy implementers are all those within the school district who are involved in putting the policy into practice. They are likely to include administrators in central office, one or more principals, and numerous teachers. Although the implementers usually want to run a good program that benefits children, they also have personal interests at stake. Their professional reputations, chances of career advancement, and (in some instances) jobs may depend on the results of the evaluation. Therefore, they want it to be favorable (Nakamura & Smallwood, 1980; Posavac, 2011).

The Clients.   Although students are the direct clients of most policies in education and of the programs or projects that embody them, their parents are the indirect, behind-the-scenes clients. The parents become players in the evaluation arena much more frequently than their children do, and those parents who are relatively well educated and affluent are most likely to be active. If the policy confers special benefits or status on their offspring, parents probably want a favorable evaluation just as the implementers do. Even if the program is failing to achieve its official objectives, they are reluctant to see it changed in significant ways or discontinued because even if ineffective, it does provide some special services for their children and may save them a certain amount of money (Nakamura & Smallwood, 1980; Posavac, 2011).

The Evaluators.   Finally, the evaluators themselves have an interest in the outcome of the evaluation. One of their motives is to produce a thorough and accurate evaluation that permits good policy decisions to be made. However, their self-interest also demands that they produce an evaluation that enhances, rather than undercuts, their careers as evaluators. In many instances this means that they seek to produce a sophisticated, technically correct evaluation report that impresses their colleagues and future clients rather than the type of evaluation really needed in a specific context; in others, it may mean that they hesitate to report extremely negative findings for fear that they will gain a reputation as hostile evaluators and find their job opportunities dwindling (Kapp & Anderson, 2010; Nakamura & Smallwood, 1980).

MANEUVERS TO PREVENT A GOOD EVALUATION.   Because all the players may use maneuvers to reduce the chances of a good evaluation, education leaders must be aware of the standard approaches to derailing a successful study. School leaders involved in an evaluation should expect to see one or more of these deployed; they should develop tentative plans well in advance for how they will respond to them. The first broad tactic is simply to block the evaluation and prevent it from occurring at all. Policymakers, acting independently or responding to pressure from the implementers or clients (or both), may vote to cancel an evaluation or reduce funding for it. Those school leaders who do want a fair evaluation of a program should therefore be on the lookout for evidence that lobbying against the evaluation is occurring and move quickly to present the case for a serious study to policymakers.

A second tactic is to shape the criteria that are to be used for the evaluation in such a way that the desired outcome is virtually guaranteed. For example, a group of parents who want a program for gifted students continued might pressure a school board to identify parental satisfaction as a major standard for judging the effectiveness of the program.

Once an evaluation is under way, a third favorite approach may surface: mobilizing the clients against the evaluators. The implementers are most likely to use this trick because they have ready access to parents and can fill their ears with frightening tales of the unsympathetic evaluation team that is gathering data on the program. Their objective is to incite conflict between the clients and the evaluators, as well as persuade the clients to contact the policymakers to voice their complaints.

The fourth scheme is also usually put into action by the implementers. They may make data gathering impossible or difficult for the evaluators—statistical records may mysteriously disappear; scheduled interviews may be abruptly cancelled; the return rate on surveys may be pitifully low. Because the implementers control most of the information about the program, they are in a good position to exercise their power in this fashion. Finally, after the evaluation has ended and the report has been issued, any of the stakeholder groups (except the evaluators) may choose the last approach: attacking the quality of the evaluation. The charges made can vary, but the most frequently heard are that the evaluators were biased or unqualified and they chose inappropriate indicators. By discrediting the evaluation, critics hope to discourage policymakers and implementers in leadership roles from using its findings to make any changes in the policy.

Clearly, the evaluation arena can be accurately described as a political minefield where many buried bombs wait to explode at the approach of unwary school leaders. Reducing (although not eliminating) the danger of this arena is possible, however, by taking some common-sense steps that can increase the likelihood of a sound evaluation, as described next.

Suggestions for Achieving a Sound Evaluation

School leaders can do several things to increase the likelihood of a sound evaluation that is neither overwhelmed by politics nor undercut by insufficient data. In this section, five key steps to a good evaluation are discussed.

BUILDING EVALUATION IN EARLY.   No good teacher would wait until the end of her course and then surprise students by suddenly unveiling the evaluation plan that she will use to determine their final grades. On the contrary, good teachers explain the evaluation plan at the beginning of the course, provide a rationale for it, and help students meet its objectives. Similarly, school leaders should not use an evaluation as an unexpected punishment that catches the implementers off guard. Such unpleasant surprises create an adversarial climate and encourage political game playing of the worst sort. Instead of using evaluation as a surprise strategy, leaders should build it in at the start. Often, a new policy, project, or program comes with a built-in evaluation system; this is frequently the case with government and foundation grants. In such instances, school leaders should not keep this information a secret. Rather, it should be shared and discussed with all the stakeholders from the beginning. On other occasions, the evaluation is not built in. This does not mean that it should be dispensed with—far from it. Instead, school leaders themselves should develop a general plan for evaluation, both formative and summative, and communicate it to stakeholders. Failure to do so may set the stage for a "surprise evaluation" several years later, creating a tense and unpleasant situation.

COMMUNICATING WITH STAKEHOLDERS.   Establishing open lines of communication with stakeholders at the beginning of the implementation of a new policy and maintaining them throughout is essential. A major subject of this communication should be the evaluation of the policy. There are two important reasons for communicating freely with stakeholders.

First, good communication helps head off major political problems. Where communication is lacking, stakeholders consider the evaluation plans secretive and cherish multiple suspicions about leaders' true intentions. In such a mistrustful atmosphere, they may react defensively, seeking to derail the evaluation if possible. However, if leaders involve them in planning the evaluation, they are less likely to try such tactics. This means that, at the outset, leaders should hold meetings with the major stakeholders or their representatives. If representatives are used, they should be selected by their own groups rather than handpicked by the leaders. In meetings with them, the objectives of the new policy should be discussed and the stakeholders should be given a chance to ask questions and raise concerns. Leaders should also ask them what information they would like to obtain from the evaluation and incorporate their ideas into the evaluation. Throughout the evaluation process, leaders should regularly inform the stakeholders of what is going on; any preliminary findings should be communicated to them. Leaders should also make sure that the final evaluation report is understandable to stakeholders, and should hold one or more meetings with them to discuss its implications for them (Yarbrough et al., 2011).

A second reason for strong communication with stakeholders is that it improves the validity and worth of the final evaluation. After all, the stakeholders are often closer to the grassroots implementation than the leaders and know more about it than they do. However, they will provide thorough information only in a climate of trust. Moreover, as suggested earlier about implementation, multiple perspectives surround all policies, and knowing what those perspectives are is helpful. Leaders can discover them only through an interactive evaluation that involves much communication.

SELECTING INDICATORS.   Even if outside evaluators are used, school leaders should select indicators to monitor at the beginning of an implementation, fully realizing that the evaluators will probably add others. Selecting indicators early reassures the implementers and also makes determining what data to collect easier. As suggested earlier, choosing indicators that do not distort the implementers' behavior is important. Open discussions with all stakeholder groups help leaders avoid serious errors in determining the best indicators (Planty & Carlson, 2010).

BUILDING IN DATA COLLECTION.   School leaders should not defer data collection until the summative evaluation is due. Just as indicators should be selected early, data collection should be ongoing, because it can be used as part of formative evaluation throughout implementation. The results of frequent monitoring can provide leaders with ideas for improving the policy and also give them an important accountability tool. Later, when a formal, summative evaluation is conducted, the evaluators will have a rich existing information base to use in conjunction with the data that they generate themselves (Holden & Zimmerman, 2009; Marshall, 2009).

CHOOSING EVALUATORS.   The choice of the individuals who conduct a policy evaluation is an important one. Any school leader responsible for this decision should think it through carefully, because it will seriously affect the quality and credibility of the final evaluation report. Basically, there are four alternatives, each with its own advantages and disadvantages.

The first possibility is an *internal evaluation conducted by the implementers.* The great advantage of this approach is that insiders have access to a great deal of information about the policy. Moreover, if they conduct the evaluation themselves, they are more willing to act on negative findings than they are if someone else has been in charge. However, this choice has serious disadvantages, too. First, the implementers may lack the research skills needed to carry out a high-quality evaluation. In addition, most outsiders will feel skeptical about their evaluation findings because of the strong probability that they are biased in favor of the policy.

A second alternative, then, is to use *internal evaluators from a specialized evaluation staff.* Many large districts, and some medium-sized ones, have a research office with personnel trained in evaluation. Such evaluators are well qualified in research methodologies and are also more impartial than the implementers. However, some credibility problems may surface with such an evaluation; after all, the evaluators and the implementers work for the same employer, and may even know each other personally. In addition, a negative evaluation could possibly incite conflict within the district (Posavac, 2011).

Using external evaluators is also possible. The school or district can contract with an *outside agency or consultant.* Universities and specialized evaluation firms are the most usual sources of researchers to conduct such evaluations. The advantages of using an external service are that the researchers are qualified and, as outsiders, have considerably more credibility than any insiders. However, there are certain drawbacks. First, outside evaluators do not know the sociopolitical environment in which the policy has been implemented. This deficiency can be partially remedied by the research methods chosen, but not all professional evaluators are sensitive to this problem. Second, they may design an evaluation oriented toward making themselves look like experts in the eyes of their colleagues rather than toward providing truly useful information to their clients. Sometimes, too, their desire for future contracts with this or other districts leads them to gloss over problems rather than address them frankly. Finally, their services are usually costly (Posavac, 2011).

The fourth alternative is to let the *organization that has funded the new policy* evaluate it. This organization might be a state legislature or a foundation; in fact, sometimes school leaders have no choice—under the terms of a grant, they must permit the funding organization to conduct the evaluation. The major advantage of this option is that such organizations usually employ skilled and professional evaluators who are capable of doing a good study. Also, of course, their evaluation is likely to be more credible than any internal one. However, the major drawback is that the funding body may have its own evaluation agenda. The result may be an evaluation that is not useful to educators, or one that is patently unfair to the policy and its implementers.

Education leaders must understand that there is no perfect choice, nor is there a single choice that is always the best one. In making this decision, school leaders must weigh many factors, including the political situation, the nature of the information that they want about the policy, and the amount of money available for evaluation. Taking into account the needs of their particular program and the overall context in which it operates is especially important. Often the best solution is to choose not one, but two evaluators: an internal one to conduct formative evaluations throughout implementation, and an external one to do all summative evaluations. This approach balances the advantages and disadvantages of internal and external evaluation while providing two relatively independent opinions of how well the policy worked. As a result, when the time comes to make major modifications in the policy, or even to terminate it, school leaders will have a broad range of data available to them that comes from different sources, thereby increasing their ability to make informed decisions (Posavac, 2011).

NEWS EDITORIAL FOR ANALYSIS

Maine's 'Worst' Schools

Ten Maine high schools have received news that they are "improvement schools," an improvement over last year's harsher designation of "persistently low-achieving schools." Superintendents of the designated schools support the purpose of the listing—to achieve the federal *No Child Left Behind Act's* requirement for "adequate yearly progress." But they object to the use of reading and math SAT scores as the chief measure of that progress. They generally express humiliation and outrage at having their high schools pilloried as the worst examples by means of a process that they consider biased and unfair. Students have resented the affronts to their pride in their schools. All of the superintendents who were questioned agreed that their schools had been given a needless and unfair black eye.

They are not the worst, and they may not be the 10 that most need federal aid, but with an influx of federal cash, they have a rare opportunity to remake themselves, which dulls the stigma. In 2005, then-Education Commissioner Susan Gendron led in switching the basis for rating progress from the Maine Educational Assessment (MEA) to the Scholastic Aptitude Test (SAT) for 11th-graders. Critics at the time called this a rushed and misguided decision because the SAT only predicts college grades and was never intended as a screening standard for educational progress.

Schools on the list face a June 1 application deadline for possible federal financial grants to help them improve. If a school wins and accepts the federal aid, it must choose between two options: Firing the principal and strengthening staff and program or replacing the principal and firing half the staff. Two other options, closing the school or converting it into a charter school, are not practical in Maine.

In Ellsworth, the RSU school board has voted to apply for the funds and replace William Conners, who has been principal of the Ellsworth High School for seven years. At the Fort Kent Community High School, Superintendent Patrick O'Neill said the board had decided to seek federal funds but would ask to redefine the role of Principal Timothy Doak rather than dismiss him.

Superintendent Terry A. Comeau said that the Southern Aroostook Community School in the tiny town of Dyer Brook will not seek additional federal money. He said the school is making adequate yearly progress, though it lost a little ground in a three-year average. Oak Hill High School in Wales will not seek federal funds, said Superintendent James Hodgkin. He added that the school is making adequate progress. He said he understood that a better rating system was being planned and that the SAT basis might be dropped even sooner. While some schools clearly need help and guidance, state officials should be receptive to such concerns.

(Adapted by permission of the publisher from an editorial, "Maine's 'Worst' Schools," from the *Bangor* [Maine] *Daily News*, April 15, 2011, p. A8.)

QUESTIONS

1. Do a little research on the SAT. To what extent are Maine educators right to object to its use as an indicator of student progress?

2. Assuming that NCLB is a program for evaluating school effectiveness, what flaws can you identify in this evaluation program as implemented in Maine?

3. In your opinion, how likely is it that replacing the principal of a high school and firing half of the staff will lead to improved student test scores? To improved student learning?

4. The educators and students are described as "humiliated," "outraged," and "resentful"— feelings that often accompany evaluations. What can evaluators do to reduce such negative feelings during and after an evaluation? ■

ACTING ON AN EVALUATION REPORT

After school leaders receive and study an evaluation report, they must decide what to do about it. The first step in this process should be assessing the quality of the report carefully, using the criteria presented earlier in this chapter. Because evaluations vary greatly in quality, leaders should never accept them uncritically, but should instead attempt to determine how good the study was; only then can they know how seriously they should take its findings and recommendations. The second step should be convening the major stakeholders to discuss with them their perceptions of the report's quality. Trying to reach consensus on the general value of the evaluation before progressing further is wise. Only after some level of agreement has been achieved should leaders decide what to do with the report. Basically, four courses of action are open to them: (1) do nothing, (2) make minor modifications, (3) make major modifications, or (4) terminate the policy (Anderson, 2003). Each possibility is discussed in turn.

Inaction

Often, the wisest course of action is to do nothing, thus maintaining the current policy in place. Two especially valid reasons exist for choosing this course of action. The first is that, in the judgment of the leaders and other stakeholders, the evaluation was questionable and they therefore do not wish to accept its recommendations. Unless obligated by a funding agency to act on a questionable evaluation, there is no good reason to do so. The second solid justification for inaction on an evaluation is that changes in the policy are not politically feasible; sometimes waiting for a propitious moment to act on the recommendations of an evaluation is necessary (Hogwood & Gunn, 1984).

Minor Modifications

It is also possible to decide to make only minor modifications in a policy, either because only a bit of fine-tuning was recommended in an evaluation report, or because more sweeping changes are impossible for political reasons (Anderson, 2003). Minor modifications do not affect the spending or staffing levels of the program, nor do they alter the objectives of the policy. Examples include changing the tests used to monitor student progress, modifying schedules, or providing additional materials similar to those already in use. Because minor modifications do not alter the substance of the policy or threaten the jobs of stakeholders, they are relatively easy to make.

Major Modifications

Table 11.1 summarizes the four broad types of major policy or program changes. They have been arranged so that the first one is the least thorough going and each successive change is increasingly serious. Clearly, each of these is threatening, because they could eliminate some stakeholders' jobs while reducing services to others. This means that in order to make them, leaders must be in a strong position: They should have both a well-conducted evaluation by expert researchers to legitimize their recommendations for change as well as the support of some of the stakeholders, particularly the policymakers. When trying to bring about major changes after an evaluation, leaders should anticipate political turbulence and plan for dealing with it (Anderson, 2003; Brewer & de Leon, 1983).

TABLE 11.1 Major Methods for Modifying Policies

Method	Explanation
Replacement	A new program with the same objectives is put in place of the old program.
Consolidation	Two or more entire programs or parts of programs are combined.
Splitting	One aspect of the program is removed and developed into a separate program or project.
Decrementing	A substantial cut in funding is imposed on the program by reducing the amount of money available to most components of the old program.

Source: Based on Brewer and de Leon (1983).

- When the administration changes
- When the economy turns down
- When budget difficulties happen
- When other jobs are available within the organization
- When the old program can easily be replaced by a new one

FIGURE 11.4   Situations conducive to policy termination

Termination

When a policy or program is terminated, it is discontinued and nothing is put in its place—usually because the government's objectives have shifted. Obviously, terminating policies is extremely difficult because most of the stakeholders resist discontinuation fiercely and fight hard to protect the policy (Anderson, 2003). Often, therefore, an ineffective policy must be continued until an opportune moment presents itself; then leaders can move swiftly, discontinuing policies whose demise is long overdue. Figure 11.4 lists several situations favorable to terminating policies (Brewer & de Leon, 1983; Hogwood & Gunn, 1984).

FINAL POINTS

As suggested by the bipartisan support for *No Child Left Behind,* we live in an age of accountability. Policymakers are not generous with tax dollars; before spending public money on education policies, they want to know how well they work and what can be done to make them more effective. They expect education leaders to act prudently, allocating funds where they make the most difference and eliminating worthless programs. This expectation is not an unreasonable one. To meet the demands of an age of accountability, however, school leaders must be literate about evaluation. They should take the lead in applying modern evaluation techniques to their own work and in acting on the findings of sound evaluations. The children in our schools, as well as the general public, deserve no less.

QUESTIONS AND ACTIVITIES FOR DISCUSSION

1. Discuss why people feel nervous about evaluations.
2. Find an evaluation that uses quantitative methods and one that uses qualitative ones. What methods of each type were used? Contrast the kinds of information yielded by each approach.
3. Find an evaluation report and evaluate it, using the criteria discussed in this chapter.
4. List the indicators used by your SDE to determine school success. Do they distort the behavior of your state's educators in any way? If so, in what ways? How would you improve them?

INTERNET ASSIGNMENT

Locate the Web sites of your state government and those of two neighboring states. Search for evaluations of education policies and be prepared to discuss your findings in class. (If you are not sure of how to locate the Web sites of state governments, refer to the Appendix.)

FOR FURTHER READING

Edwards, J. E., Scott, J. C., & Raju, N. S. (Eds.). (2003). *The human-resources program-evaluation handbook.* Thousand Oaks, CA: Sage.

This handbook provides an excellent resource for anyone who must plan a program evaluation. The practical chapters range from general ones about criteria and broad design issues to more focused ones devoted to such topics as recruiting evaluators, succession management, and evaluation coaching.

Harris, D. N. (2010). Clear away the smoke and mirrors of value-added. *Phi Delta Kappan, 91*(8), 66-69.

Harris compares value-added evaluation of schools and teachers to the more widely used approach that measures student attainment at a single point in time. His discussion provides useful information about the promises and pitfalls of value-added evaluations.

Spaulding, D. T. (2008). *Program evaluation in practice.* San Francisco: Jossey-Bass.

In this very readable book, the author first lays out the general principles of program evaluation and then presents eleven detailed case studies of program evaluation, all in education. The case studies describe evaluations of state, district, school, and community-based programs.

Wholey, J. S., Hatry, H. P., & Newcomer, K. E. (Eds.). (2004). *Handbook of practical program evaluation.* 2nd ed. San Francisco: Jossey-Bass.

This book presents the nuts and bolts of program evaluation under four broad headings: designing evaluations, data collection, data analysis, and getting people to use the findings of an evaluation. It provides a detailed overview of contemporary program evaluation.

Yarbrough, D. B., Shulha, L. M., Hopson, R. K., & Caruthers, F. A. (2011). *The program evaluation standards*. 3rd ed. Thousand Oaks, CA: SAGE.

This handbook contains a detailed discussion of each of thirty standards for evaluation, including implementation guidelines and a listing of "hazards" for many of them. Each standard is further clarified with one or two illustrative cases drawn from real life.

12

EDUCATION POLICY IN THE UNITED STATES: RETROSPECTIVE AND PROSPECTIVE

Focus Questions

▌ How has education in the United States changed through history?

▌ How do the policy proposals of today relate to those of the past?

▌ Why is the policy environment today so turbulent?

▌ What will education policy probably be like in the future?

IF WE AREN'T IN KANSAS, WHERE ARE WE?

This book opened with a quotation from *The Wizard of Oz:* "Toto, I don't think we're in Kansas anymore," the puzzled Dorothy commented to her little dog. The first chapter suggested that public education in the United States and those who lead it are no longer in quiet, stable Kansas, but in an unpredictable policy landscape that is hard to understand. Indeed, education leaders may often feel that their situation is worse than Dorothy's: Although the young heroine confronted witches and talking animals, at least she knew that the Emerald City was her destination and had magic shoes and a Yellow Brick Road to help her reach it. But in the twenty-first century, school administrators often feel perplexed by the seemingly endless streams of proposals for education reforms from politicians, businesspeople, think tanks, and universities. They ask themselves questions such as: What is happening? Why is everyone so dissatisfied with our schools? Where is it all leading?

This chapter, then, sets today's policy environment in its historical context, using four theoretical frameworks to illuminate the past and present and also to suggest what the future may hold. Two of these analytical frameworks—competing values and Lowi's policy types—were presented earlier. The third and fourth—institutional choice and international convergence—have often been implicit in previous discussions. Together, these four theoretical concepts can provide important clues to what is happening in education policy today and why. Although trying to predict the future is always risky, they can also suggest the most likely scenarios for the first decades of the new century. This chapter provides a general map of Oz so that, although it will never feel as comfortable as Kansas did to those who knew

Kansas well, education leaders will have at least an understanding of the terrain through which they are traveling.

The first section, then, briefly presents each of the theoretical frameworks. Next, each framework is used to analyze education policy during three historical periods: the Young Republic, the Common School movement, and the "Scientific" Sorting Machine. Then, the same frameworks are applied to our own era, from 1983 to the present. The final section analyzes the *No Child Left Behind Act (NCLB)*, using the theoretical frameworks. Then, based on that analysis and on recent events in Washington, it cautiously predicts what the immediate future may hold.

FOUR THEORETICAL FRAMEWORKS

Competing Values

"Policy ... [rests] ... upon value-laden public beliefs—interpretations of the American creed or dream," insists Iannaccone (1988, p. 49). Chapter 5 discusses these public values, grouping them in three categories: general social values (order and individualism), democratic values (liberty, equality, and fraternity), and economic values (efficiency, economic growth, and quality). As explained there, although all these values are always factors in education policy in the United States, their relative importance changes over time. People who analyze policy using the competing values framework argue that because only two or three values can be dominant at any given time, proponents of particular values compete with each other to move their preferred values into the top positions (Boyd, 1984). Once a value becomes the highest priority in education policy, it tends to hold that position for a long time, causing a cyclical alternation among the public values in U.S. history. Because the policies driven by each value differ considerably from each other, this means that periodically a rather dramatic shift occurs, called a *realignment.* This happens about every forty years (Iannaccone, 1988).

Lowi's Policy Types

As discussed in Chapter 9, political scientist Lowi (Lowi, 1964; Lowi & Ginsberg, 1994) developed a typology of policies (distributive, regulatory, and redistributive), arguing that each generates a distinctive political arena around itself. Although Lowi does not claim that preferred policy types move in cycles, he does assert that in different historical periods, different policy types have been favored. For example, up until the nineteenth century, governments mostly used distributive policies, but in the nineteenth century, regulations became common. In the twentieth century, however, many governments around the world pursued social goals by putting redistributive policies, such as welfare and Social Security, in place. This means that one way to understand policy shifts over time is to analyze them in terms of which policy types have been preferred in different historical periods.

Institutional Choice

Kirp (1982) argues that one way to compare and contrast the school systems of different nations is to examine the extent to which their organization reflects five types of institutions: (1) bureaucracy, (2) legalization, (3) professionalization, (4) politics, and (5) the market. He suggests that few systems are purely of one form, but that most incorporate elements of all five. However, one or two dominate, setting the tone of the overall organization and shaping its policy direction. Although he uses this framework to compare the school systems of different countries, it can also be used to compare the same system to itself across historical periods.

The first of the institutional forms that a school system can take is that of *bureaucracy*. A bureaucracy is a hierarchical organization in which everyone has a clearly defined role and directives flow from the top down. Rules and standard operating procedures are important in a bureaucracy, as are written documents such as policy manuals and minutes from meetings. Advancement within the organization is supposed to be determined by merit, as measured by a supposedly objective instrument such as a test or standard evaluation form.

A highly *legalized* institution is one in which laws are the ultimate instruments of control. Disputes are settled by taking complaints to court and letting judges make the final decision. Legalized institutions have an adversarial flavor, and all participants are concerned about protecting their rights. There is probably no organization that is predominantly legalized in structure. Nonetheless, there are many that are so torn with conflict that recourse to the judicial system is common within them.

The organizational structure encompassing the members of some occupations is that of the profession, achieved through *professionalization* at some point in the past. Members of a profession are controlled internally by norms to which they were socialized by older people working in their field. Typically, entry into a profession is competitive and highly selective; the training is long and arduous; and learners must go through various rites of passage such as difficult examinations or exhausting field experiences. On graduation from the training program, professionals have a period of supervised practice during which they are further socialized. In a profession, the members decide who gains admission and who must leave because of incompetency. Professionals work autonomously, without direct supervision. Medicine and law provide good examples of professions (Lortie, 1975). In the United States, teaching is only partially professionalized.

Politics can also be the fundamental structural principle of an education system. In political situations, people build power in order to advance their own interests or values. Political game playing usually requires negotiating to reach compromises and is frequently based on exchanging favors. Clearly, all organizations without exception include some political elements, but politics is more pronounced in some than in others. The legislative branch of democratic governments is one of the most political of institutions, and in many countries, legislatures make a high percentage of the education policy decisions. School systems vary in the extent to which policymaking is politicized.

Finally, institutions can be organized as *markets*. In a market, goods and services are produced by competing providers, who try to attract customers by offering attractive prices or distinctive product features. In a market that functions well, the presence of competing providers leads to efficient operations and high-quality products because businesses that cannot please customers lose them. Although the economic system is based heavily on market principles, many other organizations in modern societies, including school systems, use some elements of the market.

International Convergence

Comparative education specialists theorize that the school systems of the nations around the world are "converging," or becoming more like each other in structure, curriculum, and goals. The process is not new. As early as the eighteenth century, Thomas Jefferson and the Marquis de Condorcet, a French leader, corresponded about the type of schools necessary to promote democratic government; the ideas of both men were later reflected in the public schools of each nation. Cross-national influence continued in the nineteenth century. To mention just one example, under the Meiji Restoration, Japanese leaders visited schools in Europe and North America, gathering information to use in establishing their own school system as part of a broader modernization effort. Today, as the world's economies globalize, no nation can escape the impact of international forces that affect many aspects of national life, including education. The result is that, around the world, school systems are becoming increasingly similar (Coombs, 1984; Wirt & Harman, 1986). Two Canadian scholars, Davies and Guppy (1997), describe the process:

> Nation-states must increasingly react to [economic] pressures and battle constant-ly to improve their comparative advantage, which leads to a key proposition: the ever expanding web of market relations fosters a standardization of knowledge systems in all core industrialized nation-states. Since nation-states organize and distribute knowledge through formal education, this logic implies a tendency for school systems to converge across these developed nations. (p. 436)

RETROSPECTIVE ON U.S. EDUCATION POLICY

The Young Republic, 1783–1830

OVERVIEW. The first decades of the U.S. republic were shaped by the struggle to establish a viable nation—to develop political institutions, to lay the foundation for a strong economy, and to resolve the inevitable conflicts that arose among a conglomeration of former colonies with different cultures and traditions. One important cultural difference lay in their attitudes toward education; this was the major reason for omitting all mention of education from the U.S. Constitution. Thus, each state was free to follow its preferred course with regard to education; even within states, there was much diversity. Although compulsory attendance laws had not yet been passed, literacy was growing and most citizens wanted to obtain at least a rudimentary education for themselves and to provide one for their children. Parents who sought a school for their offspring could choose among a rich variety of options. Youngsters often mastered the alphabet and early elements of reading in *dame schools,* informal "home" schools where a neighbor woman taught a few children in her own residence, often in her kitchen. Special *private venture* schools offered somewhat more advanced instruction in single subjects, such as handwriting and English. Most denominations also operated elementary schools for the children of their adherents. In rural areas, semipublic *district schools* operated for two or three months annually, teaching farm children some simple notions of reading and writing. For the small number of children who pursued academic learning beyond the basic level, private academies and boarding schools provided both classical and practical curricula. Although public subsidies were available in some areas, parents bore most of the costs of these schools: paying tuition, purchasing books and materials, feeding the schoolmaster, and contributing fuel for winter heating.

Toward the end of the period, cities began to sponsor public schools for poor children. Often called *charity schools,* they had high pupil–teacher ratios and, although they taught the rudiments of reading and arithmetic, they emphasized hard work and obedience, the character traits needed in the new factories that were springing up. Because public schools were considered inferior, middle- and upper-class parents rarely chose them for their children. For example, Edward Everett Hale, son of a middle-class Boston family, attended private schools until age nine, when his parents enrolled him in the Boston Latin School that, although operated by the city, was very prestigious. Hale later wrote about his educational path: "There was no public school of any lower grade to which my father would have sent me, any more than he would have sent me to jail" (Perkinson, 1991, p. 14). His comment reveals the attitudes of this period.

THE COMPETING VALUES PERSPECTIVE.   Viewed from the perspective of the competing values framework, the values that drove education policy in the Young Republic were individualism and freedom. Memories of the Revolutionary War were fresh in people's memories, and the distrust of government that had developed during the late colonial period still flourished. As a result, most citizens were skeptical of proposals that the government operate schools, such as those that Thomas Jefferson was advocating in Virginia. Rather, they prized local—and parental—control of education and enjoyed being able to choose among many types of schools. Some parents also wanted to maintain the option of not sending children to school at all; their labor was essential on the farms and in the small shops of the period. The idea that the government should establish a public school system that all or most children would attend was therefore unappealing during this period. It reminded people too much of the high-handed ways of the British king against whom they had rebelled.

THE POLICY TYPES PERSPECTIVE.   The overall education policy orientation between 1783 and 1830 can best be described as *inaction.* For the most part, the local, state, and federal governments did little to either promote or discourage education. Nonetheless there were some policies, particularly at the local level and particularly in New England. Cities, towns, and townships provided some resources for education; toward the end of the period, they were beginning to operate schools for poor children. These policies were distributive with no regulatory strings attached other than that the funds be used for education. Similarly, the *Northwest Ordinance,* passed by Congress in 1787, was distributive, stipulating that one of the thirty-six plots in every township in the newly opened territory be rented out and the proceeds used for schools. No regulations were included in the law, and no federal monitors were provided to exercise oversight. Although these plots were often used for education as intended, misuse and fraudulent diversion of the funds were not uncommon (Kaestle, 1983).

THE INSTITUTIONAL CHOICE PERSPECTIVE.   One historian of this period observes that "schooling remained a local, voluntary, and largely entrepreneurial undertaking" (Kaestle, 1983, p. 184). The market was far and away the most dominant institutional form. Under this system, the other institutional forms were relatively insignificant. To be sure, there had to be some degree of bureaucracy within the larger schools, and

TABLE 12.1 Institutional Choices in Education Policy in Four Historical Periods

	Historical Periods			
Institutions	Young Republic	Common School	Scientific Sorting Machine	Reform Period, 1983–Present
Bureaucracy	Weak	Strong	Strong	Unsettled
Legalization	Weak	Weak	Strong	Unsettled
Professionalization	Weak	Moderate	Moderate	Unsettled
Politics	Weak	Moderate	Weak	Unsettled
Market	Strong	Weak	Weak	Unsettled

parochial schools had a church hierarchy with which to contend, but there were no central offices, no superintendents, no state departments of education, and certainly no education agencies at the federal level. Because few education laws existed, there was little possibility for legalization either. Nor were teaching or school administration professionalized; anyone who could attract students could establish a school. Teaching was regarded as a good temporary pursuit—ideal for women who wanted to earn a few dollars, for literate farmers who needed something to do in the winter months, and for young men not quite ready to enter business or read law. Finally, education policy was not particularly politicized yet. Occasionally debated in legislatures or Congress, it was not an ongoing concern. The market was clearly dominant, leading to a rich variety of choices for parents and many entrepreneurial opportunities for would-be teachers and principals. Table 12.1 summarizes the relative importance of the five institutions during this period and during the three periods that followed.

THE INTERNATIONAL CONVERGENCE PERSPECTIVE.   Because education in the United States was diverse and uncentralized, no formal exchanges could take place between U.S. educators and those from other parts of the world. Furthermore, international communication was so poor that little opportunity arose for sharing ideas through print. Nonetheless, even at this early date, the influence of other countries on U.S. education was considerable. After all, the European settlers in the New World were immigrants who had come from older, more established societies. One of the things they brought with them was the conception of schooling they had known in the Old World. For the most part, this influence was British; however, immigrants from Germany, France, and other countries also came with ideas about what constituted proper schools. Naturally, when they established schools for their children in North America, they followed these old patterns. Thus, from the start, education in the United States reflected a strong and mixed international influence.

CONCLUDING REFLECTIONS.   Political scientist Seymour Lipset (1996) observes that "the American Creed can be described in five terms: liberty, egalitarianism, individualism, populism, and laissez-faire" (p. 19). Measured against those criteria, the education policy orientation of the Young Republic can be described as quintessentially American. The high value it placed on liberty and individualism was discussed earlier. Its populism, or distrust of experts, was apparent in its relaxed attitude toward who was capable of teaching. The government definitely took a laissez-faire, "let citizens do whatever they want to," approach to education. In a sense, it was egalitarian, for all types of schools and teachers were considered good enough to participate in the education market, although they might not survive for long. Ultimately, however, it was not egalitarian enough, because the education services it provided were quite uneven, which is one reason why it came under severe attack in the 1830s.

The Rise of the Common School, 1831–1900

OVERVIEW.   By the early 1830s, the Young Republic was no longer young, and the United States was changing rapidly. The major cause of the widespread transformations of this period was industrialization. Factories sprang up throughout the Northeast, and young men and women who had grown up on farms flocked to cities to work in them. They were not the only ones who came; immigrants from Europe, primarily Ireland and Germany, joined them. Many of these were Roman Catholics, much to the dismay of the overwhelmingly Protestant population. As a result of this population growth, cities burgeoned, spreading out across former farmland, bringing with them increased crime and poverty. These rapid changes deeply disturbed many Americans, particularly in New England, and they responded in typically American fashion—by launching a variety of reform movements, each conceived as a way to save the country from the perils that threatened it. Prohibition, women's suffrage, abolition, prison reform—all these movements blossomed during the 1830s. Among them was the Common School movement, whose goal was to reform American education.

The central leader of the movement was New Englander Horace Mann, a tireless lecturer and prolific writer. He was also an educator with a reform agenda. Deeply distressed by the increasing social diversity and crime rate in the United States, Mann conceived of the Common School as a way to unify the heterogeneous population, thereby reducing the crime rate. In his view, the current school system was pitifully inadequate, "each [school] being governed by its own habits, traditions, and local customs" (cited in Perkinson, 1991, p. 22). The result was an uncoordinated educational hodgepodge, destined to keep most children ignorant and backward. Mann's solution was the Common School, which would provide an elementary education for all white children of both sexes and of every ethnic, religious, and socioeconomic group. He and his fellow reformers developed a detailed agenda for transforming education in the United States into a highly coordinated system; Figure 12.1 lists the individual planks of that platform.

- More regular school attendance
- A longer school year
- Graded schools
- The weakening of the district system
- Creation of state education agencies
- Creation of county superintendencies
- Improved occupational status for teachers
- Teacher training in normal schools

FIGURE 12.1   The platform of the Common School movement

The battle for the Common School was a long one because the advocates of the old system did not surrender without a struggle. Nor did all citizens enthusiastically welcome paying taxes to support Common Schools. Nevertheless, by 1860, the Common School was virtually universal in the North; in the South, it took considerably longer to establish, but a racially segregated version of common schooling prevailed by the end of the nineteenth century (Kaestle, 1983; Perkinson, 1991; Spring, 2005). A very large part of the "Kansas" that many educators once took for granted was in place.

THE COMPETING VALUES PERSPECTIVE.   Between the Young Republic period and the Common School era, the values that drove education policy in the United States shifted dramatically: from liberty and individualism to fraternity, order, and economic growth. *Fraternity*, defined as a sense of national unity, was the foremost value for Horace Mann and many of his fellow reformers. They feared the fragmentation of U.S. society along the lines of cleavage that had become apparent by 1830—ethnic background, religion, and, above all, social class. Their fears were dramatically reinforced by the Boston riots of 1837, during which Catholics and Protestants fought each other in the streets. In their opinion, the Common School would help prevent such conflicts by giving children from different backgrounds the opportunity to become acquainted with each other in school. All would develop a common sense of identity as Americans, forgetting the barriers that divided them. Clearly, order was also an important value for the leaders of the Common School movement. One historian even refers to "Mann's morbid fear of social unrest and instability" (Perkinson, 1991, p. 23). Although this severe judgment may reveal more about the author's inexperience with social disorder than it does about the legitimacy of Mann's fears, it does suggest the extent to which the desire for social order permeates his writings.

Somewhat less important to Mann, but a central concern for many of his supporters, was economic growth. Workers were needed for the new factories; employers wanted them to possess the rudiments of reading and arithmetic and insisted that they be hardworking and obedient. Thus, the Common School emphasized the development of a particular kind of character. Its textbooks were studded with inspirational slogans such as, "The idle boy is almost invariably poor and miserable," and "Idleness is the nest in which mischief lays its eggs" (cited in Kaestle, 1983, p. 82).

THE POLICY TYPES PERSPECTIVE.   Distributive education policy had been dominant prior to the 1830s, but the Common School reformers advocated the enactment of many regulatory policies, as indicated in Figure 12.1. Compulsory attendance laws were passed, the school year was lengthened, and a standard school organization was mandated. Moreover, a governance apparatus was instituted at both the state and county levels to enforce the new requirements and gather statistics on school performance. Schools lost their previous freedom to do whatever they wanted; now they were carefully controlled by government officials in agencies above them. The broad policy goal of the Common School movement was "systematic uniformity—uniform textbooks, a uniform curriculum, uniform teaching methods, uniform management, uniform discipline, and uniformly trained teachers" (Kaestle, 1995, p. 19). This uniformity was achieved through regulation.

THE INSTITUTIONAL CHOICE PERSPECTIVE.   The market was the dominant institution under the Young Republic, but its importance in the institutional mix dropped dramatically during the Common School era. Bureaucracy was the reformers' preferred institution; they established it at both the local and state levels. Under their guidance, state departments of education were established, directed by superintendents of public instruction. At the local level, superintendents and other supervisors made sure that state mandates were implemented. By the end of the period, bureaucracy was even beginning to appear in schools, where the roles of principals and teachers were gradually differentiated. Thus, a hierarchical and bureaucratic organizational structure was in place in U.S. education by 1900.

Although bureaucracy was the reformers' preferred institutional choice, politics and professionalism were also important to them. The education system was much more embroiled in politics during this period than it had been earlier. The fight to establish common schools was a political struggle of the first magnitude, requiring that legislatures enact statutes establishing agencies, creating the superintendency, and—above all—taxing the citizenry to support schools. All these issues were controversial. Moreover, because public education was now understood to play an important role in "ideological management" (Spring, 2005, p. 4), politicians were more interested in it than they had been previously. They saw it as a tool that could be used to shape docile workers, build patriotism, and solve a variety of youth problems. This meant that education policy issues and policy issues of other types often became intertwined. Professionalism also increased under the Common School. Although teaching was not fully professionalized, some professional elements were introduced into it. These included training in normal schools for teachers; better salaries; and journals, associations, and conferences designed especially for them. However, because teaching in common schools was feminized during this period, it remained an occupation that was relatively easy to enter. Teacher turnover was high because many young women "kept school" only until they married (Lortie, 1975).

Although legalization and the market were the least important institutions, they were not completely missing. Numerous school laws were passed during this period, and some were challenged in the courts. Taxation to support common schools was litigated frequently; the courts almost always upheld it. As for the market, the Common School reformers merely weakened the old district system; they did not eliminate it. This meant that parents, especially in urban areas, could still choose schools for their children by choosing in which district they would live. Table 12.1 summarizes the relative importance of the five institutions during the Common School era.

THE INTERNATIONAL CONVERGENCE PERSPECTIVE.   The government and business leaders of the Common School era worried about international economic competition, just as they do today. Great Britain was the dominant world power, and Americans did not idealize the mother country as they sometimes do now; their memories of the Revolutionary War and the War of 1812 were too vivid. They perceived Great Britain, with her navy and global ambitions, as a serious threat. A newer concern was Prussia (the northern region of modern Germany), which was building both economic and military might. Of less concern but also worrisome were France, Japan, and Russia. The leaders of the period were convinced that education was a major weapon for winning the international competition that was developing. Therefore, Mann and other Common School reformers made a point of visiting European schools, especially those in Prussia and France, to obtain ideas. The European influence is apparent in many elements of the common schools and of the early normal schools, which trained teachers. Indeed, the very term *normal school* is a literal translation of the French term, *école normale* (Kaestle, 1983). Thus, the Common School reforms can be understood as a movement away from a distinctively American educational institution and toward emerging international norms for school systems.

CONCLUDING REFLECTIONS.   In many respects, the Common School was a typical nineteenth-century institution. As with many other organizations developed during the period, including the business firm and the government agency, its structure was bureaucratic and hierarchical. In its reliance on regulations as its preferred policy type, it was also typical; in general, the nineteenth century saw a geometric increase in the number of government regulations in effect and also in the ability to enforce them (Lowi, 1964). Finally, its nationalistic goals were characteristic of an age during which nation-states grew in power, self-consciousness, and influence. However, the twentieth century presented challenges that the Common School could not fully meet. Therefore, the early 1900s, like the 1830s, would be a period of school reform.

The "Scientific" Sorting Machine, 1900–1982

OVERVIEW.   Like the 1830s, the early twentieth century was a period of change; indeed, many of these changes paralleled those of the earlier era. For example, immigration reached high levels with 8.5 million immigrants entering the United States between 1900 and 1910, and another four million between 1910 and 1920 (Perkinson, 1991). The now highly industrialized economy was booming, conferring on business high credibility with the public and great influence on civic affairs. Numerous scientific inventions and advances made daily life more comfortable and dramatically improved health and life expectancy. However, storm clouds were gathering over Europe as the new century began. International tensions were mounting since the competition among the European powers had intensified during the late nineteenth century. This period was marked by major international conflict, with World War I breaking out in 1914, World War II raging between 1939 and 1945, and the Cold War driving policy after that. The major result for Americans was the changed international status of the United States. It emerged from World War I as a major world power, and from World War II as one of two superpowers dominating the world stage. Inevitably, all these changes made an impact on education policy (Perkinson, 1991; Ravitch, 1983; Spring, 2005).

At the beginning of the twentieth century, the two central education policy issues were modifying the governance structures of public education and deciding how to deal with growing enrollment in secondary schools. The Progressive reformers of the turn of the twentieth century sought local government reforms, including reforms of school governance, because they believed that in recent decades city governments had become thoroughly corrupt. Therefore, they advocated a number of legal changes, all designed to reduce partisanship, nepotism, and graft. Unfortunately, they also had the effect of reducing public participation in local politics. In education, the Progressive reforms involved reducing the size of school boards, making school board elections nonpartisan, and expanding central office staffs by adding to them various experts trained in the scientific management approach then popular in business circles. Confidence in experts—especially if they claimed to be "scientific"—was high, and many decisions that elected officials, teachers, and principals had previously made were shifted to central offices (Callahan, 1962; Tyack, 1974).

Burgeoning enrollment in secondary schools also posed a major policy problem, and two distinctly different proposals for dealing with it were offered. The first was best represented by the recommendations of the Committee of Ten on Secondary School Studies that—significantly—issued its report in 1892, late in the Common School era. The Committee of Ten proposed a high school in which all children would pursue the same curriculum, one that would be academically oriented. In short, it proposed the extension of the Common School concept into secondary education. The alternative proposal was for a differentiated secondary curriculum, all of whose components (or "tracks") would be offered in the same building. A concrete example of this policy proposal was the *Cardinal Principles of Secondary Education,* a report published by the National Education Association (NEA) in 1918. It called for a differentiated secondary curriculum that would be driven "by the needs of the society to be served, the character of the individuals to be educated, and the knowledge of educational theory and practice available" (cited in Ravitch, 1983, p. 48). This was the position that won out because the federal government, which was becoming increasingly active in education policy, supported it with both rhetoric and money. In 1917, for example, it had passed the *Smith–Hughes Act*, providing federal resources for vocational education. During the first quarter of the twentieth century, a number of other policy mechanisms (Figure 12.2) developed to facilitate and support the differentiation of the secondary curriculum into tracks.

Throughout the rest of this period, leaders considered the public schools a major instrument of public policy, which the government could (and did) use to meet a broad range of social and economic needs: training future workers, identifying young people's ability levels and channeling them into the "right" career directions, helping the United States maintain its economic and military supremacy, and encouraging most youngsters to "adjust" rather than to develop high-level cognitive skills that would not be needed in their workplace (Perkinson, 1991; Ravitch, 1983; Spring, 1989). Historian Joel Spring (1989) aptly dubbed this version of the American school "the great sorting machine." This was the other half of the school system that many educators considered their "familiar Kansas," largely in place by 1930.

- Ability grouping
- Extracurricular activities
- Guidance counseling
- I.Q. testing
- Junior high schools
- School psychology
- Standardized achievement tests
- Vocational guidance

FIGURE 12.2   Policy mechanisms in support of the differentiated curriculum

A major contradiction lay at the heart of the Scientific Sorting Machine, however. Although it was surrounded by the rhetoric of equal education opportunity for all children, people did not have to score at the genius level on one of the new intelligence tests to be able to figure out that a considerable gap separated rhetoric from reality. In both the North and South, African Americans attended racially segregated schools that were almost always inferior to those that white children attended. Moreover, in some parts of the country, Hispanic, Native American, and Asian American children were required to go to separate, unequal schools. The Scientific Sorting Machine also discriminated against girls, who, in the eyes of the writers of the *Cardinal Principles,* did not need to prepare for college but rather for lives as homemakers. This gender discrimination was expressed both in the courses that guidance counselors urged young women to take and in the fact that they had unequal access to some aspects of the extracurricular program, especially athletics. As for children with handicaps, they were originally excluded, shunted off into special schools or deprived of education altogether. After World War II, these incongruities were experienced as increasingly unacceptable and, one by one, they were either reduced or abolished. Such changes did not occur without a struggle, however, and the federal government had to play an increasingly important role in enforcing the new policies designed to enhance equal education opportunity. Unfortunately, the continued existence of multiple school districts, especially in metropolitan areas, allowed families to "vote with their feet" by moving to the suburbs, where school populations were more homogeneous. The result was school systems that were increasingly segregated by class and in which a new form of racial segregation continued (Perkinson, 1991; Ravitch, 1983; Spring, 2005). By the end of the period, dissatisfaction with public education was mounting, suggesting that another period of reform might be on the horizon.

THE COMPETING VALUES PERSPECTIVE.   During the era of the Scientific Sorting Machine, efficiency was the dominant value, with equality second most important. Efficiency was so paramount in the thinking of this period that Callahan (1962) entitled his classic study of the transformation of school administration in the early twentieth century *Education and the Cult of Efficiency.* This preoccupation with efficiency was manifested in many ways. The superintendency evolved into a job having more to do with school finance than with education leadership. Decisions about children's learning were increasingly based on test scores rather than on teachers' professional judgment. Testing itself changed; as time passed, essay examinations (which were time-consuming to evaluate and therefore costly) were progressively replaced by multiple-choice tests (which could be quickly and cheaply scored by machines). In fact, the whole purpose of the sorting machine was to improve social efficiency by expeditiously channeling young people into tracks that would lead them into the occupations that U.S. society most needed (Perkinson, 1991; Ravitch, 1983). As the period moved toward its end, however, equality assumed ever greater importance. Understood as equal opportunity to succeed in the Scientific Sorting Machine, it became the driving value behind the various rights movements of the 1960s and 1970s. However, none of these movements seriously challenged the basic assumptions of the sorting machine or argued that other types of equality should be pursued by U.S. schools.

THE POLICY TYPES PERSPECTIVE.   During the Scientific Sorting Machine period, the preferred policy types were regulation and the redistribution of resources. Early in the period, regulations were emphasized, and many new ones were put on the books. For example, in line with the era's confidence in expertise, the requirements for teacher certification were substantially increased and administrative certification was introduced. As time passed and redistributive policies became increasingly popular, detailed regulations were usually attached to them. Title I, one of the compensatory education sections of the *Elementary and Secondary Education Act* of 1965, was accompanied by complex guidelines that changed frequently. Legislation governing children with handicaps, passed in the 1970s, also came with numerous guidelines. As regulations accumulated, the redistributive policies of the 1960s and 1970s also began to shift many educational resources away from the "regular" classroom and toward poor children, children with handicaps, non–English-speaking children, and others. Predictably, the political arena became increasingly turbulent as the dynamics of regulatory and redistributive policies were set in motion simultaneously. Ravitch (1983) describes the politics of the last decade of the period:

> Whoever the claimant, whether representing blacks, women, the handicapped, or non-English-speaking minority groups, the avenue of political remedy was the same: to bypass educational authorities by working directly with sympathetic congressional committees and by gaining judicial supervision. Each victory led to the imposition of mandates on school . . . officials, requiring them to do promptly what they otherwise would have done slowly, reluctantly, or not at all. By their very nature, these outside interventions diminished the authority of educational administrators. (p. 311)

THE INSTITUTIONAL CHOICE PERSPECTIVE.   Even more than the leaders of the Common School movement, the key figures during the Scientific Sorting Machine era preferred bureaucracy, for it was consistent with their great faith in expertise. Therefore, they not only maintained the bureaucracy that had been put in place during the nineteenth century, but extended and strengthened it as well. Their additions increased the specialization and division of labor that already existed. By the 1960s, a host of experts of various kinds worked in school systems—guidance counselors, school psychologists, reading teachers, special education teachers, curriculum specialists, vocational placement officers, and so forth. Increasingly, educational roles and authority were moved out of the classrooms and principals' offices and into the domains of these specialists.

Professionalization was also used, but within clear limits. As people who admired knowledge and those individuals who possessed it, the leaders of the period had great confidence in credentials. Not surprisingly, therefore, they raised education requirements for teachers, developed administrator preparation programs, and emphasized inservice education. At the same time, however, their tendency to increase specialization and reinforce the existing division of labor undermined the professional autonomy of principals and teachers. Increasingly, the former were managers rather than education leaders, whereas the latter found themselves carrying out the directives of others and basing their instruction on supposedly "teacher-proof" curricula devised by experts (Ravitch, 1983; Spring, 2005).

The leaders of this period distrusted politics; but, ironically, this distrust led to the legalization of education in the United States, which in turn sparked fierce political controversy. The Progressive reforms of the early twentieth century had sought to "get the politics out of education," and to a certain extent they had succeeded. The nonpartisan school boards established at that time were so removed both from ordinary citizens and from the mainstream of state and federal politics that exercising political influence on them was difficult. As a result, citizens bypassed them, taking their grievances into the state and federal court systems. The degree of the legalization of education is suggested by the fact that although federal courts decided only 112 education cases in the decade between 1946 and 1956, they decided 729 between 1956 and 1966, and 1,200 in the four years from 1966 to 1970 (Ravitch, 1983). Not surprisingly, this judicial activism was deeply resented in many quarters, setting the stage for political revolt on the part of both legislators and citizens' groups (Perkinson, 1991; Ravitch, 1983).

Although education leaders of the Scientific Sorting Machine period also distrusted the market, they unwittingly reinforced it. Urban parents who were disgruntled with court-ordered desegregation and busing policies fled to the suburbs, where many small, competing school districts sought to lure them with shiny new facilities and low tax rates. The result was the development of an education market around most large cities in which suburbs competed for residents, drawing most middle-class children out of city school districts (Weeres, 1988).

THE INTERNATIONAL CONVERGENCE PERSPECTIVE.   Like the education system of the Common School era, that of the Scientific Sorting Machine period reflected international influence. The major developed nations of Europe as well as Japan had established highly differentiated school systems during the nineteenth century. Although both bipartite and tripartite systems existed, the same basic concept prevailed in all of them: children whose probable career paths differed should pursue different education programs, and these should be offered in different, separate schools. Typically, youngsters who would ultimately seek professional positions studied in prestigious schools that prepared them for university admission. The others pursued less academically-oriented curricula in vocational and technical schools. Although all these schools were funded by the government and were therefore public, they did not have equal status. Not coincidentally, pupils' social class background was a major determinant of the type of school they attended (Fowler, 1995a). Thus, the adoption of "tracks" in U.S. schools represented a movement toward the dominant international education model of the time. In fact, those who established vocational programs in the United States were especially influenced by the tripartite German school system.

International convergence was not a one-way street, however. As time passed and the United States became increasingly powerful in world affairs, other countries became familiar with the comprehensive high school found in the United States and adopted their own versions of it. In the 1950s, 1960s, and 1970s, many of them reformed their systems, bringing them closer to the U.S. Common School model. Indeed, by the end of this period, Japan and several nations of Western Europe, including France, Italy, and the Scandinavian countries, were actually closer to having Common Schools than was the United States (Fowler, 1995a).

CONCLUDING REFLECTIONS.   In many ways, the Scientific Sorting Machine was the ideal school system for most of the twentieth century. Organizationally modeled on the factories of the time, it produced the sort of workers that both business and the military wanted. It offered an intellectually challenging curriculum to the top 20% of youngsters while providing the rest with a basic education that emphasized rote memory, "adjusting" to society, and practical skills (Reich, 1991). Considering the great economic and military success of the United States during the period, this education system cannot be regarded as a complete failure. Nonetheless, times change, and by the 1980s, the Scientific Sorting Machine was under sustained attack.

In Search of a New Paradigm, 1983–Present

OVERVIEW.   By the 1980s, dissatisfaction with public education was growing again; much of it crystallized around a federal commission report, *A Nation at Risk,* that appeared in 1983. Blaming most of the problems in the United States on the failure of schools to prepare their graduates adequately for the competitive global economy, the writers of the report sketched a broad outline of the reforms that they thought necessary to save the endangered nation. Many leaders of education reform movements rallied to its call, even though they did not always agree with the report on the exact nature of the required changes (Lugg, 1996). The result was a vigorous education reform movement (or, rather, several overlapping and contradictory reform movements) that flourish to this day.

The movements of the 1980s and 1990s must be understood against the backdrop of the 1970s. During that decade, the economic boom launched by the end of World War II ended. This event, which was not recognized immediately, brought with it disquieting economic symptoms: double-digit inflation, unexpectedly high unemployment, and a slowing of economic growth. At the same time, Americans began to realize that the economic gap between them and other developed countries was narrowing. Although they still had the highest standard of living in the world, the Japanese and the Western Europeans were catching up, and in some areas they were moving ahead. The success of the Japanese in selling automobiles in the United States and the growing presence of European products in U.S. stores jolted many out of their previous complacency. The world was shrinking; our long-time allies were emerging as competitors for global markets; obviously something had to be done to solve the problem (Reich, 1991; Thurow, 1992). One solution was school reform.

Several observers have argued that the school reform movement was a red herring, designed to divert public attention away from the errors of business and political leaders (see, e.g., Berliner & Biddle, 1995). Some truth is probably inherent in this position; Americans have long regarded education as a cure-all for whatever ails the nation (Perkinson, 1991; Tyack & Cuban, 1995), and therefore are particularly receptive to the notion that economic problems can be solved by tinkering with the school system. Nonetheless, dismissing the school reform movement as merely a "manufactured" crisis, to use Berliner and Biddle's (1995) term, would be simplistic. For one thing, education reform is not a purely U.S. phenomenon; it has international dimensions, and virtually all developed countries have implemented major changes in their school systems since 1980 (Fowler, 1995a). This suggests that there are deeper reasons for the movement in the United States than purely political ones. No doubt one of these is simply that because most of the school systems in the developed world were established in the nineteenth century, as institutions they were beginning to show their age by the 1980s.

In the United States, several proposals for updating the school system coexisted in the policy arena from 1983 on. Joseph Murphy (1990) grouped them in three broad categories: (1) intensifying the old bureaucracy, (2) restructuring, and (3) redesigning. His basic concept has been adapted with some alterations for the following discussion. The first set of reforms, summarized in Figure 12.3, was proposed earliest and advocates the least thorough going changes. Basically, the proponents of these reforms, although sometimes dubious about certain aspects of the Scientific Sorting Machine, accepted the basic structure of the U.S. school system, especially its Common School components. Implicitly, however, they believed that the Common School model was never fully achieved and advocated its completion. Thus, some of them pushed for reforms such as national standards and curriculum reform, which would further systematize education. Some were more interested in reforms such as school finance equalization, detracking, and inclusion, which would bring the school system closer to the old Common School ideal.

The second set of reforms, summarized in Figure 12.4, called for the restructuring of the school system in the direction of greater professionalization. Those who advocated these reforms argued that children cannot be taught to be critical and creative thinkers by teachers who are required to conform to the old factory model of teaching. They believed that if teachers were given more autonomy within the classroom and more power to make decisions within their school and to govern their profession outside it, they would be better able to educate the type of workers the United States needs in the twenty-first century.

Finally, proposed reforms of the third type, summarized in Figure 12.5, advocated restructuring education to make it more like a market. According to advocates of these changes, the main cause of the problems of public education is that it is a government monopoly, and therefore unresponsive to consumer demands.

- Curriculum alignment
- Detracking
- Inclusion
- Increased graduation requirements
- Longer school day/year
- New technology
- Paideia Proposal
- School finance reform
- State/national standards
- State/national subject matter tests
- State proficiency tests
- Subject-matter standards
- Systemic reform

FIGURE 12.3   Reforms to complete, restore, or update the Common School

- Authentic assessment
- Career ladders
- Differentiated staffing
- Five-year teacher preparation programs
- Increased teacher salaries
- New teacher induction programs
- Peer evaluation
- Portfolio assessment
- Professional development schools
- Professional standards boards
- Site-based decision making
- Teacher mentoring
- Teacher teams

FIGURE 12.4   Reforms to professionalize teaching

- Charter schools
- Interdistrict open enrollment
- Intradistrict open enrollment
- Magnet schools
- Merit pay plans
- Postsecondary open enrollment options
- Privatization of support services
- Privatization of management
- Subsidies for private schools
- Vouchers

FIGURE 12.5   Reforms to marketize education

They suggested making it into a market, or at least introducing market elements into it, so that the resulting competition could increase its responsiveness and efficiency.

Different policy networks and coalitions advocate these reforms, competing in Congress and in state legislatures to gain official acceptance for their ideas. Lawmakers freely borrowed from all three groups of reforms, unaware that in practice they are not always compatible. However, for those who were leading schools and school systems, the constant flood of new policies and policy proposals created an education landscape that was sometimes very Oz-like indeed.

THE COMPETING VALUES PERSPECTIVE.   Some observers have identified freedom and excellence as the two core values of the education reform movement that began in the late twentieth century (Boyd & Kerchner, 1988; Iannaccone, 1988). Certainly, *freedom*—understood primarily as *freedom of choice*—was central to the movement. Not only was freedom the value that drove every aspect of most school choice proposals, but it was also implicit in many policies that would increase teacher professionalism, understood as professional autonomy. Certainly, too, the rhetoric that surrounded the movement resonates with the discourse of excellence, whether it was conceived as higher standards, greater emphasis on critical thinking, or more challenging forms of assessment. Nonetheless, few advocated excellence for the sake of excellence; rather, what they really sought was economic growth, and higher standards of excellence were seen as a way to produce a workforce better able to compete in the global economy. Thus, the dominant core values seemed to be freedom and economic growth, with excellence seen as the best way to achieve the latter.

THE POLICY TYPES PERSPECTIVE.   Different branches of the reform movement preferred different policy types. Consistent with their fundamental loyalty to the old Common School, those who advocated completing it often expressed their policy choices through regulatory mechanisms. During the 1980s, for example, many legislatures increased graduation requirements and lengthened the school day or year by voting in laws that imposed new mandates on schools (Murphy, 1990). However, those who advocated either form of restructuring backed redistributive policies. Unlike their predecessors in the 1960s and 1970s, they wished to reallocate power rather than money. Advocates of greater professionalism wished to shift power from central offices to school buildings and from principals to teachers. School-choice proponents, however, sought to shift power away from educators of all types toward parents.

THE INSTITUTIONAL CHOICE PERSPECTIVE.   Each of the three branches of the reform movement favored a different institutional choice for the new education paradigm. Those who advocated the completion of the old Common School model wished to perfect several aspects of its bureaucracy, clarifying its rules, requirements, and organizational hierarchy. Proponents of increased professionalism argued for the greater professionalization of the teaching occupation, making it more like law and medicine. Choice supporters favored the market with its diversity of producers and products as well as its competition. Although all three movements were very politically active, only the first implied the ongoing use of politics as an institution; the perfected bureaucracy would continue to be part of the government, and its basic mandates would have to be voted by legislatures. However, although some proponents of the old Common School model—especially advocates of school finance equalization and inclusion—relied heavily on the courts, no proposals implied the ongoing use of legalization as an ideal.

THE INTERNATIONAL CONVERGENCE PERSPECTIVE.   From an international perspective, all three branches of the current reform movement could be interpreted as movements toward greater conformity with international education norms. As those who pushed for the completion of the Common School model liked to point out, most other developed countries and many developing ones have national or state standards, a national or state curriculum, and national or state tests. Moreover, most other school systems in the world are more "coherent," "systemic," or "aligned" (that is, more fully bureaucratic) than ours (Fuhrman, 1993). Similarly, teaching is more fully professionalized in most other developed countries than it is in the United States, a point that the American Federation of Teachers (AFT) has demonstrated through its research and publicity (see, e.g., AFT, 1995). Finally, although the education market is not particularly favored on the European continent or in Japan, the "marketization" of education has been popular throughout the English-speaking world since the early 1980s (Cooper, 1988). Each group, then, drew on international models for ideas.

CONCLUDING REFLECTIONS.   The education reform movement of the 1980s and 1990s can be seen as a revolt against the aging school organization inherited from the nineteenth and early twentieth centuries and as a search for a new paradigm. The revolt against the Scientific Sorting Machine elements of the old system was particularly strong, with all three movements rejecting many of its components. Both the people who advocated the completion of the Common School and those who favored "marketization" somewhat idealized a past phase of the American school system, with the former preferring the Common School era, and the latter, the approach of the Young Republic. Proponents of increased professionalization could not refer readily to an earlier period, because teaching in the United States has never been fully professionalized (Lortie, 1975). They had to look abroad for models, but both other groups had international connections as well. This is not surprising, because school reform is an international movement, not peculiar to the United States. One would expect, then, that the final education paradigm that emerges today will almost certainly reflect not just American elements, but the results of education experimentation elsewhere as well.

IS NO CHILD LEFT BEHIND THE NEW PARADIGM?

Overview

Early in 2002, President Bush signed into law the latest reauthorization of ESEA, entitled *No Child Left Behind*. Since then, much of the energy of education leaders at every level has been devoted to implementing—or resisting—this far-reaching piece of legislation. It is reasonable to ask, then, if *No Child Left Behind* represents the new education paradigm toward which the reformers of the 1980s and 1990s were struggling.

The first edition of this book, written in 1997 and published two years later, made some predictions about what the new education paradigm would look like; these predictions were repeated in the second edition, which was prepared in 2001–2002. It predicted that the teacher professionalism movement would not have much impact on the new paradigm because "[a]ppealing as the full professionalism of teaching may be to many educators, it would be inconsistent with core American values" (Fowler, 2004, p. 346) such as individualism and freedom. Instead, it predicted that the new paradigm would include numerous elements from both the updated Common School and the marketization models, arguing that

> Together, these two models fulfill all the requirements for the new paradigm: they express the dominant values of freedom and economic growth based on excellence, they have broad political support from a range of constituencies, and they are consistent with the theory of international convergence. (Fowler, 2004, p. 347)

Finally, it predicted that the new paradigm, when it appeared, would spark controversy and conflict that would last for many years.

The concluding portion of this chapter argues the thesis that *No Child Left Behind* does, in fact, represent the resolution of the education reform movements of the 1980s and 1990s. However, it also argues that the paradigm represented by NCLB has not yet reached its final form, and that many of the political struggles of the immediate future will revolve around refining this paradigm. In presenting this argument, first the politics behind the passage of the law are described. Next, its major provisions are summarized. Then, it is analyzed using the four theoretical lenses used throughout this chapter. Finally, it concludes with several recommendations to educational leaders who dislike some (or all) of the provisions of the law.

The Passage of NCLB

As with most laws, NCLB was the product of a series of political compromises. As early as 1989, President George H. W. Bush met with the nation's governors at the first "Education Summit" in American history. They agreed on the importance of establishing national education goals, and in his 1990 State of the Union speech, the president spelled out six goals that American schools were to reach by 2000. The first President Bush was, of course, a one-term president; however, his successor, Bill Clinton, shared his desire for stronger academic standards and some sort of testing program that would encourage schools to strive to meet them. The reauthorization of ESEA in 1994 gave the Clinton Administration an opportunity to push American education in the direction of national standards and testing. The result was *Goals 2000*, a companion bill to the ESEA reauthorization bill. Eventually approved by a fairly large congressional majority, *Goals 2000* and the 1994 version of ESEA called for states to adopt content standards in the major school subjects, as well as to develop assessment programs to measure progress toward meeting those standards. However, the Clinton Administration was unable to get bills with real teeth approved by Congress; in order to get the ESEA reauthorization and *Goals 2000* passed, it had to water down the enforcement components of the original bills (Hess & Petrilli, 2006; McGuinn, 2006).

In November 1994, the momentum toward enforceable national standards and tests was slowed when the Republicans won a landslide victory, taking control of both houses of Congress. A large number of ultraconservative Republicans, who favored weak government, came to Washington. The power of the Republican Right was reduced two years later when Clinton was reelected, strengthening the position of moderate Republicans, who favored a stronger role for the federal government in education policy. As the Clinton Administration approached its end, three general positions on federal education policy could be identified. Conservative Republicans favored a weak Department of Education, the devolution of more power over education to the states, and several forms of school choice. The liberal wing of the Democratic Party favored generous financial support for education for poor children with few strings attached; they strongly opposed most forms of school choice. Moderates in both parties supported stronger accountability policies for public education and some forms of school choice. Meanwhile, key constituents were pressuring both parties toward more accountability in public education. On the Republican side, the influential business community strongly favored national standards and tests. Two important

Democratic constituencies—African Americans and Latinos—were increasingly dis-satisfied with public education and wanted substantive changes in it. Consensus for tougher accountability reforms was building (Abernathy, 2007; Hess & Petrilli, 2006; McGuinn, 2006).

In 2001, the second President Bush was inaugurated. Both he and his opponent, Al Gore, had argued for higher academic standards and more school choice during their campaigns. Even so, the second Bush Administration might have found it im-possible to pull together the votes to pass an education reform law if nineteen ter-rorists had not flown airplanes into the World Trade Center and the Pentagon on September 11, 2001. In the aftermath of those tragic events, the two parties pulled to-gether to enact *No Child Left Behind*. The law was the result of a bipartisan effort, and even the ranking liberals on the two congressional education committees—Sen. Ted Kennedy of Massachusetts and Rep. George Miller of California—supported it (Hess & Petrilli, 2006; McGuinn, 2006).

Major Provisions of NCLB

NCLB is 670 pages long and has been accurately described as "large and ponderous" (Abernathy, 2007, p. 3). Its 670 pages include numerous components, many of which are relatively insignificant. This summary focuses on the provisions of the law that establish what political scientist Patrick McGuinn (2006) calls the new "accountability regime" in American education. Basically, NCLB requires states that receive federal funds under ESEA to develop academic standards, to establish an assessment system based on those standards, and to test students in reading and mathematics to see if they are meeting those standards. Unlike *Goals 2000*, however, NCLB includes enforcement mechanisms. The explicit goal of the legislation is for 100% of American children to be proficient in reading and mathematics by 2014, and schools and school districts must make "adequate yearly progress" (AYP) toward this goal. An added wrinkle is that not only must students in schools and districts make AYP on the whole, but each of several subgroups, such as whites, African Americans, low-income students, and students with disabilities, must also make AYP. Schools and districts that do not make their AYP goals are subject to various sanctions that escalate with each passing year. For example, schools that do not make AYP for two consecutive years are designated "in need of improvement." They must develop a school improvement plan, and their students must be offered the opportunity to transfer to a school within the district that is reaching its AYP goals. After three years of inadequate progress, schools must offer tutoring services to their students. The fourth year is supposed to lead to changes in the school, such as bringing in new teachers and lengthening the school day. Finally, in the fifth year, schools are supposed to be restructured (Hess & Petrilli, 2006; Irons & Harris, 2007; McGuinn, 2006). As Hess and Petrilli say, "These sanctions are the 'teeth' of *No Child Left Behind*" (p. 43). NCLB differs from past federal education laws in that it does actually have "teeth," or enforcement mechanisms. The federal government can use the threat of withdrawing ESEA funds to bring formidable pressure to bear on states, school districts, and schools to meet the demands of the law.

A related component of NCLB is the "highly qualified teacher" provision, which requires that all teachers of core academic subjects be "highly qualified." Several criteria are used to establish that a teacher is highly qualified; he or she must have a bachelor's degree, be licensed by the state, and be knowledgeable about the subject taught. Although the full rigor of the law is supposed to be applied to new teachers, requirements are somewhat looser for veteran ones. States have the authority to develop ways to assess whether teachers who are already practicing are highly qualified. These may include experience; advanced credentials, such as a master's degree; or high student achievement. Although states have more flexibility in implementing the highly qualified teacher component of the law than they do in implementing the rest of the "accountability regime," the law does put some pressure on them in this area. For instance, if a teacher who is not "highly qualified" teaches a class for more than four weeks, then the district must notify the students' parents of this fact (Hess & Petrilli, 2006; Irons & Harris, 2007; McGuinn, 2006).

In short, NCLB is structured in such a way that noncompliant school districts and states experience at least public embarrassment if they do not meet the requirements of the law. If their noncompliance is extensive, they may find that large numbers of their schools are labeled "failing" and must be reorganized. Federal ESEA funds can be withheld, of course. Nonetheless, the major threat of NCLB is probably the massive loss of legitimacy in the eyes of parents and the general public that schools and districts labeled "failing" will, no doubt, experience.

Applying Four Theoretical Lenses to NCLB

COMPETING VALUES.   On the surface, two values are predominant in NCLB: freedom and equality. The concern for promoting freedom is apparent in the fact that the law does not impose standards or testing programs on the states. In order to receive federal funds, states *must* develop academic content standards and they *must* develop a testing program to assess the progress of schools and school districts toward meeting them; however, they do have the freedom to develop their own programs within the broad framework of NCLB. The school-choice provisions in the law also promote freedom. The law gives the parents of children who attend schools that have not made AYP the right to transfer their children to more successful schools within the district, as well as the right to avail themselves of tutoring services. Concern for equality is indicated by the requirement that test scores be disaggregated to reveal how well various subgroups are doing, and also by the fact that a school does not make AYP unless all of its subgroups make it as well. This provision of NCLB pressures educators to pay more attention to certain children than they have in the past. Especially in schools whose enrollment was heavily middle class, it was easy to neglect poor and minority children, not to mention those children who did not speak English at home or who had disabilities. Historically, such children have not performed as well as native-born, nondisabled, white, middle- and upper-middle class youngsters, leading to significant achievement gaps among these populations. Under NCLB, such children can no longer be ignored; on the contrary, educators have a strong incentive to try to understand why these children do not achieve well in school, and to try to teach them more effectively. Moreover, one important dimension of NCLB is that in some respects it changed the prevailing definition of *equality* in American education. Throughout most of American history, the dominant understanding of *equality* has been equal opportunity. With NCLB, the definition has broadened to include equality of outcome. As Crawford (2007) observes: "Eliminating achievement gaps is paramount among the law's goals; equal educational opportunity is not" (p. 31).

Although freedom and equality appear to be the major values undergirding NCLB, a study of the law's history suggests that economic growth is actually the dominant value. The achievement gap between white children and most minority children, as well as the gap between the middle class and the poor, is a matter of great concern to many of the nation's leaders. This concern is not necessarily grounded in altruism or compassion. As the economic and demographic data presented in chapter 3 reveal, American school children are increasingly poor and increasingly minority. In addition, large numbers of them do not speak English at home. In the not-too-distant future, these hard to educate children—who historically have not thrived in U.S. schools—will make up a large proportion of the workforce. If they do not achieve well in school, they are likely to lower the overall quality of the labor pool, making it difficult for the American economy to compete well with other countries. It is primarily for this reason that business and political leaders are so concerned about the achievement gap, not because they are champions of equality in the abstract.

LOWI'S POLICY TYPES.   Although technically states are free to decide whether to accept funding under NCLB, in reality, after having received hundreds of millions of dollars in ESEA funding annually since the mid-1960s, few states found it easy to suddenly start to refuse those funds in 2002. Yet operating under NCLB means dealing with a heavy regulatory burden. The law is filled with mandates that have dramatically changed the way that many American schools operate. Teachers must teach to the state content standards; students must be tested regularly; districts must worry about which teachers are "highly qualified" and which are not; test data must be studied and plans developed to improve the learning of certain groups of students. If schools are found to be "failing" under the law, then states and districts must impose sanctions that are spelled out in detailed regulations. Thus, it would seem that the new "accountability regime" is also very much a "regulatory regime."

The strongly regulatory nature of the law should not, however, blind observers to its redistributive potential. As school districts strive to eliminate the achievement gaps revealed by their test data, they may find that they have to pour more resources into the education of poor children, minority children, children with disabilities, and English language learners. Because it is unlikely that the federal government will provide all the funding necessary for such remedial efforts, districts may have to reduce their financial support for programs geared toward those students who do well on the tests, such as gifted programs, AP classes, and the like. As they begin to pursue this course of action, NCLB will be revealed as redistributive as well as regulatory, leading to some very interesting political conflicts.

INSTITUTIONAL CHOICE.   Both Democrats and Republicans have gone on record as wanting to "reinvent" government, making it less complex and bureaucratic; therefore, it is ironic that NCLB greatly increases the bureaucratic complexity of American education. Yet, this is exactly what the reforms advocated by those who would extend the Common School through more standardized curriculum and assessment have long implied. Implementing a law like NCLB requires a lot of work for a lot of people; inevitably, many of these people are bureaucrats. At the federal level, the law clearly expands the size and power of the U.S. Department of Education. In Washington, people have had to take on such tasks as evaluating state standards and assessment programs to see if they meet the requirements of the law. Not surprisingly, since the passage of NCLB, the U.S. Department of Education "has been reorganized to facilitate the agency's new focus on student achievement and state compliance" (McGuinn, 2006, p. 182). The impact on state departments of education has also been great. At the state level, people—most of whom work in state departments of education—have had to develop academic content standards, plan testing programs, assess the credentials of teachers and instructional aides to determine if they are "highly qualified," develop methods of assessing AYP, and perform many other tasks related to NCLB. In an interview with McGuinn (2006), Sally Sullivan, a spokesperson for the Council of Chief State School Officers, described NCLB's impact on the states this way: "NCLB is a huge, huge shift for states. . . . Under the new law it's 'you have to have these things in place, you've got to do it on this timeframe, you have to produce and report the information this way'" (p. 182). Nor is the bureaucratization limited to the national and state levels of education governance. Many school districts have had to expand their central offices in order to deal effectively with such tasks as running the testing program, analyzing test data, and planning professional development for teachers. To be sure, NCLB includes a small component of marketization; parents of children in schools that do not make AYP must be allowed to send their children to a public school within the district that is successful. However, currently, the institution that NCLB most promotes is bureaucracy, not the market.

INTERNATIONAL CONVERGENCE.   Not surprisingly, NCLB also represents considerable convergence toward international norms. After all, during the 1980s and 1990s, many education reformers enjoyed making negative comparisons of American education to the educational systems of such countries as Japan, South Korea, and Germany, often implying that the clearest path to education improvement was the emulation of the methods used in other nations. Frequently, these reformers mentioned one particular aspect of the education systems in other countries that they admired: their national curricula, standards, and tests. Significantly, they usually did not mention other important components of family and education policy, such as universal health care, widely available preschools, and highly professionalized teaching staffs. Nor did they point out that few other countries use standardized or multiple-choice tests for their national assessments. Instead, guided both by their values and their pocketbooks, they carefully selected some aspects of the education systems of other countries while ignoring others. Nonetheless, it is true that under NCLB, American public education has moved closer to the education policies typical of most other developed countries. With its new powers, the U.S. Department of Education resembles the ministries of education in other countries more than it used to. Also, of course, the adoption of standards and tests throughout the nation moves the United States closer to the education paradigms seen abroad.

Will NCLB Be Repealed?

Technically, the ESEA—of which NCLB was the 2002 version—should have been reauthorized by the 2007-2008 Congress, but the reauthorization stalled at that time. The 2009-2010 Congress, which met during the first two years of the Obama Administration, focused on economic policy and ways to bring the country out of the Great Recession, rather than on education policy. In the spring of 2010, the Obama Administration signaled its intention to move forward with ESEA by publishing *A Blueprint for Reform*, which maintained NCLB's emphasis on standards and accountability while arguing that NCLB was flawed and that those flaws should be addressed by the new federal education law. Among the flaws identified were the earlier law's focus on punishing failure rather than rewarding success, its unrealistic timeline for reaching 100% proficiency, and its method of assessing annual yearly progress, which did not distinguish fundamentally good schools that had problems in one or two areas from very weak schools that were failing in virtually every way possible (Berry & Herrington, 2011). Clearly, the Obama Administration hoped that Congress would reauthorize ESEA in 2010 or early 2011.

The 2010 congressional election, however, greatly slowed down the process. Not only did the Republicans take control of the House of Representatives, but many of the newly elected representatives were members of the Tea Party Movement and firmly opposed to any federal role in education policy. Moreover, the Obama Administration's espousal of such controversial policies as using student test scores in evaluating teachers somewhat alienated the teachers' unions, traditionally strong supporters of Democratic administrations. As a result, the politics involved in passing a reauthorization bill became extremely complex, and still are as of this writing in mid-2011 (Jennings, 2010; Toch, 2011). Therefore, at this point it is impossible to predict what will ultimately happen to NCLB.

What *is* currently happening, however, is that although NCLB officially remains on the books, the Department of Education is increasingly willing to make exceptions to its harsher provisions. For example, in 2008—when George Bush was still president—the Department developed a program called Differentiated Accountability and invited states to apply for waivers from NCLB's rigid accountability components if they proposed more flexible yet acceptable ways to deal effectively with schools that did not make AYP (Berry & Herrington, 2011). Obama's Secretary of Education, Arne Duncan, has been an even more liberal granter of waivers from various NCLB requirements. In 2009 alone he granted 315 waivers. In comparison, Secretary Rod Paige granted only 8 waivers from 2002 to 2004, and Secretary Margaret Spellings granted only 91 in her four years as secretary (McNeil, 2011). For the time being, then, NCLB will probably remain on the books but be implemented flexibly.

However, no one should interpret these developments as meaning that standards-based accountability is going to suddenly vanish from the American policy landscape. Support for this general approach to education reform is broad-based and strong. NCLB may be progressively altered through a generous approach to implementation, and the next iteration of ESEA may be more realistic, but the basic concepts that undergird NCLB are likely to remain popular for the foreseeable future.

What, Then, Should Education Leaders Do?

Faced with the continuation of an unpopular law, education leaders must think and plan carefully as they steer their schools and school systems through the troubled seas created by NCLB. Following are three recommendations.

Education leaders should not launch a frontal attack on the concept of accountability. When schools are struggling under the burden of excessive testing and many find themselves unfairly labeled "failing," a lot of people in education are tempted to believe that the problem is accountability itself; therefore, they launch criticisms of this central component of NCLB. However, educators who choose this course of action are choosing to wield a double-edged sword that has the potential to damage them more than it damages their opponents. It is extremely difficult for people whose salaries are paid with public money and who operate schools and school systems using public money to sound credible when they object to standards and assessments. Rather, they sound as if they fear public scrutiny by politicians, the media, and the general public. Therefore, education leaders must be careful not to appear to oppose accountability in and of itself.

Rather than oppose the accountability system included in NCLB, education leaders should say that they support accountability, but believe that the NCLB form of it must be improved. A careful reading of Chapter 11 suggests that as an evaluation plan, NCLB is deeply flawed. Numerous flaws could be identified, but this discussion focuses on just one. NCLB relies on a single measure of school success; depending on what sorts of tests states choose to use, that measure is likely to be extremely inaccurate. Moreover, because the law relies on such a very restricted indicator—test scores—it encourages pathological effects. These include narrowing the curriculum to those subjects tested; teaching to the tests; and cheating on the tests by students as well as, unfortunately, by teachers and administrators. Therefore, education leaders should first study the testing program adopted by their state carefully, asking themselves such questions as: Are the tests used norm-referenced or criterion-referenced? Are they really aligned with our state's academic standards? Are all the questions multiple choice or other types of objective questions, or are the children also given a chance to write essays or demonstrate how to solve a problem? If the tests fall short in any of these areas, then they should work with state officials to modify the assessment program.

Next, education leaders must inform themselves about more holistic approaches to educational evaluation and encourage both state and federal officials to use them. For example, it is possible to rate schools not only on how many children have reached a certain level of proficiency at a given point in time, as NCLB currently does, but also on how much the students have improved over time. This latter type of assessment is called *value-added evaluation*, and often yields results strikingly different from those approaches that merely assess children's average scores at a given point in time. A 2004 study supported by the Educational Testing Service found that when scores on the National Assessment of Educational Progress (NAEP) were reanalyzed to see how much

African American students improved between fourth and eighth grades in various states, an interesting picture emerged. Although the District of Columbia had the lowest average proficiency score in the study, it also led the country in the degree of improvement shown by African American students over a four-year period. Similarly, California's average score was close to the bottom, but it ranked second in student improvement. Of course, some states, such as Virginia and New York, ranked close to the top on both measures; and others, such as Alabama, were close to the bottom on both (Reid, 2004). One problem with NCLB as originally written is that a school in which students are making good progress, but still rate low on the tests, is rated "failing," as is a school that is low in *both* areas. Surely, some distinction should be made between such schools.

Education leaders should also encourage state and federal officials to consider using indicators other than test scores. For example, drop-out and attendance rates could also be determined as well as measures of school climate; and educators could be asked to keep student work samples for evaluation (Popham, 2004). Using a broader range of indicators would provide a more accurate picture of how well schools are doing; it would also reduce some of the pathological effects apparent under the first version of NCLB.

Education leaders should learn more about the foreign school systems with which American schools are often compared. Unfortunately, few American education leaders have ever visited a school in another country, much less taught in one. Probably they have not read many books or articles about them, either. However, they should begin to make learning about other school systems a top priority. For many years, policymakers and other national leaders have used comparisons of American education with its international competitors as a powerful way to argue for changes in American schools. Yet often their arguments are based on shallow and incomplete knowledge of what really happens in other school systems; as a result, they advocate reforms that are based on serious misconceptions. NCLB is one of these reforms. Although it is true that many other developed countries have adopted a national curriculum and require children to take state or national tests over that curriculum, it is not true that their assessment programs resemble those set up under NCLB. For example, the United Kingdom has long had a testing program for school children that includes the famous "A" and "O" level tests. However, it also has a long tradition of school "inspection." Periodically, school "inspectors" visit British schools to observe what is going on in them. They look at test scores, to be sure, but also at many other measures of successful work with young people. The school inspection adds a qualitative element to the evaluation of British schools (Grace, 1995). Thus, the tests are balanced by a more holistic assessment of the work of teachers and principals. Similarly, France has had a national testing program since the nineteenth century. However, the tests are not objective ones, but are based on essay writing, problem solving, and performance. At the high school level, they even include oral examinations. These tests, which measure higher-level thinking skills as well as factual knowledge, do not have as many pathological effects as purely objective tests do. Moreover, although the high school tests are high-stakes tests that determine students' academic futures, the tests given at lower levels of the school system are used formatively both to plan instruction in the schools and to identify areas where more professional development is necessary (Fowler, 2001). Both the British and French assessment systems are more holistic—and probably more accurate—than NCLB. It is time for American educational leaders to start using international examples of accountability systems to counter the narrowly focused ones that political leaders in the United States favor.

FINAL POINTS

This book was originally written to give education leaders the theoretical foundation and practical knowledge that they would need if they wanted to try to influence the policy process. In 1997, when the first edition was written, it was important for education leaders to have input into education policy—with the passage of NCLB, it became crucial. Standards-based accountability is not going to vanish in the foreseeable future, but it is going to change. An ongoing policy debate will surround those changes. Education leaders should be involved in that debate at the local, state, and federal levels. Such involvement is not an optional activity for a few leaders who enjoy politics; it is a central component of leading an education organization in an age of accountability.

QUESTIONS FOR DISCUSSION

1. What elements of the education policy of the Young Republic, the Common School Movement, and the Scientific Sorting Machine are evident in your school district?
2. List the major education reforms and reform proposals that have emerged in your state in the past decade. Group them into the three categories discussed in this chapter. What tendencies do you notice?
3. How have standards-based accountability and high-stakes tests affected education in your school?
4. What evidence have you seen of the "pathological effects" of the indicators embedded in NCLB?

INTERNET ASSIGNMENT

Use the Internet to explore the Web site of the Ministry of Education in another country. What are the major education policy issues mentioned on the site? What type of accountability system does this country seem to have?

FOR FURTHER READING

Bryk, A. S., Sebring, P. B., Allensworth, E., Luppescu, S., & Easton, J. Q. (2010). *Organizing schools for improvement: Lessons from Chicago.* Chicago: University of Chicago Press.

Drawing on a 15-year longitudinal study of reform in Chicago elementary schools, Bryk and his team identified five key factors that distinguished schools that improved from those that did not. The authors concluded that it is possible for urban schools to improve, but that facing unpleasant facts about race and class is the prerequisite for widespread school improvement in our big cities.

Callahan, R. E. (1962). *Education and the cult of efficiency*. Chicago: University of Chicago Press.

This is a classic study of the efficiency revolution of the early twentieth century, which transformed schools and education administration. It clearly indicates the educational costs associated with early attempts to make schools more business-like.

Chubb, J., & Moe, T. (1990). *Politics, markets, and America's schools*. Washington, D.C.: Brookings Institution.

This very readable book critiques the institutional structure of schools as it existed in 1990 and argues that school choice (in the form of vouchers) will solve many of the current ills of public education in the United States. It helped to launch the movement to expand school choice, which is still popular in the United States.

Perkinson, H. J. (1991). *The imperfect panacea*, 4th ed. New York: McGraw-Hill.

Perkinson's history of education in the United States focuses on how Americans have sought over the years to solve broader social problems by reforming education. It alerts readers to the ways that the schools are still used to address problems that originate elsewhere.

Ravitch, D. (2010). *The death and life of the great American school system*. New York: Basic Books.

The subtitle of Ravitch's book says it all: *How testing and choice are undermining education*. Once a strong supporter of both high-stakes tests and school choice, Ravitch has changed her mind. In her book she presents the evidence that persuaded her.

GLOSSARY

agenda Those policy issues that politicians and other influential people are seriously considering.

agenda setting The process of deciding which policy issues will be on the agenda; the second stage of the policy process.

bill A draft of a proposed statute law that has been introduced into a legislature for its consideration, or is about to be introduced.

budget process The steps involved in proposing a budget for the federal government or a state government, negotiating its content, and getting it passed into law.

capacity building A policy instrument that involves investing large sums of money in developing, over time, the ability of individuals or groups to act more effectively.

case law The body of opinions written by judges to explain how they have interpreted or applied the law in specific cases.

cost analysis A procedure for estimating all the tangible costs of a policy.

cost-effectiveness analysis A procedure for comparing alternative policy options to determine which of them offers the best combination of effectiveness and reasonable cost.

evaluation A form of applied research designed to determine how well a policy is working; the sixth stage of the policy process.

federalism A system of government in which the central government and subsidiary governments share sovereign power; the United States, Canada, and Germany have federal governments.

foundation An endowed organization that sponsors policy research and its dissemination.

hortatory policy A policy instrument that involves the government using various methods to persuade citizens to perform a desired action.

ideology A systematic but rather simplified understanding of how the economy, the political system, and society actually work and should ideally work.

implementation Putting a policy into practice; the fifth stage of the policy process.

inducement A policy instrument that governments use when they offer special funds or privileges to citizens in order to get them to behave in a desired way; grants are inducements.

interest group An organization that works actively to influence policy.

issue definition The process by which a problem is transformed into an issue that a government could address; the first stage of the policy process.

lobbying The process of trying to influence policy, especially a legislature.

mandate A policy instrument that requires everyone to perform a desired action or suffer some kind of penalty.

mobilization of bias The institutionalization of power in organizations, traditions, and customs in such a way that people are differentially empowered and disempowered without any individual acting overtly to influence them; the second dimension of power.

policy actors People and groups who are involved in the policy process.

policy adoption The process by which a legislature, an agency, or a court approves a written version of a policy.

policy analysis A systematic procedure for describing a policy and making its implications clear.

policy formulation The process by which a legislature, an agency, or a court develops a written version of a potential policy.

policy issue A public controversy over how the government should act in a particular instance.

policymaker Any policy actor who has the authority to approve or promulgate a policy.

policy network Loose national coalitions of organizations that work to influence policy in a specific area; the Education Commission of the States is a policy network.

political culture A collective way of thinking about politics that includes an understanding of the political process and beliefs about how politicians should act.

power The ability to influence the behavior or beliefs of others.

program An institutionalized project.

project A short-term activity, often associated with a grant.

rules Regulations that are developed by administrative agencies and interpret or provide details to go with a statute.

shaping of consciousness The systematic inculcation of a set of ideas about the general worth and proper role of another person or a group of people; the third dimension of power.

statute A law passed by a legislative body.

system change A policy instrument that involves shifting power or resources from one set of people to another.

terminate Ending a policy because it has accomplished its purpose or is ineffective; ideally, the final stage of the policy process.

think tanks Policy-planning organizations, often funded by private money, that do research or disseminate their positions in an effort to affect policy, especially issue definition and agenda setting.

APPENDIX

USEFUL WEB SITES FOR FOLLOWING EDUCATION POLICY*

U.S. Government

House of Representatives—*house.gov/*

United States Senate—*senate.gov/*

U.S. Department of Education—*ed.gov/*

U.S. Supreme Court—*supremecourt.gov/*

White House—*whitehouse.gov/*

Education Organizations

American Association of School Administrators—*aasa.org/*

American Federation of Teachers—*aft.org/*

Association for Supervision and Curriculum Development—*ascd.org/*

Council for Exceptional Children—*cec.sped.org/*

National Association for Elementary School Principals—*naesp.org/*

National Association for Secondary School Principals—*nassp.org/*

National Education Association—*nea.org/*

National School Boards Association—*nsba.org/*

Parent–Teacher Association—*pta.org/*

Foundations, Think Tanks, and Policy Research Institutes

Achieve, Inc.—*achieve.org/*

American Enterprise Institute—*aei.org/*

Bill & Melinda Gates Foundation– *gatesfoundation.org/*

Brookings Institution—*brookings.edu/*

Carnegie Corporation of New York—*carnegie.org/*

Center on Education Policy—*cep-dc.org/*

Consortium for Policy Research in Education—*cpre.wceruw.org/*

Economic Policy Institute—*epi.org/*

Education Trust—*edtrust.org*

Ford Foundation—*fordfoundation.org/*

Heritage Foundation—*heritage.org/*

RAND—*rand.org/*

Rockefeller Foundation—*rockefellerfoundation.org/*

Thomas B. Fordham Foundation— *edexcellence.net/*

Urban Institute—*urban.org/*

Interest Groups

Americans United for the Separation of Church and State—*au.org/*

Children's Defense Fund—*childrensdefense.org/*

Christian Coalition—*cc.org/*

*Accurate as of August 2011.

National Association for the Advancement of Colored People—*naacp.org/*

National Council of La Raza—*nclr.org/*

Intergovernmental Organizations

Education Commission of the States—*ecs.org/*

National Association of State Boards of Education—*nasbe.org/*

National Conference of State Legislators—*ncsl.org/*

National Governors Association—*nga.org/*

Business Groups

Business Roundtable—*businessbroundtable.org/*

Committee for Economic Development—*ced.org/*

Farm Bureau—*fb.org/*

National Association of Manufacturers—*nam.org/*

U.S. Chamber of Commerce—*uschamber.com/*

Media

Chicago Tribune—chicagotribune.com/

CNN—*cnn.com/*

C-SPAN—*c-span.org/*

Education Week—edweek.org/

FOX News—*foxnews.com/*

Los Angeles Times—latimes.com/

New York Times—nytimes.com/

NPR—*npr.org/*

PBS—*pbs.org/*

USA Today—usatoday.com/

Washington Post—washingtonpost.com/

HOW TO LOCATE GOVERNMENT WEB SITES FOR SPECIFIC STATES*

GO TO: USA.GOV

Select: *State Government,* under "Find Government Agencies"

Select: The specific state that interests you.

*Accurate as of July 2011.

REFERENCES

AASA/American Association of School Administrators. (2011). Available at http://www.aasa.org. Retrieved May 10, 2011.

Abernathy, S. F. (2007). *No Child Left Behind and the public schools*. Ann Arbor, MI: The University of Michigan Press.

About us. Available at http://www.stopopts.org/us.html. Retrieved September 3, 2000.

Abraham, H. J. (1998). *The judicial process* (7th ed.). New York: Oxford University Press.

Abrams, M. H., Donaldson, E. T., Smith, H., Adams, R. M., Monk, S. H., Ford, G. H., & Daiches, D. (Eds.). (1962). *The Norton anthology of English literature*. New York: Norton.

Access: Education Finance Litigation, School Funding Policy and Advocacy. (n.d.). "State by State." Available at http://www.schoolfunding.info/states/state_by_state.php3. Retrieved January 23, 2007.

Ackerman, K. (2004, March 10). Study: Schools shift from liberal arts. [Hamilton, OH] *Journal–News*, D4.

AFT: A Union of Professionals. (2011). Available at http://www.aft.org. Retrieved May 9, 2011.

Alexander, K., & Alexander, M. D. (2008). *American public school law* (6th ed.). Belmont, CA: Thomson West.

Almond, G. A. (1990). *A discipline divided: Schools and sects in political science*. Newbury Park, CA: Sage.

American Federation of Teachers. (1995). *What college-bound students abroad are expected to know*. Washington, D.C.: Author.

American heritage dictionary of the English language, The (4th ed.) (2000). Available at http://www.bartleby.com/reference. Retrieved December 1, 2006.

Anderson, J. E. (2003). *Public policymaking* (5th ed.). Boston: Houghton Mifflin.

Apple, M. W. (1985). *Education and power*. Boston: Ark Paperbacks.

Apple, M. W. (2006). *Educating the "right" way* (2nd ed.). New York: Routledge.

Arendt, H. (1986). Communicative power. In S. Lukes (Ed.), *Power* (pp. 59–74). New York: New York University Press.

Bachrach, P., & Baratz, M. S. (1962). Two faces of power. *American Political Science Review, 56*, 947–952.

Bachrach, P., & Botwinick, A. (1992). *Power and empowerment*. Philadelphia: Temple University Press.

Bailey, M. R., Rich, B. A., & Bennett, S. (2010). Crisis planning to manage risks posed by animal rights extremists. *ILAR Journal, 51*, 138–148.

Baker, K. (1991). Yes, throw money at schools. *Phi Delta Kappan, 72*, 628–631.

Ball, S. J. (1990). *Politics and policy making in education: Explorations in policy sociology*. London: Routledge.

Bannon, B. (2011, June 2). Is the Tea Party killing the Republican Party? [Opinion]. Available at http://www.usnews.com/opinion/blogs/brad-bannon/2011/06/02/is-tea-party-killing-the-republican-party. Retrieved June 5, 2011.

Bardach, E. (1977). *The implementation game*. Cambridge, MA: The MIT Press.

Barstow, D. (2010, February 16). Tea Party lights fuse for rebellion on right. *New York Times*. Available at http://www.nytimes.com/2010/02/16/us/politics/16teaparty.html. Retrieved May 10, 2011.

Bartlett, B. (2009). *The new American economy*. New York: PalgraveMacmillan.

Bartlett, B. R. (1981). *Reaganomics*. Westport, CT: Arlington House.

Bartow Parents Against Bullying. (2011). Available at http://www.bartowparentsagainstbullying.org. Retrieved May 24, 2011.

Baum, L. (2006). State courts in their political environment. In C. E. Van Horn (Ed.), *The state of the states* (4th ed., pp. 81–100). Washington, D.C.: CQ Press.

Baum, L. (2010). *The Supreme Court* (10th ed.). Washington, D.C.: CQ Press.

Baumann, E. A. (1989). Research, rhetoric and the social construction of elder abuse. In J. Best (Ed.), *Images of issues* (pp. 55–74). New York: deGruyter.

Baumgartner, F. R., & Jones, B. D. (2009). *Agendas and instability in American politics* (2nd ed.). Chicago: University of Chicago Press.

Beem, K. (2006). Caught in the middle. *School Administrator, 63*(9), 16–25.

Bell, C. A. (2009). All choices created equal? The role of choice sets in the selection of schools. *Peabody Journal of Education, 84*, 191–208.

Bellah, R. N., Madsen, R., Sullivan, W. M., Swidler, A., & Tipton, S. M. (1996). *Habits of the heart* (updated ed.). Berkeley, CA: University of California Press.

Bendix, R. (1977). *Max Weber*. Berkeley, CA: University of California Press.

Berkman, M. B., & Plutzer, E. (2005). *Ten thousand democracies: American governance and public policy*. Washington, D.C.: Georgetown University Press.

Berliner, D. C., & Biddle, B. J. (1995). *The manufactured crisis: Myths, fraud, and the attack on*

America's public schools. Reading, MA: Addison Wesley.

Berman, P., & McLaughlin, M. W. (1976). Implementation of educational innovation. *The Educational Forum, 40,* 345–370.

Berman, P., & McLaughlin, M. W. (1978). *Federal programs supporting educational change, Vol. VIII: Implementing and sustaining innovations.* Santa Monica, CA: Rand.

Bernhard-Bubb, H. (2004a, August 3). Divided Dover board OKs biology text; Minority also wants book on 'intelligent design' *The York Dispatch* (York, PA). Available at http://web.lexis-nexis.com/universe/docum. Retrieved, October 13, 2006.

Bernhard-Bubb, H. (2004b, November 2). 'Design' bedevils school board. *The York Dispatch* (York, PA). Available at http://web.lexis-nexis.com/universe/docum. Retrieved October 13, 2006.

Bernhard-Bubb, H. (2004c, November 19). Four get seats in Dover. *The York Dispatch* (York, PA). Available at http://web.lexis-nexis.com/universe/docum. Retrieved October 13, 2006.

Bernhard-Bubb, H. (2004d, December 2). Dover lawsuit looms. *The York Dispatch* (York, PA). Available at http://web.lexis-nexis.com/universe/docum. Retrieved October 13, 2006.

Bernhard-Bubb, H. (2004e, December 7). Another Dover school board member quits. *The York Dispatch* (York, PA). Available at http://web.lexis-nexis.com/universe/docum. Retrieved, October 13, 2006.

Bernstein, B. (1996). *Pedagogy, symbolic control, and identity.* London: Taylor & Francis.

Berry, K. S., & Herrington, C. D. (2011). States and their struggles with NCLB: Does the Obama blueprint get it right? *Peabody Journal of Education, 86,* 272–290.

Best, J. (1989a). Afterword. In J. Best (Ed.), *Images of issues* (pp. 243–253). New York: deGruyter.

Best, J. (1989b). Claims. In J. Best (Ed.), *Images of issues* (pp. 1–3). New York: deGruyter.

Best, J. (1989c). Dark figures and child victims: Statistical claims about missing children. In J. Best (Ed.), *Images of issues* (pp. 21–37). New York: deGruyter.

Beyer, B. K. (1995). *How to conduct a formative evaluation.* Alexandria, VA: Association for Curriculum and Program Development.

Beyle, T. L. (2001). *State and local government, 2001–2002.* Washington, D.C.: Congressional Quarterly Press.

Björk, L. G., & Gurley, D. K. (2005). Superintendent as educational statesman and political strategist.

In L. G. Björk & T. J. Kowalski (Eds.), *The contemporary superintendent* (pp. 163–185). Thousand Oaks, CA: Corwin Press.

Blank, R. M. (2000). Strong employment, low inflation: How has the US economy done so well? *Canadian Public Policy, 26* (Special Supplement), S175–S186.

Bodilly, S. J. (1998). *Lessons from New American Schools' scale-up phase.* Santa Monica, CA: RAND Education.

Bootel, J. A. (1995). *CEC special education advocacy handbook.* Reston, VA: Council for Exceptional Children.

Bowen, B. (n.d.). History of the Tea Party movement. Available at http://www.infoplease.com/us/government/tea-party-history.html. Retrieved June 17, 2011.

Bowman, A. O., & Kearney, R. C. (1986). *The resurgence of the states.* Upper Saddle River, NJ: Prentice Hall.

Bowman, A. O'M., & Kearney, R. C. (2004). *State and local government: The essentials.* Boston: Houghton Mifflin Harcourt.

Boyd, W. L. (1984). Competing values in educational policy and governance: Australian and American developments. *Educational Administration Review, 2,* 4–24.

Boyd, W. L., & Kerchner, C. T. (1988). Introduction and overview: Education and the politics of excellence and choice. In W. L. Boyd & C. T. Kerchner (Eds.), *The politics of excellence and choice in education* (pp. 1–11). London: Taylor & Francis.

Boyd, W. L., Lugg, C. A., & Zahorchak, G. L. (1996). Social traditionalists, religious conservatives, and the politics of outcome-based education. *Education and Urban Society, 28,* 347–365.

Brainard, E. A. (1996). *A hands-on guide to school program evaluation.* Bloomington, IN: Phi Delta Kappa Educational Foundation.

Brewer, G. D., & de Leon, P. (1983). *The foundations of policy analysis.* Homewood, IL: Dorsey.

Brouwer, S. (1998). *Sharing the pie.* New York: Henry Holt.

Brown, C. A., & Wright, T. S. (2011). The rush toward universal public Pre-K: A media analysis. *Educational Policy, 25,* 115–133.

Brunner, C. C., & Björk, L. G. (Eds.). (2001). *The new superintendency.* Kidlington, Oxford, U.K.: Elsevier Science, Ltd.

Brunner, C. C., & Grogan, M. (2007). *Women leading school systems.* Lanham, MD: Rowman & Littlefield Education.

Buchholz, T. G. (1989). *New ideas from dead economists*. New York: New American Library.

Bundy, A. L. (2005, Fall). Aligning systems to create full-service schools: The Boston experiences, so far. *New Directions for Youth Development, 107,* 71–80.

Burbules, N. C. (1986). A theory of power in education. *Educational Theory, 36,* 95–114.

Burke, F. G. (1990). *Public education: Who's in charge?* New York: Praeger.

Burron, A. (1994). Traditionalist Christians and OBE: What's the problem? *Educational Leadership, 51*(6), 73–75.

Business cycle expansions and contractions. Available at http://www.nber.org/cycles.html. Retrieved August 23, 2006.

Callahan, R. E. (1962). *Education and the cult of efficiency*. Chicago: University of Chicago Press.

Carl, J. (1994). Parental choice as national policy in England and the United States. *Comparative Education Review, 38,* 294–322.

Carter, G. R., & Cunningham, W. G. (1997). *The American school superintendent*. San Francisco: Jossey-Bass.

Cavanagh, S. (2011). States hurt as stimulus loses steam. *Education Week, 30*(27), 1, 32–33.

Children's Defense Fund. (n.d.). Available at http://www.childrensdefense.org. Retrieved June 30, 2011.

Chubb, J., & Moe, T. (1990). *Politics, markets, and America's schools*. Washington, D.C.: Brookings Institution.

Cibulka, J. G. (1995). Policy analysis and the study of the politics of education. In J. D. Scribner & D. Layton (Eds.), *The study of educational politics* (pp. 105–125). London: Falmer Press.

Clark, E. (2000, December 16). School leaders advocate state testing reform. [Hamilton, OH] *Journal-News*, pp. A1, A2.

Clemons, R. S., & McBeth, M. K. (2008). *Public policy praxis* (2nd ed.). New York: Pearson Longman.

Clune, W. H. (1994a). The cost and management of program adequacy: An emerging issue in educational policy and finance. *Educational Policy, 8,* 365–375.

Clune, W. H. (1994b). The shift from equity to adequacy in school finance. *Educational Policy, 8,* 376–394.

Cobb, P., McClain, K., Lamberg, T. S., & Dean, C. (2003). Situating teachers' instructional practices in the institutional setting of the school and district. *Educational Researcher, 32*(6), 13–24.

Cobb, R. W., & Elder, C. D. (1972). *Participation in American politics: The dynamics of agenda building*. Boston: Allyn & Bacon.

Coburn, C. E. (2001). Collective sensemaking about reading: How teachers mediate reading policy in their professional communities. *Educational Evaluation and Policy Analysis, 23,* 145–170.

Coburn, C. E. (2003). Rethinking scale: Moving beyond numbers to deep and lasting change. *Educational Researcher, 32*(6), 3–12.

Coburn, C. E. (2005). The role of nonsystem actors in the relationship between policy and practice: The case of reading instruction in California. *Educational Evaluation and Policy Analysis, 27,* 23–52.

Coburn, C. E., & Stein, M. K. (2006). Communities of practice theory and the role of teacher professional community in policy implementation. In M. I. Honig (Ed.), *New directions in education policy implementation* (pp. 25–46). Albany, NY: State University of New York Press.

Cohen, D. K., & Spillane, J. P. (1993). Policy and practice: The relations between governance and instruction. In S. H. Fuhrman (Ed.), *Designing coherent education policy* (pp. 35–95). San Francisco: Jossey-Bass.

Colorado General Assembly. (2011). Available at http://www.leg.state.co.us. Retrieved July 14, 2011.

Congress A to Z. (3rd ed.) (1999). Washington, D.C.: Congressional Quarterly Press.

Consortium for Policy Research in Education. (n.d.). *Research agenda and recent publications list*. N.P.: Author.

Cookson, P. W., Jr. (1994). *School choice: The struggle for the soul of American education*. New Haven, CT: Yale University Press.

Coombs, P. H. (1984). *The world crisis in education*. New York: Oxford University Press.

Cooper, B. S., Fusarelli, L. D., & Carella, V. A. (2000). *Career crisis in the school superintendency?* Arlington, VA: American Association of School Administrators.

Cooper, R., Slavin, R. E., & Madden, N. A. (1998). Success for All: Improving the quality of implementation of whole-school change through the use of a national reform network. *Education and Urban Society, 30,* 385–408.

Coplin, W. D., & O'Leary, M. K. (1981). *Basic policy studies skills*. Croton-on-Hudson, NY: Policy Studies Associates.

Coplin, W. D., & O'Leary, M. K. (1998). *Basic policy studies skills* (3rd ed.). Croton-on-Hudson, NY: Policy Studies Associates.

Corson, D. (1993). *Language, minority education and gender*. Clevedon, U.K.: Multilingual Matters.

Corson, D. (1995). Discursive power in educational organizations: An introduction. In D. Corson (Ed.),

Discourse and power in educational organizations (pp. 3–15). Cresskill, NJ: Hampton Press.

Coulter, E. M. (1997). *Principles of politics and government* (6th ed.). Madison, WI: Brown & Benchmark Publishers.

CPRE. (2007). Available at http://cpre.wceruw.org/. Retrieved May 24, 2011.

Crawford, J. (2007). A diminished vision of civil rights. *Education Week, 26*(39), 40, 41.

Crosby, B. C., & Bryson, J. M. (2005). *Leadership for the common good* (2nd ed.). San Francisco: Jossey-Bass.

Dahl, R. (1984). *Modern political analysis* (4th ed.). Upper Saddle River, NJ: Prentice Hall.

Dahl, R. (1986). Power as the control of behavior. In S. Lukes (Ed.), *Power* (pp. 37–58). New York: New York University Press.

Darden, E. C. (2007, November). Dealing with the culture wars. *American School Board Journal*, 42–43.

Datnow, A., Hubbard, L., & Mehan, H. (2002). *Extending educational reform*. London: RoutledgeFalmer.

Datnow, A., McHugh, B., Stringfield, S., & Hacker, D. J. (1998). Scaling up the Core Knowledge Sequence. *Education in Urban Society, 30*, 409–432.

Davies, S., & Guppy, N. (1997). Globalization and educational reforms in Anglo-American democracies. *Comparative Education Review, 41*, 435–459.

Deal, T. E., & Kennedy, A. A. (1982). *Corporate cultures*. Reading, MA: Addison-Wesley.

DeBray, E., Parson, G., & Woodworth, K. (2001). Patterns of response in four high schools under state accountability policies in Vermont and New York. In S. H. Fuhrman (Ed.), *From the capitol to the classroom: Standards-based reform in the states* (pp. 170–192). Chicago: University of Chicago Press.

deKieffer, D. E. (2007). *The citizen's guide to lobbying Congress*. Revised and updated. Chicago: Chicago Review Press.

Delpit, L. D. (1988). The silenced dialogue: Power and pedagogy in educating other people's children. *Harvard Educational Review, 58*, 280–298.

Detwiler, F. (1993/1994, December/January) A tale of two districts. *Educational Leadership, 51*(4), 24–28.

Diane Ravitch: Curriculum vitae. (n.d.). Available at http://www.dianeravitch.com/vita.html. Retrieved May 24, 2011.

Domenech, D. A. (2010). AASA's status check on the superintendency. *School Administrator, 67*(11), 47.

Domestic policy of the George W. Bush administration. (2007). From *Wikipedia, the free encyclopedia*. Available at http://en.wikipedia.org.

George_W._Bush_administration. Retrieved March 26, 2007.

Draut, T. (2005). *Strapped*. New York: Doubleday.

Dreier, P., Mollenkopf, J., & Swanstrom, T. (2001). *Place matters: Metropolitics for the twenty-first century*. Lawrence, KS: The University Press of Kansas.

Dunlap, D. M., & Goldman, P. (1991). Rethinking power in schools. *Educational Administration Quarterly, 27*, 5–29.

Dunn, W. N. (2004). *Public policy analysis* (3rd ed.). Upper Saddle River, NJ: Prentice Hall.

Dye, T. R. (2002). *Who's running America?* (7th ed.). Upper Saddle River, NJ: Prentice Hall.

Ebbing, L. (2000, September 6). Proficiency tests create additions to school curriculum. [Hamilton, OH] *Journal-News*, p. A7.

Economic policy of the George W. Bush administration. (2007). From *Wikipedia, the free encyclopedia*. Available at http://en.wikipedia.org/wiki/Economic_policy_of_the_George_W._Bush_administration. Retrieved March 26, 2007.

ECRI: Economic Cycle Research Institute. (2011). Business cycle peak and trough dates, 22 countries, 1948-2010. Available at http://www.businesscycle.com/resources.cycles. Retrieved August 5, 2011.

Edelman, M. (1964). *The symbolic uses of politics*. Urbana, IL: University of Illinois Press.

Education Commission of the States. (2011). Available at http://www.ecs.org. Retrieved May 24, 2011.

El Nasser, H., & Overberg, P. (2011, June 3). Ratio of US kids shrinking. *Cincinnati Enquirer*, A1.

Elazar, D. J. (1994). *The American mosaic*. Boulder, CO: Westview Press.

Elazar, D. J. (2003). *The metropolitan frontier and American politics*. New Brunswick, NJ: Transaction.

Encyclopedia Britannica Online: Academic Edition. (n.d.) Available at Miami University Library Web Site: http://searcheb.com.proxy.lib.muohio.edu/eb/article-9055605. Retrieved October 14, 2006.

English, F. W. (1994). Politics in the nation's schools: The battle for the principalship. *NASSP Bulletin, 78*(558), 18–25.

Fabian, J. (2010). Palin urges Republican Party to 'absorb' Tea Party movement. *The Hill*. Available at http://thehill.com/homenews/campaign/80065-palin-urges-republican-party-to-absorb-tea-party-movement. Retrieved June 15, 2011.

Fairclough, N. (2003). *Analyzing discourse*. London: Routledge.

Febey, K. S., & Louis, K. S. (2008). Political cultures in education at the state and local levels: Views from three states. In B. S. Cooper, J. G. Cibulka, & L. D. Fusarelli (Eds.), *Handbook of education politics and policy* (pp. 52–72). New York: Routledge.

Federal Register. January 18, 2002.

Federal Register. February 28, 2002.

Fendler, L. (2010). *Michel Foucault.* London: Continuum.

Firestone, W. A., & Corbett, H. D. (1988). Planned organizational change. In N. J. Boyan (Ed.), *Handbook of research on educational administration* (pp. 321–340). New York: Longman.

First, P. F., Curcio, J. L., & Young, D. L. (1994). State full-service initiatives: New notions of policy development. In L. Adler & S. Gardner (Eds.), *The politics of linking schools and social services* (pp. 63–73). Bristol, PA: Falmer Press.

Foer, F. (2004). Center forward? The fate of the New Democrats. In P. Berkowitz (Ed.), *Varieties of progressivism in America* (pp. 87–104). Stanford, CA: Hoover Institution Press.

Foldvary, F. E. (2007). *The depression of 2008.* Berkeley, CA: The Gutenberg Press.

Ford, P. (1992). American Enterprise Institute for Public Policy Research. In C. H. Weiss (Ed.), *Organizations for policy analysis* (pp. 29–47). Newbury Park, CA: Sage.

Fowler, F. C. (1985). Why reforms go awry. *Education Week, 5*(10), 24, 17.

Fowler, F. C. (1987). The politics of school reform in Tennessee: A view from the classroom. In W. L. Boyd & C. T. Kerchner (Eds.), *The politics of excellence and choice in education* (pp. 183–197). London: Taylor & Francis.

Fowler, F. C. (1992). Challenging the assumption that choice is all that freedom means. In F. C. Wendel (Ed.), *Reforms in empowerment, choice, and adult learning* (pp. 15–28). University Park, PA: University Council of Education Administration.

Fowler, F. C. (1995a). The international arena: The global village. In J. Scribner & D. Layton (Eds.), *Politics of Education Association 1994 commemorative yearbook.* London: Taylor & Francis.

Fowler, F. C. (1995b). The neoliberal value shift and its implications for federal education policy under Clinton. *Educational Administration Quarterly, 31,* 38–60.

Fowler, F. C. (1996, April). *Meaningful competition? A study of student movement under interdistrict open enrollment.* Paper presented at the annual meeting of the American Educational Research Association, New York.

Fowler, F. C. (2000). Converging forces: Understanding the growth of state authority over education. In N. D. Theobald & B. Malen (Eds.), *Balancing local control and state responsibility for*

K–12 education (pp. 123–146). Larchmont, NY: Eye on Education.

Fowler, F. C. (2001). Testing, French style. *The Clearing House, 74*(4), 197–200.

Fowler, F. C. (2004). *Policy studies for educational leaders: An introduction* (2nd ed.). Upper Saddle River, NJ: Pearson Education.

Fraser, S., & Freeman, J. B. (2010). The strange history of Tea Party populism. *Salon.* Available at http://www.salon.com/news/feature/2010/05/03/tea-party-populism-history. Retrieved June 11, 2011.

Frieden, J. A. (2006). *Global capitalism.* New York: W. W. Norton.

Friedman, M. (1962). *Capitalism and freedom.* Chicago: University of Chicago Press.

Fuhrman, S. H. (1993). The politics of coherence. In S. H. Fuhrman (Ed.), *Designing coherent education policy* (pp. 1–34). San Francisco: Jossey-Bass.

Fuhrman, S. H. (2001). Introduction. In S. H. Fuhrman (Ed.), *From the capitol to the classroom: Standards-based reform in the states* (pp. 1–12). Chicago: University of Chicago Press.

Fullan, M. (2001). *The new meaning of educational change* (3rd ed.). New York: Teachers College Press.

Fullan, M. (2007). *The new meaning of educational change* (4th ed.). New York: Teachers College Press.

Galbraith, J. K. (1994). *A journey through economic time.* Boston: Houghton Mifflin.

Garda, R. (2011). The politics of education reform: Lessons from New Orleans. *Journal of Law & Education, 40,* 57–103.

Gaventa, J. (1980). *Power and powerlessness.* Urbana, IL: University of Illinois Press.

Gerth, H., & Mills, C. W. (Eds.). (1946). *From Max Weber: Essays in sociology.* New York: Oxford University Press. Quoted in D. H. Wrong, *Power* (New York: Harper & Row, 1979), 230.

Gewirtz, S. (2000). Bringing the politics back in: A critical analysis of quality discourses in education. *British Journal of Educational Studies, 48,* 352–370.

Gewirtz, S., Ball, S. J., & Bowe, R. (1995). *Markets, choice and equity in education.* Buckingham, U.K.: Open University Press.

Giroux, H. A. (1999). *The mouse that roared.* Lanham, MD: Rowman & Littlefield.

Goldstein, L. (2004). Harvard analysis is critical of 'No Child' law. *Education Week, 23*(23), 9.

Goode, E. (1994). *Site-based management in public education: A challenge for critical pragmatism.* Unpublished doctoral dissertation, Miami University, Oxford, OH.

Graber, D. A. (2010). *Mass media and American politics* (8th ed.). Washington, D.C.: CQ Press.

Grace, G. (1995). *School leadership*. London: Falmer Press.

Grafton, C., & Permaloff, A. (2005). The behavioral study of political ideology and public policy formulations. In C. Grafton & A. Permaloff (Eds.), *The behavioral study of political ideology and public policy formulation* (pp. 173–192). Lanham, MD: University Press of America.

Gray, V. (1996). The socioeconomic and political context of states. In V. Gray & H. Jacob (Eds.), *Politics in the American states* (6th ed., pp. 1–34). Washington, D.C.: Congressional Quarterly Press.

Gronn, P. C. (1983). Talk as the work: The accomplishment of school administration. *Administrative Science Quarterly, 28,* 1–21.

Gross, D. (2009). The recession is . . . over? *The Daily Beast.* Available at www.thedailybeast.com/newsweek/2009/07/13/the-recession-is-over.print.html. Retrieved August 5, 2011.

Gross, N., Giacquinta, J. B., & Bernstein, M. (1971). *Implementing organizational innovations.* New York: Basic Books.

Guthrie, J. W. (2002). Education policy, United States. In J. W. Guthrie (Ed.), *Encyclopedia of Education* (2nd ed., Vol. 2, 668–676). New York: Macmillan Reference.

Guthrie, J. W., & Koppich, J. (1987). Exploring the political economy of national education reform. In W. L. Boyd & C. T. Kerchner (Eds.), *The politics of excellence and choice in education* (pp. 25–47). London: Falmer Press.

Hagan, J. P. (1988). Patterns of activism on state supreme courts. *Publius: The Journal of Federalism, 18*(1), 297–315.

Halberstam, D. (1986). *The reckoning.* New York: Morrow.

Hall, E. T. (1990). *The hidden dimension.* New York: Anchor Books.

Hall, M. G. (2008). State courts: Politics and the judicial process. In V. Gray & R. L. Hanson (Eds.), *Politics in the American states* (9th ed., pp. 229–255). Washington, D.C.: CQ Press.

Halston, W. A. (2004). Incomplete victory: The rise of the New Democrats. In P. Berkowitz (Ed.), *Varieties of progressivism in America* (pp. 59–85). Stanford, CA: Hoover Institution Press.

Hamann, E. T., & Lane, B. (2004). The roles of state departments of education as policy intermediaries: Two cases. *Educational Policy, 18*(3), 426–255.

Hamm, K. E., & Moncrief, G. R. (1999). Legislative politics in the states. In V. Gray, R. L. Hanson, & H. Jacob (Eds.), *Politics in the American states* (7th ed., pp. 144–190). Washington, D.C.: CQ Press.

Hamm, K. E., & Moncrief, G. R. (2004). Legislative politics in the states. In V. Gray, R. L. Hanson, & H. Jacob (Eds.), *Politics in the American states* (8th ed., pp. 157–193). Washington, D.C.: CQ Press.

Hamm, K. E., & Moncrief, G. R. (2008). Legislative politics in the states. In V. Gray & R. L. Hanson (Eds.), *Politics in the American states* (9th ed., pp. 154–191). Washington, D.C.: CQ Press.

Hannaway, J., & Kimball, K. (2001). Big isn't always bad: School district size, poverty, and standards-based reform. In S. H. Fuhrman (Ed.), *From the capitol to the classroom: Standards-based reform in the states* (pp. 99–123). Chicago: University of Chicago Press.

Hanson, R. L. (2004). Intergovernmental relations. In V. Gray & R. I. Hanson (Eds.), *Politics in the American states* (8th ed.). Washington, D.C.: CQ Press.

Hanushek, E. A. (1989). The impact of differential expenditures on school performance. *Educational Researcher, 18*(4), 45–51, 62.

Hanushek, E. A. (1994). A jaundiced view of "adequacy" in school finance reform. *Educational Policy, 8,* 460–469.

Harragan, B. L. (1977). *Games mother never taught you.* New York: Warner Books.

Hatch, J., & Clinton, A. (2000, December). Job growth in the 1990s: A retrospect. *Monthly Labor Review,* 3–18.

Heclo, H. (1978). Issue networks and the executive establishment. In A. King (Ed.), *The new American political system* (pp. 87–124). Washington, D.C.: American Enterprise Institute for Public Policy Research.

Heilbroner, R. L. (1985). *The nature and logic of capitalism.* New York: Norton.

Henig, J. R. (2009). The politics of localism in an era of centralization, privatization, and choice. *Yearbook of the National Society for the Study of Education (Wiley-Blackwell), 108*(1), 112–129.

Hess, F. M., & Petrilli, M. J. (2006). *No Child Left Behind.* New York: Peter Lang.

Heywood, A. (2007). *Political ideologies: An introduction.* New York: Palgrave Macmillan.

Hilgartner, S., & Bosk, C. L. (1988). The rise and fall of social problems: A public arenas model. *American Journal of Sociology, 94,* 53–78.

Hirschman, A. O. (1970). *Exit, voice, and loyalty.* Cambridge, MA: Harvard University Press.

Historical CPI. (n.d.) Available at http://inflationdat.com/inflation/Consumer_Price_Index/HistoricalCPI.aspx. Retrieved August 23, 2006.

Historical Labor Force/Unemployment Data for UNITED STATES. Available at http://www.nidataplus.com/lfeus1.htm. Retrieved August 23, 2006.

History of Ohio proficiency tests. (n.d.) Available at http://www.stopopts.org/histotybocy.html. Retrieved, September 3, 2000.

Hobbes, T. (1958). *Leviathan.* Indianapolis: BobbsMerrill. Quoted in Wrong, D. H. (1979). *Power* (p. 218). New York: Harper & Row.

Hodgkinson, H. (2000/2001). Educational demographics: What teachers should know. *Educational Leadership, 58*(4), 6–11.

Hoff, D. J. (2002). Panel to examine standards-based math curricula, *Education Week, 21*(40), 5.

Hoff, D. J. (2004). Utah House softens stand on federal education law. *Education Week, 23*(23), 30.

Hoff, D. J. (2006). NCLB panel favors retaining law's core measures. *Education Week, 26*(6), 21–22.

Hofstede, G., & Bond, M. H. (2001). The Confucius connection: From cultural roots to economic growth. In M. J. Gannon (Ed.), *Cultural metaphors* (pp. 31–50). Thousand Oaks, CA: Sage.

Hogwood, B. W., & Gunn, L. A. (1984). *Policy analysis for the real world.* London: Oxford University Press.

Holden, D. J., & Zimmerman, M. A. (2009). Evaluation planning here and now. In D. J. Holden & M. A. Zimmerman (Eds.), *A practical guide to program evaluation planning* (pp. 7–31). Thousand Oaks, CA: SAGE.

Honig, M. I. (2006). Complexity and policy implementation: Challenges and opportunities for the field. In M. I. Honig (Ed.), *New directions in education policy implementation* (pp. 1–23). Albany, NY: State University of New York Press.

House Committee on the Budget, Democratic Staff and Joint Economic Committee, Democratic Staff. (2006). Some perspective on Bush Administration economic claims. Available at http://jec.senate.gov/Documents/Reports/annualreportfinal-2006.pdf. Retrieved March 26, 2007.

Huberman, A. M., & Miles, M. B. (1984). *Innovation up close.* New York: Plenum Press.

Hulten, C. R., & Sawhill, I. V. (1984). *The legacy of Reaganomics: An overview.* Washington, D.C.: Urban Institute.

Hunt, S., Tortora, A., & Mrozowski, J. (2000, September 3). High-stakes state tests raise stress, controversy. *Cincinnati Enquirer,* pp. A1, A10.

Iannaccone, L. (1988). From equity to excellence: Political context and dynamics. In W. L. Boyd & C. T. Kerchner (Eds.), *The politics of excellence and choice in education* (pp. 49–65). London: Falmer Press.

Iannaccone, L., & Lutz, F. W. (1995). The crucible of democracy: The local arena. In J. D. Scribner & D. Layton (Eds.), *The study of educational politics* (pp. 39–52). Washington, D.C.: Falmer Press.

Illinois State University, College of Education. (1997). Status of school finance constitutional litigation. Available at http://www.ilstu.edu/depts/coe/boxscore.htm. Retrieved January 12, 1997.

The immigration wave. (2000, September 27). *Education Week on the Web.* Available at http://www.edweek.org/ew/ewstory.cfm. Retrieved February 25, 2002.

Irons, E. J., & Harris, S. (2007). *The challenges of No Child Left Behind.* Lanham, MD: Rowman & Littlefield Education.

Isaak, A. (1987). *Politics.* Glenview, IL: Scott, Foresman.

Isidore, C. (2008, December 1). It's official: Recession since Dec. '07. *CNN.* Available at http://money.cnn.com/2008/12/01/news/economy/recession/index.htm, Retrieved August 5, 2011.

It's all relative. (2000, September 27). *Education Week on the Web.* Available at http://www.edweek.org/ew/ewstory.cfm. Retrieved February 25, 2002.

Jackson, J. E., & Kingdon, J. W. (1992). Ideology, interest group scores, and legislative votes. *American Journal of Political Science, 36,* 805–823.

Jacob, H. (1996). Courts: The least visible branch. In V. Gray & H. Jacob (Eds.), *Politics in the American states* (6th ed., pp. 253–285). Washington, D.C.: Congressional Quarterly Press.

Jacobs, J. A., & Gerson, K. (2000). Who are the overworked Americans? In L. Golden & D. M. Figart (Eds.), *Working time* (pp. 89–105). London: Routledge.

Jennings, J. F. (1998). *Why national standards and tests?* Thousand Oaks, CA: Sage Publications.

Jennings, J. (2010). The policy and politics of rewriting the nation's main education law. *Phi Delta Kappan, 92*(4), 44–49.

Jensen, D. N. (1985). Judicial activism and special education. (Project Report No. 85–A10, sponsored by the National Institute of Education, Grant No. NIE-G-83-0003.)

Johnson, S. M. (1996). *Leading to change: The challenge of the new superintendency.* San Francisco: Jossey-Bass.

Johnson, S. M., & Papay, J. R. (2010, May). Merit pay for a new generation. *Educational Leadership,* 49–52.

Joint Committee on Standards for Educational Evaluation. (1994). *The program evaluation standards* (2nd ed.). Thousand Oaks, CA: Sage.

Kaestle, C. F. (1983). *Pillars of the republic.* New York: Hill & Wang.

Kagan, R. A. (1986). Regulating business, regulating schools: The problem of regulatory unreasonableness. In D. L. Kirp & D. N. Jensen (Eds.), *School days, rule days* (pp. 64–90). Philadelphia: Falmer Press.

Kahne, J. (1996). *Reframing educational policy.* New York: Teachers College Press.

Kalodner, H. I. (1990). Overview of judicial activism in education litigation. In B. Flicker (Ed.), *Justice and school systems* (pp. 3–22). Philadelphia: Temple University Press.

Kaplan, G. R., & Usdan, M. D. (1992). The changing look of education's policy networks. *Phi Delta Kappan, 73,* 664–672.

Kaplan, M., & O'Brien, S. (1991). *The governors and the new federalism.* Boulder, CO: Westview Press.

Kapp, S. A., & Anderson, G. R. (2010). *Agency-based program evaluation.* Thousand Oaks, CA: SAGE.

Kauffman, C. (2005a, March 14), 18 seek seven school board seats in Dover. *The York Dispatch* (York, PA). Available at http://web.lexis-nexis.com/universe/docum. Retrieved November 9, 2006.

Kauffman, C. (2005b, May 18), Issue draws large number of voters. *The York Dispatch* (York, PA). Available at http://web.lexis-nexis.com/universe/docum. Retrieved November 9, 2006.

Kerwin, C. M., & Furlong, S. R. (2011). *Rulemaking* (4th ed.). Washington, D.C.: CQ Press.

King, J. A. (1994). Meeting the educational needs of at-risk students: A cost analysis of three models. *Educational Evaluation and Policy Analysis, 16,* 1–19.

Kingdon, J. W. (2003). *Agendas, alternatives, and public policies* (3rd ed.). New York: Longman.

Kirp, D. L. (1982). Professionalization as a policy choice: British special education in comparative perspective. *World Politics, 34,* 137–174.

Kirp, D. L. (1986). Introduction: The fourth R: Reading, writing, 'rithmetic—and rules. In D. L. Kirp & D. N. Jensen (Eds.), *School days, rule days* (pp. 1–17). Philadelphia: Falmer Press.

Kirst, M., & Jung, R. (1980). The utility of a longitudinal approach in assessing implementation. *Educational Evaluation and Policy Analysis, 2,* 17–34.

Knoepfel, P., Larrue, C., Varnone, F., & Hill, M. (2007). *Public policy analysis.* Bristol, U.K.: The Policy Press.

Kowalski, T. J. (1995). *Keepers of the flame.* Thousand Oaks, CA: Corwin Press.

Kowalski, T. J. (1999). *The school superintendent.* Upper Saddle River, NJ: Prentice Hall.

Kraft, M. E., & Furlong, S.R. (2007). *Public policy* (2nd ed.). Washington, D.C.: CQ Press.

Krugman, P. (2009). *The return of depression economics and the crisis of 2008.* New York: W. W. Norton.

Kruschke, E. R., & Jackson, B. M. (1987). *The public policy dictionary.* Santa Barbara, CA: ABC–CLIO.

Kuttner, R. (1984). *The economic illusion.* Boston: Houghton Mifflin.

Lagemann, E., & de Forest, J. (2007). What might Andrew Carnegie want to tell Bill Gates? Reflections on the hundredth anniversary of the Carnegie Foundation for the Advancement of Teaching. In R. Bacchetti & T. Ehrlich (Eds.), *Reconnecting education and foundations* (pp. 47–67). San Francisco: Jossey-Bass.

La Morte, M. W. (2005). *School law: Cases and concepts* (8th ed.). Boston: Pearson.

Lawton, M. (1997, August 6). Feds position national tests on fast track. *Education Week,* 1, 34.

Lebo, L. (2004, December 14). Parents plan suit over intelligent design. *The Evening Sun* (Hanover, PA). Available at http://web.lexis-nexis.com/universe/docum. Retrieved October 13, 2006.

Lemke, J. L. (1995). *Textual politics.* London: Taylor & Francis.

Lenkowsky, L., & Piereson, J. (2007). Education and the conservative foundations. In R. Bacchetti & T. Ehrlich (Eds.), *Reconnecting education and foundations* (pp. 347–378). San Francisco: Jossey-Bass.

Levin, H. M., & McEwan, P. J. (2001). *Cost-effectiveness analysis* (2nd ed.). Thousand Oaks, CA: Sage Publications.

Levine, J., Carmines, E. G., & Huckfeldt, R. (2008). The rise of ideology in the post-New Deal party system. In C. Grafton & A. Permaloff (Eds.), *The behavioral study of political ideology and public policy formulation* (pp. 27–42). Lanham, MD: University Press of America.

Lewis, D. A., & Maruna, S. (1996). The politics of education. In V. Gray & H. Jacob (Eds.), *Politics in the American states* (6th ed., pp. 438–477). Washington, D.C.: Congressional Quarterly Press.

Lieberman, J. M. (2002). Three streams and four policy entrepreneurs converge. *Education and Urban Society, 34,* 438–450.

Lindblom, C. E., & Woodhouse, E. J. (1993). *The policy-making process* (3rd ed.). Upper Saddle River, NJ: Prentice Hall.

Lipset, S. M. (1996). *American exceptionalism.* New York: Norton.

Little, J. W. (2003). Inside teacher community: Representations of classroom practice. *Teachers College Record, 105*, 913–945.

Liu, X., Lindquist, E., Vedlitz, A., & Vincent, K. (2010). Understanding local policy-making: Policy elites' perceptions of local agenda setting and alternative policy selection. *Policy Studies Journal 38*, 69–70.

Loomis, B. A. (1994). *Time, politics and policies.* Lawrence, KS: University Press of Kansas.

Lorch, R. S. (1987). *Colorado's government* (4th ed.). Colorado Associated University Press.

Lortie, D. C. (1975). *Schoolteacher.* Chicago: University of Chicago Press.

Louis, K. S., Febey, K., Gordon, M., Meath, J., & Thomas, E. (2006). *Educational leadership in the states: A cultural analysis.* Minneapolis, MN: Center for Applied Research and Educational Improvement, University of Minnesota.

Louis, K. S., & Miles, M. B. (1990). *Improving the urban high school.* New York: Teachers College Press.

Louis, K. S., Leithwood, K., Wahlstrom, K. L., & Anderson, S. E. (2010). *Investigating the links to improved student learning.* St. Paul, MN: University of Minnesota.

Louis, K. S., Thomas, E., Gordon, M. F., & Febey, K. S. (2008). State leadership for school improvement: An analysis of three states. *Educational Administration Quarterly, 44*, 562–592.

Lowi, T. J. (1964, July). American business, public policy, case studies, and political theory. *World Politics*, 677–715.

Lowi, T. J. (1979). *The end of liberalism* (2nd ed.). New York: Norton.

Lowi, T. J. (1995). *The end of the Republican era.* Norman, OK: University of Oklahoma Press.

Lowi, T. J., & Ginsberg, B. (1994). *American government* (brief 3rd ed.). New York: Norton.

Lowi, T.J., Ginsberg, B., & Shepsle, K. A. (2007). *American government: Power and purpose* (10th brief edition). New York: W. W. Norton.

Lugg, C. A. (1996). *For God and country.* New York: Peter Lang.

Lukes, S. (2005). *Power: A radical view* (2nd ed.). Houndsmills, U.K.: Palgrave Macmillan.

Lutz, F. W., & Merz, C. (1992). *The politics of school/community relations.* New York: Teachers College Press.

Madaus, G. F., Stufflebeam, D. L., & Scriven, M. (1983). Program evaluation: A historical overview. In G. F. Madaus, M. Scriven, & D. L. Stufflebeam (Eds.), *Evaluation models* (pp. 23–43). Boston: Kluwer–Nijhoff.

Madsen, J. (1994). *Educational reform at the state level.* Bristol, PA: Falmer Press.

Makin, J. H. (1996). How low should inflation go? *AEI Economic Outlook* [Online serial]. Available at http://www.aei.org/eo/eo6981.htm.

Makin, J. H. (1997). Perils of prosperity. *AEI Economic Outlook* [Online serial]. Available at http://www.aei.org/eo/eo8270.htm.

Maldonado, J. (2005, January 7). Teachers: Statement violates school code. *The Evening Sun* (Hanover, PA). Available at http://web.lexis-nexis.com/universe/docum. Retrieved November 9, 2006.

Malen, B., & Ogawa, R. T. (1988). Professional patron influence on site-based management. *Educational Evaluation and Policy Analysis, 10*, 251–270.

Mann, M. (1992). *The sources of social power. Vol. 1.* Cambridge, England: Cambridge University Press.

Marshall Smith. (n.d.). *Business Week.* Available at http://investing.businessweek.com/businessweek/research/stocks/private/person. Retrieved May 24, 2011.

Marshall, C., Mitchell, D., & Wirt, F. (1989). *Culture and education policy in the American states.* New York: Falmer Press.

Marshall, J. A. (2009). Planning for an education evaluation. In D. J. Holden & M. A. Zimmerman (Eds.), *A practical guide to program evaluation planning* (pp. 33–61). Thousand Oaks, CA: SAGE.

Martin, J. M. (1994). *Lessons from the hill.* New York: St. Martin's Press.

Masters, J. (2011). Militant extremists in the United States. A backgrounder of the Council on Foreign Relations. Available at http://www.cfr.org/terrorist-organizations/militant-extremists-united-states/p9236. Retrieved June 14, 2011.

Mather, M., Pollard, K., & Jacobsen, L. A. (2011). *First results from the 2020 census.* Washington, D.C.: Population Reference Bureau.

Mauriello, T. (2005, December 21). Defeat for intelligent design in U.S. court; Dover, PA, school board requirement unconstitutional, 'sham,' judge says. *Pittsburgh Post-Gazette.* Available at http://web.lexis-nexis.com/universe/docum. Retrieved November 9, 2006.

Mazzoni, T. L. (1993). The changing politics of state education policy making: A 20 year Minnesota perspective. *Educational Evaluation and Policy Analysis, 15*, 357–379.

Mazzoni, T. L. (1995). State policymaking and school reform: Influences and influentials.

In J. D. Scribner & D. H. Layton (Eds.), *The study of educational politics* (pp. 53–73). London: Falmer Press.

McCarthy, M., Langdon, C., & Olson, J. (1993). *State education governance structures.* Denver, CO: Education Commission of the States.

McCarthy, M. M., Cambron-McCabe, N. H., & Thomas, S. B. (2004). *School law: Teachers' and students' rights* (5th ed.). Boston: Pearson.

McDonnell, L. M. (1991). Ideas and values in implementation analysis. In A. R. Odden (Ed.), *Education policy implementation* (pp. 241–258). Albany, NY: State University of New York Press.

McDonnell, L. M. (1994). Assessment policy as persuasion and regulation. *American Journal of Education, 102,* 391–420.

McDonnell, L. M., & Elmore, R. F. (1987). Getting the job done: Alternative policy instruments. *Educational Evaluation and Policy Analysis, 9,* 133–152.

McGann, J. G. (1995). *The competition for dollars, scholars, and influence in the public policy research industry.* Lanham, MD: University Press of America.

McGuinn, P. J. (2006). *No Child Left Behind and the transformation of federal education policy, 1965–2005.* Lawrence, KS: University Press of Kansas.

McLaughlin, M. W. (1976). Implementation as mutual adaptation: Change in classroom organization. *Teachers College Record, 77,* 339–351.

McLaughlin, M. W. (1987). Learning from experience: Lessons from policy implementation. *Educational Evaluation and Policy Analysis, 9,* 171–178.

McNeil, M. (2011). NCLB waivers are plentiful under Duncan. *Education Week, 30*(29), 1, 30.

Miles, M. B., & Louis, K. S. (1990). Mustering the will and skill for change. *Educational Leadership, 47*(8), 57–61.

Mintrom, M. (1997). Policy entrepreneurs and the diffusion of innovation. *American Journal of Political Science, 41,* 738–770.

Mirel, J. (1994). School reform unplugged: The Bensenville New American School project, 1991–93. *American Educational Research Journal, 31,* 481–518.

Mixed needs of immigrants pose challenges for schools. (2000, September 27). *Education Week on the Web.* Available at http://www.edweek .org/ew/ewstory.cfm. Retrieved February 25, 2002.

Morken, H., & Formicola, J. R. (1999). *The politics of school choice.* Lanham, MD: Rowman & Littlefield.

Morrison, P. A. (2001). *A demographic perspective on our nation's future.* Santa Monica, CA: Rand.

Muller-Hill, B. (1988, December 22). Heroes and villains. *Nature,* pp. 721–722.

Mulloy, D. J. (2004). *American extremism.* London: Routledge.

Murphy, J. (1990). *The educational reform movement of the 1980s.* Berkeley, CA: McCutchan.

Murphy, J. T. (1971). Title I of ESEA: The politics of implementing federal education reform. *Harvard Educational Review, 41,* 35–63.

Murray, S. E., Rueben, K., & Rosenberg, C. (2007). State education spending: Current pressures and future trends. *National Tax Journal, 60*(2), 325–345.

Muth, R. (1984). Toward an integrative theory of power and educational organizations. *Educational Administration Quarterly, 20,* 25–42.

Nakamura, R. T., & Smallwood, F. (1980). *The politics of policy implementation.* New York: St. Martin's Press.

NASBE. (n.d.) Available at http://nasbe.org. Retrieved June 30, 2011.

National Association of College and University Business Officers and Commonfund Institute. (2011). NACUBO-Commonfund study of endowments. Available at http://www.nacubo.org/ Research/NACUBO_Endowment_Study.html. Retrieved May 24, 2011.

National Governors Association. (2011). Available at http://www.nga.org. Retrieved April 27, 2011.

National PTA. (2011). Available at http://www.pta. org. Retrieved May 10, 2011.

NEA/National Education Association. (2011). Available at http://www.nea.org. Retrieved May 5, 2011.

Neustadt, R. E. (1960). *Presidential power.* New York: Wiley.

New York Times, The. (1996). *The downsizing of America.* New York: Times Books.

Noguera, P. (2010, September 27). Schools vs. slogans. *The Nation,* 6–8.

NSBA/National School Boards Association. (2011). Available at http://www.nsba.org. Retrieved May 10, 2011.

Nuttall, D. L. (1994). Choosing indicators. In K. A. Riley & D. L. Nuttall (Eds.), *Measuring quality* (pp. 17–40). London: Falmer Press.

Obama administration's education reform plan emphasizes flexibility, resources and accountability for result. Available at http://www2.ed.gov/news/ pressreleases/2010/03/03152010.html. Retrieved November 16, 2010.

O'Brien, D. M. (2005). *Storm center: The Supreme Court in American politics* (7th ed.). New York: W.W. Norton & Co.

OEA Online News. (n.d.). Available at http://www.ohea.org/news/news.htm. Retrieved September 3, 2000.

Ogawa, R. T. (1994). The institutional sources of educational reform: The case of school based management. *American Educational Research Journal, 31*, 519–548.

Ohio State University. (1991). Department of Policy and Leadership. Policy Research for Ohio Based Education. *How to lobby the legislature: An interview with Representative Michael Fox*. Produced by Robert Donmoyer. [Videotape].

Okun, A. (1975). *Equality and efficiency: The big tradeoff*. Washington, D.C.: Brookings Institution.

Okun, A. M. (1982). Customer markets and the costs of inflation. In M. N. Baily & A. K. Okun (Eds.), *The battle against unemployment and inflation* (pp. 35–39). New York: Norton.

Oleszek, W. J. (1996). *Congressional procedures and the policy process* (4th ed.). Washington, D.C.: CQ Press.

Oleszek, W. J. (2007). *Congressional procedures and the policy process* (7th ed.). Washington, D.C.: CQ Press.

Oregon. (2002). *Oregon Administrative Rules, 2002 Compilation*. Available at http://arc.web.sos.state.or.us/rules/OAR. Retrieved May 23, 2002.

Orfield, M. (2002). *American metropolitics: The new suburban reality*. Washington, D.C.: Brookings Institution.

Paris, D. C., & Reynolds, J. F. (1983). *The logic of policy inquiry*. New York: Longman.

Pascopella, A. (2008). State of the superintendency. *District Administration, 44*(2), 32–36.

Patterson, S. C. (1996). Legislative politics in the states. In V. Gray & H. Jacob (Eds.), *Politics in the American states* (6th ed., pp. 159–206). Washington, D.C.: Congressional Quarterly Press.

PDA: Progressive Democrats of America. (n.d.). Available at http://www.pdaamerica.org. Retrieved June 18, 2011.

Peck, M. S. (1978). *The road less traveled*. New York: Simon & Schuster.

Penner, R. G., Sawhill, I. V., & Taylor, T. (2000). *Updating America's social contract*. New York: W. W. Norton & Co.

Perkinson, H. J. (1991). *The imperfect panacea* (4th ed.). New York: McGraw-Hill.

Perot, R. (1993). *Not for sale at any price*. New York: Hyperion.

Perry, L. B. (2009). Conceptualizing education policy in democratic societies. *Educational Policy, 23*, 423–450.

Peschek, J. G. (1987). *Policy-planning organizations*. Philadelphia: Temple University Press.

Peshkin, A. (2001). *Permissible advantage? The moral consequences of elite schooling*. Mahwah, NJ: Lawrence Erlbaum Associates.

Peterson, P., Rabe, B., & Wong, K. (1986). *When federalism works*. Washington, D.C.: Brookings Institution.

Peterson, P., Rabe, B., & Wong, K. (1991). *When federalism works*. Washington, D.C.: Brookings Institution.

Pew Center on the States. (2010). *How the recession might change the states*. Washington, D.C.: The Pew Charitable Trusts.

Phillips, K. (1994). *Arrogant capital*. Boston: Little, Brown.

Planty, M., & Carlson, D. (2010). *Understanding education indicators*. New York: Teachers College Press.

Plotkin, S., & Scheuerman, W. E. (1994). *Private interests, public spending*. Boston, MA: South End Press.

Popham, W. J. (1988). *Educational evaluation* (2nd ed.). Upper Saddle River, NJ: Prentice Hall.

Popham, W. J. (2004). *America's "failing" schools*. New York: RoutledgeFalmer.

Porter, A. C., Archbald, D. A., & Tyree, A. K., Jr. (1991). Reforming the curriculum: Will empowerment policies replace control? In S. H. Fuhrman & B. Malen (Eds.), *The politics of curriculum and testing* (pp. 11–36). London: Falmer Press.

Porter, M. C. (1982). State supreme courts and the legacy of the Warren court: Some inquiries for a new situation. In M. C. Porter & G. A. Tarr (Eds.), *State supreme courts* (pp. 3–21). Westport, CT: Greenwood Press.

Porter, M. C., & Tarr, G. A. (1982). Introduction. In M. C. Porter & G. A. Tarr (Eds.), *State supreme courts* (pp. xi–xxvii). Westport, CT: Greenwood Press.

Portner, J. (1996a, May 11). Minn. student leaders push for place at policy table. *Education Week,* 11.

Portner, J. (1996b, June 19). Study tracks violent deaths at school or related activities. *Education Week,* 10.

Posavac, E. J. (2011). *Program evaluation: Methods and case studies*. Upper Saddle River, NJ: Prentice Hall.

Prestine, N., & McGreal, T. L. (1997). Fragile changes, sturdy lives: Implementing authentic assessment in schools. *Educational Administration Quarterly, 33*, 371–400.

Putnam, R. D. (2000). *Bowling alone*. New York: Simon & Schuster.

Putnam, R. D. (2002). Bowling together. *American Prospect, 13*(3), 20–22.

Quarles, C. L. (2004). *Christian identity*. Jefferson, NC: McFarland & Company.

Raffaele, M. (2004, November 11). Pa. school district mandates "intelligent design" in curriculum. The Associated Press State & Local Wire. Available at http://web.lexis-nexis.com/universe/docum. Retrieved October 13, 2006.

Raffaele, M. (2005, November 9). Voters oust Pa. school board that backed 'intelligent design.' The Associated Press State & Local Wire. Available at http://web.lexis-nexis.com/universe/docum. Retrieved November 9, 2006.

Ravitch, D. (1983). *The troubled crusade*. New York: Basic Books.

Ravitch, D. (1995). *National standards in American education*. Washington, D.C.: Brookings Institution.

Rawls, J. (1971). *A theory of justice*. Cambridge, MA: Harvard University Press.

Ray, C. A., & Mickelson, R. A. (1990). Business leaders and the politics of school reform. In D. E. Mitchell & M. E. Goertz (Eds.), *Education politics for the new century* (pp. 119–135). London: Falmer Press.

Reeve, E. (2011, February 8). Why is the Democratic Leadership Council shutting down? *The Atlantic*. Available at http://www.theatlanticwire.com/politics/2011/02/why-is-the-democratic-leadership-council-shutting-down/21183/. Retrieved June 11, 2011.

Reich, R. (1991). *The work of nations*. New York: Knopf.

Reich, R. B. (2010). *Aftershock*. New York: Vintage Books.

Reid, K. S. (2001, March 21). U.S. census underscores diversity. *Education Week on the Web*. Available at http://www.edweek.org/ew/ewstory.cfm. Retrieved February 25, 2002.

Reid, K. S. (2004, March 17). 'Value added' study finds NAEP gains for black students. *Education Week, 7*.

Reif, J., Whittle, J., Woznick, A., Thurmond, M. E., & Kelly, J. (1997). *Services: The export of the 21st century*. San Rafael, CA: World Trade Press.

Rich, A. (2004). *Think tanks, public policy, and the politics of expertise*. Cambridge, U.K.: Cambridge University Press.

Ritter, G. W., & Jensen, N. C. (2010). The delicate task of developing an attractive merit pay plan for teachers. *Phi Delta Kappan, 91*(8), 32–37.

Robinson, V. M. J. (1995). The identification and evaluation of power in discourse. In D. Corson (Ed.), *Discourse and power in educational organizations* (pp. 111–130). Cresskill, NJ: Hampton Press.

Rochefort, D. A., & Cobb, R. W. (Eds.). (1994). *The politics of problem definition*. Lawrence, KS: University of Kansas Press.

Rosenthal, A. (1981). *Legislative life*. New York: Harper & Row.

Rosenthal, A. (2009). *Engines of democracy*. Washington, D.C.: CQ Press.

Rubin, I. S. (2006). *The politics of public budgeting* (5th ed.). Washington, D.C.: CQ Press.

Sabatier, P. (1975). Social movements and regulatory agencies: Toward a more adequate—and less pessimistic—theory of "clientele capture." *Policy Sciences, 6*, 301–342.

Samuels, C. A. (2011, July 13). Test tampering found rampant in Atlanta system. *Education Week, 1*, 22.

Sarason, S. B. (1996). *Revisiting "The culture of the school and the problem of change."* New York: Teachers College Press.

Sargent, L. T. (Ed.). (1995). *Extremism in America*. New York: New York University Press.

Schattschneider, E. E. (1935). *Politics, pressures, and the tariff*. New York: Prentice Hall. Cited in Lowi, T. J. (1964, July). American business, public policy, case studies, and political theory. *World Politics, 677*–715.

Schattschneider, E. E. (1960). *The semisovereign people*. New York: Holt, Rinehart & Winston.

Schor, J. B. (1998). *The overspent American*. New York: Basic Books.

Schroeder, R. (1992). *Max Weber and the sociology of culture*. London: Sage.

Sidoti, L. (2000, September 5). Schools feel pressure from test-driven ratings. [Hamilton, OH] *Journal-News*, pp. A1, A2.

Skrla, L. (2000). The social construction of gender in the superintendency. *Journal of Education Policy, 15*, 293–316.

Smith, A. (1976 [1776]). *An inquiry into the nature and causes of the wealth of nations*. Oxford, England: Clarendon Press. Quoted in Buchholz, T. G. (1989). *New ideas from dead economists* (pp. 21–22). New York: New American Library.

Smith, J. A. (1991). *Brookings at seventy-five*. Washington, D.C.: Brookings Institution.

Sommerfeld, M. (1996, April 24). California parents target math frameworks. *Education Week, 1*, 11.

Spicker, P. (2006). *Policy analysis for practice*. Bristol, U.K.: The Policy Press.

Spillane, J. P. (1998). A cognitive perspective on the role of the local educational agency in implementing instructional policy: Accounting for local variability. *Educational Administration Quarterly, 34*, 31–57.

Spillane, J. P. (1999). External reform initiatives and teachers' efforts to reconstruct their practice: The mediating role of teachers' zones of enactment. *Journal of Curriculum Studies, 31*, 143–175.

Spillane, J. P. (2000). Cognition and policy implementation: District policymakers and the reform of mathematics education. *Cognition and Instruction, 18*, 141–179.

Spillane, J. P. (2005). Distributed leadership. *The Educational Forum, 69*(2), 143–150.

Spillane, J. P. (2006). *Distributed leadership*. San Francisco: Jossey-Bass.

Spillane, J. P., & Callahan, K. A. (2000). *Journal of Research in Science Teaching, 37*, 401–425.

Spillane, J. P., Reiser, B. J., & Reimer, T. (2002). Policy implementation and cognition: Reframing and refocusing implementation research. *Review of Educational Research, 72*, 387–431.

Spring, J. (1989). *The sorting machine revisited*. New York: Longman.

Spring, J. (2005). *The American school, 1642–2004* (6th ed.). New York: McGraw-Hill.

Spring, J. (2010). *Political agendas for education*. New York: Routledge.

Squire, P., & Moncrief, G. (2010). *State legislatures today*. Boston, MA: Longman.

Sroufe, G. E. (1995). Politics of education at the federal level. In J. D. Scribner & D. H. Layton (Eds.), *The study of educational politics* (pp. 75–88). London: Falmer Press.

State boards of education. (2011). Available at http://nasbe.org. Retrieved June 28, 2011.

Stecher, B. M., Epstein, S., Hamilton, L. S., Marsh, J. A., Robyn, A., McCombs, J. S., Russell, J., & Naftel, S. (2008). *Pain and gain*. Santa Monica, CA: RAND.

Steiner, L. (2000). Comprehensive school reform: A review of the research literature on scaling up in education. Available at the Web site of the North Central Regional Educational Laboratory, http://www.ncrel.org. Retrieved March 2, 2007.

Stone, D. A. (1989). Causal stories and the formation of policy agendas. *Political Science Quarterly, 104*, 281–300.

Stringfield, S., & Datnow, A. (1998). Scaling up school restructuring designs in urban schools. *Education and Urban Society, 30*, 269–276.

Stufflebeam, D. L. (1983). The CIPP model for program evaluation. In G. F. Madaus, M. Scriven, & D. L. Stufflebeam (Eds.), *Evaluation models* (pp. 117–141). Boston: Kluwer–Nijhoff.

Stufflebeam, D. L., & Webster, W. J. (1983). An analysis of alternative approaches to evaluation. In G. F. Madaus, M. Scriven, & D. L. Stufflebeam (Eds.), *Evaluation models* (pp. 23–43). Boston: Kluwer–Nijhoff.

Summers, L. H. (1984). The long-term effects of current macroeconomic policies. In C. R. Hulten & I. V. Sawhill (Eds.), *The legacy of Reaganomics: An overview* (pp. 179–198). Washington, D.C.: Urban Institute.

Susser, B. (1995). *Political ideology in the modern world*. Boston: Allyn & Bacon.

Swanson, C. B., & Barlage, J. (2006). *Influence: A study of the factors shaping education policy*. N.P.: Editorial Projects in Education Research Center.

Tennessee Code Commission. (1995). *Tennessee code annotated: 1995 supplement. Vol. 9*. Charlottesville, VA: Michie.

Thomas, C. S., & Hrebenar, R. J. (2004). Interest groups in the states. In V. Gray & H. Jacob (Eds.), *Politics in the American states* (8th ed., pp. 113–143). Washington, D.C.: CQ Press.

Thurow, L. C. (1985, November). The "big tradeoff" debunked: The efficiency of a fair economy. *The Washington Monthly*, 47–54.

Thurow, L. C. (1992). *Head to head*. New York: Morrow.

Thurow, L. C. (1996). *The future of capitalism*. New York: Morrow.

Toch, Thomas. (2011). In the game. *Phi Delta Kappan, 92*(8), 72–73.

Tucker, R., & Wilson, D. (2011, July 24). Household debt $13.4T last year. *Hamilton* [Ohio] *Journal News*, A7.

Turner, D. W. (1995). Building legislative relationships: A guide for principals. *Here's How, 13*(5), 1–4.

Tyack, D. (1974). *The one best system*. Cambridge, MA: Harvard University Press.

Tyack, D. (1986). Toward a social history of law and public education. In D. L. Kirp & D. N. Jensen (Eds.), *School days, rule days* (pp. 212–237). Philadelphia: Falmer Press.

Tyack, D., & Cuban, L. (1995). *Tinkering toward utopia*. Cambridge, MA: Harvard University Press.

Tyack, D., & Tobin, W. (1994). The "grammar" of schooling: Why has it been so hard to change? *American Educational Research Journal, 31*, 453–479.

Unfulfilled promises: School finance remedies and state courts. (1991). *Harvard Law Review 104*, 1072–1092.

UNICEF. (2007). *Child poverty in perspective: An overview of child well-being in rich countries*. (Innocenti

Report Card 7, 2007). Available at http://www
.unicef.org/media/files/ChildPovertyReport.pdf.
Retrieved August 5, 2011.

U.S. Census Bureau. (2001). *Series A: Population projections by age, sex, and Hispanic origin for 1999 to 2100.*

U.S. Department of Education. (1999). *A back to school special report on the baby boom echo: No end in sight.* Available at http://www.ed.gov/pubs/bbecho99/index.html. Retrieved February 25, 2002.

U.S. Department of Labor. Bureau of Labor Statistics. (2011). *U.S. CPI—All items (1982-84+100).* Available at http://www.bls.gov/. Retrieved August 5, 2011.

U.S. Unemployment Rate—1948-2010, The. (2011). Available at http://www.miseryindex.us/urbyyear.asp. Retrieved August 8, 2011.

Van Horn, C. E. (2006). Power, politics, and public policy in the states. In C. E. Van Horn (Ed.), *The state of the states* (4th ed., pp. 1–13). Washington, D.C.: CQ Press.

Verba, S., & Orren, G. R. (1985). *Equality in America.* Cambridge, MA: Harvard University Press.

Vinovskis, M. A. (1996). An analysis of the concept and uses of systemic educational reform. *American Educational Research Journal, 33,* 53–85.

Waite, D. (1995). Teacher resistance in a supervision conference. In D. Corson (Ed.), *Discourse and power in educational organizations* (pp. 71–86). Cresskill, NJ: Hampton Press.

Weber, M. (1968). *Economy and society.* Three volumes. New York: Bedminster Press. Quoted in Wrong, D. H. (1979). *Power* (p. 21). New York: Harper & Row.

Weber, M. (1986). Domination by economic power and by authority. In S. Lukes (Ed.), *Power* (pp. 28–36). New York: New York University Press.

Weeres, J. G. (1988). Economic choice and the dissolution of community. In W. L. Boyd & C. T. Kerchner (Eds.), *The politics of excellence and choice in education* (pp. 117–129). New York: Falmer Press.

Weimer, D. L., & Vining, A. R. (2004). *Policy analysis* (4th ed.). Upper Saddle River, NJ: Prentice Hall.

Weiss, C. (Ed.). (1992). *Organizations for policy analysis.* Newbury Park, CA: Sage.

Weiss, C. H. (1988). Where politics and evaluation research meet. In D. Palumbo (Ed.). *The politics of program evaluation* (pp. 47–70). Newbury Park, CA: Sage.

Weiss, C. H. (1992). Helping government think: Functions and consequences of policy analysis organizations. In C. H. Weiss (Ed.), *Organizations for policy analysis* (pp. 1–18). Newbury Park, CA: Sage.

Weiss, I. R., & Pasley J. D. (2006, March). Scaling up instructional improvement through teacher professional development: Insights from the Local Systemic Change Initiative. *CPRE Policy Briefs,* 1–16.

Welsh-Huggins, A. (2000, September 5). State tests raise angst. *Cincinnati Enquirer,* pp. B1, B4.

Welsh-Huggins, A. (2000, November 30). Overhaul of Ohio's proficiency test procedure may be forthcoming. [Hamilton, OH] *Journal-News,* p. A7.

Wiget, L. A. (1995). *Effective government relations for public education.* Bloomington, IN: Phi Delta Kappa Educational Foundation.

Williams, B. R., & Palmatier, M. A. (1992). The RAND Corporation. In C. H. Weiss (Ed.). *Organizations for policy analysis* (pp. 48–68). Newbury Park, CA: Sage.

Wilson, J. Q. (1989). *Bureaucracy.* New York: Basic Books.

Wirt, F. M., & Harman, G. (1986). *Education, recession, and the world village.* London: Falmer Press.

Wodak, R. 1995. Power, discourse, and styles of female leadership in school committee meetings. In D. Corson (Ed.), *Discourse and power in educational organizations* (pp. 31–54). Cresskill, NJ: Hampton Press.

Wolf, R. M. (1990). *Evaluation in education* (3rd ed.). New York: Praeger.

Wrong, D. H. (1995). *Power* (2nd ed.). New York: Harper & Row.

Yarbrough, D. B., Shulha, L. M., Hopson, R. K., & Caruthers, F. A. (2011). *The program evaluation standards* (3rd ed.). Thousand Oaks, CA: SAGE.

Yen, H. (2010, October 10). Suburban poverty is up 37% since 2000, analysis finds. *Hamilton [Ohio] Journal News,* A8.

Young, T. V., Shepley, T. V., Miskel, C., & Song, M. (2010). Understanding agenda setting in state policy: An application of Kingdon's multiple streams model to the formation of state reading policy. *Education Policy Analysis Archives, 18*(15), 1–18.

NAME INDEX

SUBJECT INDEX